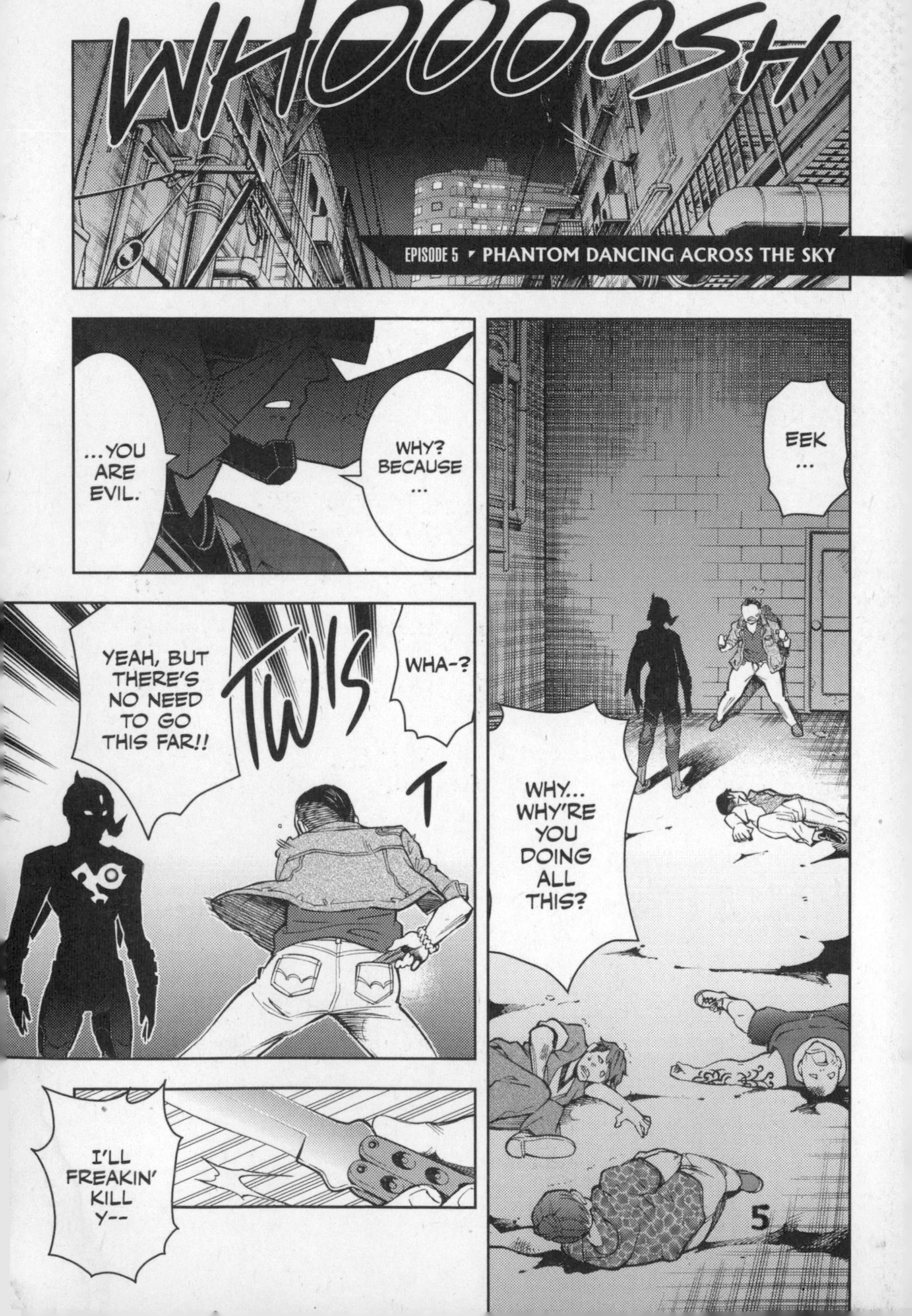
WHOOOOSH
EPISODE 5 ▾ PHANTOM DANCING ACROSS THE SKY
EEK ...
WHY... WHY'RE YOU DOING ALL THIS?
WHY? BECAUSE ...
...YOU ARE EVIL.
WHA-?
TWIST
YEAH, BUT THERE'S NO NEED TO GO THIS FAR!!
I'LL FREAKIN' KILL Y--

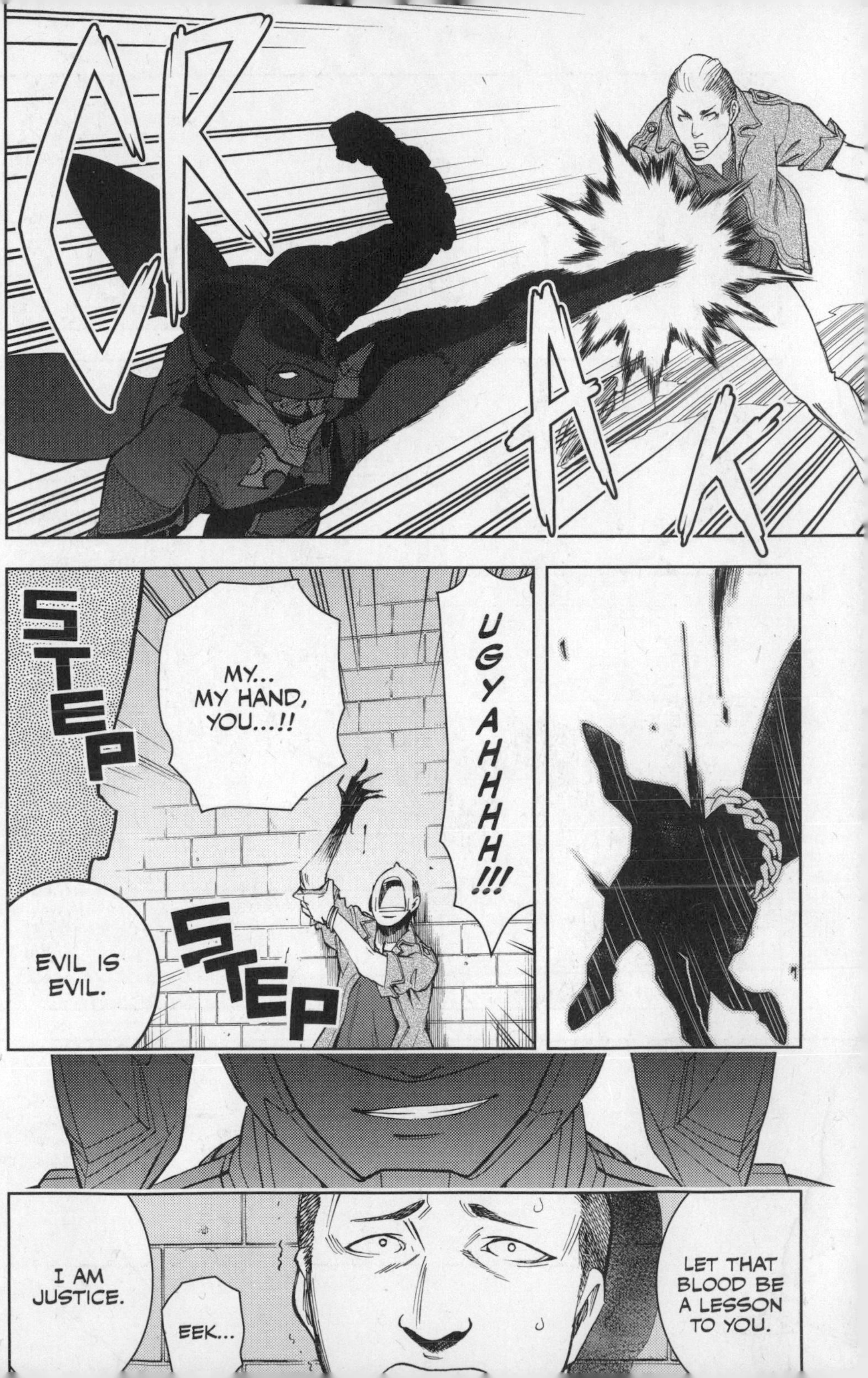
CRAK
UGYAHHHHH!!!
MY... MY HAND, YOU...!!
STEP
STEP
EVIL IS EVIL.
LET THAT BLOOD BE A LESSON TO YOU.
EEK...
I AM JUSTICE.

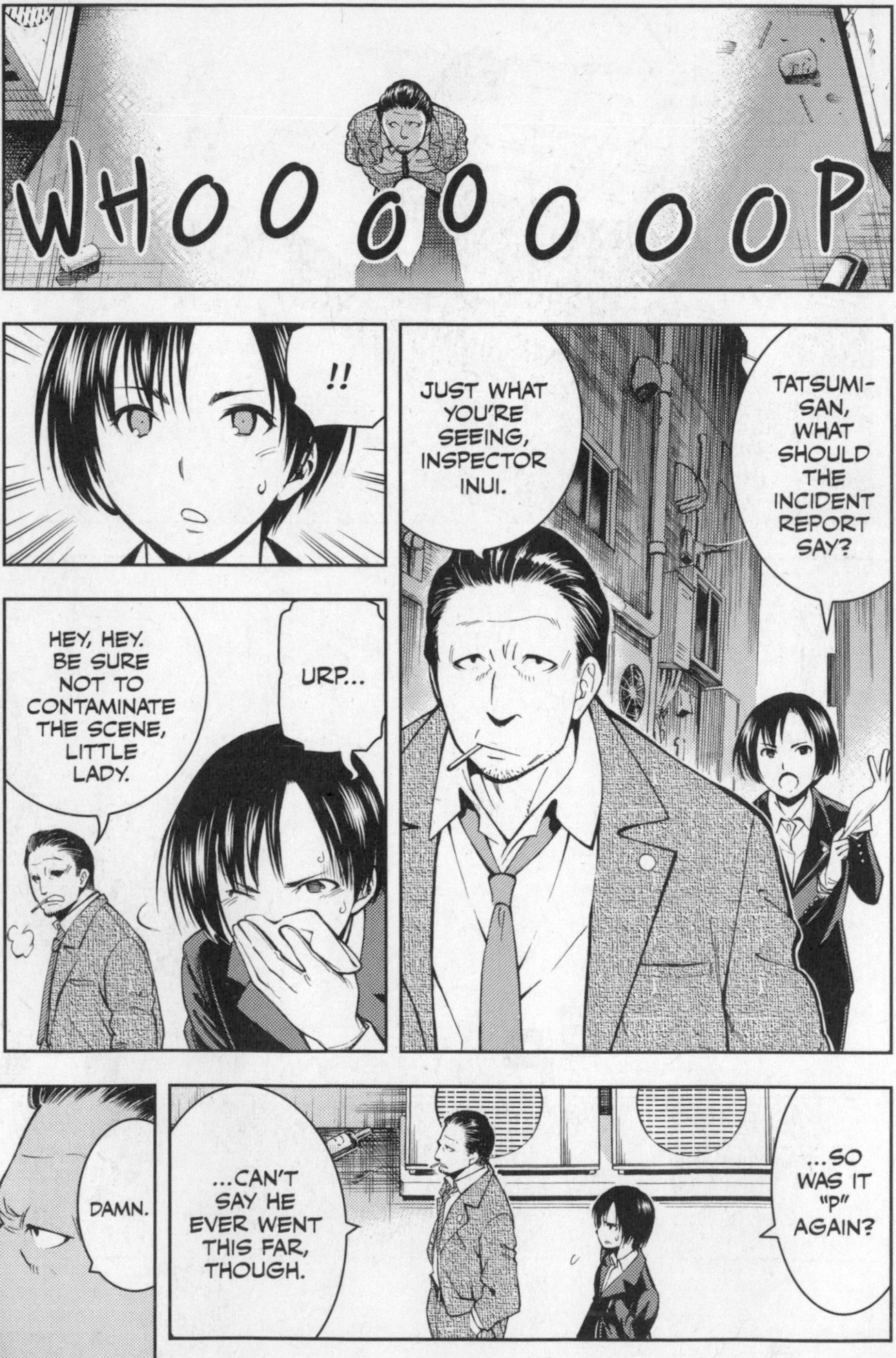
WHOOOOOOOP
TATSUMI-SAN, WHAT SHOULD THE INCIDENT REPORT SAY?
JUST WHAT YOU'RE SEEING, INSPECTOR INUI.
!!
URP...
HEY, HEY. BE SURE NOT TO CONTAMINATE THE SCENE, LITTLE LADY.
...SO WAS IT "P" AGAIN?
...CAN'T SAY HE EVER WENT THIS FAR, THOUGH.
DAMN.

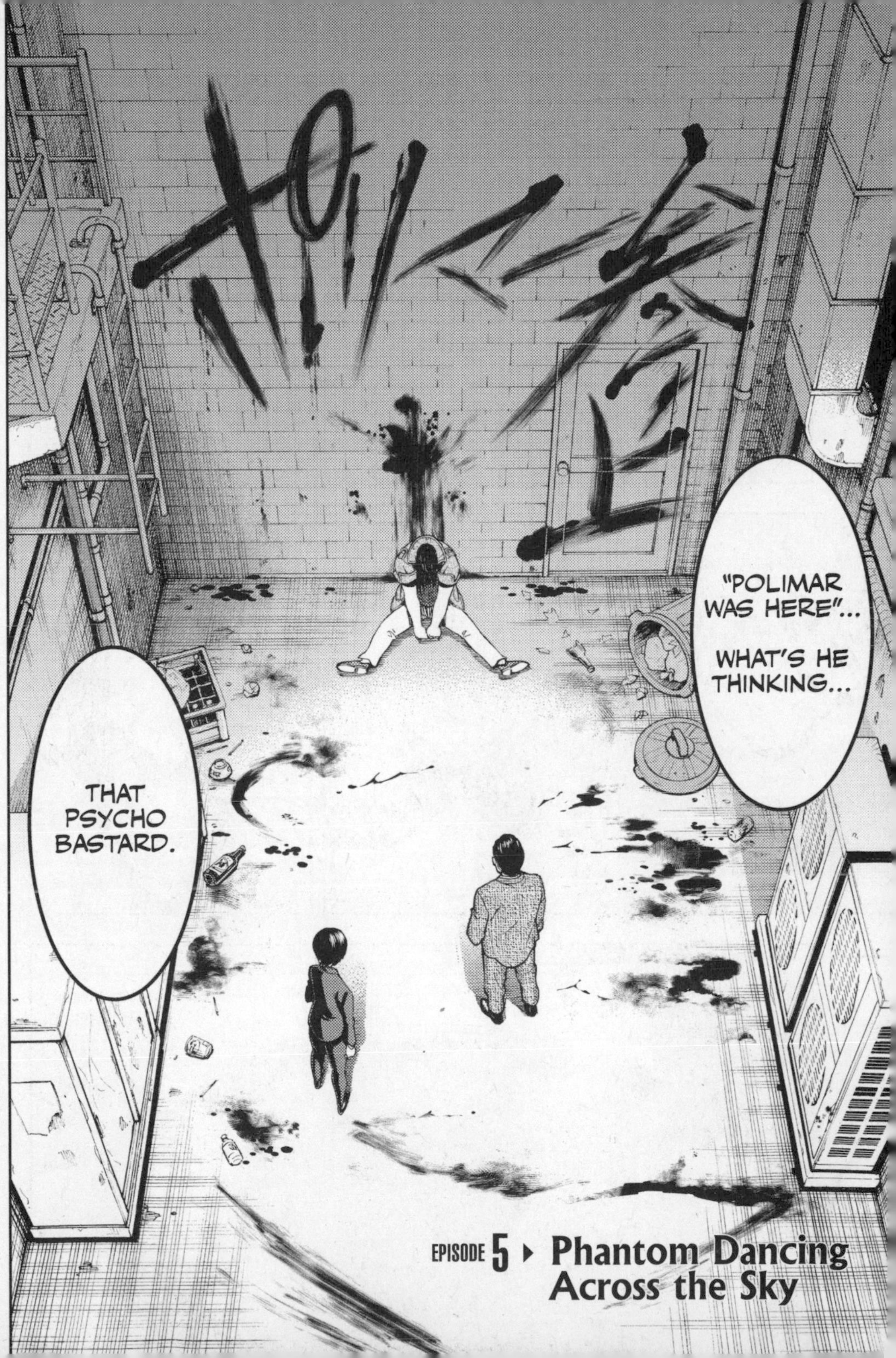
ポリマ参上
"POLIMAR WAS HERE"... WHAT'S HE THINKING...
THAT PSYCHO BASTARD.
EPISODE 5 ▸ Phantom Dancing Across the Sky

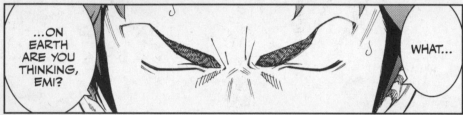

...ON EARTH ARE YOU THINKING, EMI?

WHAT...

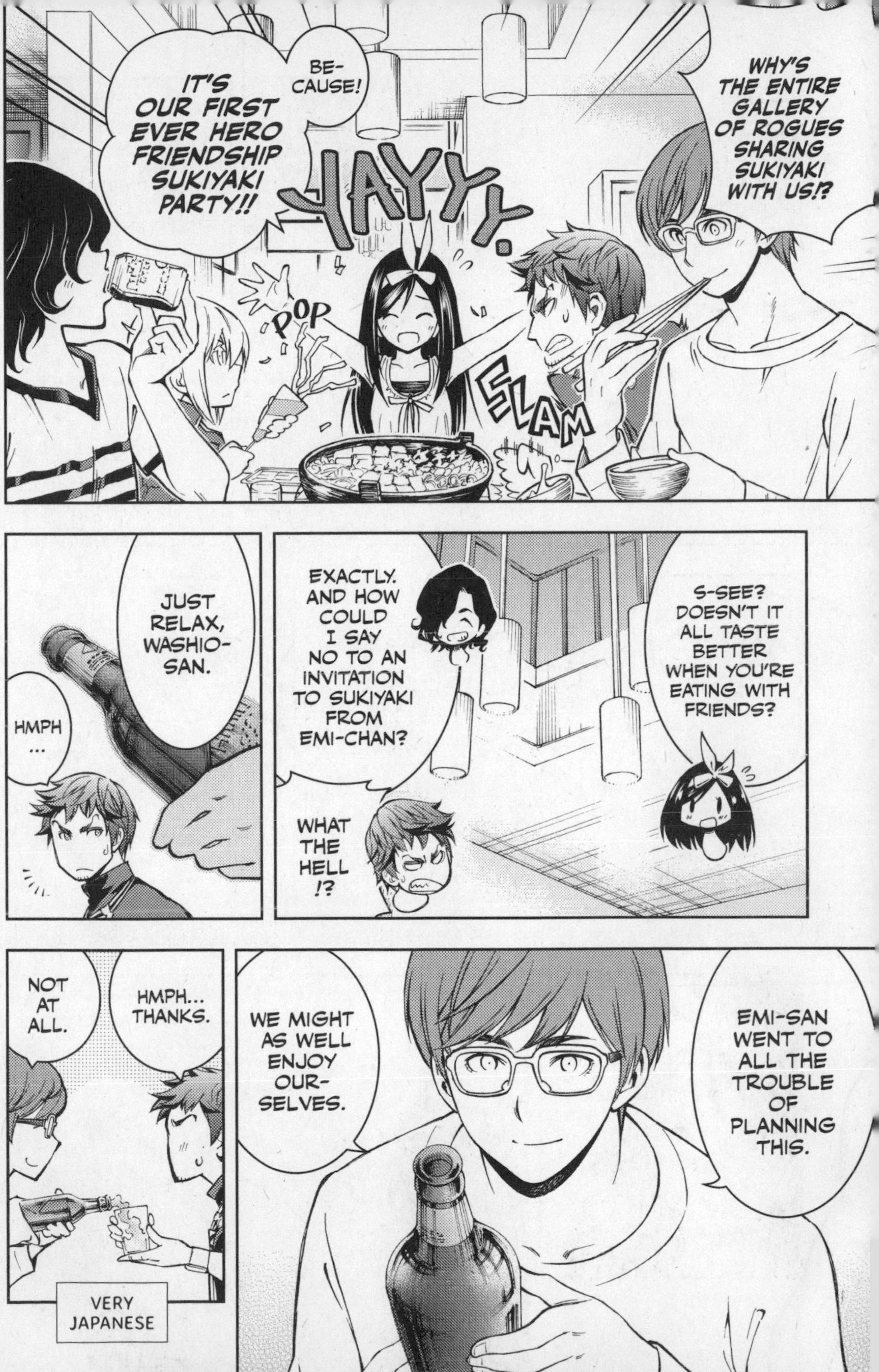
WHY'S THE ENTIRE GALLERY OF ROGUES SHARING SUKIYAKI WITH US!?
BE-CAUSE!
IT'S OUR FIRST EVER HERO FRIENDSHIP SUKIYAKI PARTY!!
YAYYY.
POP
SLAM
S-SEE? DOESN'T IT ALL TASTE BETTER WHEN YOU'RE EATING WITH FRIENDS?
EXACTLY. AND HOW COULD I SAY NO TO AN INVITATION TO SUKIYAKI FROM EMI-CHAN?
WHAT THE HELL !?
JUST RELAX, WASHIO-SAN.
HMPH ...
EMI-SAN WENT TO ALL THE TROUBLE OF PLANNING THIS.
WE MIGHT AS WELL ENJOY OUR-SELVES.
HMPH... THANKS.
NOT AT ALL.
VERY JAPANESE

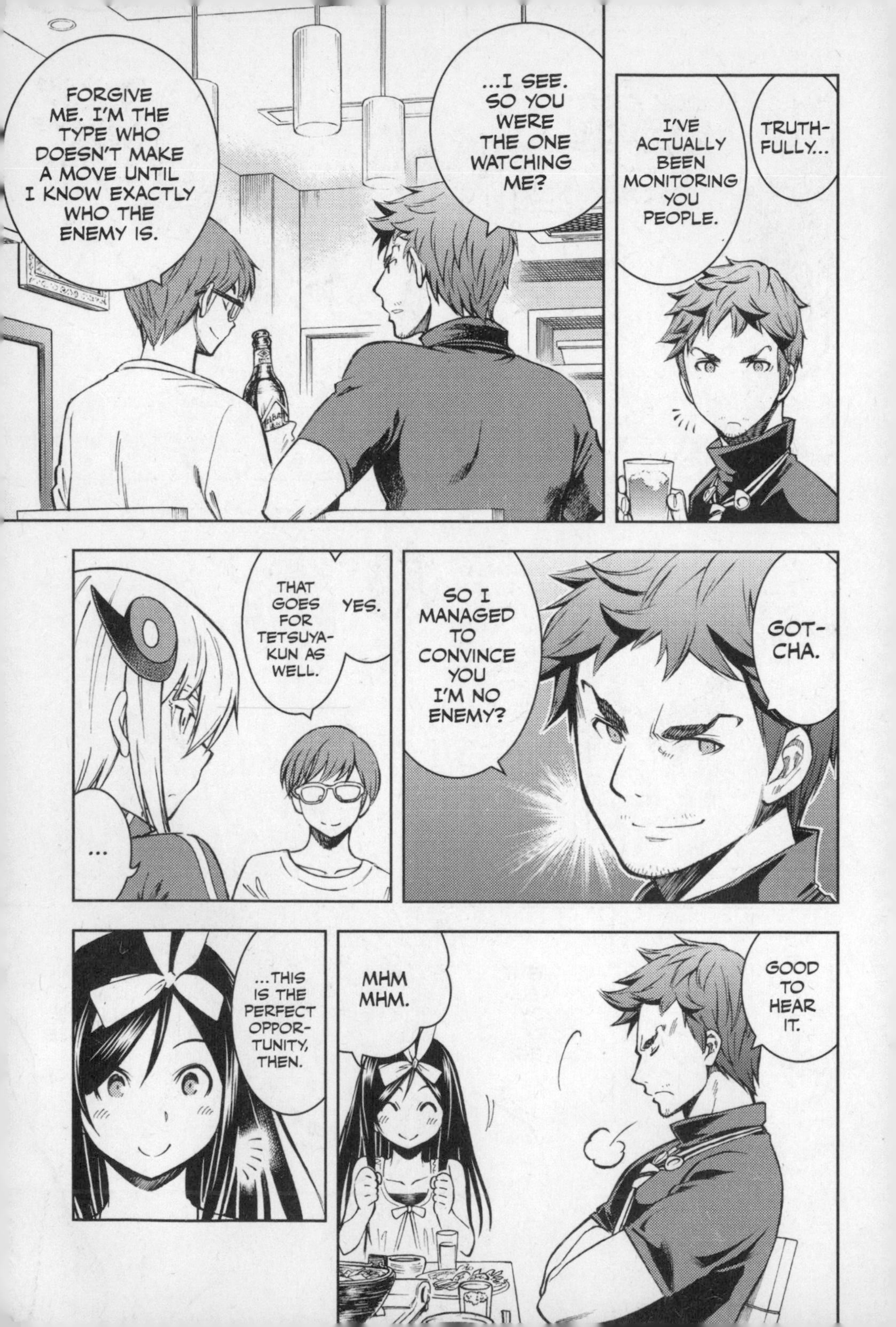
TRUTH-FULLY...
I'VE ACTUALLY BEEN MONITORING YOU PEOPLE.
...I SEE. SO YOU WERE THE ONE WATCHING ME?
FORGIVE ME. I'M THE TYPE WHO DOESN'T MAKE A MOVE UNTIL I KNOW EXACTLY WHO THE ENEMY IS.
GOT-CHA.
SO I MANAGED TO CONVINCE YOU I'M NO ENEMY?
YES.
THAT GOES FOR TETSUYA-KUN AS WELL.
...
GOOD TO HEAR IT.
MHM MHM.
...THIS IS THE PERFECT OPPOR-TUNITY, THEN.

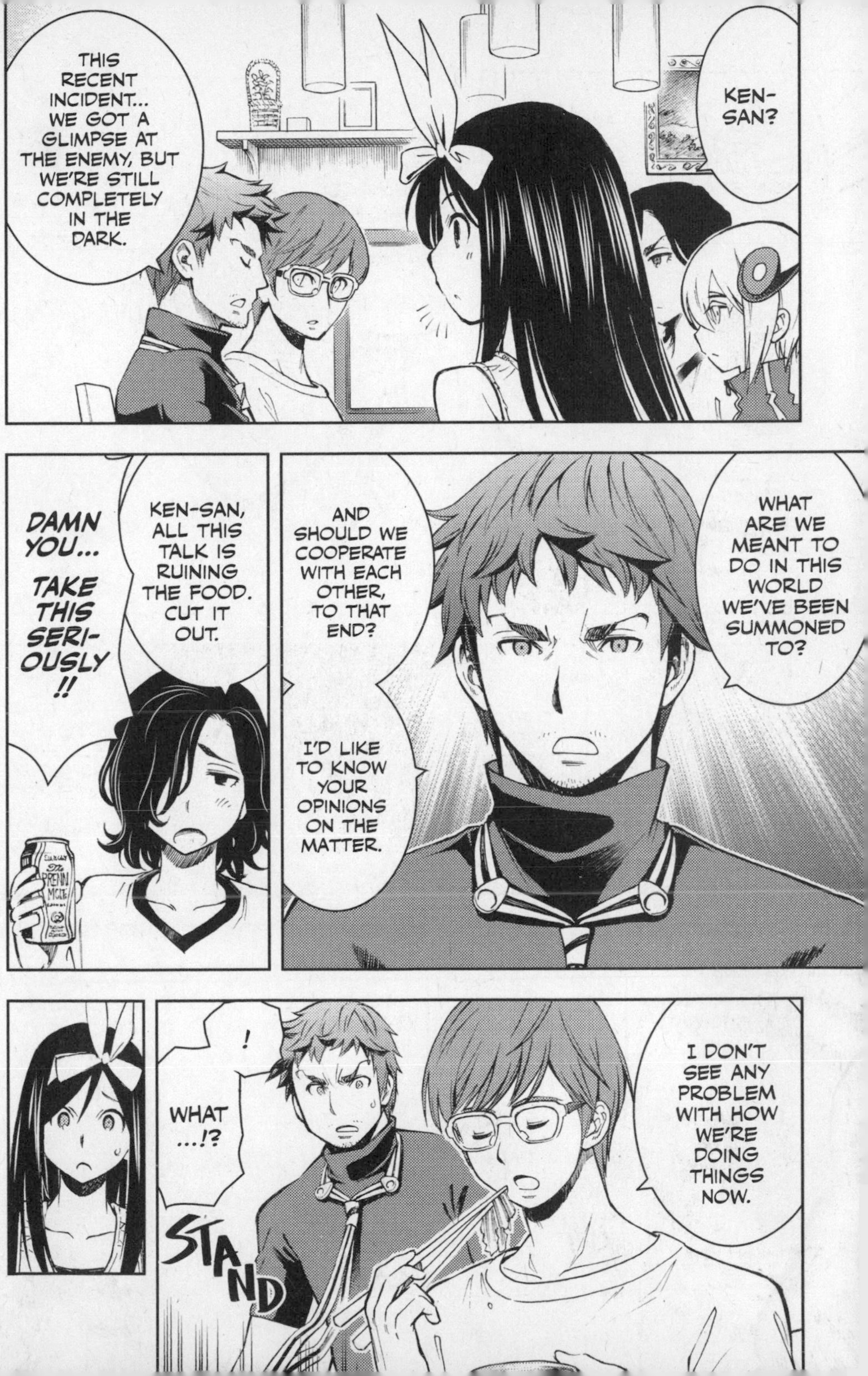
KEN-SAN?
THIS RECENT INCIDENT... WE GOT A GLIMPSE AT THE ENEMY, BUT WE'RE STILL COMPLETELY IN THE DARK.
WHAT ARE WE MEANT TO DO IN THIS WORLD WE'VE BEEN SUMMONED TO?
AND SHOULD WE COOPERATE WITH EACH OTHER, TO THAT END?
I'D LIKE TO KNOW YOUR OPINIONS ON THE MATTER.
KEN-SAN, ALL THIS TALK IS RUINING THE FOOD. CUT IT OUT.
DAMN YOU...
TAKE THIS SERI-OUSLY!!
I DON'T SEE ANY PROBLEM WITH HOW WE'RE DOING THINGS NOW.
!
WHAT ...!?
STAND

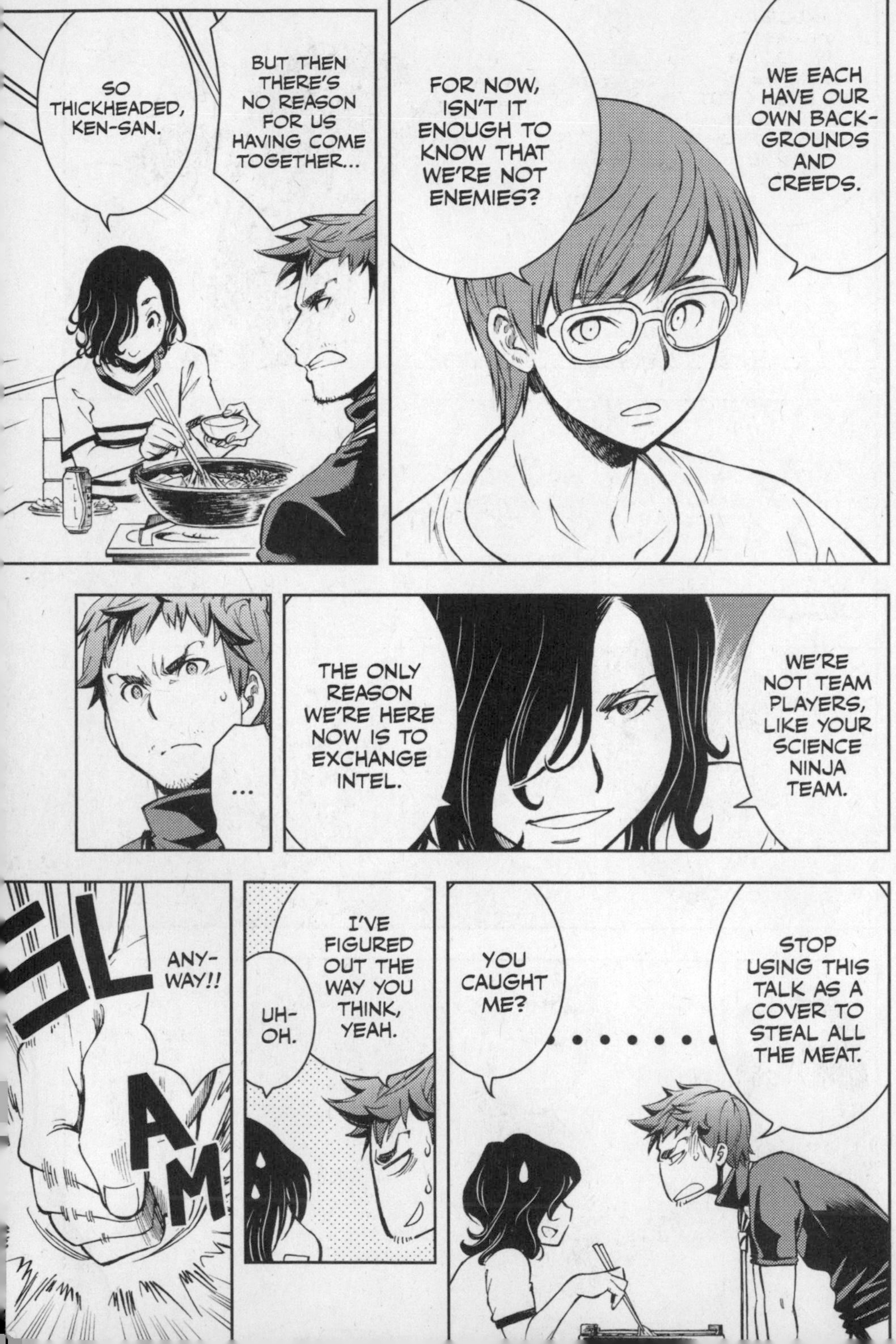
WE EACH HAVE OUR OWN BACK-GROUNDS AND CREEDS.
FOR NOW, ISN'T IT ENOUGH TO KNOW THAT WE'RE NOT ENEMIES?
BUT THEN THERE'S NO REASON FOR US HAVING COME TOGETHER...
SO THICKHEADED, KEN-SAN.
WE'RE NOT TEAM PLAYERS, LIKE YOUR SCIENCE NINJA TEAM.
THE ONLY REASON WE'RE HERE NOW IS TO EXCHANGE INTEL.
...
STOP USING THIS TALK AS A COVER TO STEAL ALL THE MEAT.
.......
YOU CAUGHT ME?
I'VE FIGURED OUT THE WAY YOU THINK, YEAH.
UH-OH.
ANY-WAY!!
SLAM

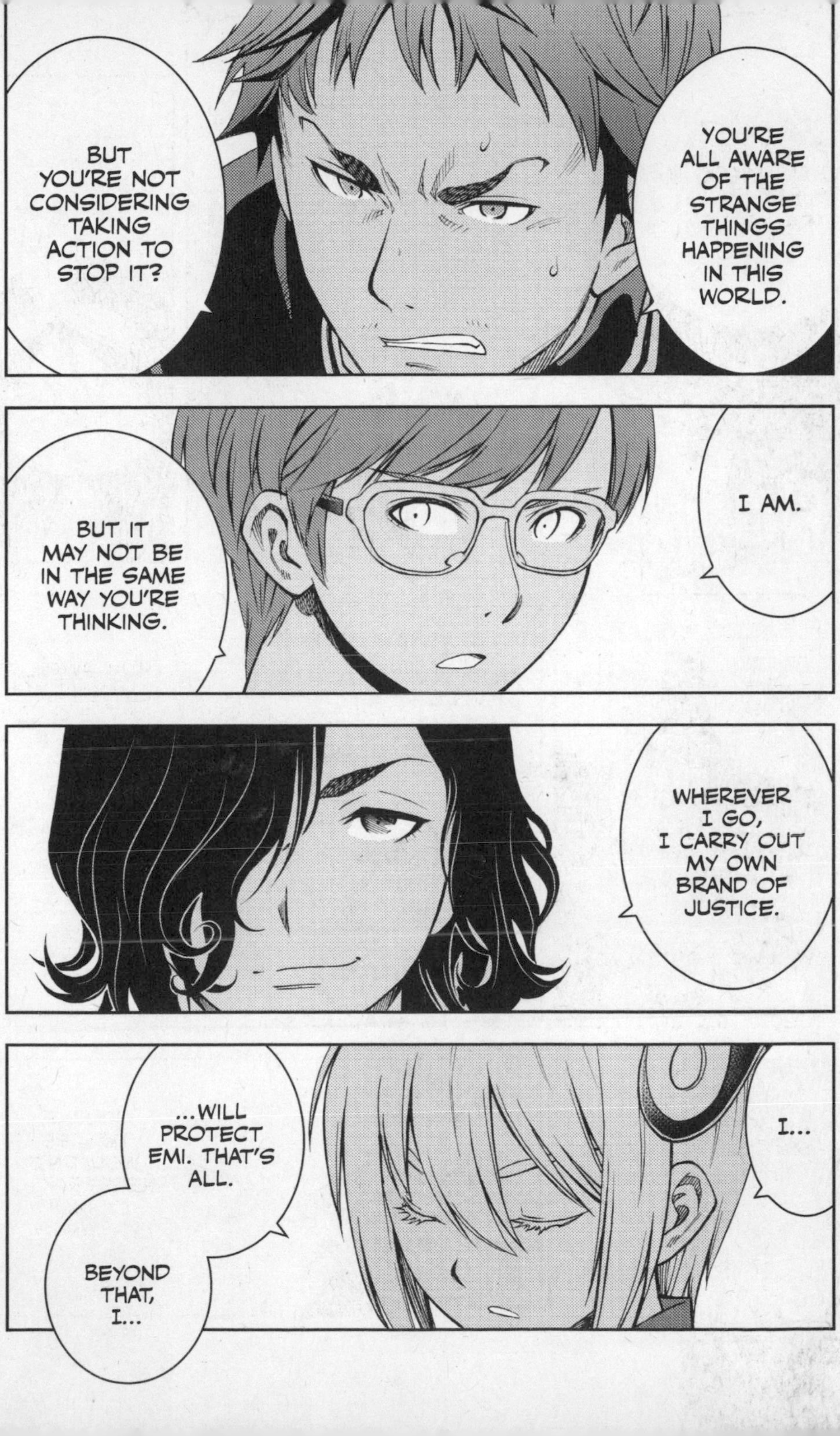
YOU'RE ALL AWARE OF THE STRANGE THINGS HAPPENING IN THIS WORLD.
BUT YOU'RE NOT CONSIDERING TAKING ACTION TO STOP IT?
I AM.
BUT IT MAY NOT BE IN THE SAME WAY YOU'RE THINKING.
WHEREVER I GO, I CARRY OUT MY OWN BRAND OF JUSTICE.
I...
...WILL PROTECT EMI. THAT'S ALL.
BEYOND THAT, I...

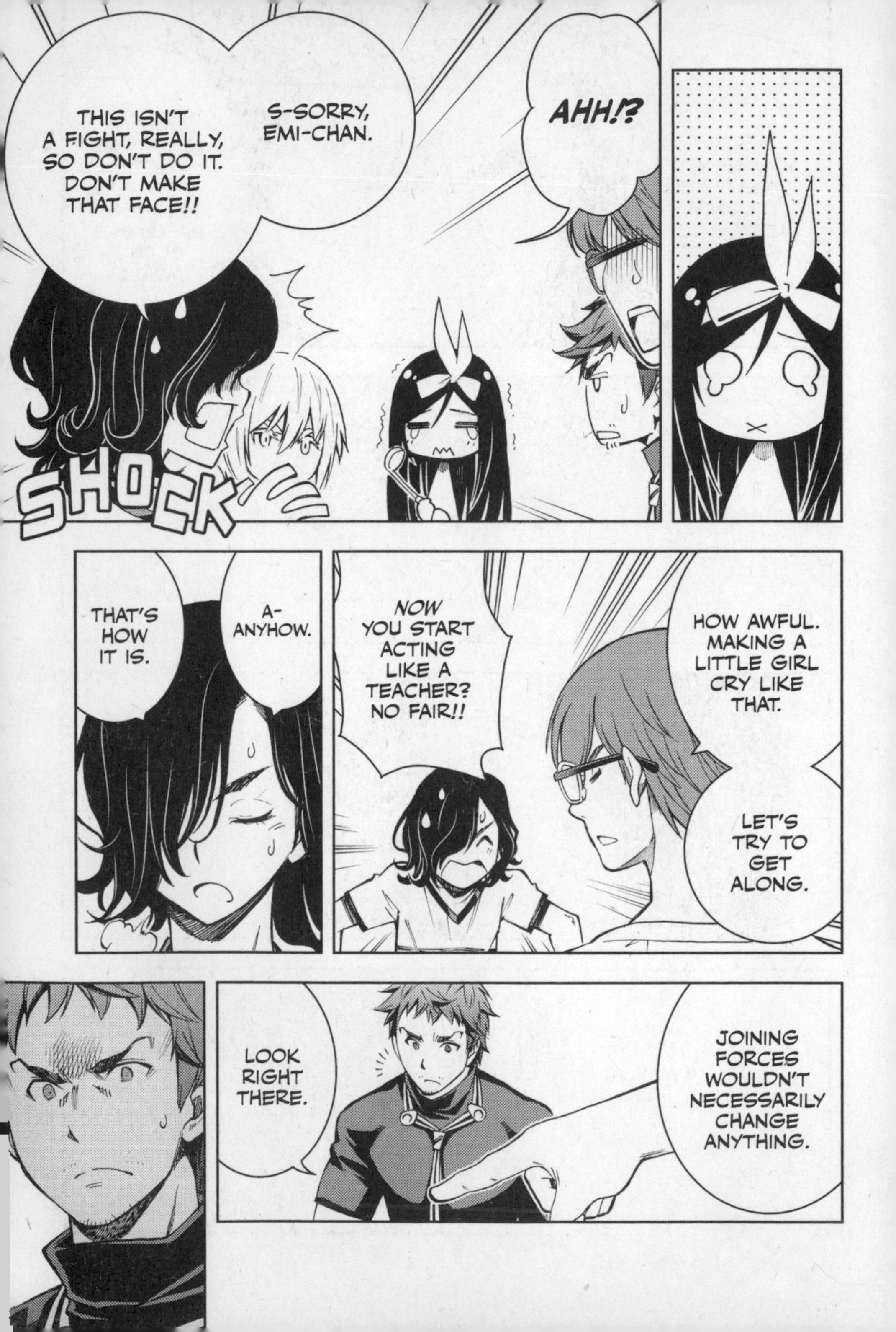
AHH!?
S-SORRY, EMI-CHAN.
THIS ISN'T A FIGHT, REALLY, SO DON'T DO IT. DON'T MAKE THAT FACE!!
SHOCK
HOW AWFUL. MAKING A LITTLE GIRL CRY LIKE THAT.
LET'S TRY TO GET ALONG.
*NOW* YOU START ACTING LIKE A TEACHER? NO FAIR!!
A- ANYHOW.
THAT'S HOW IT IS.
JOINING FORCES WOULDN'T NECESSARILY CHANGE ANYTHING.
LOOK RIGHT THERE.

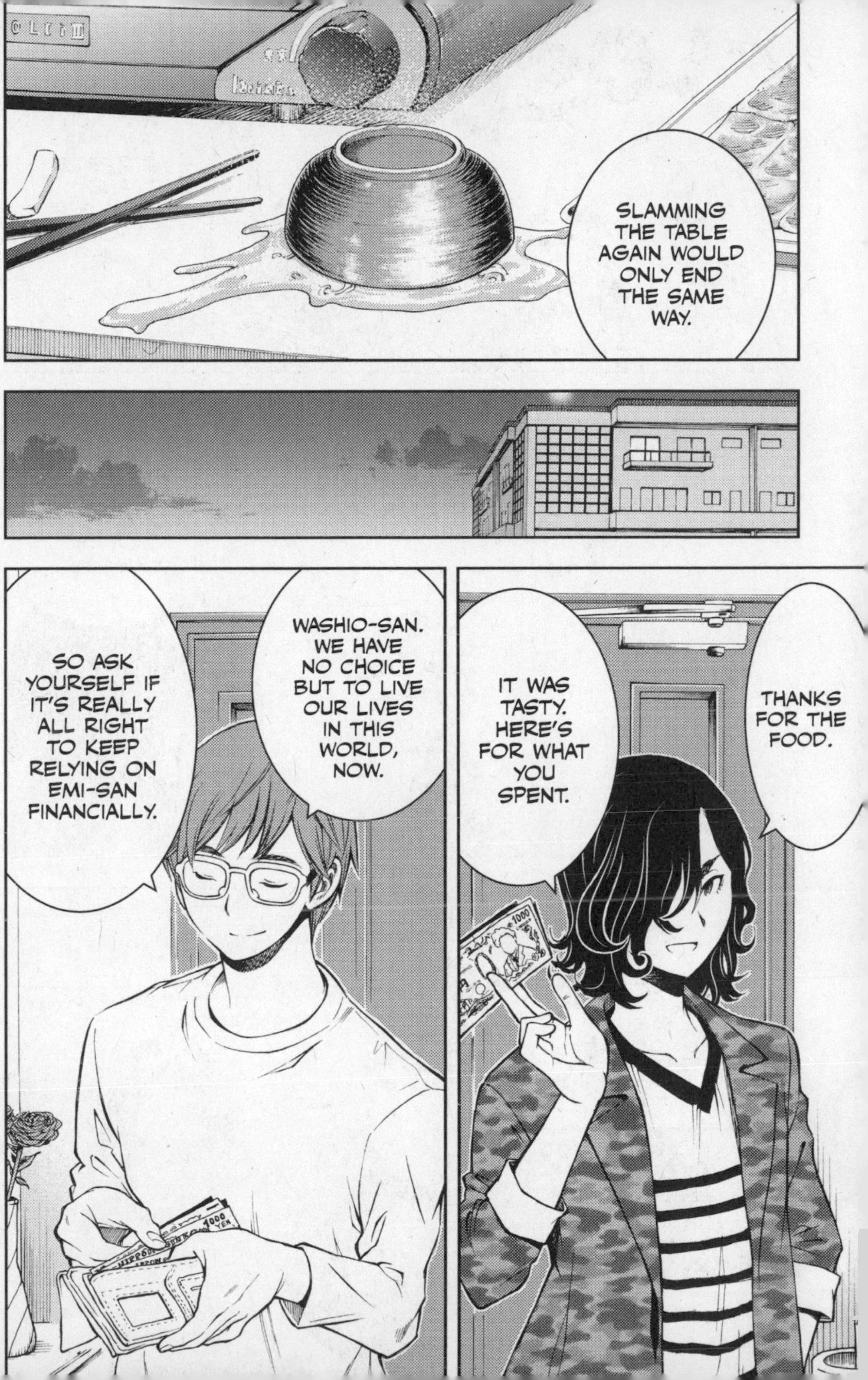
SLAMMING THE TABLE AGAIN WOULD ONLY END THE SAME WAY.
THANKS FOR THE FOOD.
IT WAS TASTY. HERE'S FOR WHAT YOU SPENT.
WASHIO-SAN. WE HAVE NO CHOICE BUT TO LIVE OUR LIVES IN THIS WORLD, NOW.
SO ASK YOURSELF IF IT'S REALLY ALL RIGHT TO KEEP RELYING ON EMI-SAN FINANCIALLY.

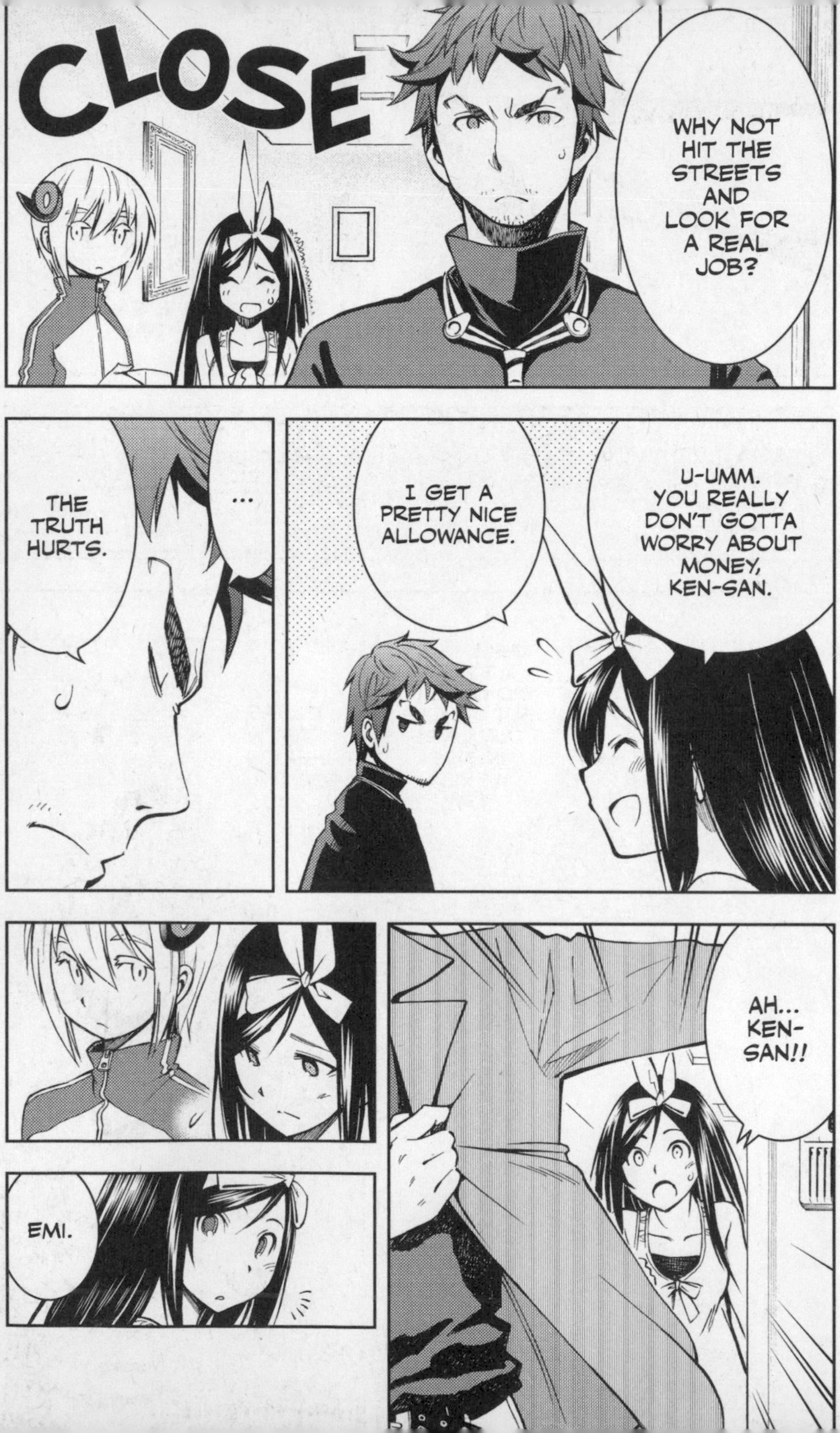
WHY NOT HIT THE STREETS AND LOOK FOR A REAL JOB?
CLOSE
U-UMM. YOU REALLY DON'T GOTTA WORRY ABOUT MONEY, KEN-SAN.
I GET A PRETTY NICE ALLOWANCE.
...
THE TRUTH HURTS.
AH... KEN-SAN!!
EMI.

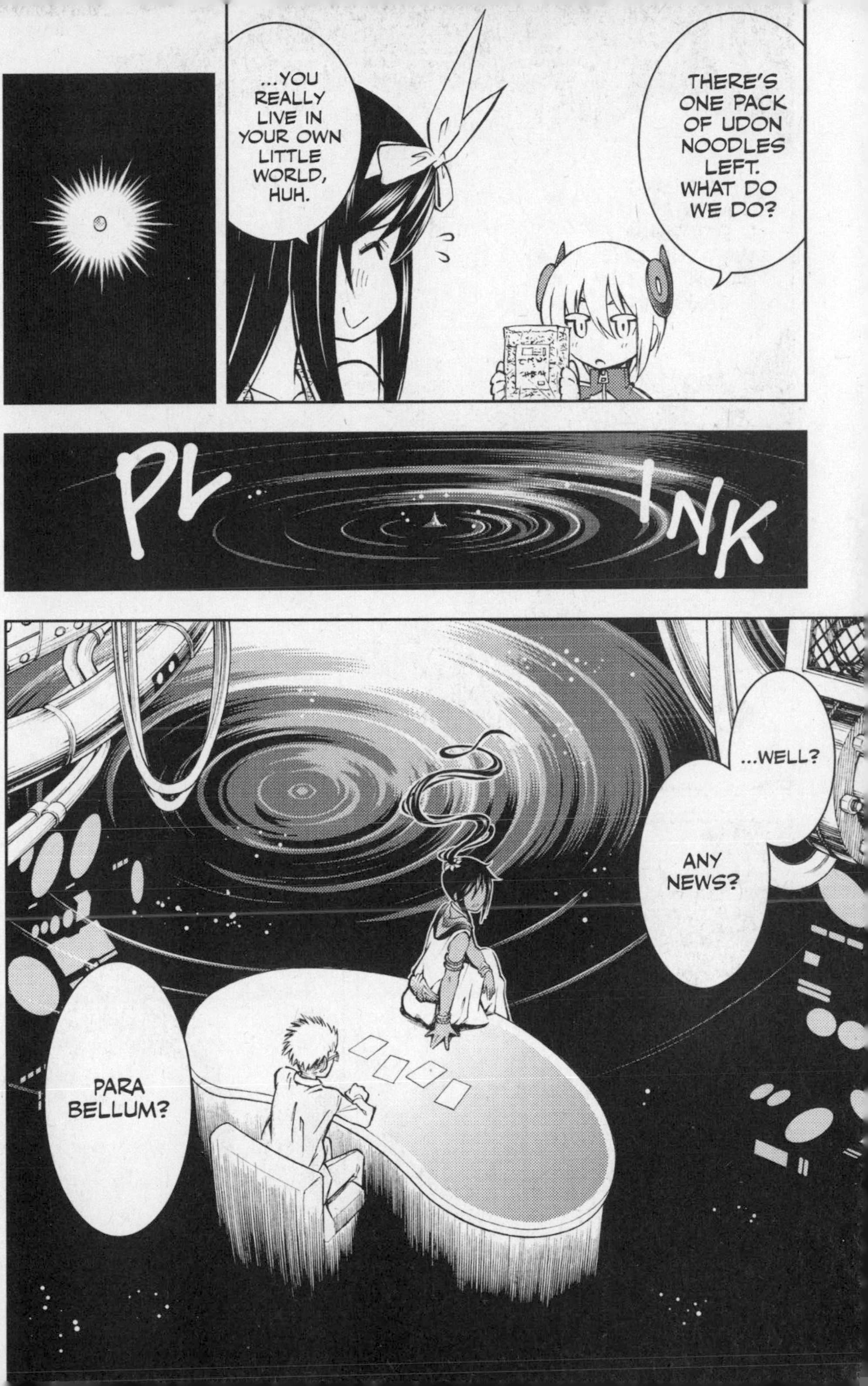
THERE'S ONE PACK OF UDON NOODLES LEFT. WHAT DO WE DO?
...YOU REALLY LIVE IN YOUR OWN LITTLE WORLD, HUH.
PL INK
...WELL?
ANY NEWS?
PARA BELLUM?

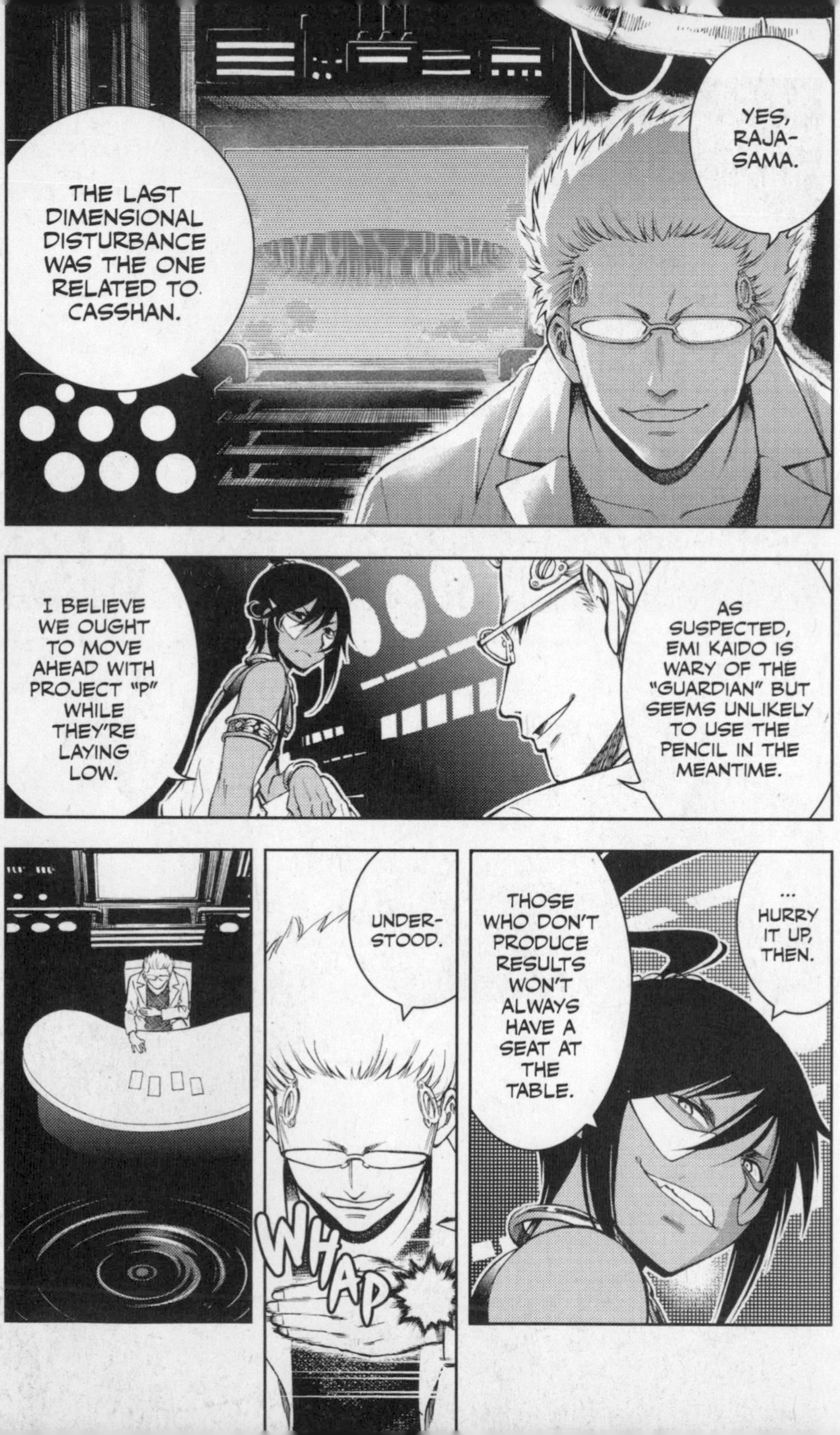
YES, RAJA-SAMA.
THE LAST DIMENSIONAL DISTURBANCE WAS THE ONE RELATED TO CASSHAN.
AS SUSPECTED, EMI KAIDO IS WARY OF THE "GUARDIAN" BUT SEEMS UNLIKELY TO USE THE PENCIL IN THE MEANTIME.
I BELIEVE WE OUGHT TO MOVE AHEAD WITH PROJECT "P" WHILE THEY'RE LAYING LOW.
... HURRY IT UP, THEN.
THOSE WHO DON'T PRODUCE RESULTS WON'T ALWAYS HAVE A SEAT AT THE TABLE.
UNDER-STOOD.
WHAP

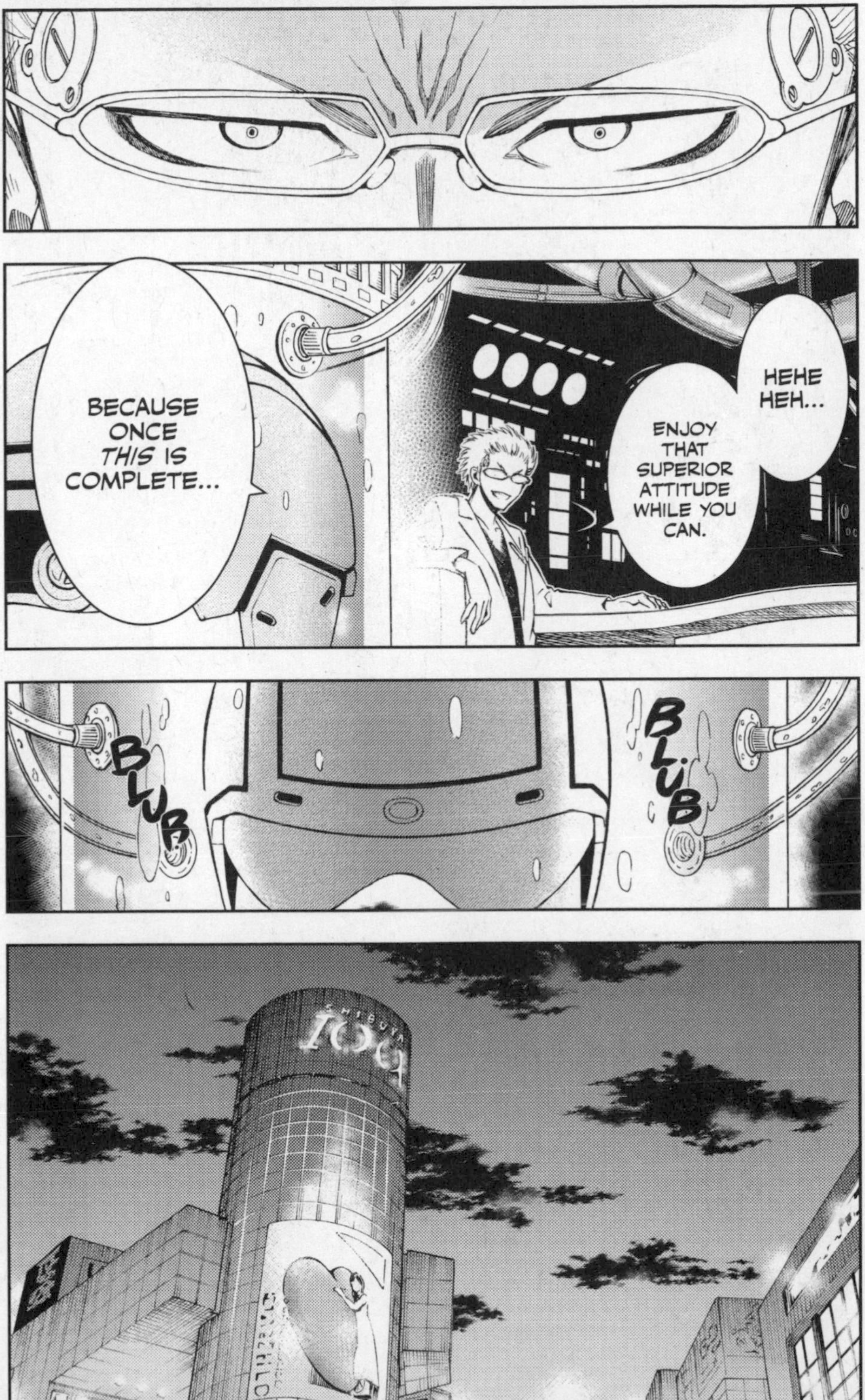
HEHE HEH...
ENJOY THAT SUPERIOR ATTITUDE WHILE YOU CAN.
BECAUSE ONCE *THIS* IS COMPLETE...
BLUB
BLUB

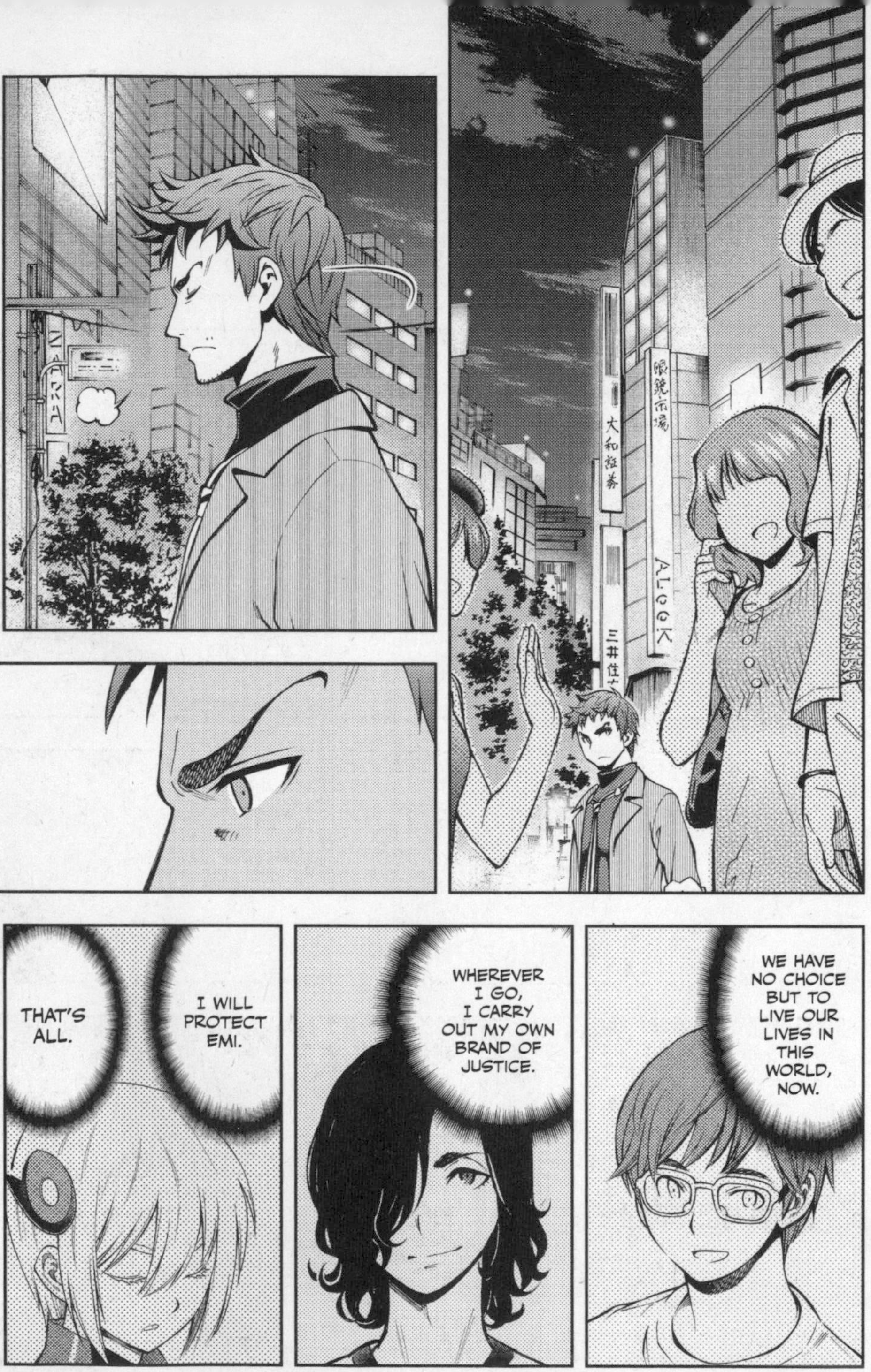
眼鏡市場
大和証券
ALOOK
WE HAVE NO CHOICE BUT TO LIVE OUR LIVES IN THIS WORLD, NOW.
WHEREVER I GO, I CARRY OUT MY OWN BRAND OF JUSTICE.
I WILL PROTECT EMI.
THAT'S ALL.

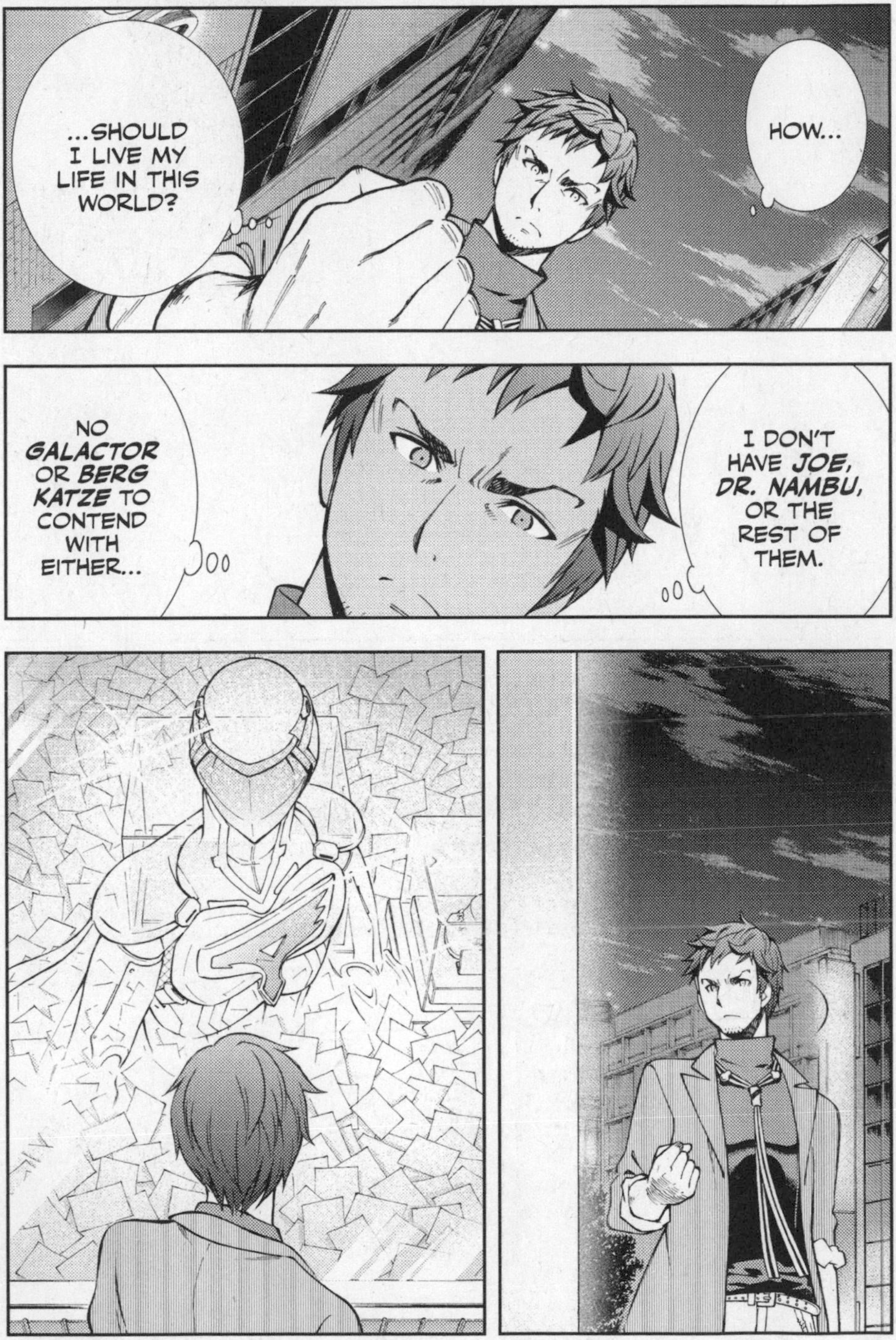
HOW...
...SHOULD I LIVE MY LIFE IN THIS WORLD?
I DON'T HAVE JOE, DR. NAMBU, OR THE REST OF THEM.
NO GALACTOR OR BERG KATZE TO CONTEND WITH EITHER...

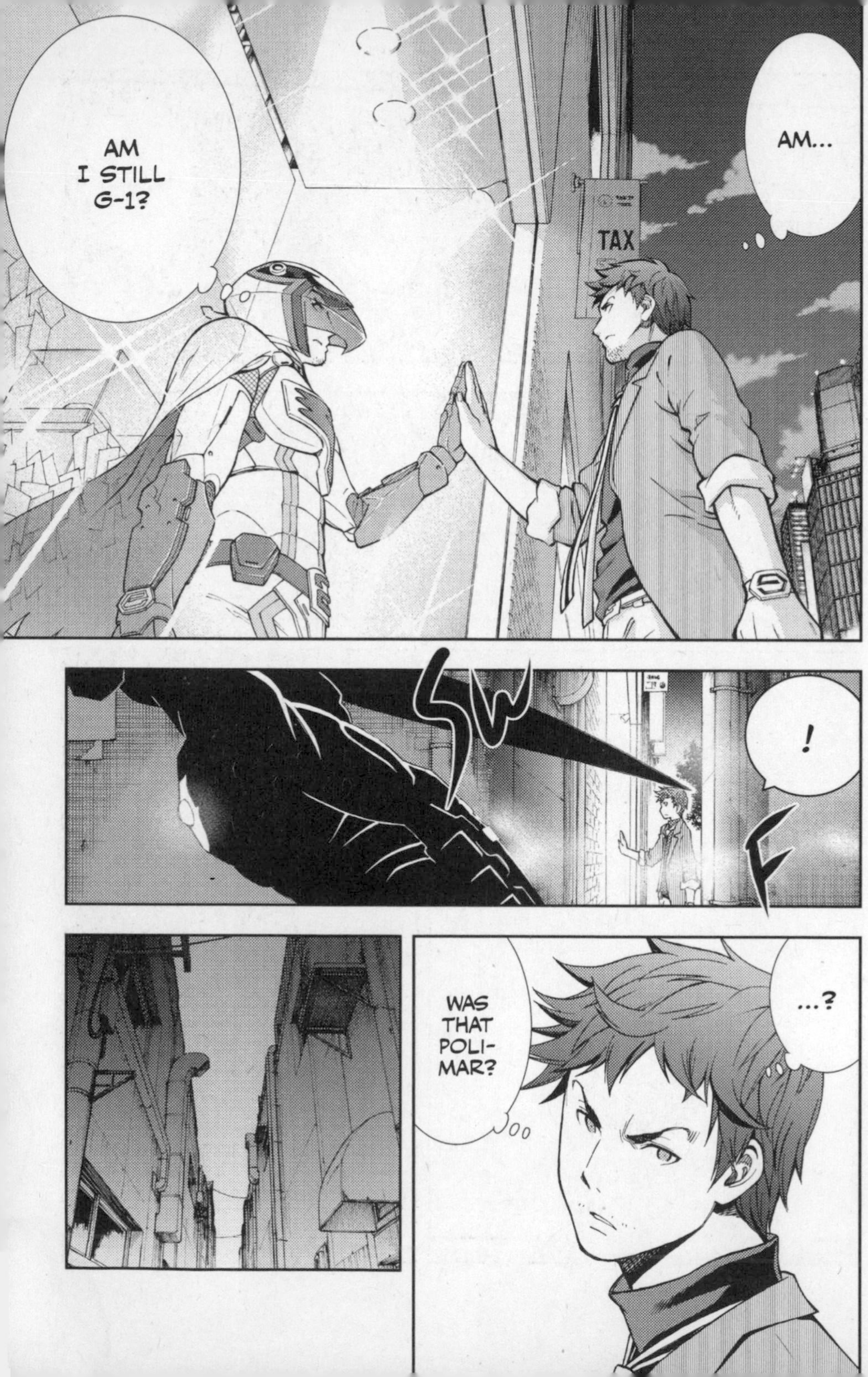
AM...
TAX
AM I STILL G-1?
!
F
SW
...?
WAS THAT POLI-MAR?

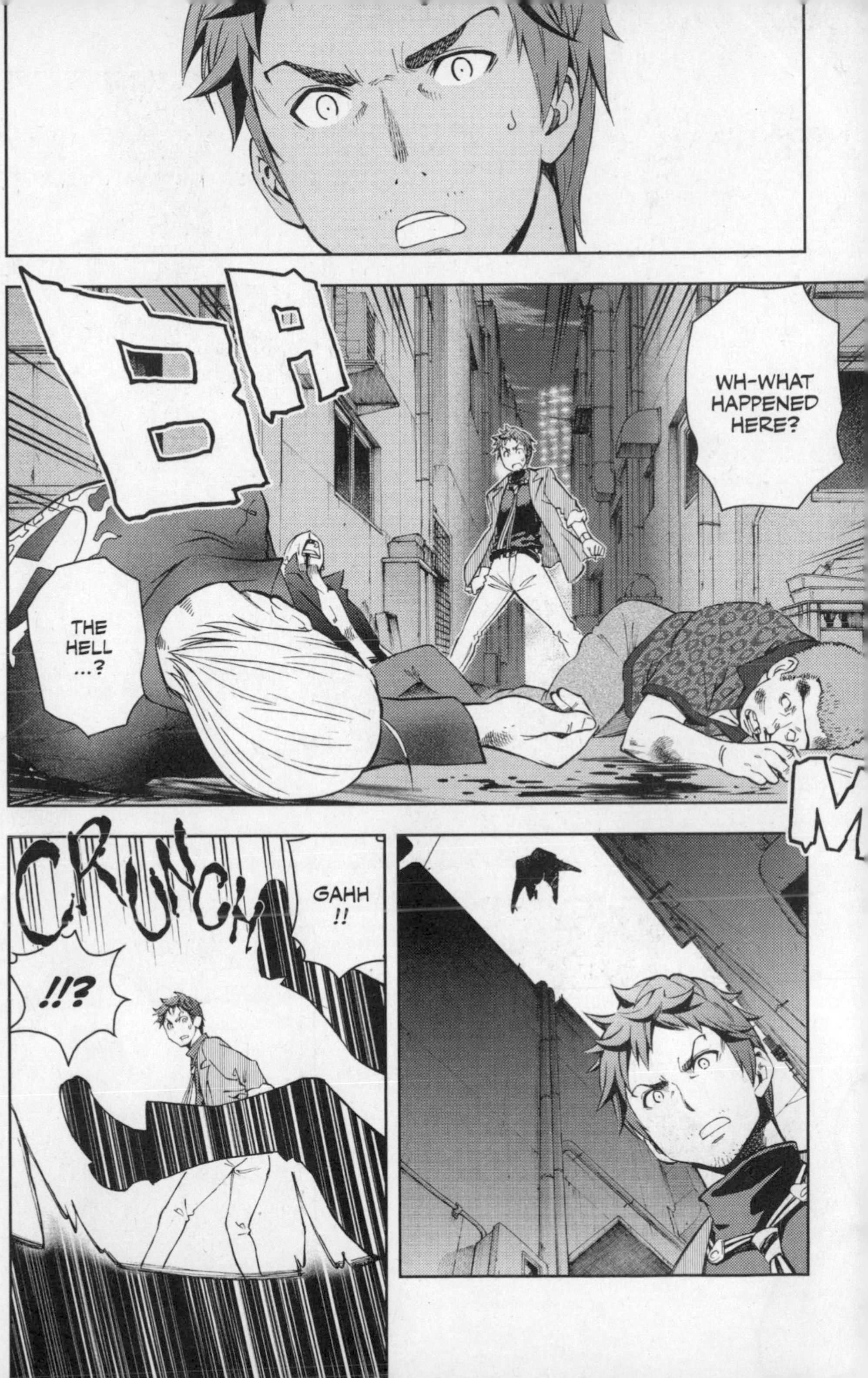
WH-WHAT HAPPENED HERE?
BA
THE HELL ...?
CRUNCH
GAHH !!
!!?

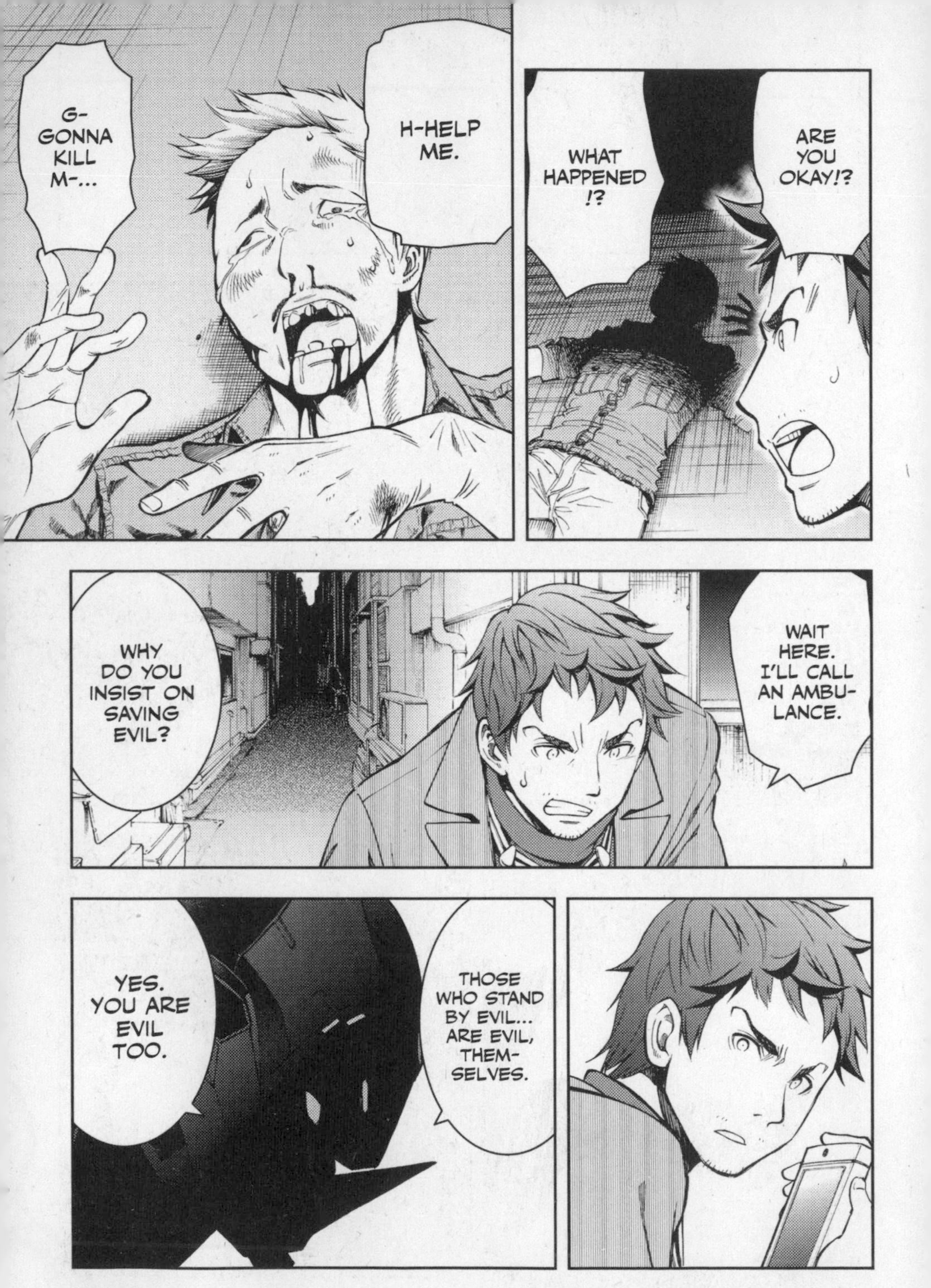
ARE YOU OKAY!?
WHAT HAPPENED !?
H-HELP ME.
G- GONNA KILL M-...
WAIT HERE. I'LL CALL AN AMBU- LANCE.
WHY DO YOU INSIST ON SAVING EVIL?
THOSE WHO STAND BY EVIL... ARE EVIL, THEM- SELVES.
YES. YOU ARE EVIL TOO.

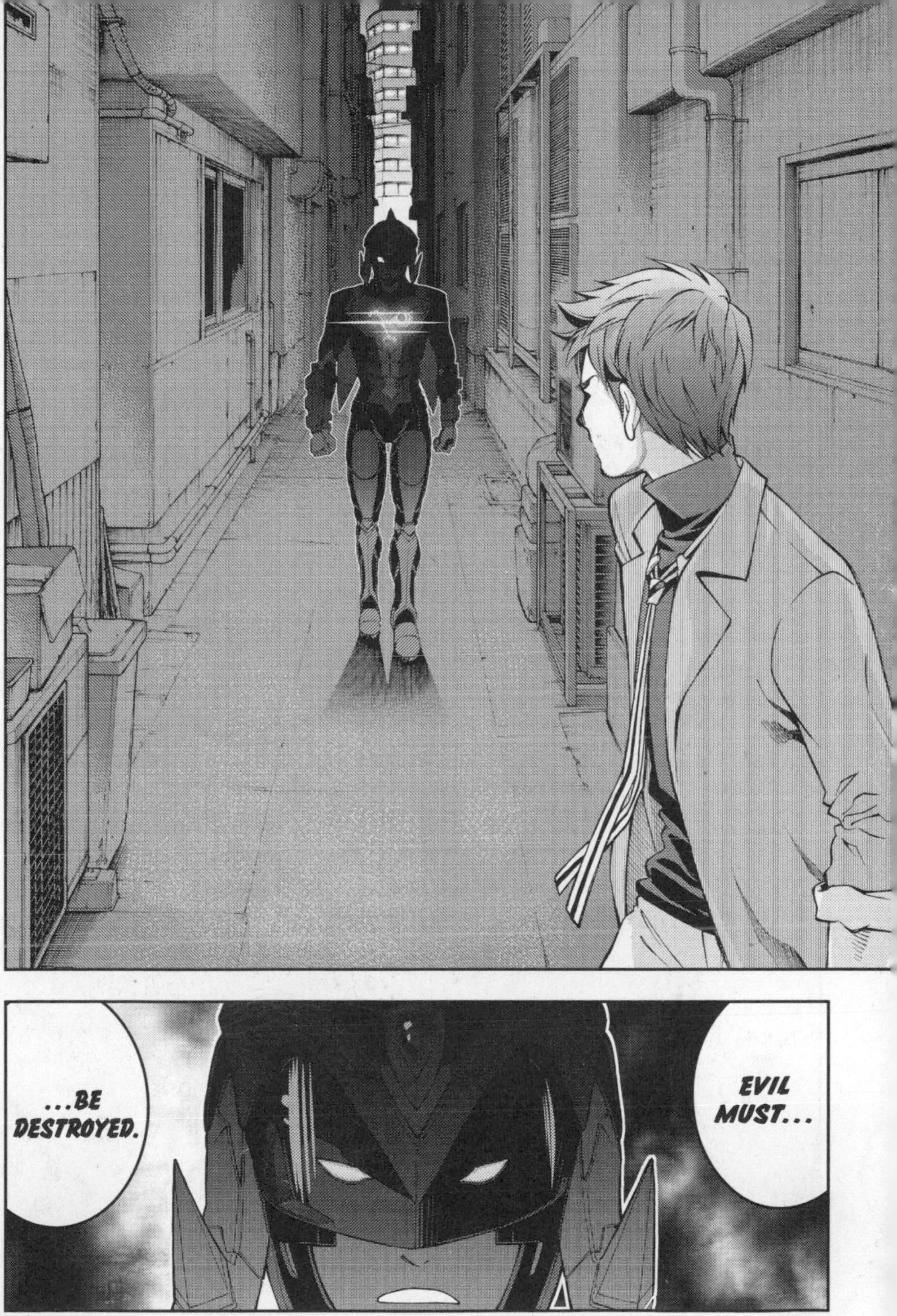
EVIL MUST...
...BE DESTROYED.

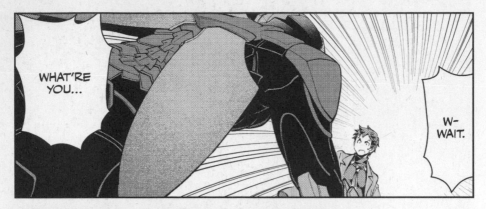

WHAT'RE YOU...

W-WAIT.

DON'T MOVE, POLIMAR !!

YOU'RE UNDER ARREST !!

FZASH

!!

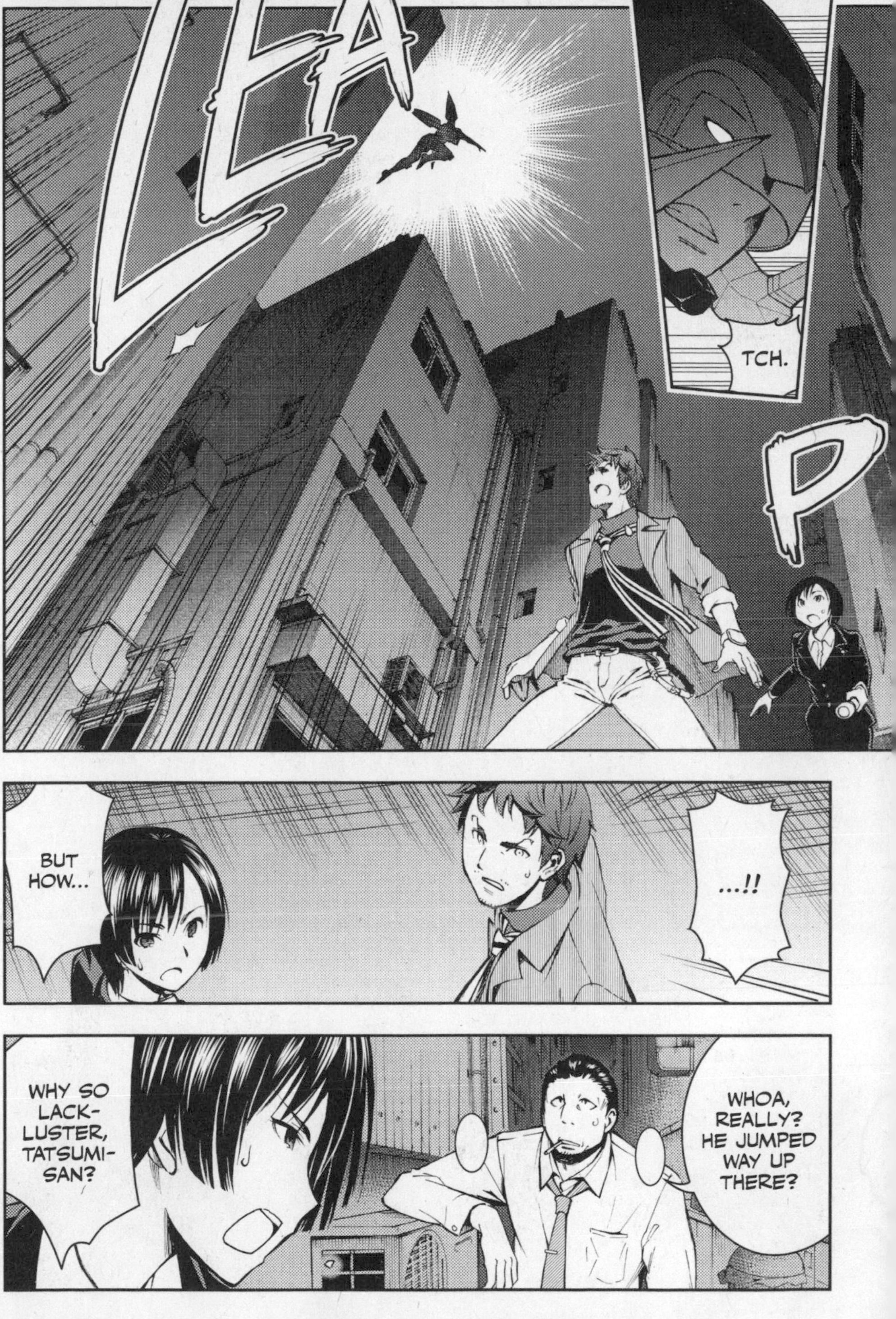
TCH.
LEAP
...!!
BUT HOW...
WHOA, REALLY? HE JUMPED WAY UP THERE?
WHY SO LACK-LUSTER, TATSUMI-SAN?

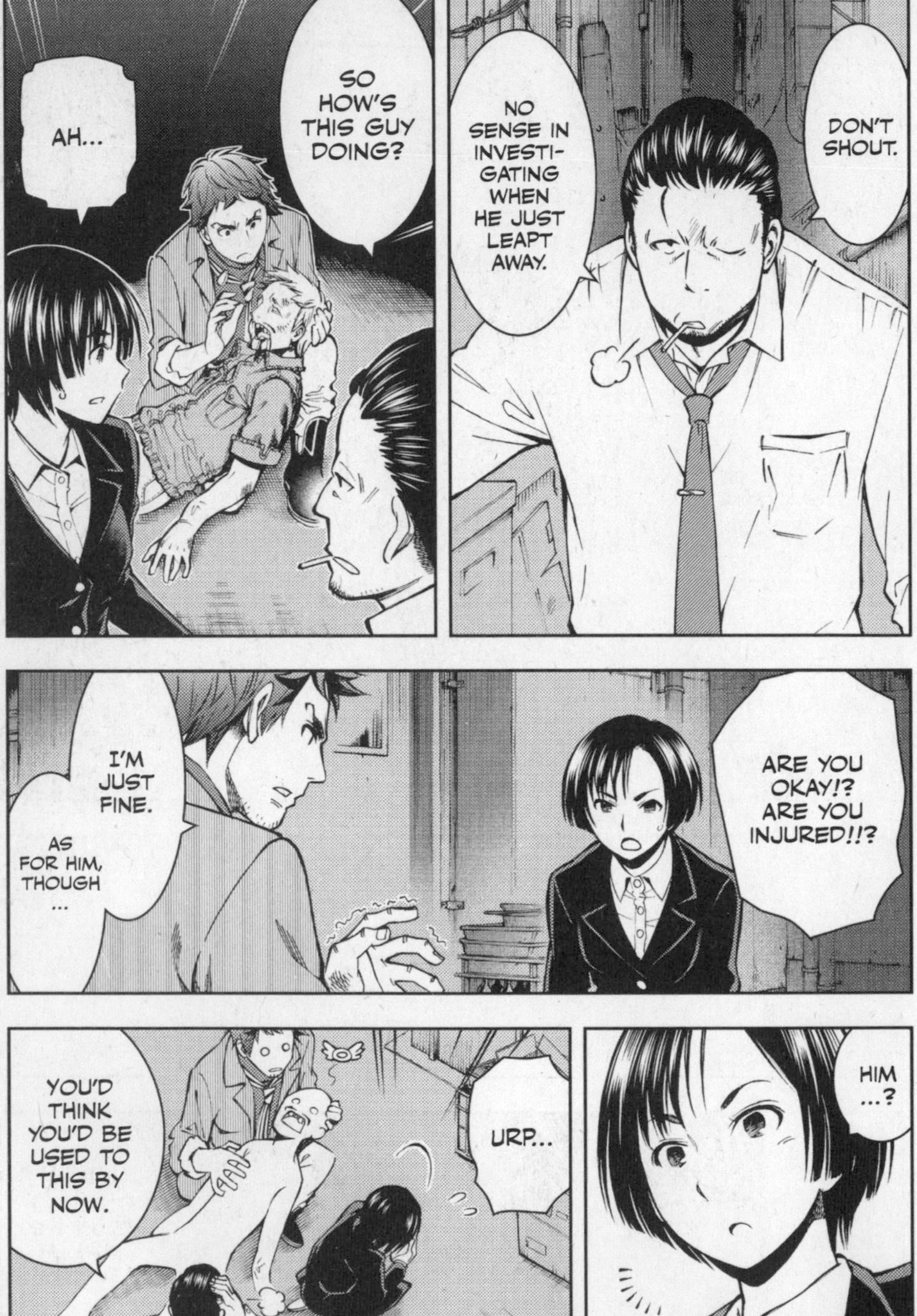
DON'T SHOUT.
NO SENSE IN INVESTIGATING WHEN HE JUST LEAPT AWAY.
SO HOW'S THIS GUY DOING?
AH...
ARE YOU OKAY!? ARE YOU INJURED!!?
I'M JUST FINE.
AS FOR HIM, THOUGH ...
HIM ...?
URP...
YOU'D THINK YOU'D BE USED TO THIS BY NOW.

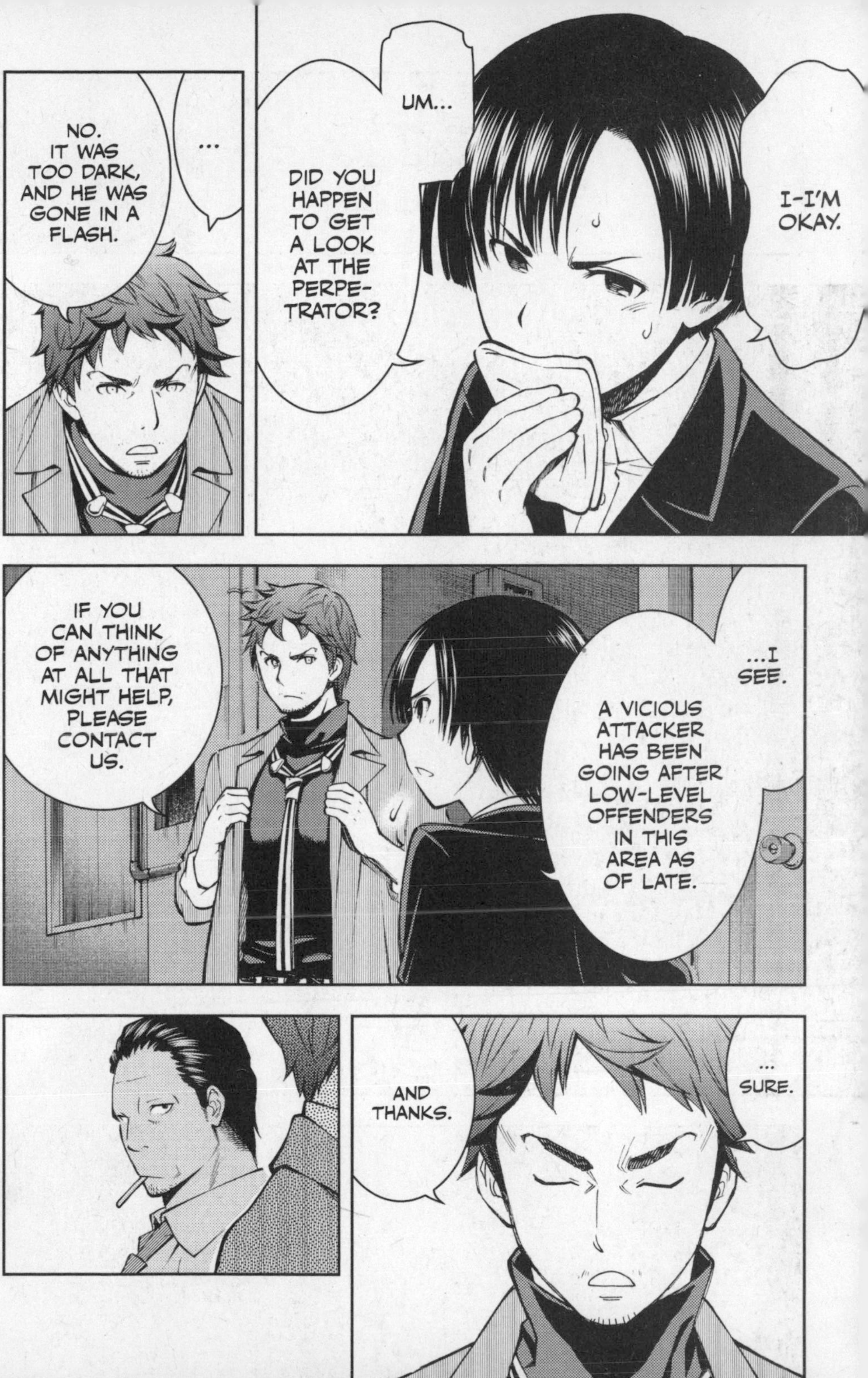
I-I'M OKAY.
UM...
DID YOU HAPPEN TO GET A LOOK AT THE PERPE-TRATOR?
...
NO. IT WAS TOO DARK, AND HE WAS GONE IN A FLASH.
...I SEE.
A VICIOUS ATTACKER HAS BEEN GOING AFTER LOW-LEVEL OFFENDERS IN THIS AREA AS OF LATE.
IF YOU CAN THINK OF ANYTHING AT ALL THAT MIGHT HELP, PLEASE CONTACT US.
... SURE.
AND THANKS.

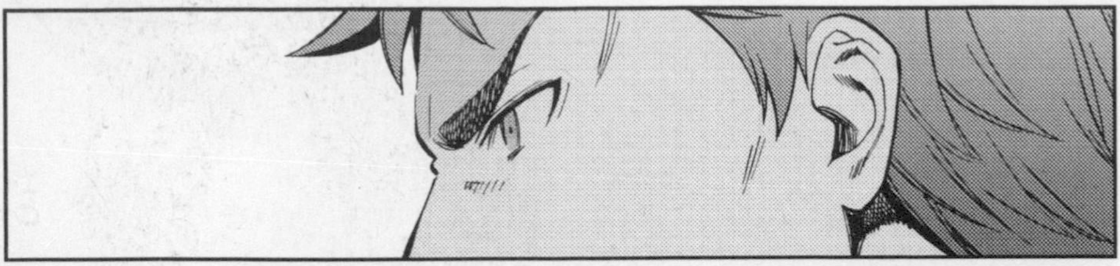
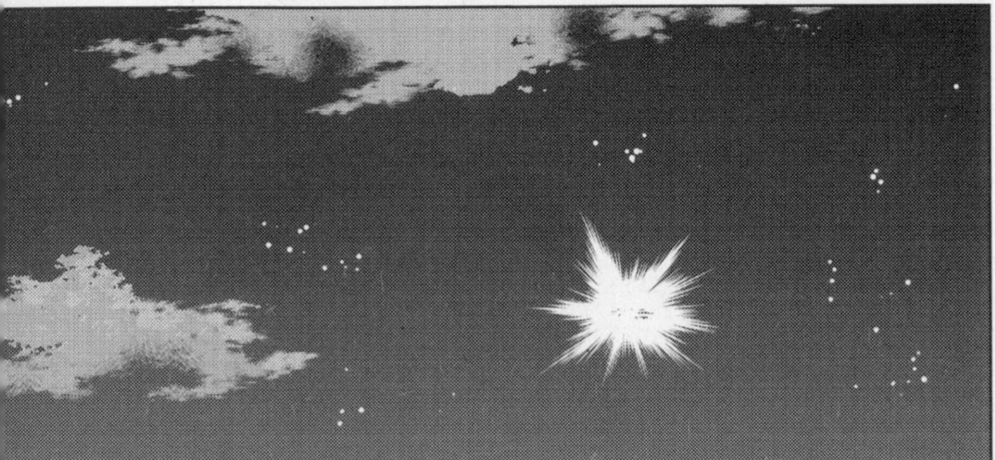
CON MALL
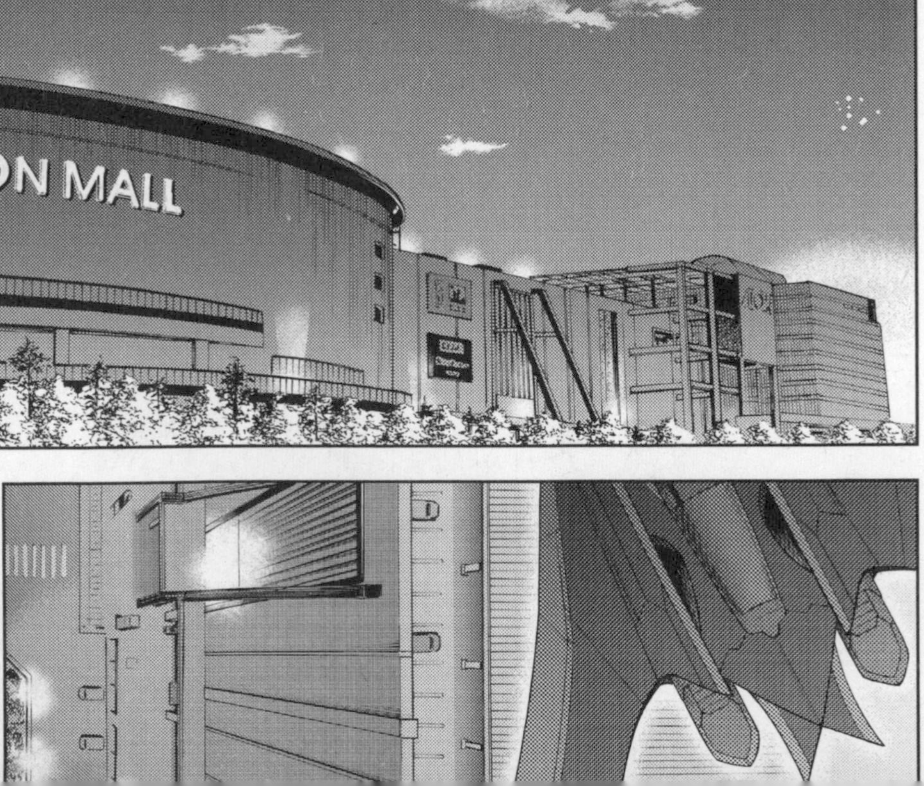

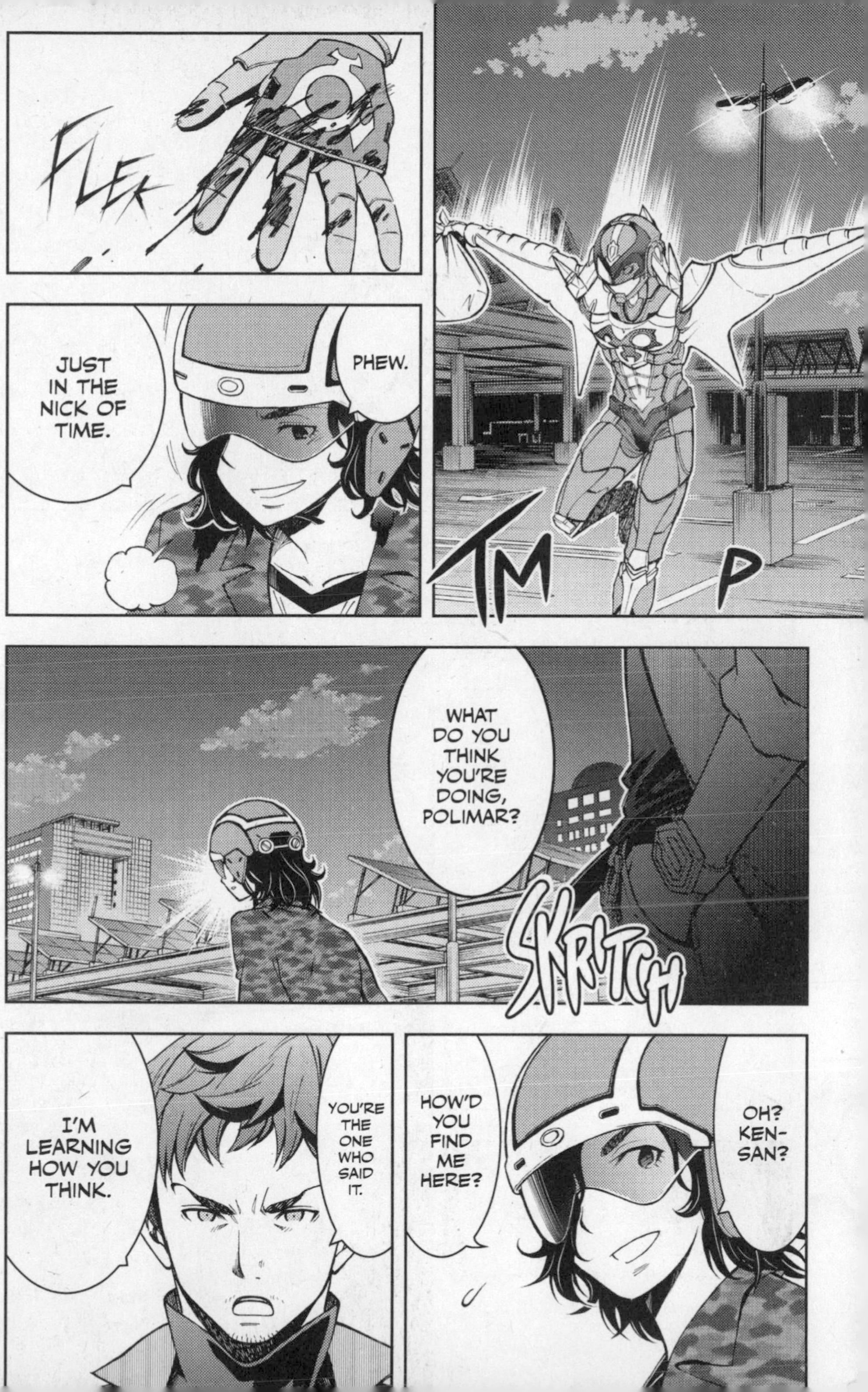
TMP
FLEK
PHEW.
JUST IN THE NICK OF TIME.
WHAT DO YOU THINK YOU'RE DOING, POLIMAR?
SKRITCH
OH? KEN-SAN?
HOW'D YOU FIND ME HERE?
YOU'RE THE ONE WHO SAID IT.
I'M LEARNING HOW YOU THINK.

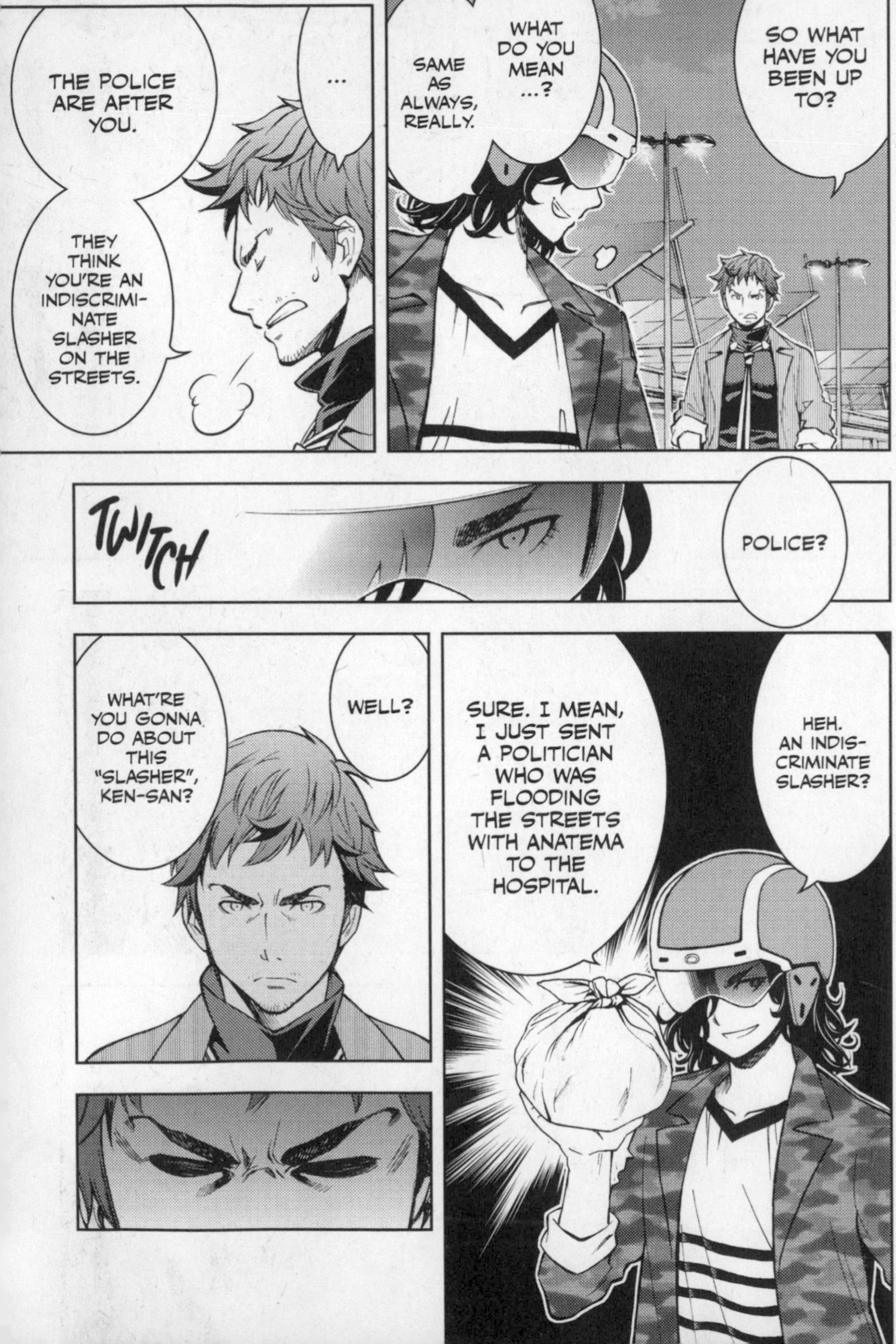
SO WHAT HAVE YOU BEEN UP TO?
WHAT DO YOU MEAN ...?
SAME AS ALWAYS, REALLY.
...
THE POLICE ARE AFTER YOU.
THEY THINK YOU'RE AN INDISCRIMINATE SLASHER ON THE STREETS.
POLICE?
TWITCH
HEH. AN INDISCRIMINATE SLASHER?
SURE. I MEAN, I JUST SENT A POLITICIAN WHO WAS FLOODING THE STREETS WITH ANATEMA TO THE HOSPITAL.
WELL?
WHAT'RE YOU GONNA DO ABOUT THIS "SLASHER", KEN-SAN?

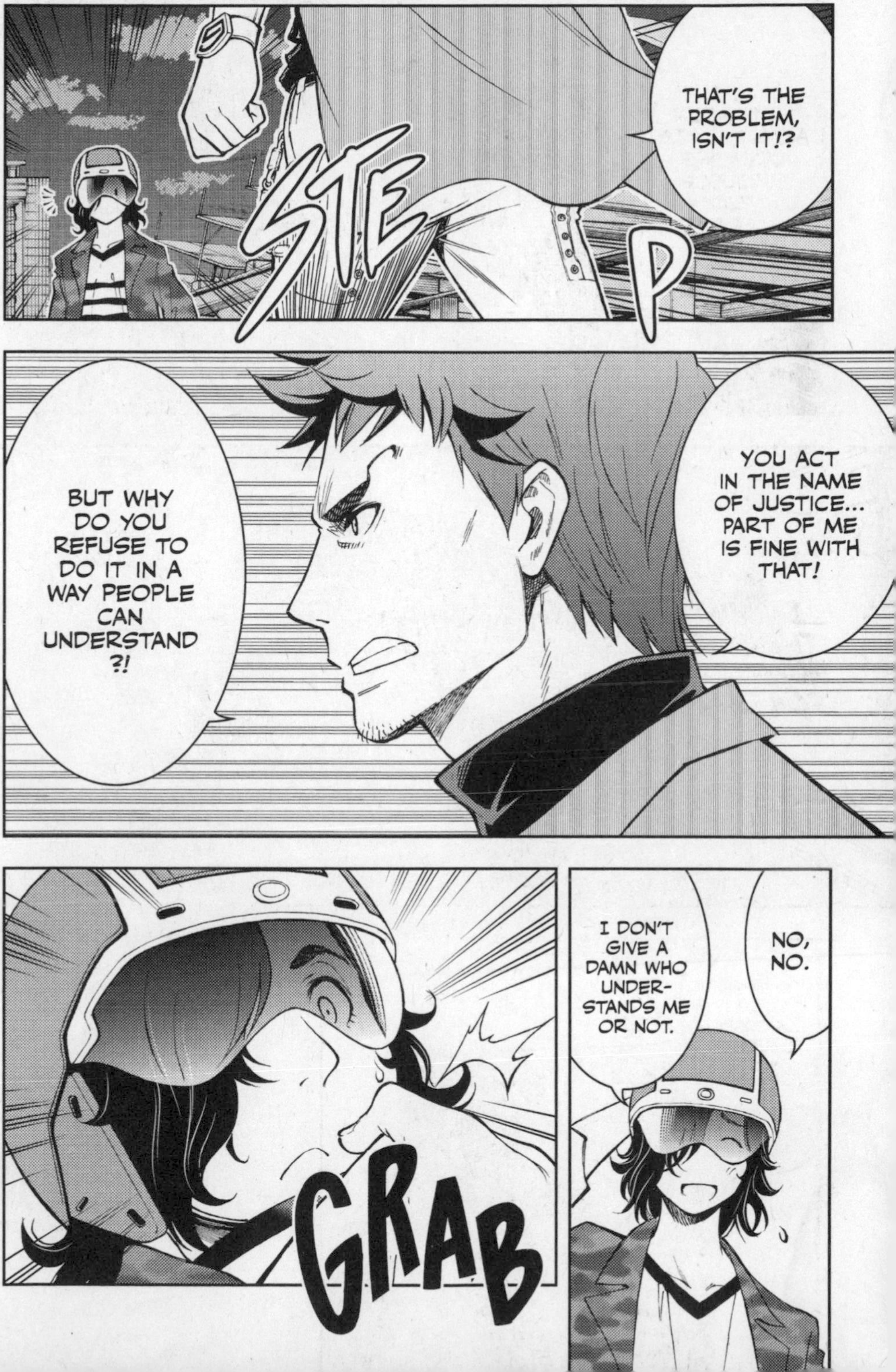
THAT'S THE PROBLEM, ISN'T IT!?
STEP
YOU ACT IN THE NAME OF JUSTICE... PART OF ME IS FINE WITH THAT!
BUT WHY DO YOU REFUSE TO DO IT IN A WAY PEOPLE CAN UNDERSTAND ?!
NO, NO.
I DON'T GIVE A DAMN WHO UNDER- STANDS ME OR NOT.
GRAB

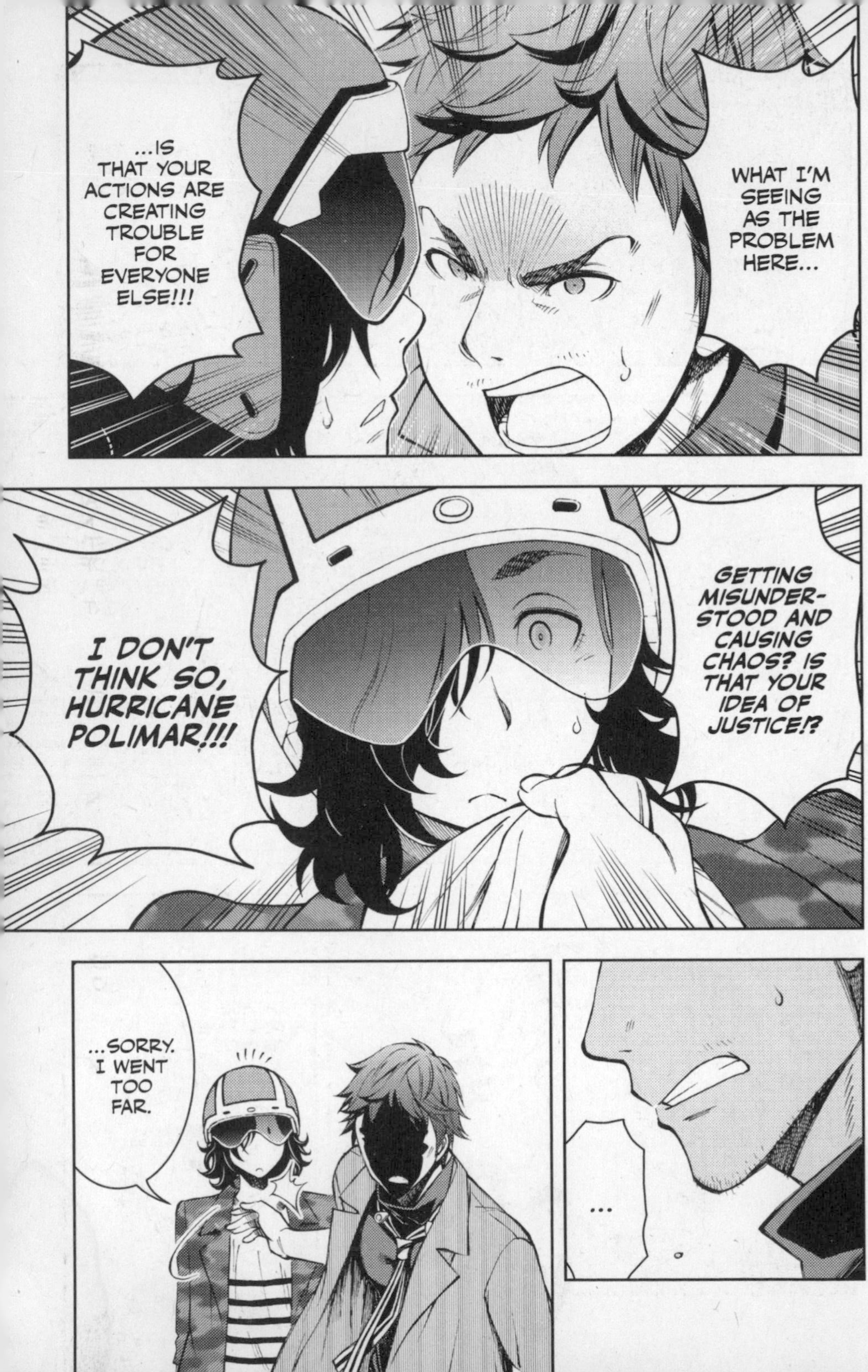
WHAT I'M SEEING AS THE PROBLEM HERE...
...IS THAT YOUR ACTIONS ARE CREATING TROUBLE FOR EVERYONE ELSE!!!
GETTING MISUNDER-STOOD AND CAUSING CHAOS? IS THAT YOUR IDEA OF JUSTICE!?
I DON'T THINK SO, HURRICANE POLIMAR!!!
...
...SORRY. I WENT TOO FAR.

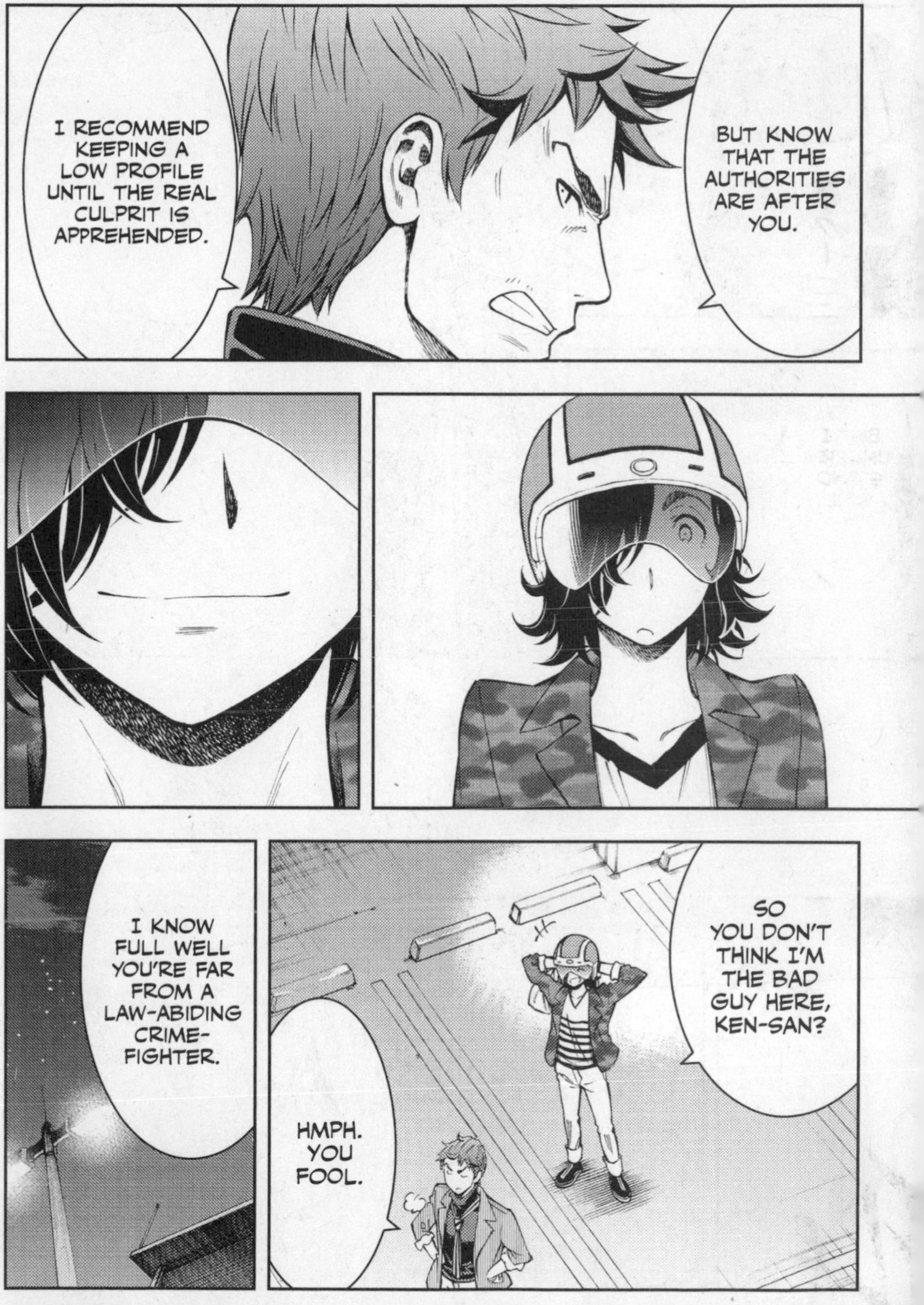
BUT KNOW THAT THE AUTHORITIES ARE AFTER YOU.
I RECOMMEND KEEPING A LOW PROFILE UNTIL THE REAL CULPRIT IS APPREHENDED.
SO YOU DON'T THINK I'M THE BAD GUY HERE, KEN-SAN?
HMPH. YOU FOOL.
I KNOW FULL WELL YOU'RE FAR FROM A LAW-ABIDING CRIME-FIGHTER.

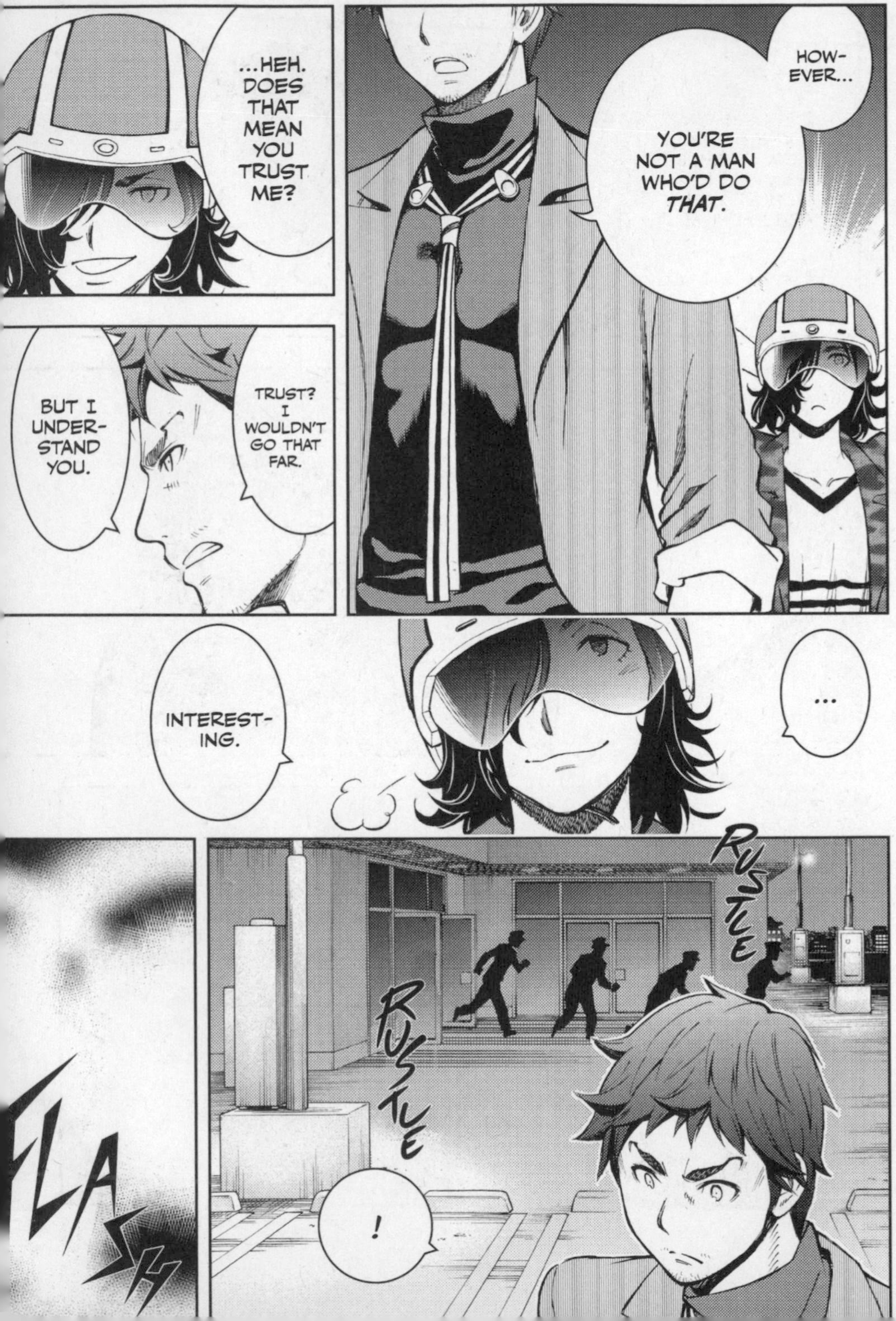
HOW-EVER...
YOU'RE NOT A MAN WHO'D DO *THAT*.
...HEH. DOES THAT MEAN YOU TRUST ME?
TRUST? I WOULDN'T GO THAT FAR.
BUT I UNDER-STAND YOU.
...
INTEREST-ING.
RUSTLE
RUSTLE
!
FLASH

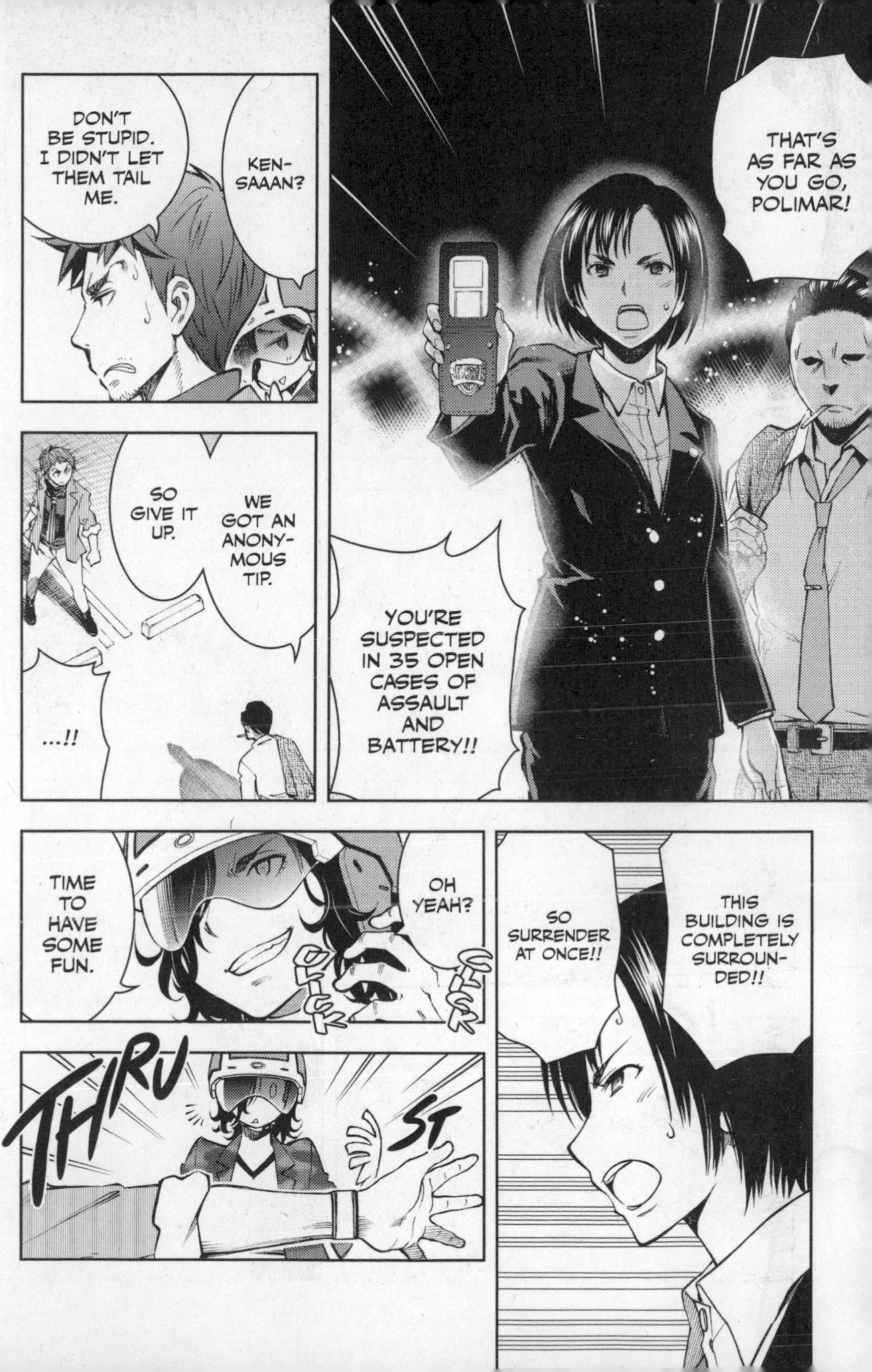
THAT'S AS FAR AS YOU GO, POLIMAR!
YOU'RE SUSPECTED IN 35 OPEN CASES OF ASSAULT AND BATTERY!!
KEN-SAAAN?
DON'T BE STUPID. I DIDN'T LET THEM TAIL ME.
WE GOT AN ANONYMOUS TIP.
SO GIVE IT UP.
...!!
THIS BUILDING IS COMPLETELY SURROUNDED!!
SO SURRENDER AT ONCE!!
OH YEAH?
TIME TO HAVE SOME FUN.
CLICK
CLICK
THRUST

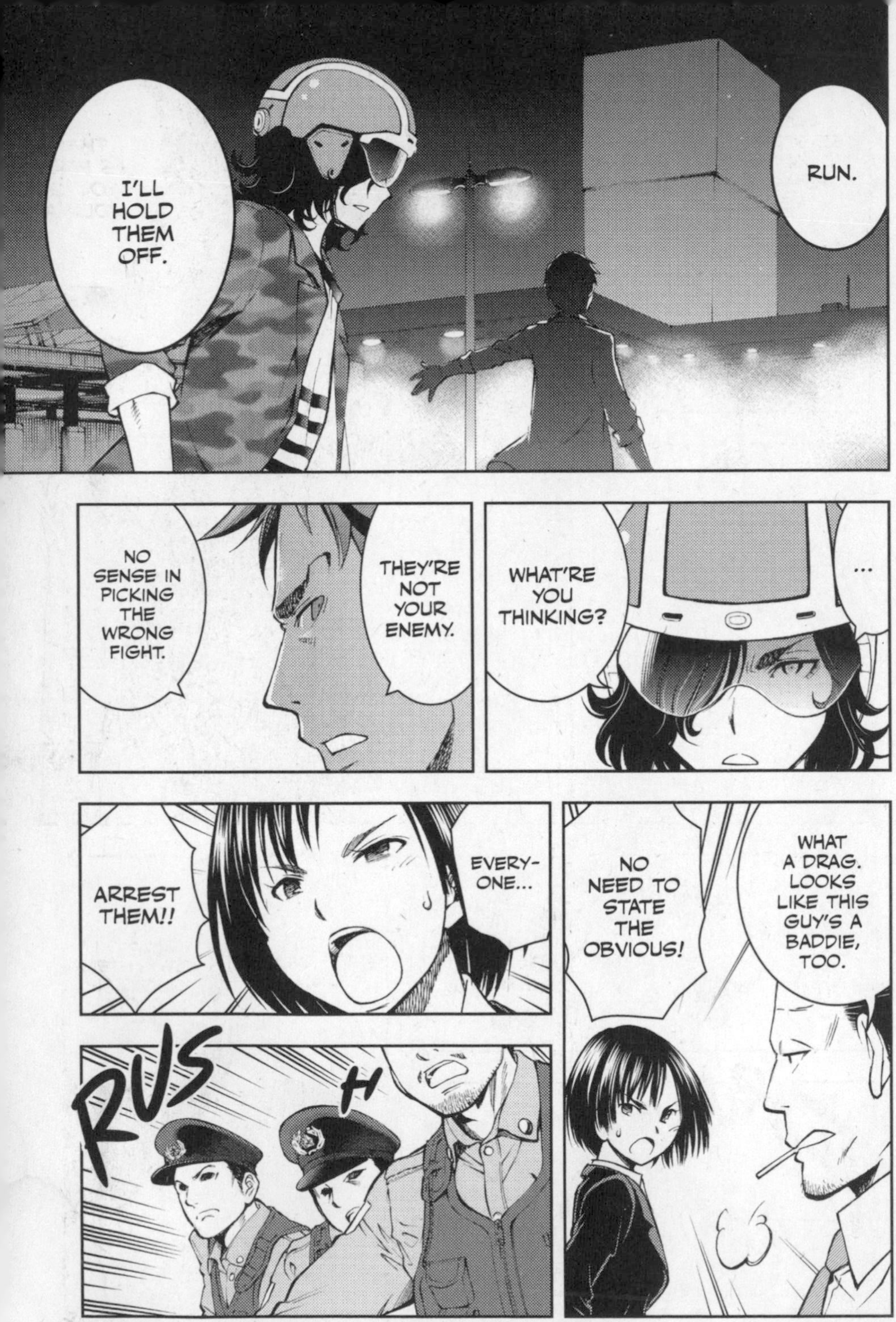
RUN.
I'LL HOLD THEM OFF.
...
WHAT'RE YOU THINKING?
THEY'RE NOT YOUR ENEMY.
NO SENSE IN PICKING THE WRONG FIGHT.
WHAT A DRAG. LOOKS LIKE THIS GUY'S A BADDIE, TOO.
NO NEED TO STATE THE OBVIOUS!
EVERY-ONE...
ARREST THEM!!
RUSH

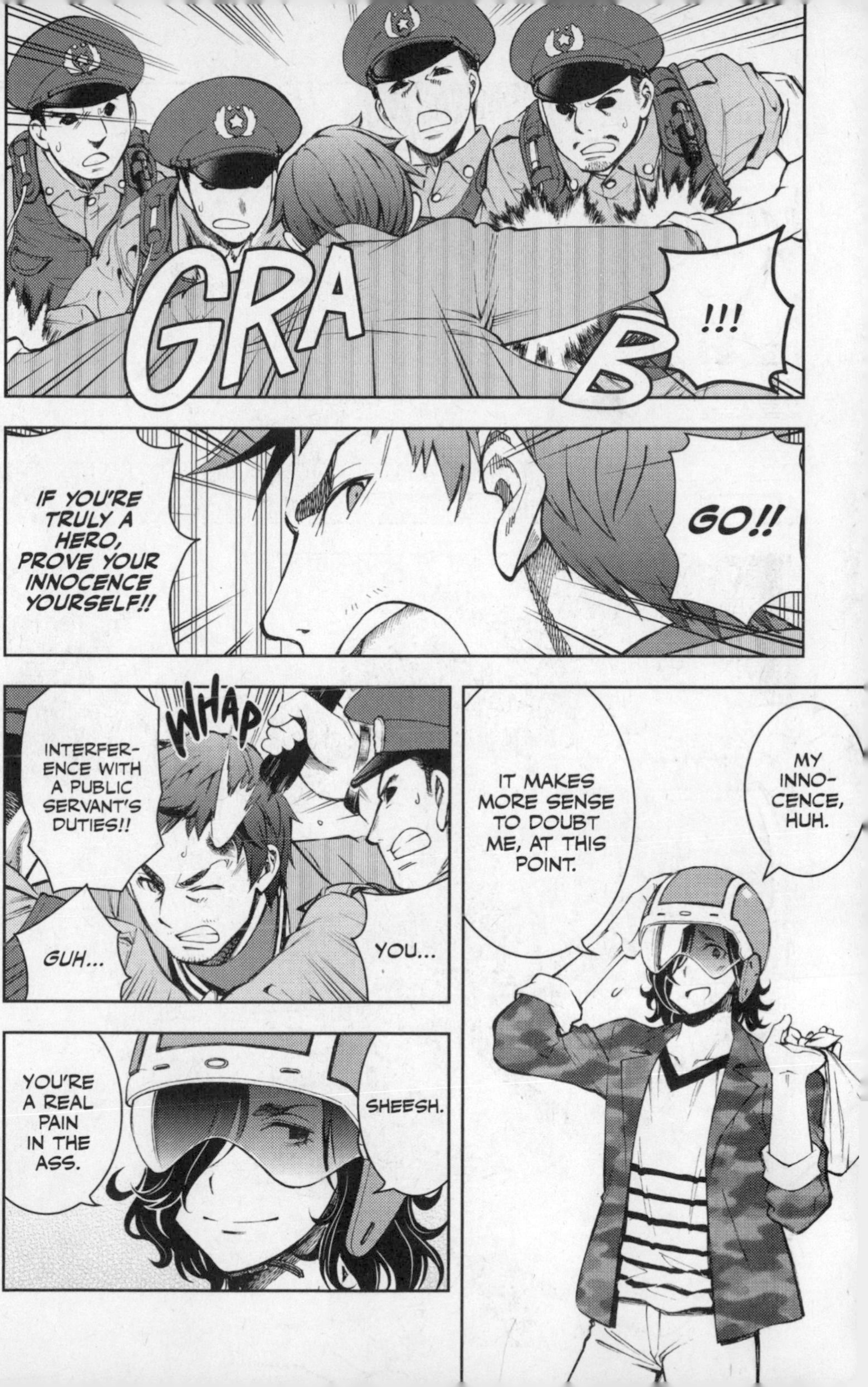
GRAB
!!!
GO!!
IF YOU'RE TRULY A HERO, PROVE YOUR INNOCENCE YOURSELF!!
MY INNO-CENCE, HUH.
IT MAKES MORE SENSE TO DOUBT ME, AT THIS POINT.
WHAP
INTERFER-ENCE WITH A PUBLIC SERVANT'S DUTIES!!
YOU...
GUH...
SHEESH.
YOU'RE A REAL PAIN IN THE ASS.

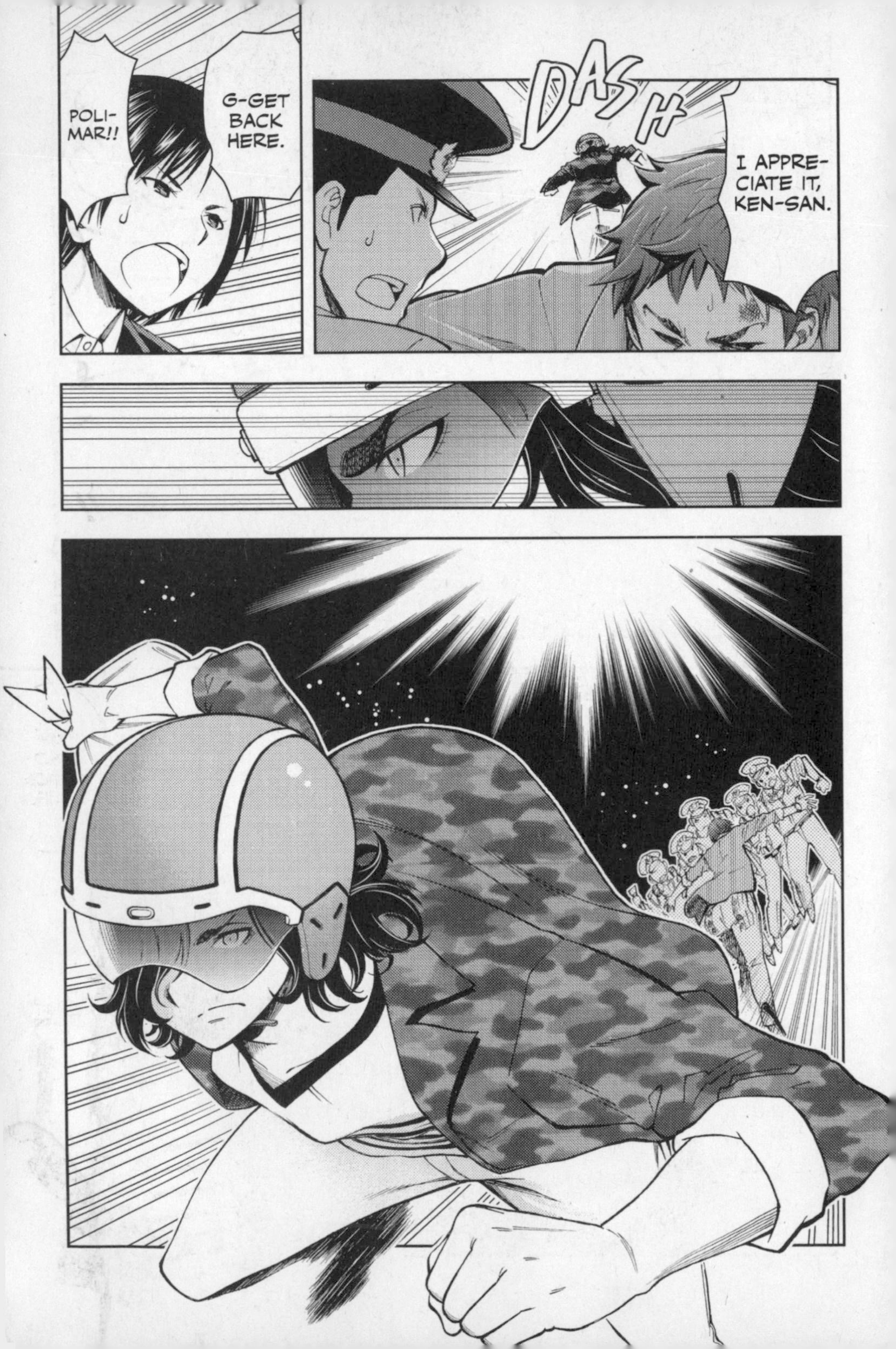
DASH
I APPRECIATE IT, KEN-SAN.
G-GET BACK HERE.
POLIMAR!!

NOW WHERE'VE WE SEEN THIS POSE BEFORE?

Infini-T Force
インフィニティフォース
ARC TO THE FUTURE

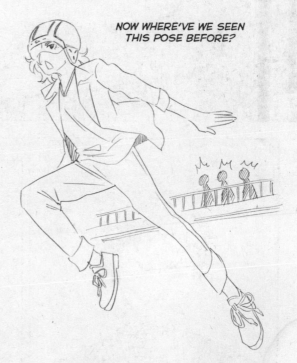

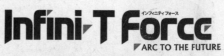

# EPISODE 6 ▸ FIST OF STEEL

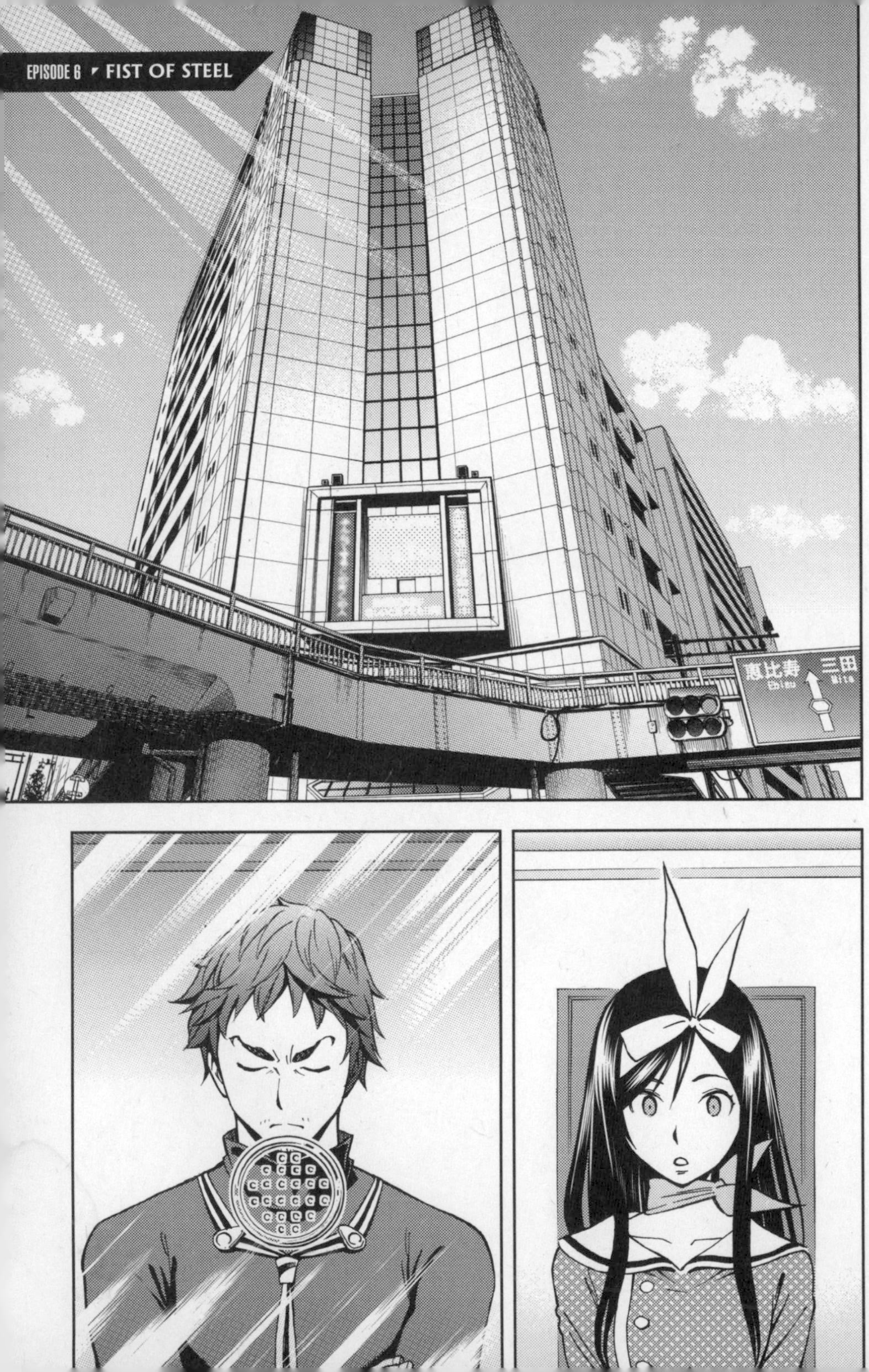
恵比寿
Ebisu
三田
Mita

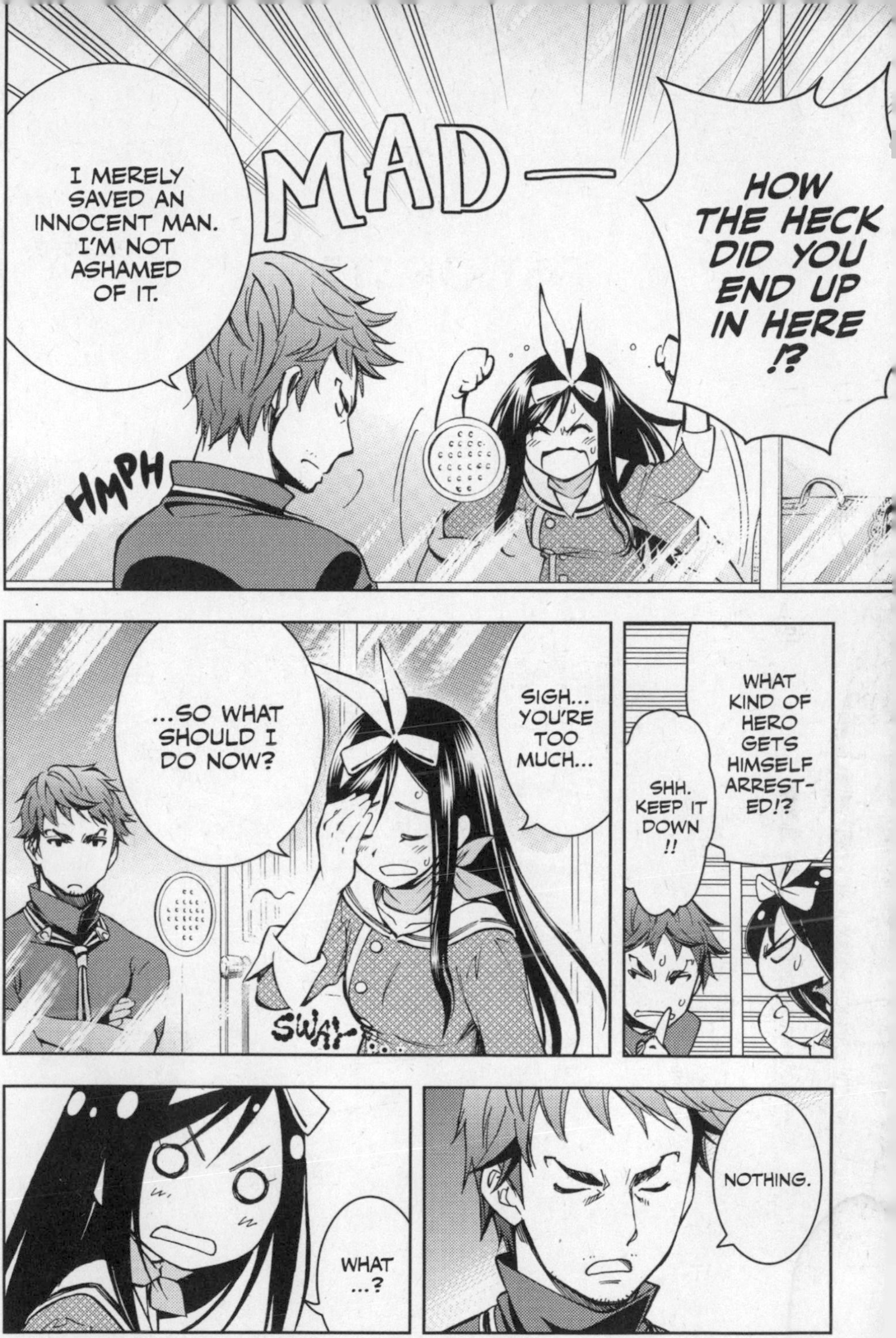
HOW THE HECK DID YOU END UP IN HERE!?
MAD—
I MERELY SAVED AN INNOCENT MAN. I'M NOT ASHAMED OF IT.
HMPH
WHAT KIND OF HERO GETS HIMSELF ARREST-ED!?
SHH. KEEP IT DOWN!!
SIGH... YOU'RE TOO MUCH...
...SO WHAT SHOULD I DO NOW?
SWAY
NOTHING.
WHAT ...?

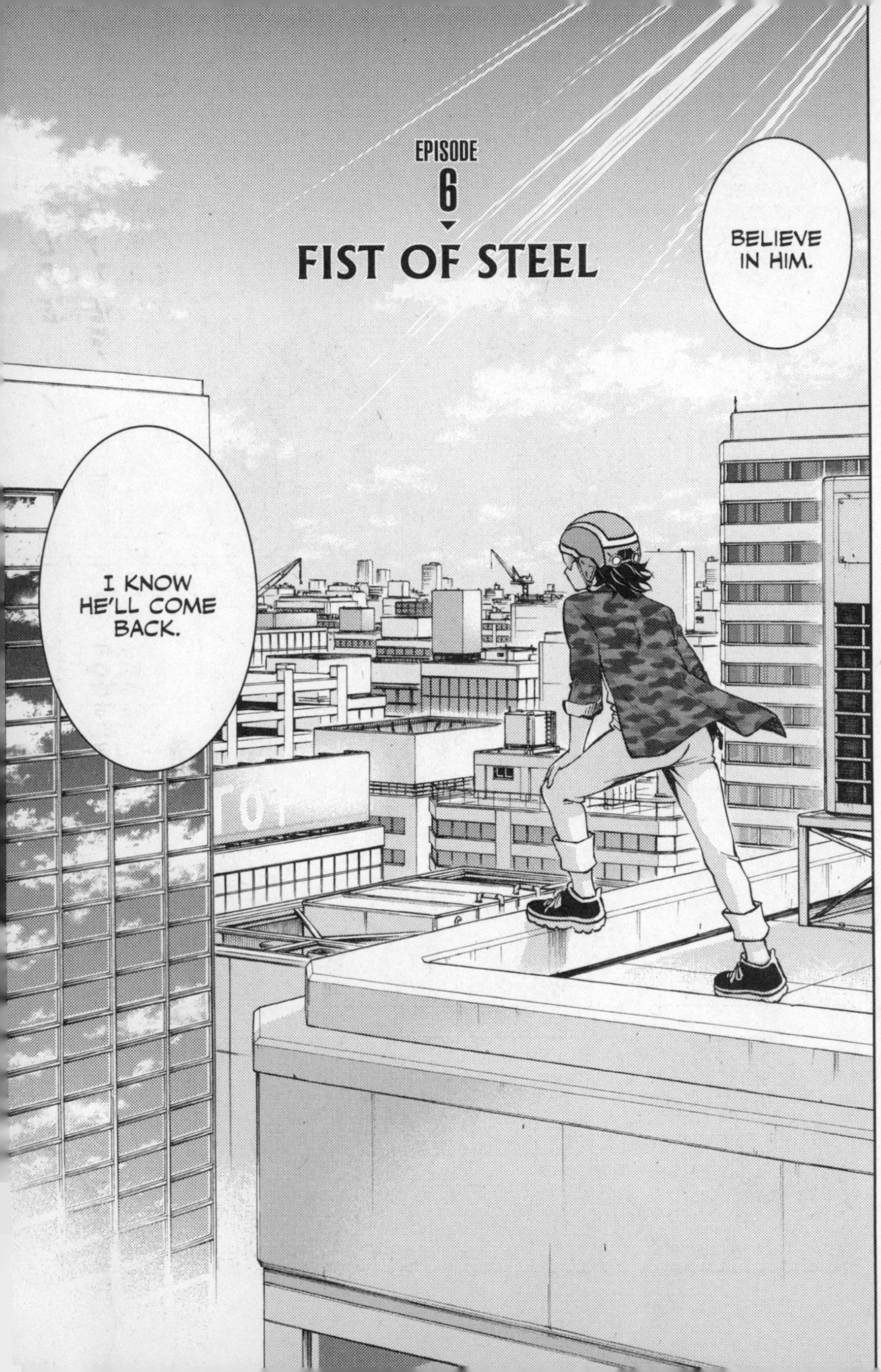
EPISODE
6
FIST OF STEEL
BELIEVE IN HIM.
I KNOW HE'LL COME BACK.

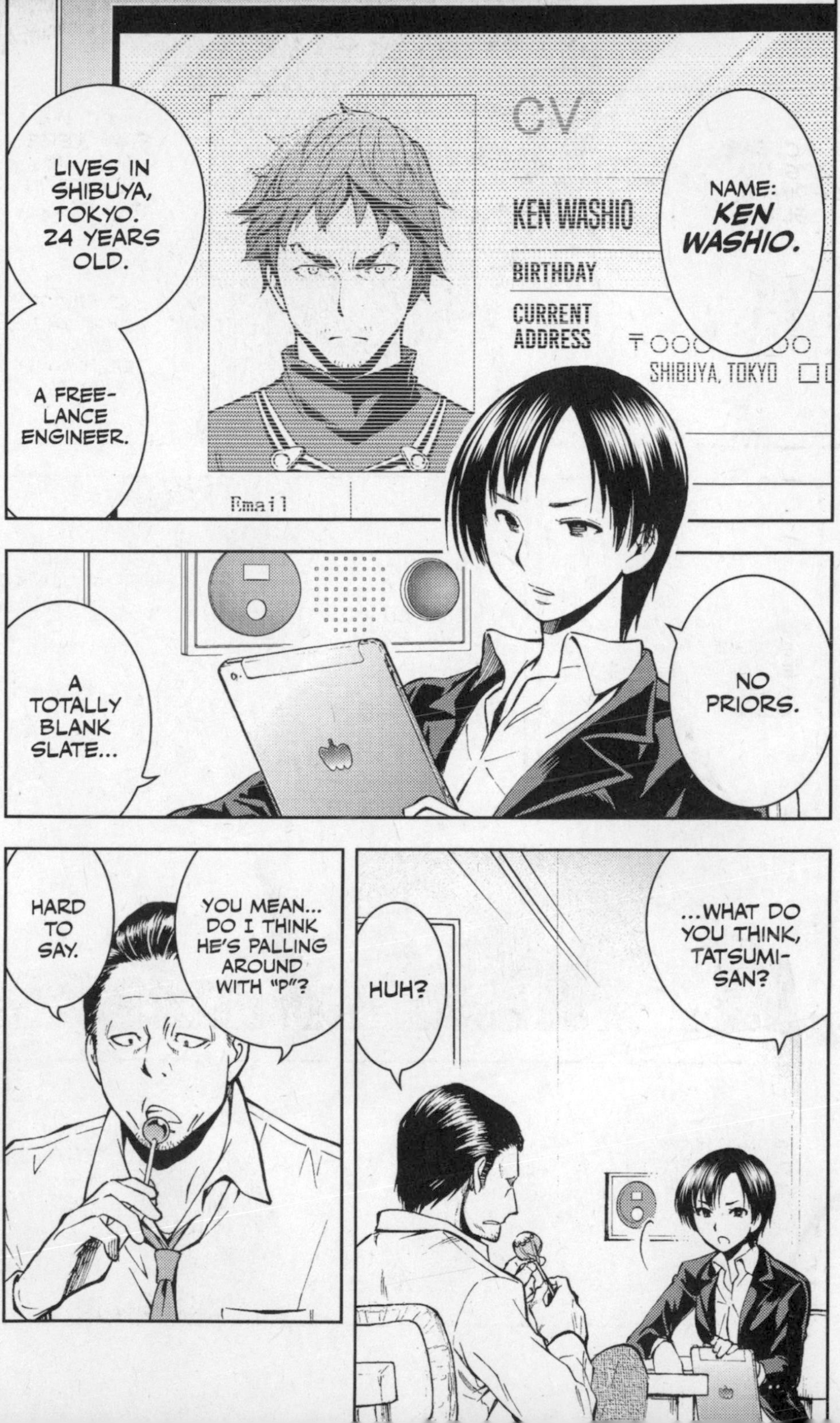
CV
KEN WASHIO
BIRTHDAY
CURRENT ADDRESS
SHIBUYA, TOKYO
Email
NAME: KEN WASHIO.
LIVES IN SHIBUYA, TOKYO. 24 YEARS OLD.
A FREE-LANCE ENGINEER.
NO PRIORS.
A TOTALLY BLANK SLATE...
...WHAT DO YOU THINK, TATSUMI-SAN?
HUH?
YOU MEAN... DO I THINK HE'S PALLING AROUND WITH "P"?
HARD TO SAY.

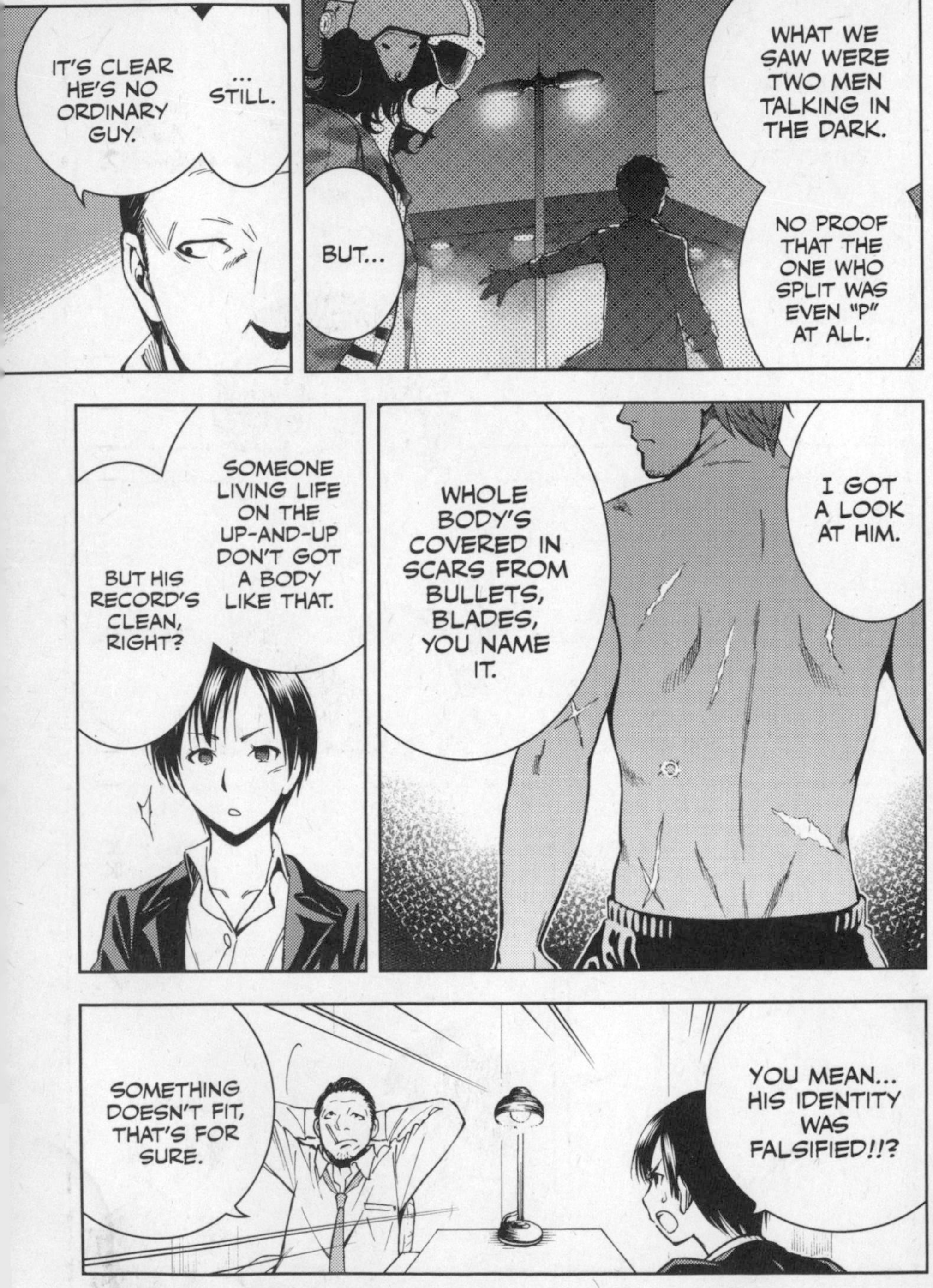
WHAT WE SAW WERE TWO MEN TALKING IN THE DARK.
NO PROOF THAT THE ONE WHO SPLIT WAS EVEN "P" AT ALL.
BUT...
...STILL.
IT'S CLEAR HE'S NO ORDINARY GUY.
I GOT A LOOK AT HIM.
WHOLE BODY'S COVERED IN SCARS FROM BULLETS, BLADES, YOU NAME IT.
SOMEONE LIVING LIFE ON THE UP-AND-UP DON'T GOT A BODY LIKE THAT.
BUT HIS RECORD'S CLEAN, RIGHT?
YOU MEAN... HIS IDENTITY WAS FALSIFIED!!?
SOMETHING DOESN'T FIT, THAT'S FOR SURE.

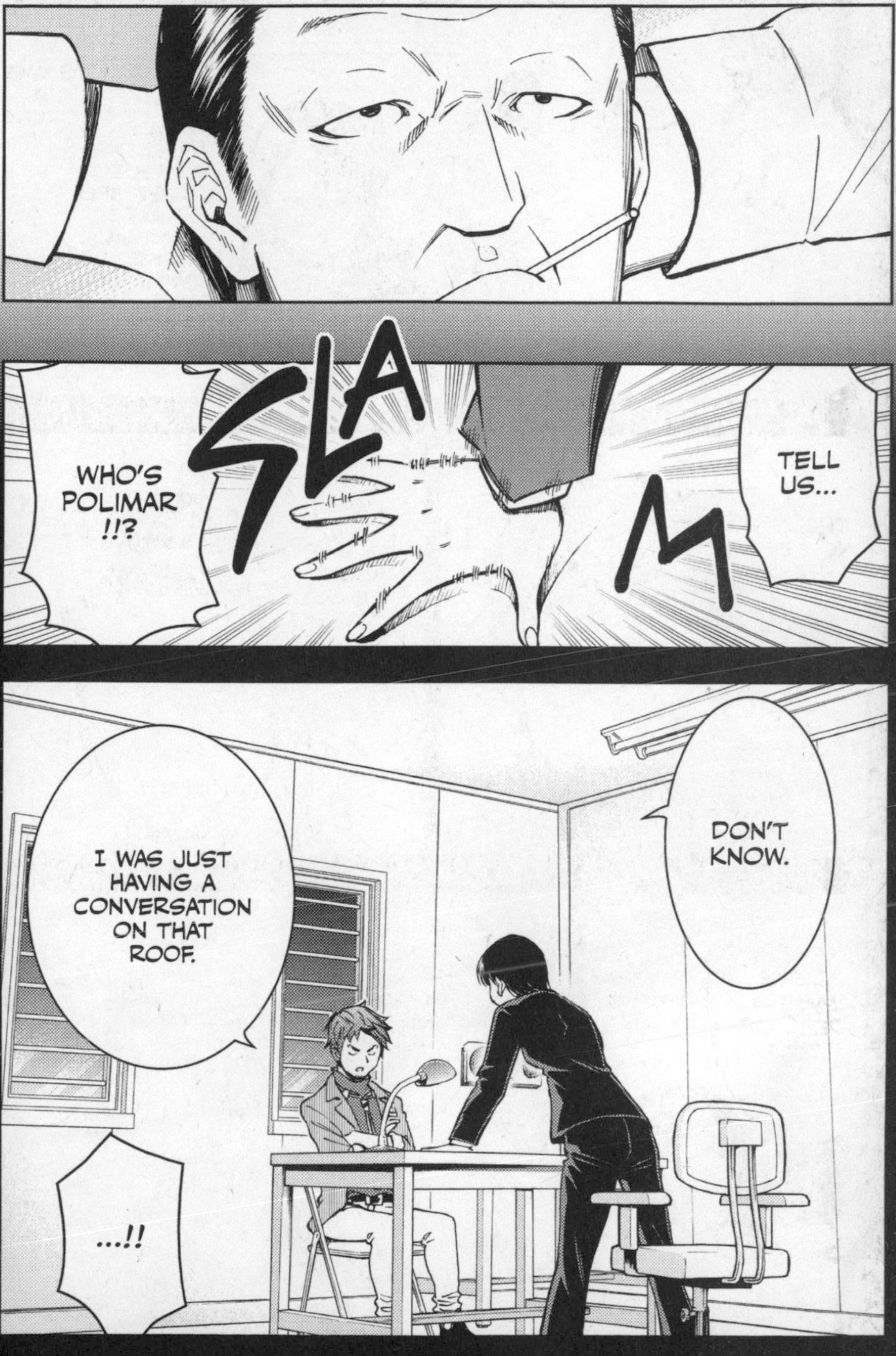
TELL US...
SLAM
WHO'S POLIMAR!!?
DON'T KNOW.
I WAS JUST HAVING A CONVERSATION ON THAT ROOF.
...!!

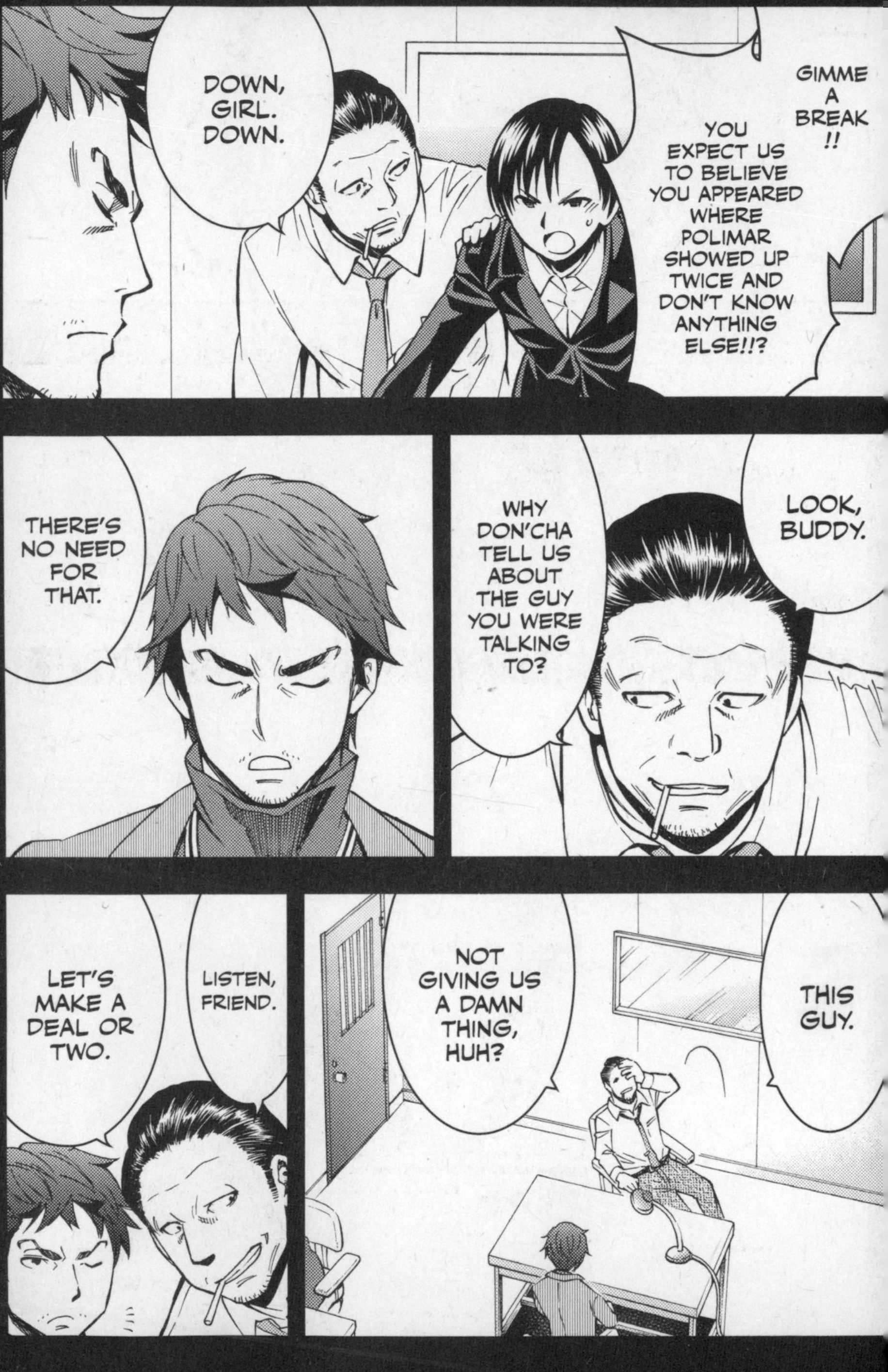
GIMME A BREAK!!
YOU EXPECT US TO BELIEVE YOU APPEARED WHERE POLIMAR SHOWED UP TWICE AND DON'T KNOW ANYTHING ELSE!!?
DOWN, GIRL. DOWN.
LOOK, BUDDY.
WHY DON'CHA TELL US ABOUT THE GUY YOU WERE TALKING TO?
THERE'S NO NEED FOR THAT.
THIS GUY.
NOT GIVING US A DAMN THING, HUH?
LISTEN, FRIEND.
LET'S MAKE A DEAL OR TWO.

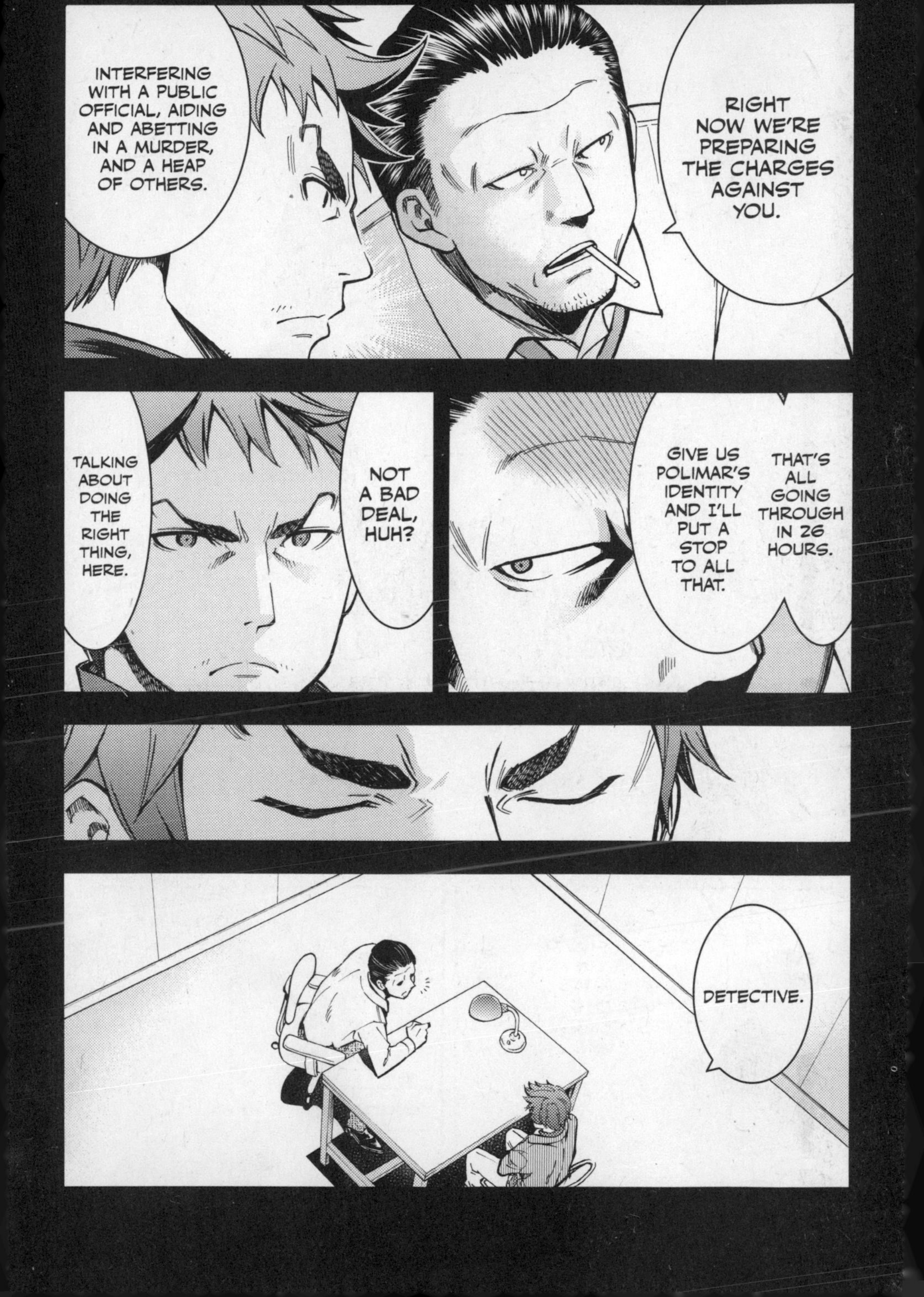
RIGHT NOW WE'RE PREPARING THE CHARGES AGAINST YOU.
INTERFERING WITH A PUBLIC OFFICIAL, AIDING AND ABETTING IN A MURDER, AND A HEAP OF OTHERS.
THAT'S ALL GOING THROUGH IN 26 HOURS.
GIVE US POLIMAR'S IDENTITY AND I'LL PUT A STOP TO ALL THAT.
NOT A BAD DEAL, HUH?
TALKING ABOUT DOING THE RIGHT THING, HERE.
DETECTIVE.

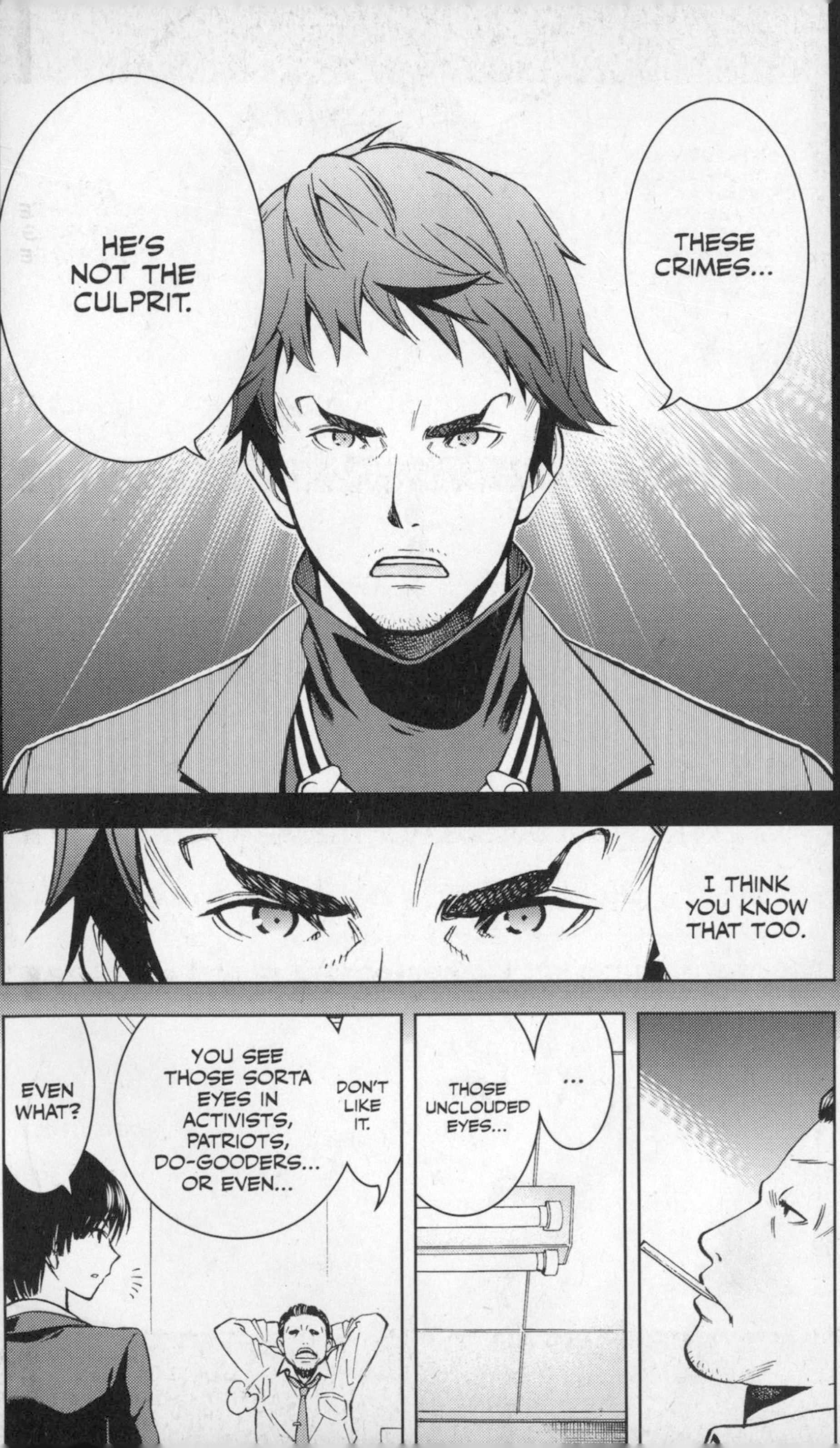
THESE CRIMES...
HE'S NOT THE CULPRIT.
I THINK YOU KNOW THAT TOO.
...
THOSE UNCLOUDED EYES...
DON'T LIKE IT.
YOU SEE THOSE SORTA EYES IN ACTIVISTS, PATRIOTS, DO-GOODERS... OR EVEN...
EVEN WHAT?

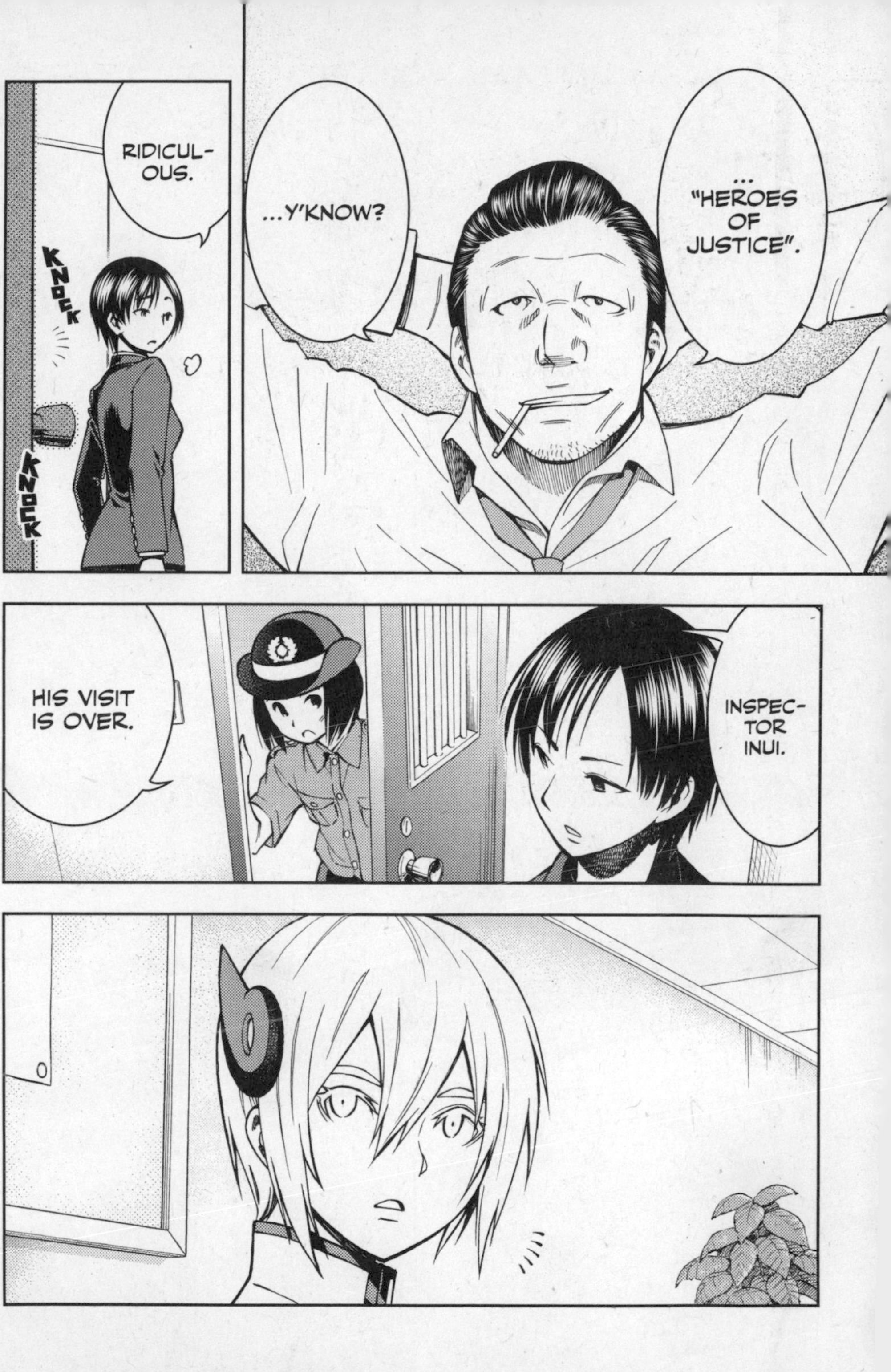

... "HEROES OF JUSTICE".
...Y'KNOW?
RIDICUL- OUS.
KNOCK
KNOCK
INSPEC- TOR INUI.
HIS VISIT IS OVER.

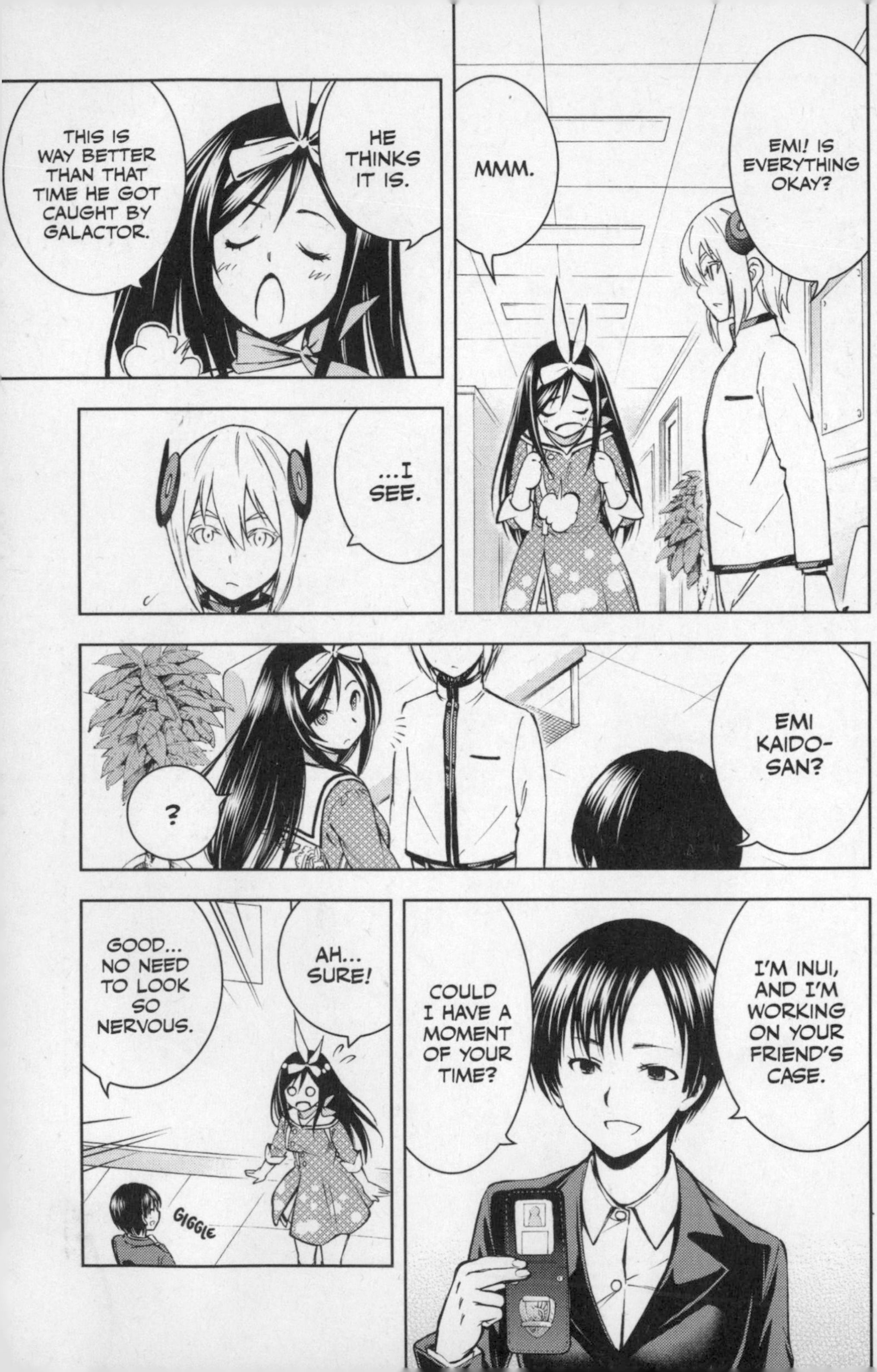
EMI! IS EVERYTHING OKAY?
MMM.
HE THINKS IT IS.
THIS IS WAY BETTER THAN THAT TIME HE GOT CAUGHT BY GALACTOR.
...I SEE.
EMI KAIDO-SAN?
?
I'M INUI, AND I'M WORKING ON YOUR FRIEND'S CASE.
COULD I HAVE A MOMENT OF YOUR TIME?
AH... SURE!
GOOD... NO NEED TO LOOK SO NERVOUS.
GIGGLE

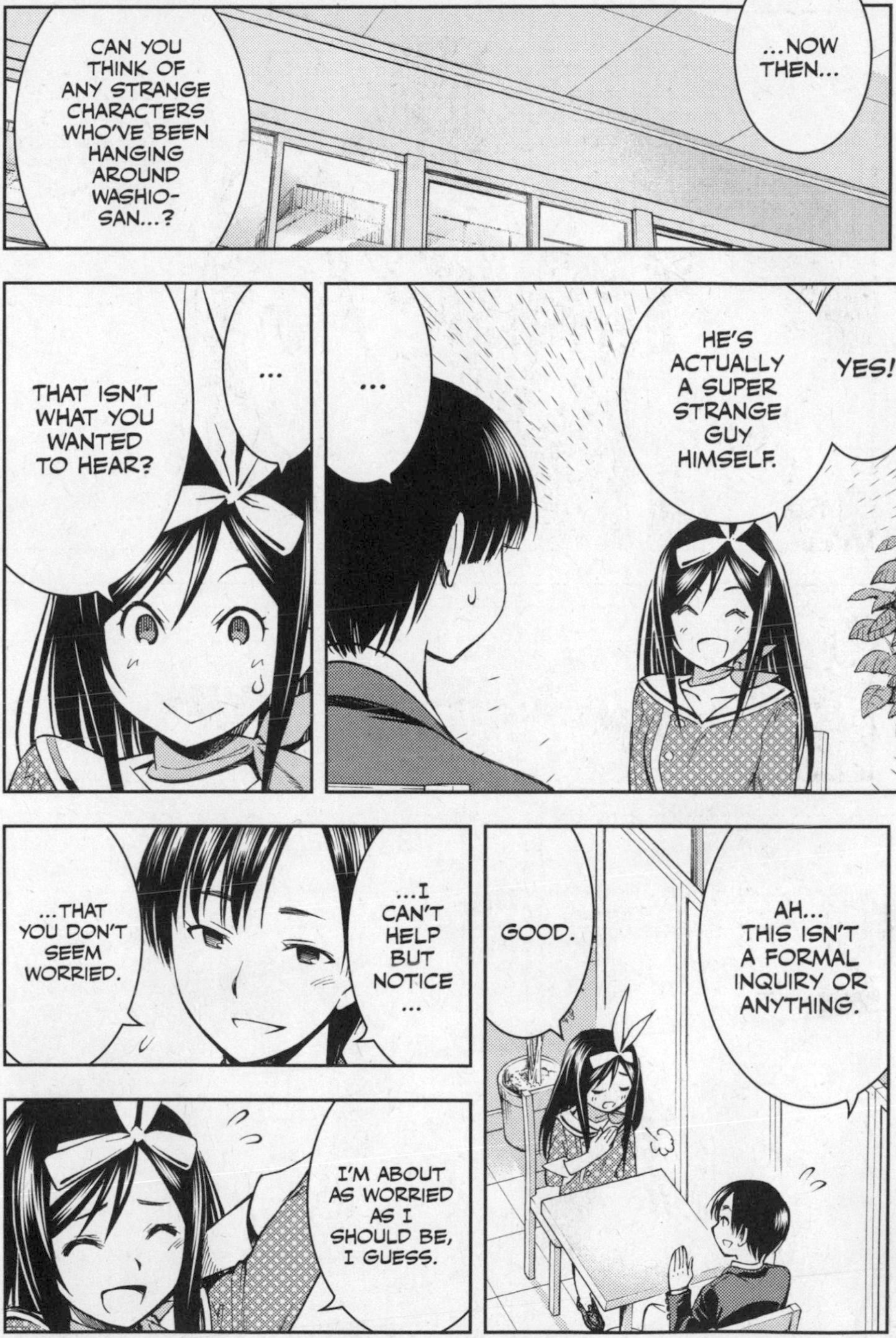
...NOW THEN...
CAN YOU THINK OF ANY STRANGE CHARACTERS WHO'VE BEEN HANGING AROUND WASHIO-SAN...?
YES!
HE'S ACTUALLY A SUPER STRANGE GUY HIMSELF.
...
...
THAT ISN'T WHAT YOU WANTED TO HEAR?
AH... THIS ISN'T A FORMAL INQUIRY OR ANYTHING.
GOOD.
...I CAN'T HELP BUT NOTICE...
...THAT YOU DON'T SEEM WORRIED.
I'M ABOUT AS WORRIED AS I SHOULD BE, I GUESS.

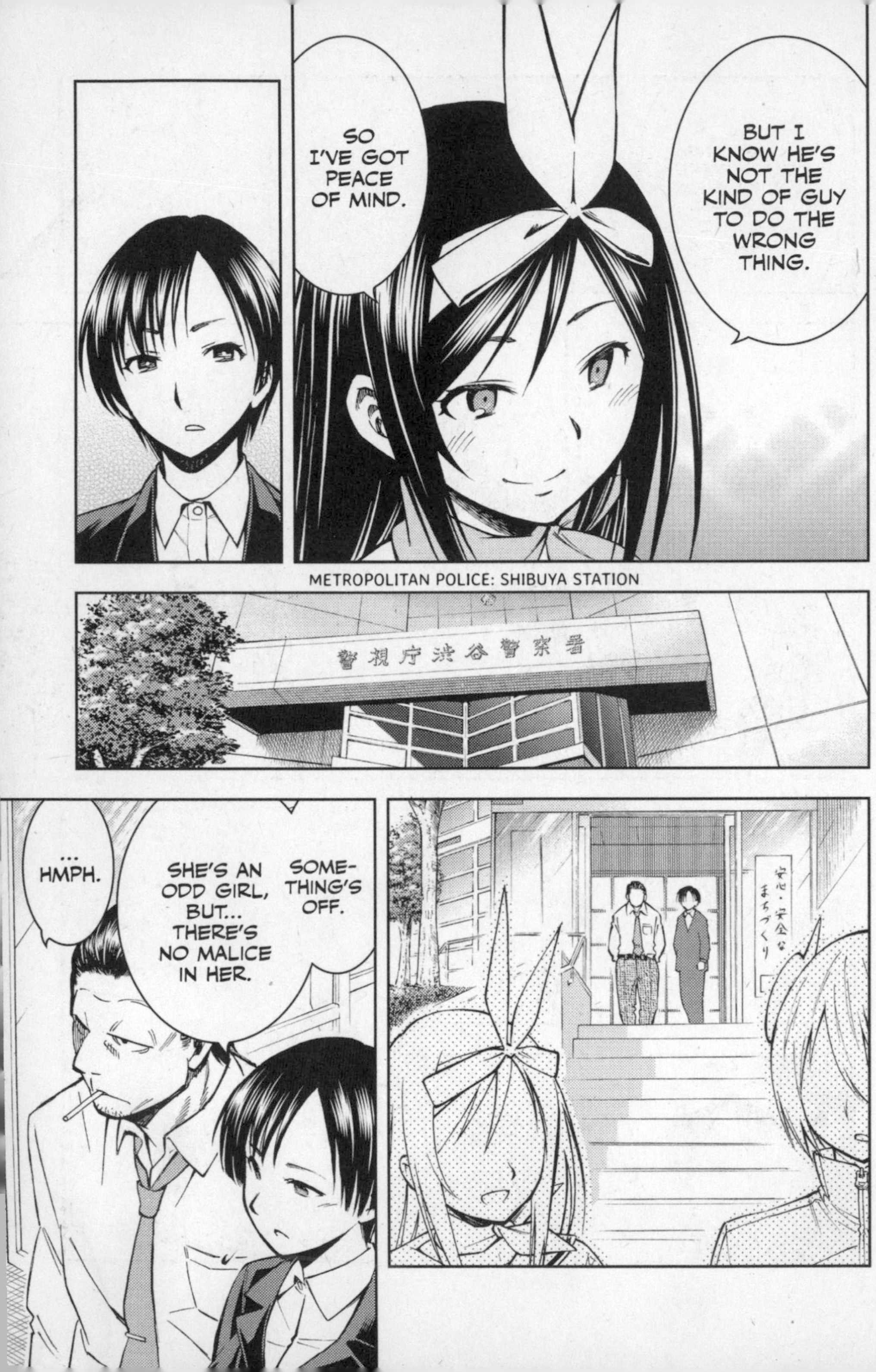
BUT I KNOW HE'S NOT THE KIND OF GUY TO DO THE WRONG THING.
SO I'VE GOT PEACE OF MIND.
METROPOLITAN POLICE: SHIBUYA STATION
警視庁渋谷警察署
安心・安全なまちづくり
SOME-THING'S OFF.
SHE'S AN ODD GIRL, BUT... THERE'S NO MALICE IN HER.
... HMPH.

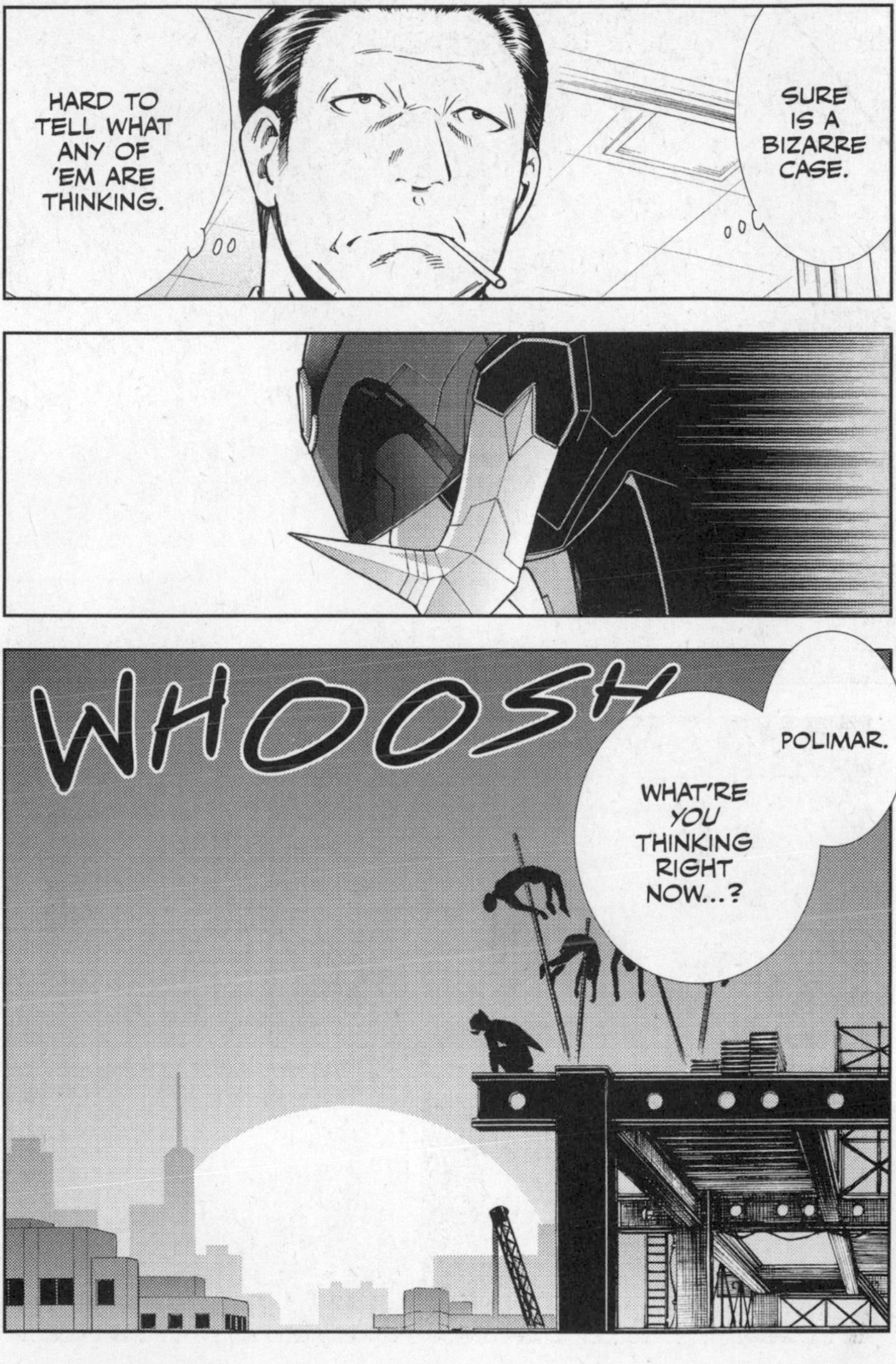
SURE IS A BIZARRE CASE.
HARD TO TELL WHAT ANY OF 'EM ARE THINKING.
POLIMAR.
WHAT'RE *YOU* THINKING RIGHT NOW...?
WHOOSH

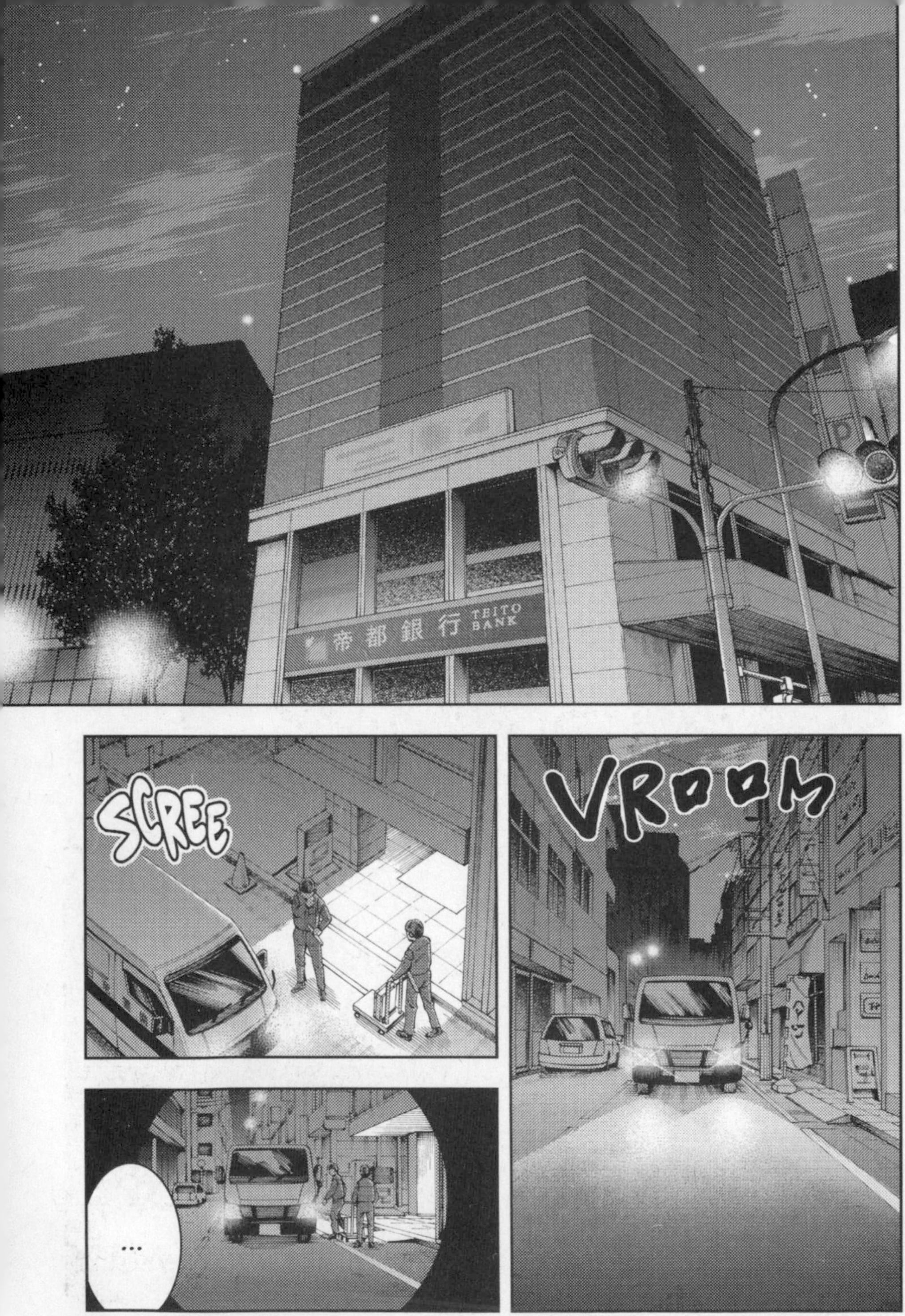
帝都銀行 TEITO BANK
VROOM
SCREE
...

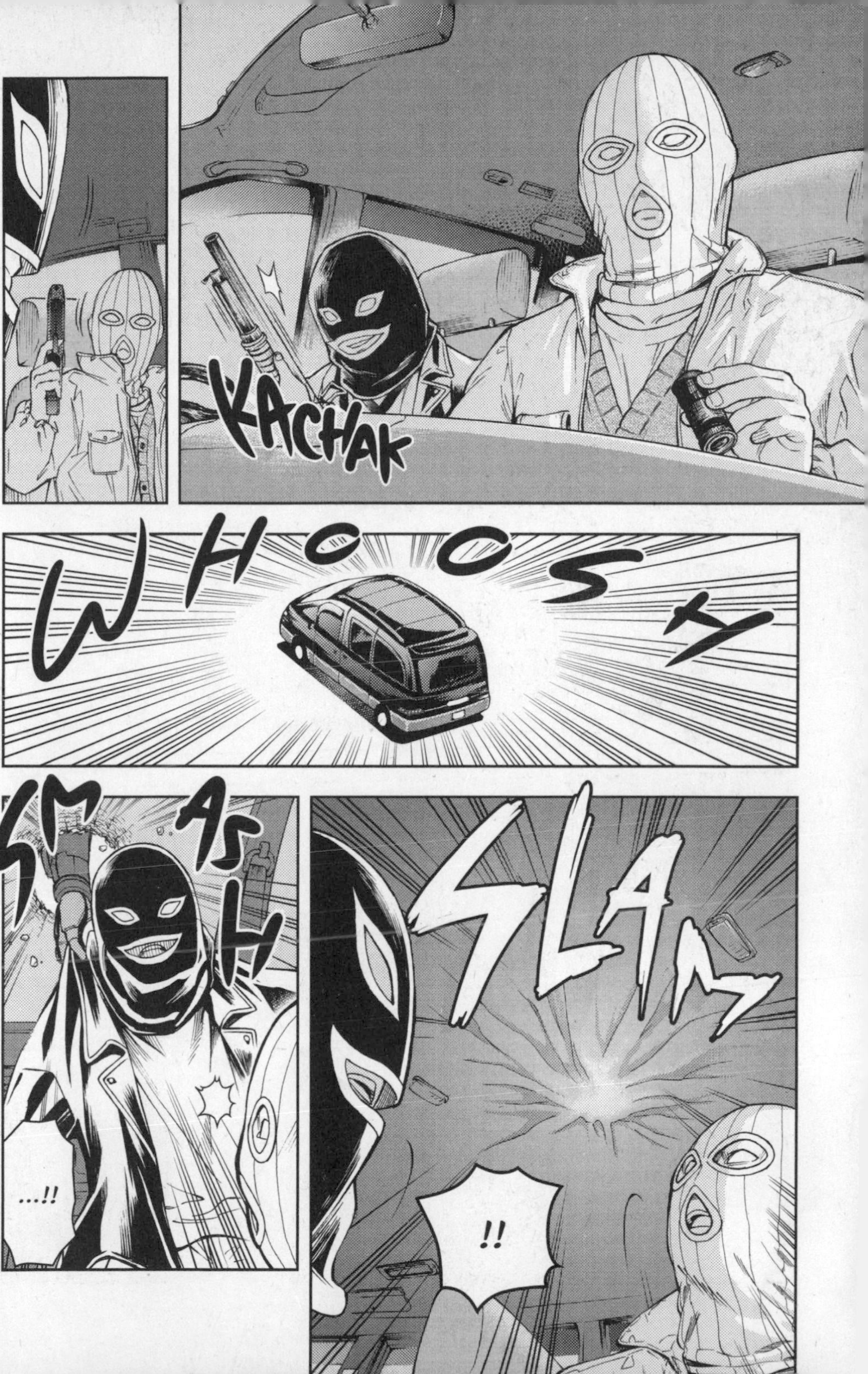
KACHAK
WHOOSH
SLAM
!!
SMASH
...!!

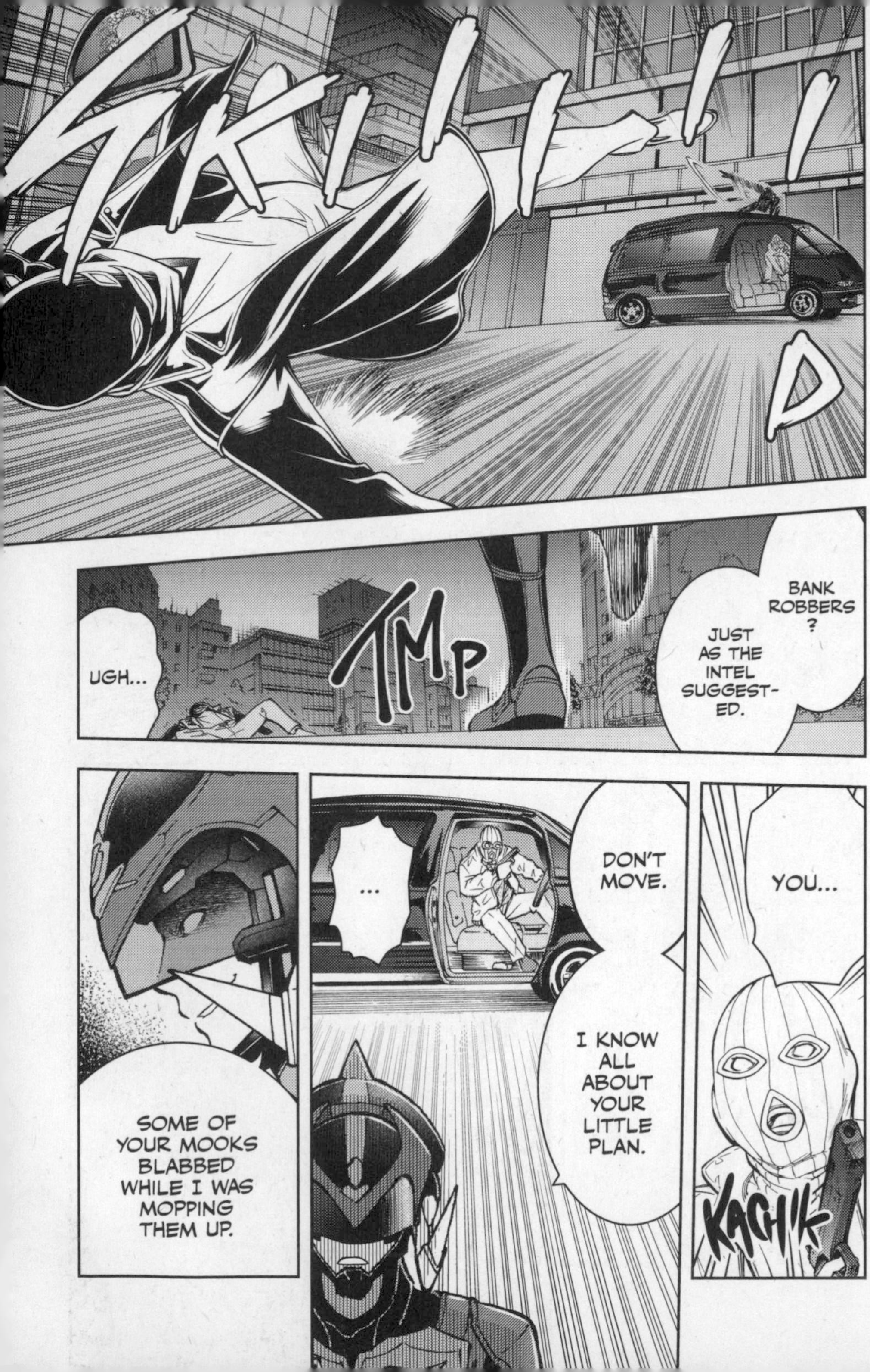
SKIIIIID
BANK ROBBERS?
JUST AS THE INTEL SUGGESTED.
TMP
UGH...
YOU...
KACHIK
DON'T MOVE.
I KNOW ALL ABOUT YOUR LITTLE PLAN.
...
SOME OF YOUR MOOKS BLABBED WHILE I WAS MOPPING THEM UP.

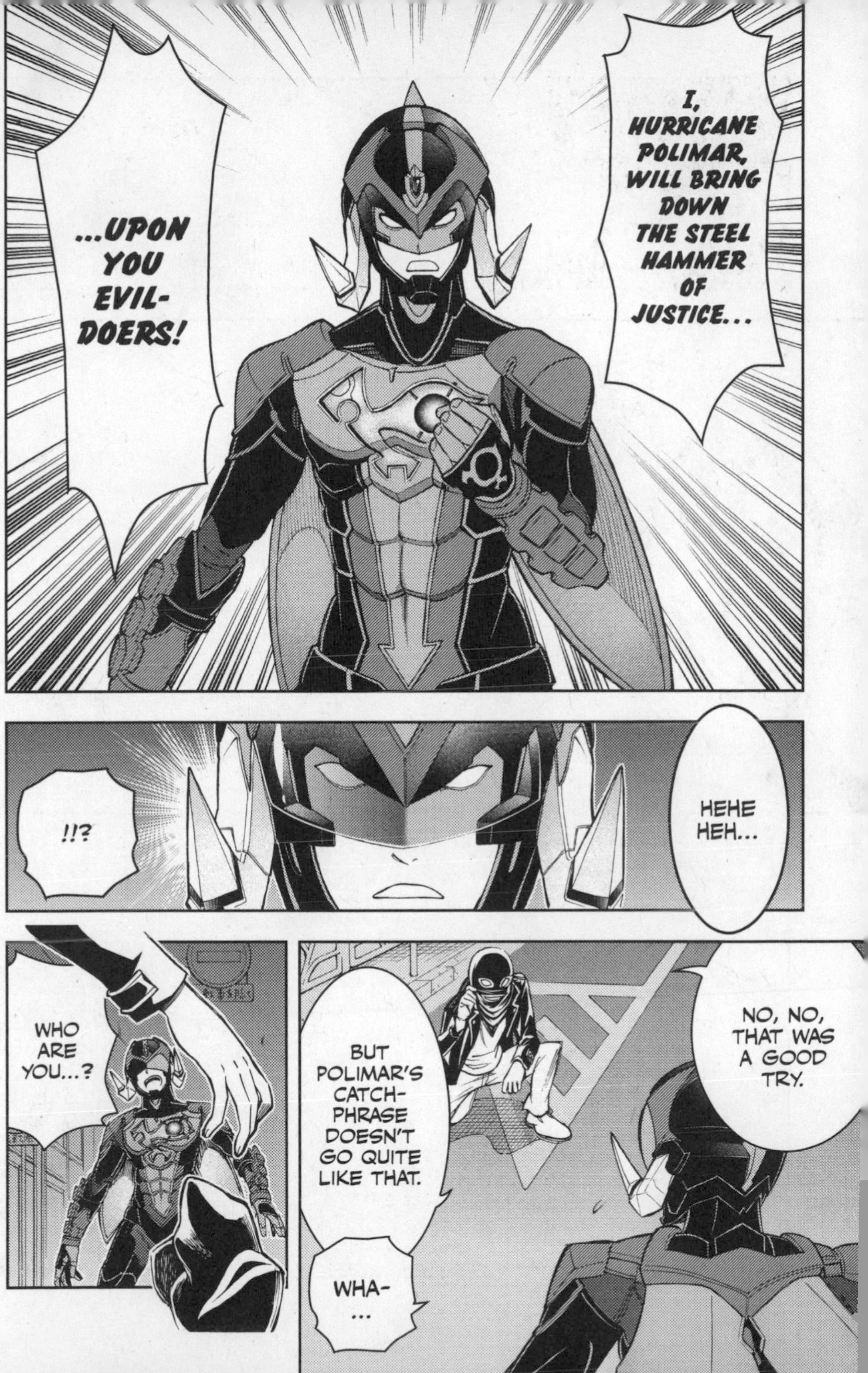
I, HURRICANE POLIMAR, WILL BRING DOWN THE STEEL HAMMER OF JUSTICE...
...UPON YOU EVIL-DOERS!
HEHE HEH...
!!?
NO, NO, THAT WAS A GOOD TRY.
BUT POLIMAR'S CATCH-PHRASE DOESN'T GO QUITE LIKE THAT.
WHA-...
WHO ARE YOU...?

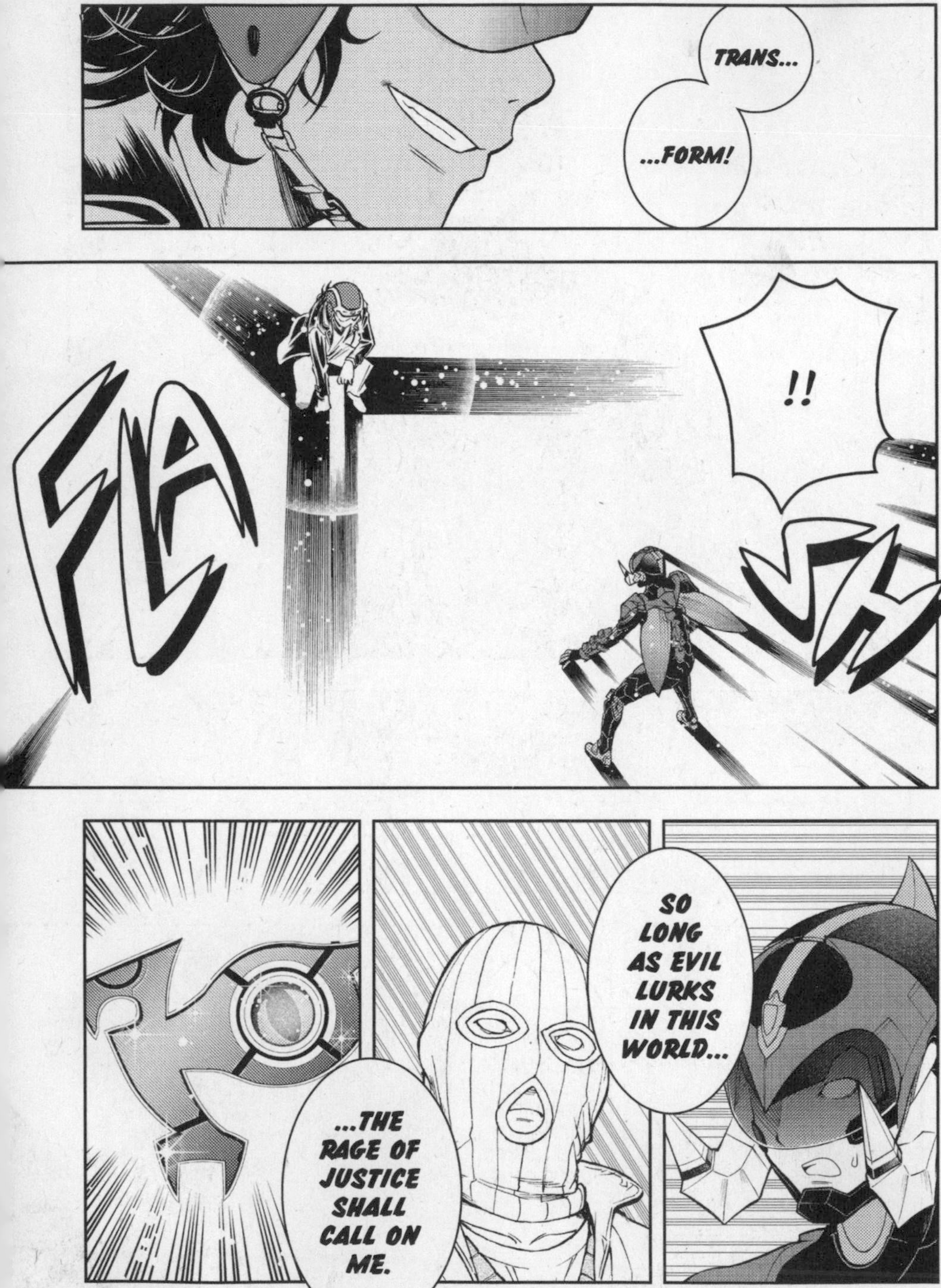
TRANS...
...FORM!
!!
FLA
SH
SO LONG AS EVIL LURKS IN THIS WORLD...
...THE RAGE OF JUSTICE SHALL CALL ON ME.

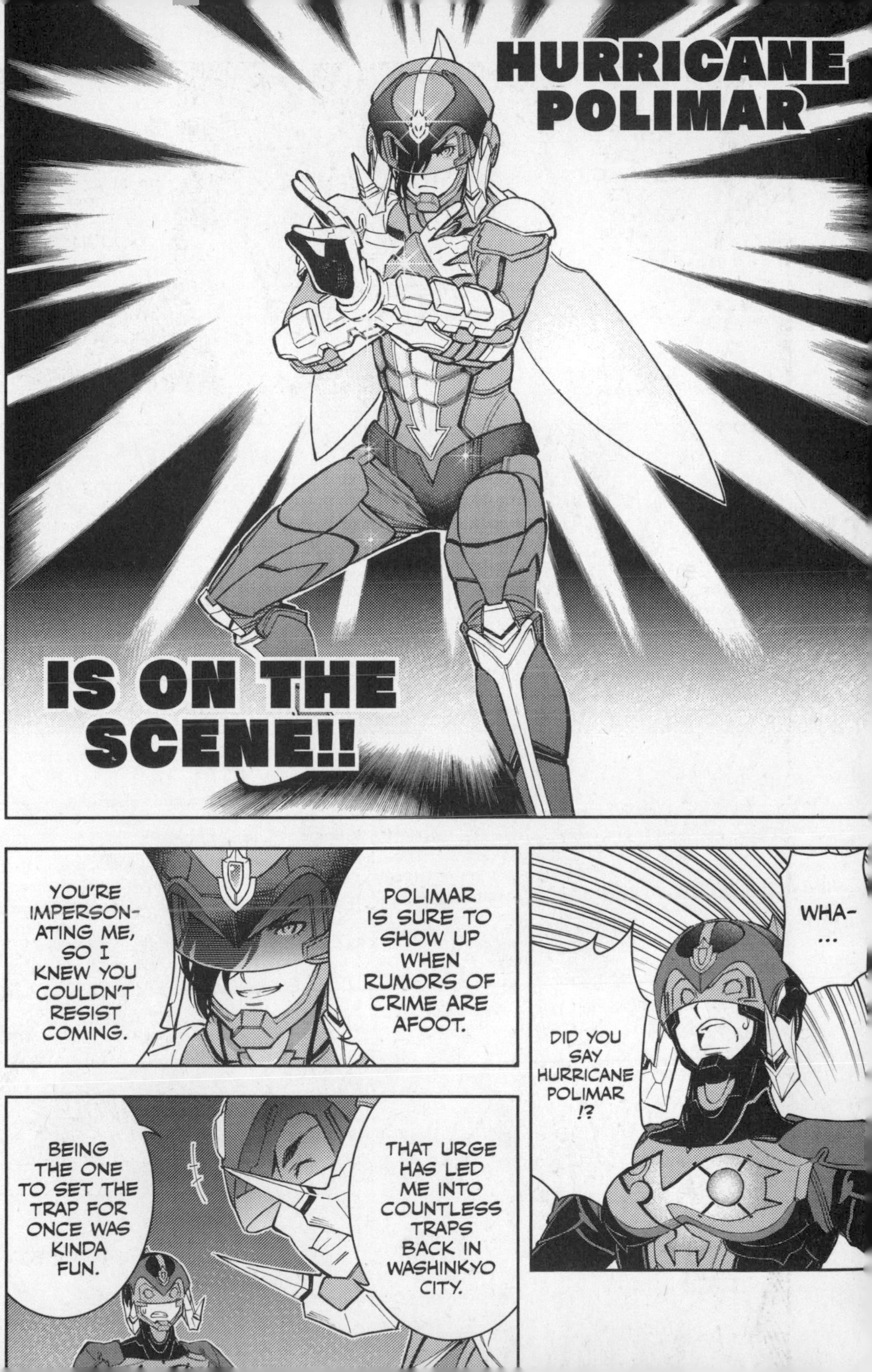
HURRICANE POLIMAR
IS ON THE SCENE!!
WHA-...
DID YOU SAY HURRICANE POLIMAR!?
POLIMAR IS SURE TO SHOW UP WHEN RUMORS OF CRIME ARE AFOOT.
YOU'RE IMPERSON-ATING ME, SO I KNEW YOU COULDN'T RESIST COMING.
THAT URGE HAS LED ME INTO COUNTLESS TRAPS BACK IN WASHINKYO CITY.
BEING THE ONE TO SET THE TRAP FOR ONCE WAS KINDA FUN.

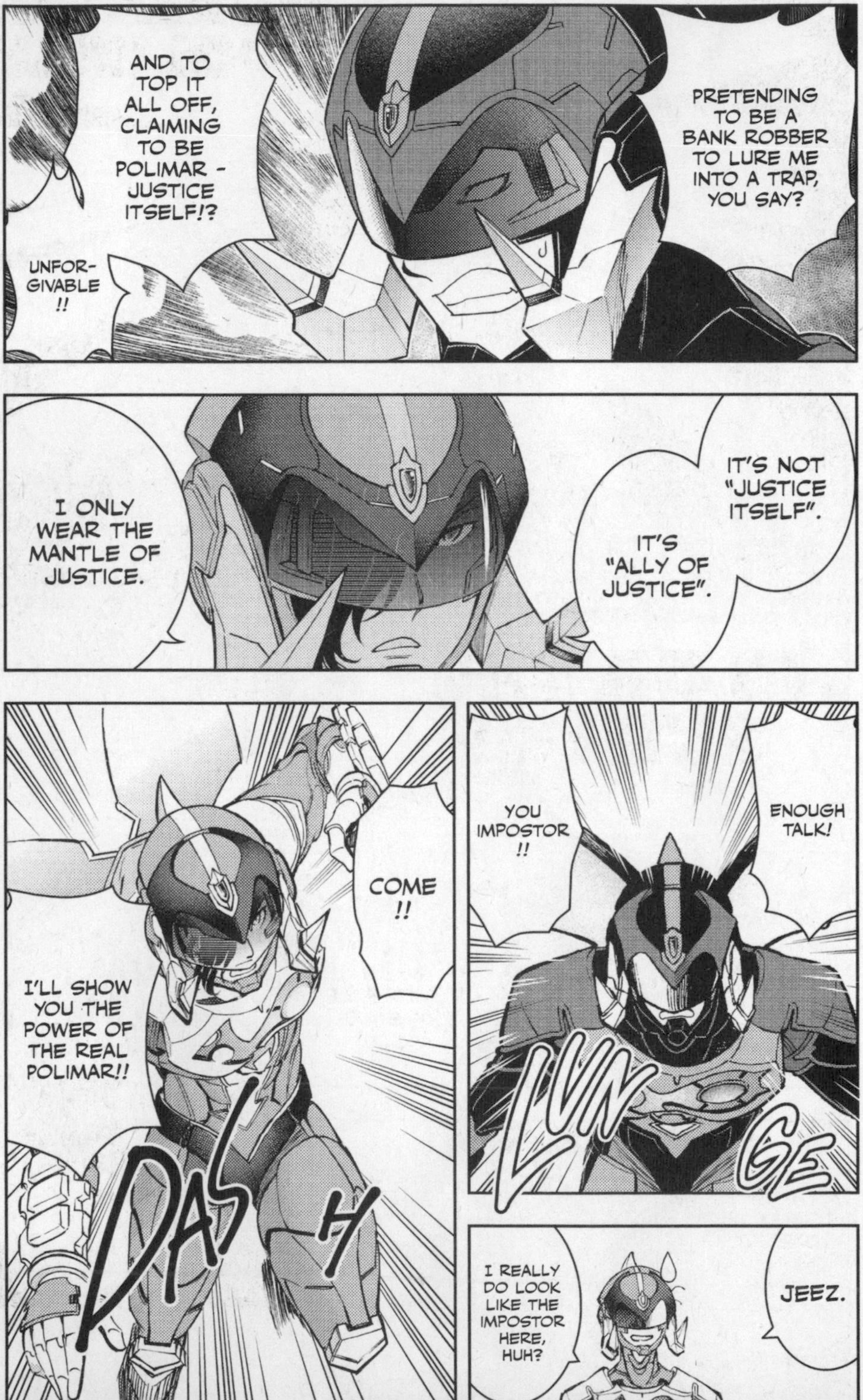
PRETENDING TO BE A BANK ROBBER TO LURE ME INTO A TRAP, YOU SAY?
AND TO TOP IT ALL OFF, CLAIMING TO BE POLIMAR - JUSTICE ITSELF!?
UNFOR-GIVABLE !!
IT'S NOT "JUSTICE ITSELF".
IT'S "ALLY OF JUSTICE".
I ONLY WEAR THE MANTLE OF JUSTICE.
ENOUGH TALK!
YOU IMPOSTOR !!
LUNGE
JEEZ.
I REALLY DO LOOK LIKE THE IMPOSTOR HERE, HUH?
COME !!
I'LL SHOW YOU THE POWER OF THE REAL POLIMAR!!
DASH

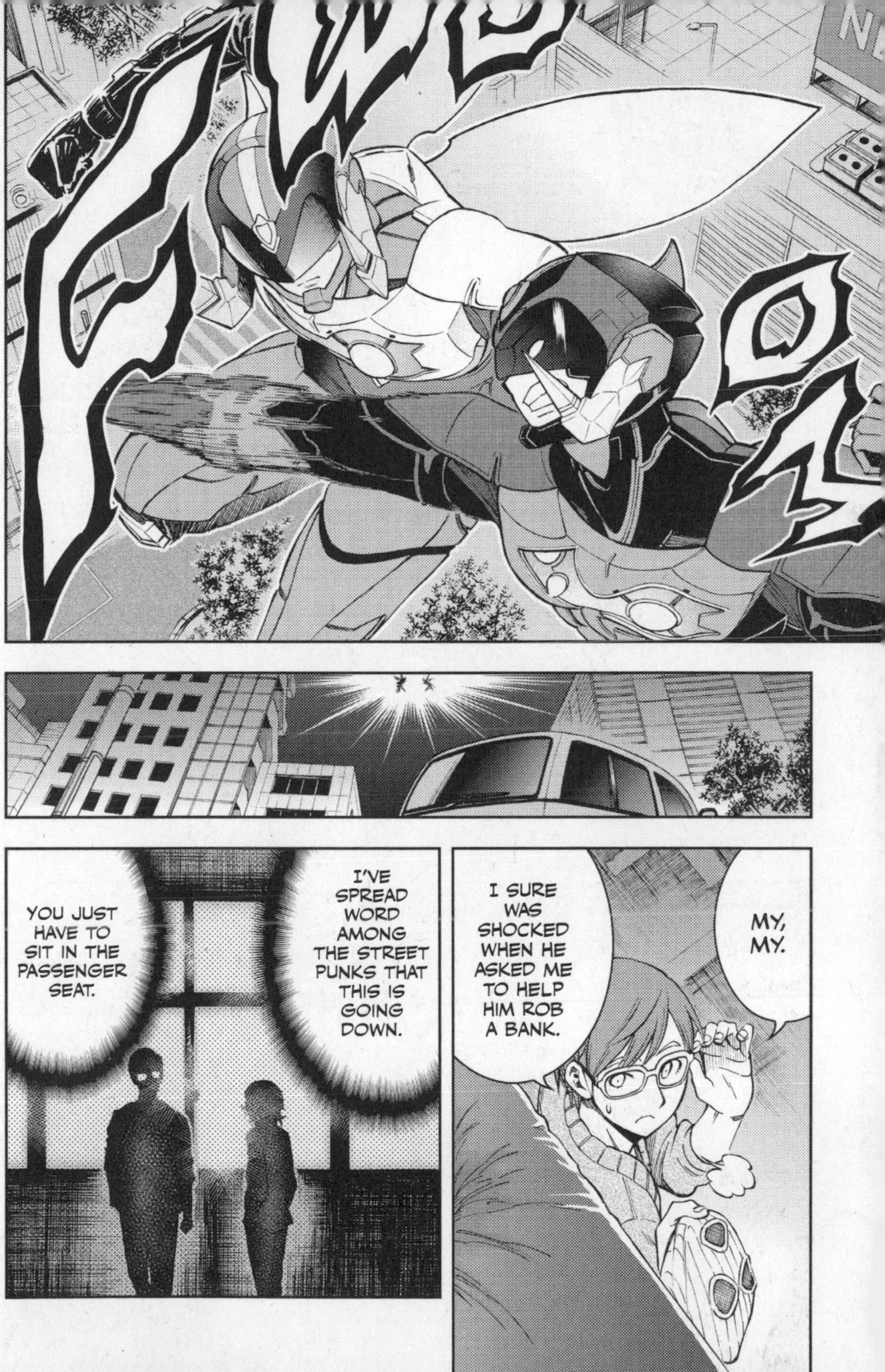
MY, MY.
I SURE WAS SHOCKED WHEN HE ASKED ME TO HELP HIM ROB A BANK.
I'VE SPREAD WORD AMONG THE STREET PUNKS THAT THIS IS GOING DOWN.
YOU JUST HAVE TO SIT IN THE PASSENGER SEAT.

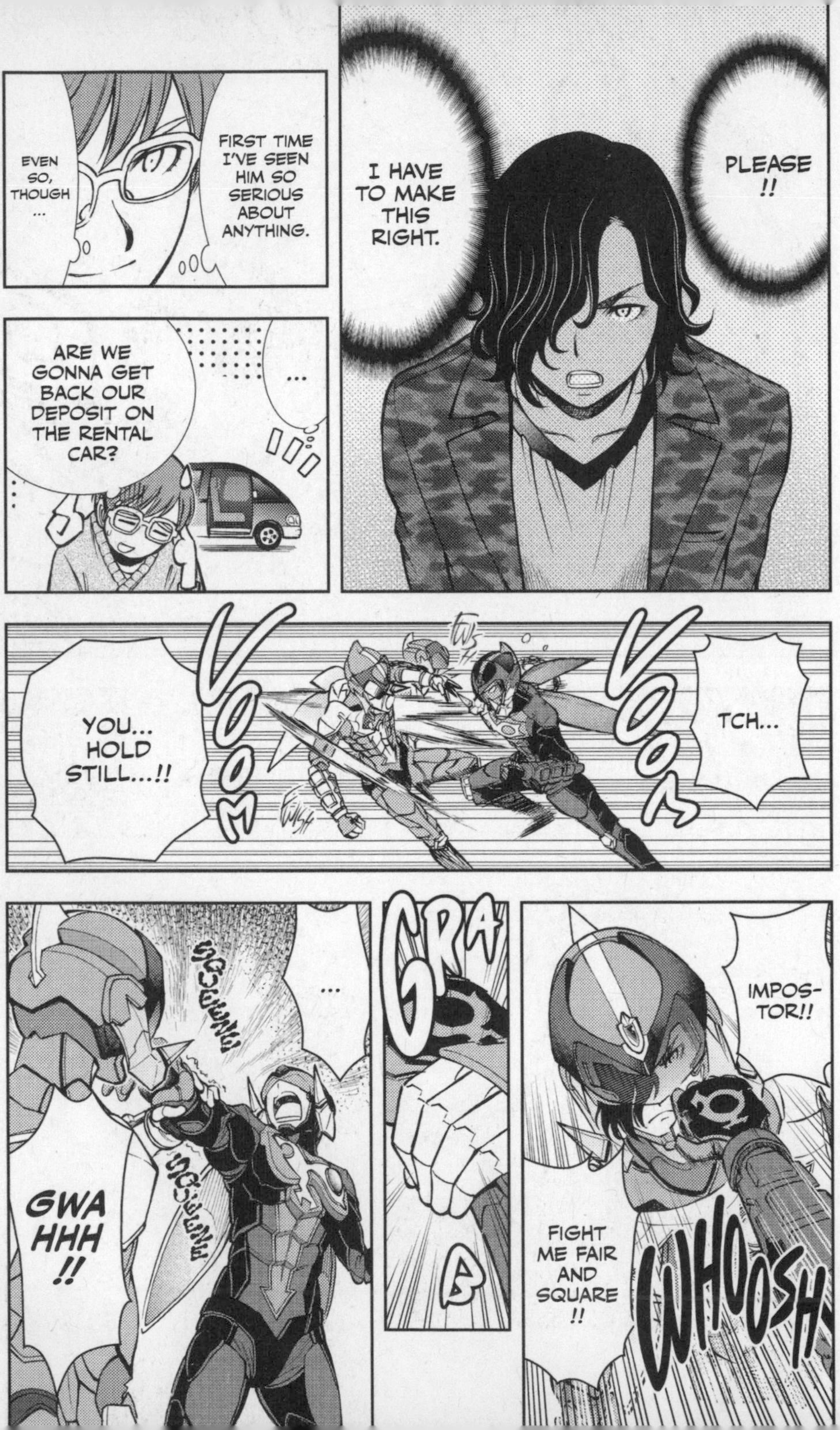
PLEASE !!
I HAVE TO MAKE THIS RIGHT.
FIRST TIME I'VE SEEN HIM SO SERIOUS ABOUT ANYTHING.
EVEN SO, THOUGH ...
...
ARE WE GONNA GET BACK OUR DEPOSIT ON THE RENTAL CAR?
TCH...
VOOOM
VOOM
YOU... HOLD STILL...!!
IMPOSTOR!!
FIGHT ME FAIR AND SQUARE !!
WHOOSH
GRAB
...
GWA HHH !!

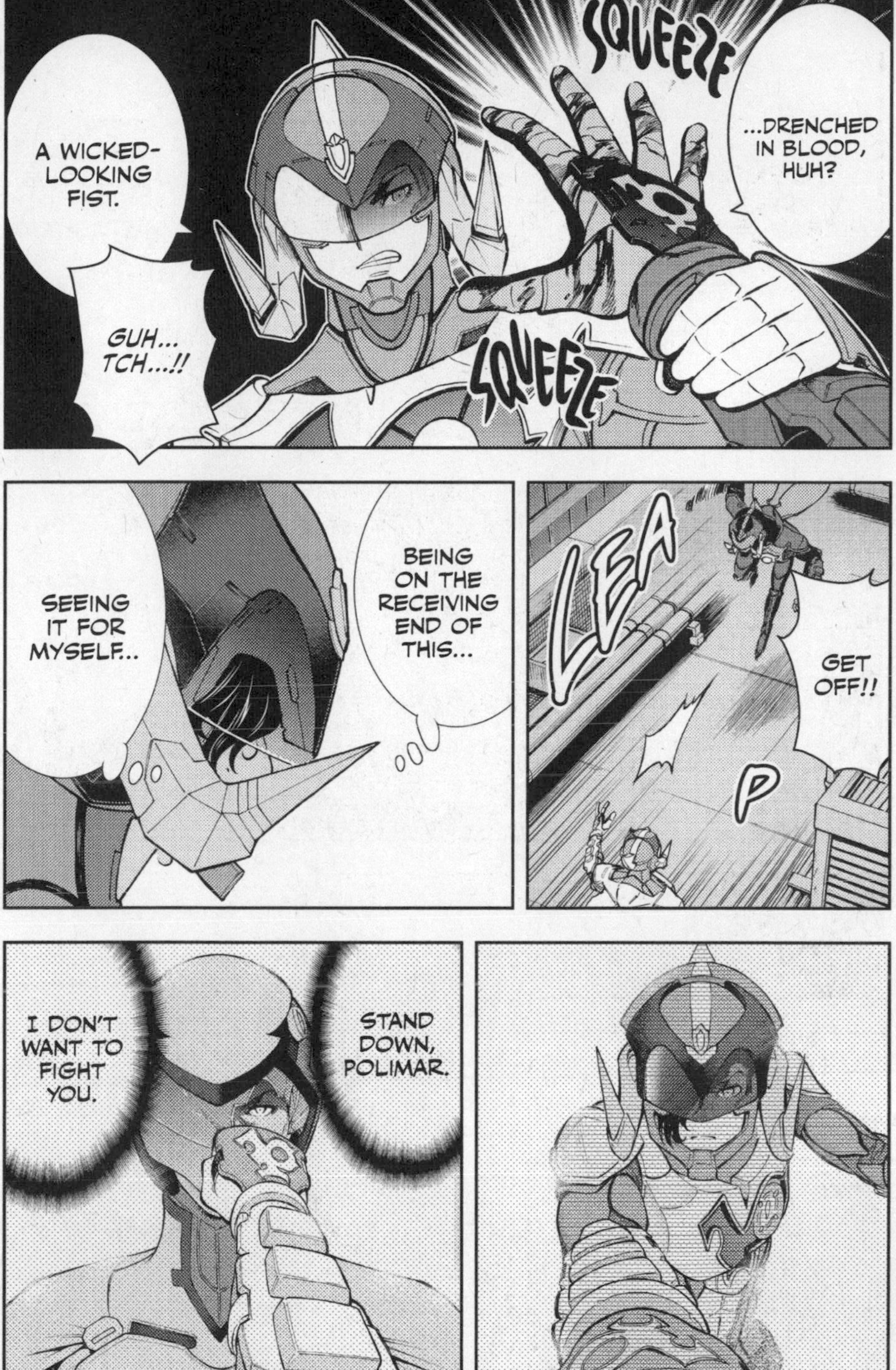
SQUEEZE
...DRENCHED IN BLOOD, HUH?
A WICKED-LOOKING FIST.
SQUEEZE
GUH... TCH...!!
LEA
GET OFF!!
P
BEING ON THE RECEIVING END OF THIS...
SEEING IT FOR MYSELF...
STAND DOWN, POLIMAR.
I DON'T WANT TO FIGHT YOU.

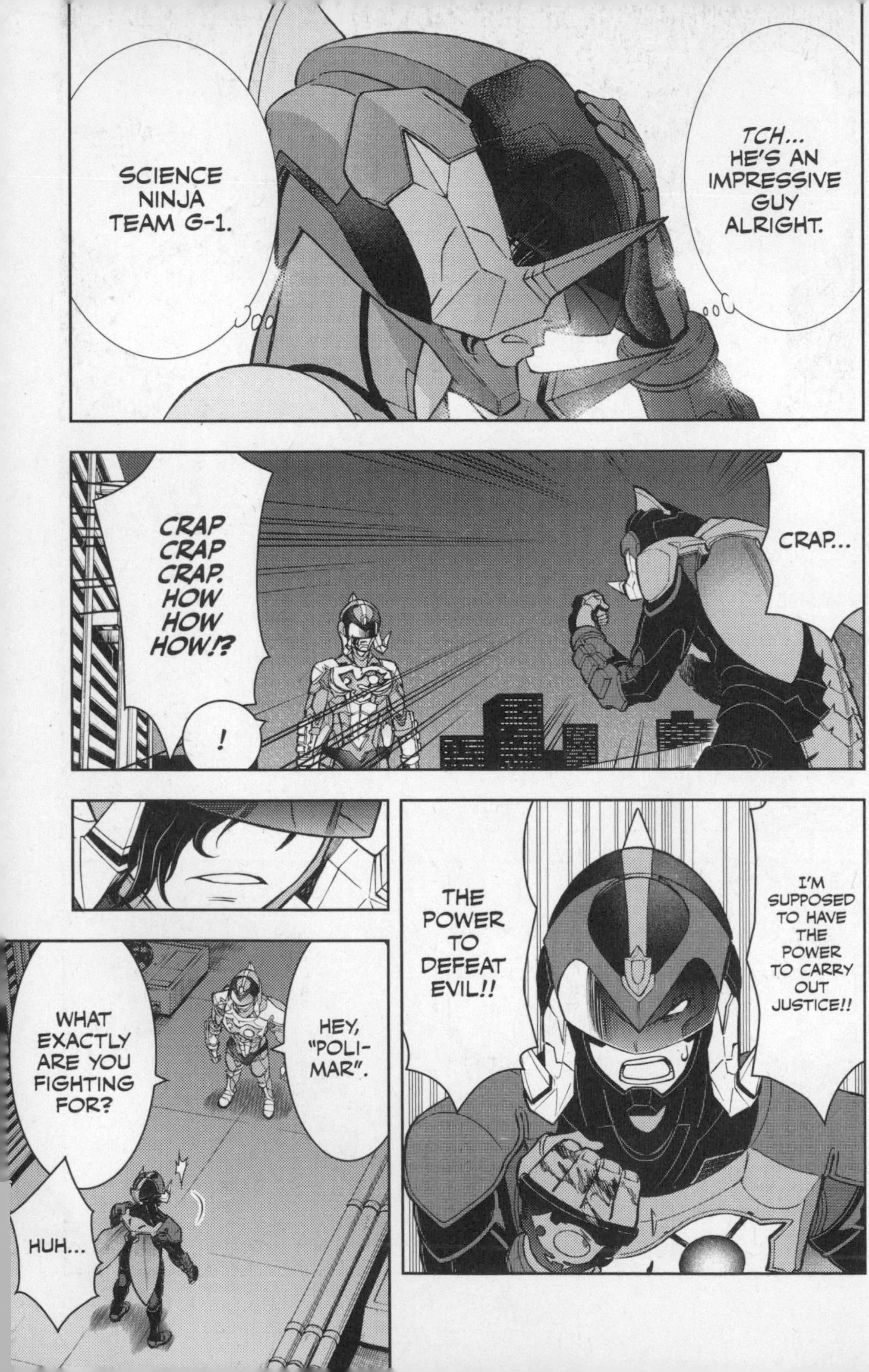
TCH... HE'S AN IMPRESSIVE GUY ALRIGHT.
SCIENCE NINJA TEAM G-1.
CRAP...
CRAP CRAP CRAP. HOW HOW HOW!?
!
I'M SUPPOSED TO HAVE THE POWER TO CARRY OUT JUSTICE!!
THE POWER TO DEFEAT EVIL!!
HEY, "POLI-MAR".
WHAT EXACTLY ARE YOU FIGHTING FOR?
HUH...

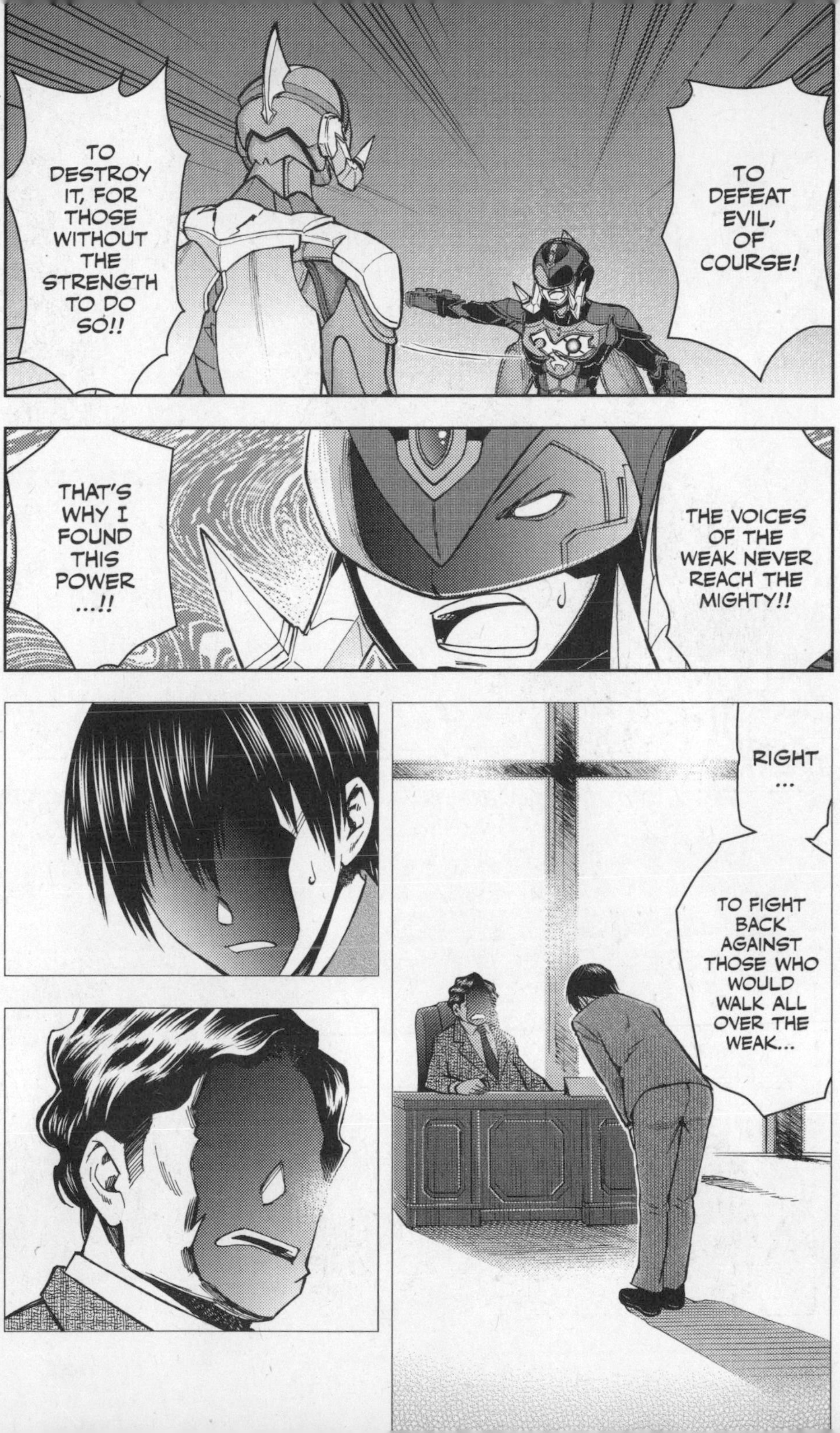
TO DEFEAT EVIL, OF COURSE!
TO DESTROY IT, FOR THOSE WITHOUT THE STRENGTH TO DO SO!!
THE VOICES OF THE WEAK NEVER REACH THE MIGHTY!!
THAT'S WHY I FOUND THIS POWER ...!!
RIGHT ...
TO FIGHT BACK AGAINST THOSE WHO WOULD WALK ALL OVER THE WEAK...

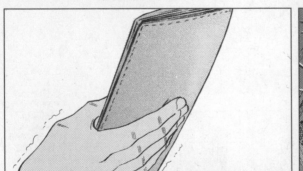

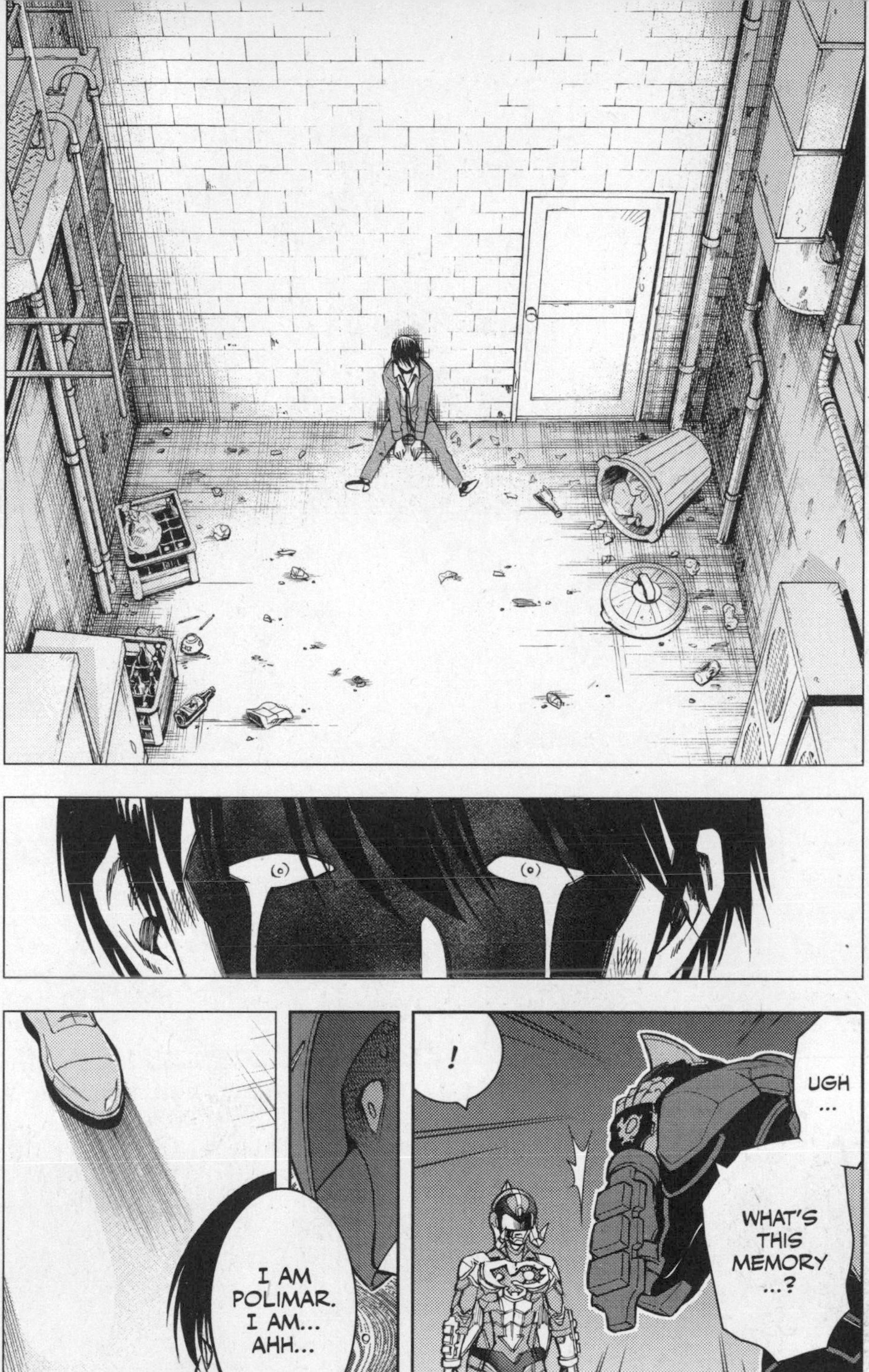
UGH ...
!
WHAT'S THIS MEMORY ...?
I AM POLIMAR. I AM... AHH...

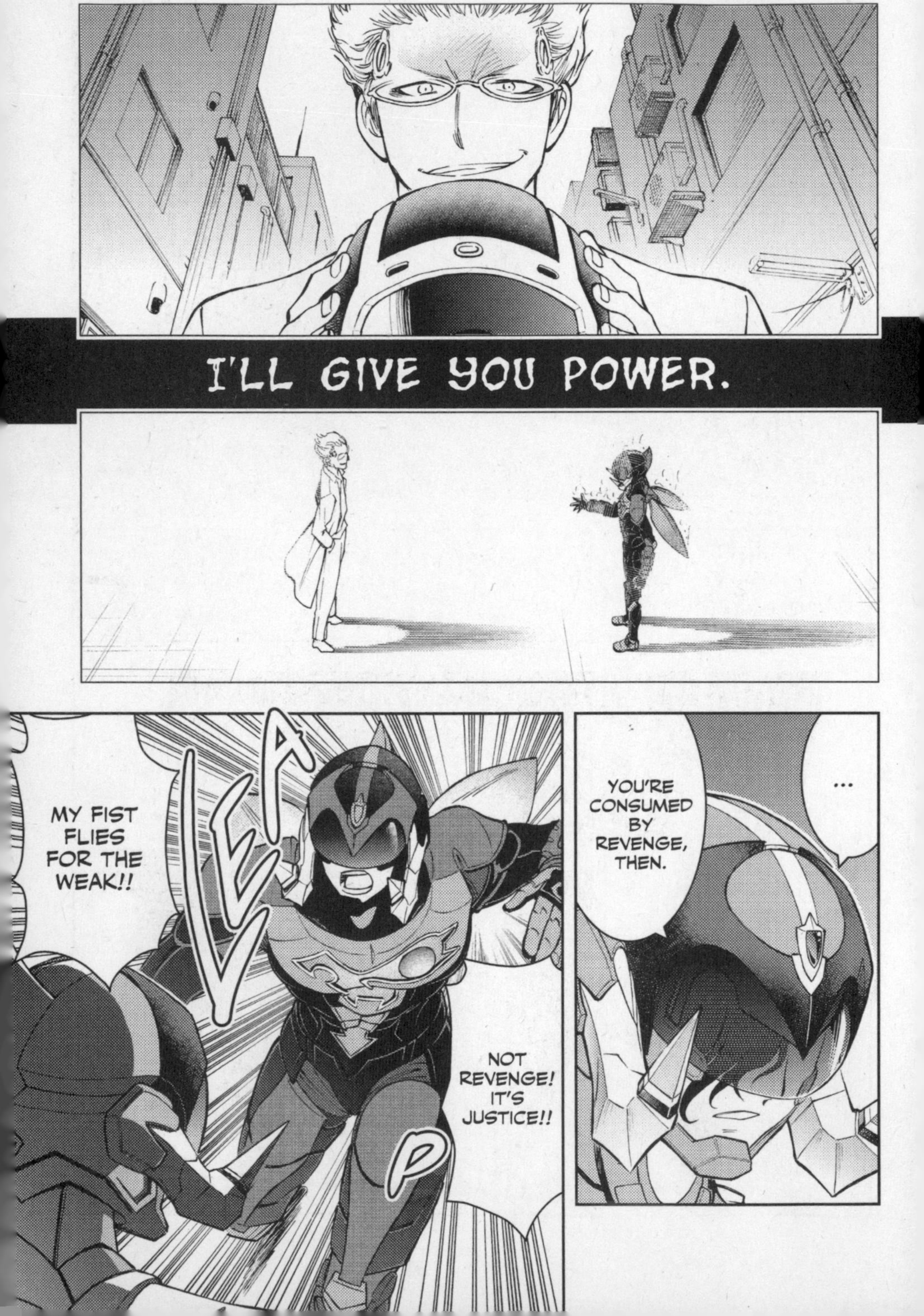
I'LL GIVE YOU POWER.
...
YOU'RE CONSUMED BY REVENGE, THEN.
LEAP
NOT REVENGE! IT'S JUSTICE!!
MY FIST FLIES FOR THE WEAK!!

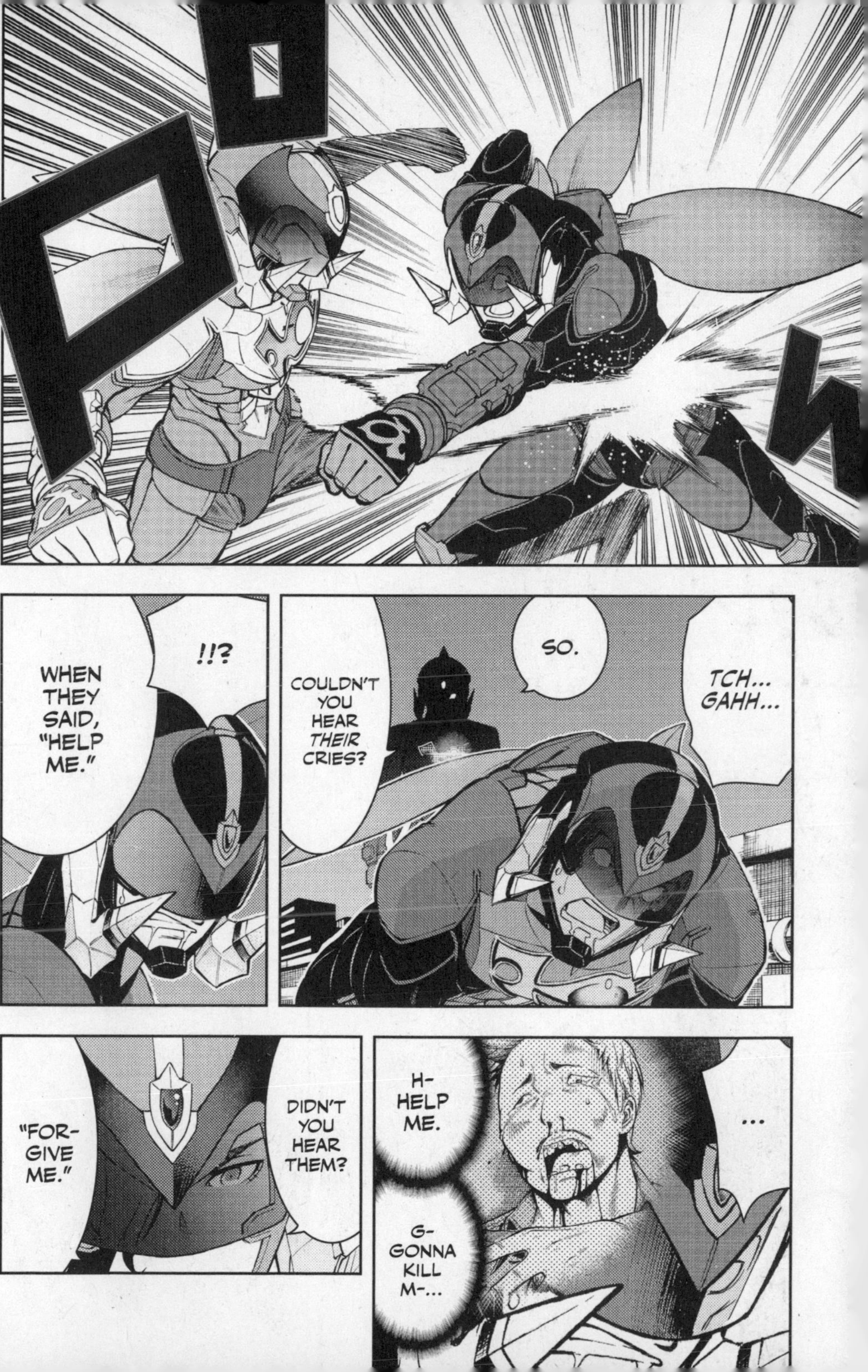
POW
TCH... GAHH...
SO.
COULDN'T YOU HEAR *THEIR* CRIES?
!!?
WHEN THEY SAID, "HELP ME."
...
H- HELP ME.
G- GONNA KILL M-...
DIDN'T YOU HEAR THEM?
"FOR-GIVE ME."

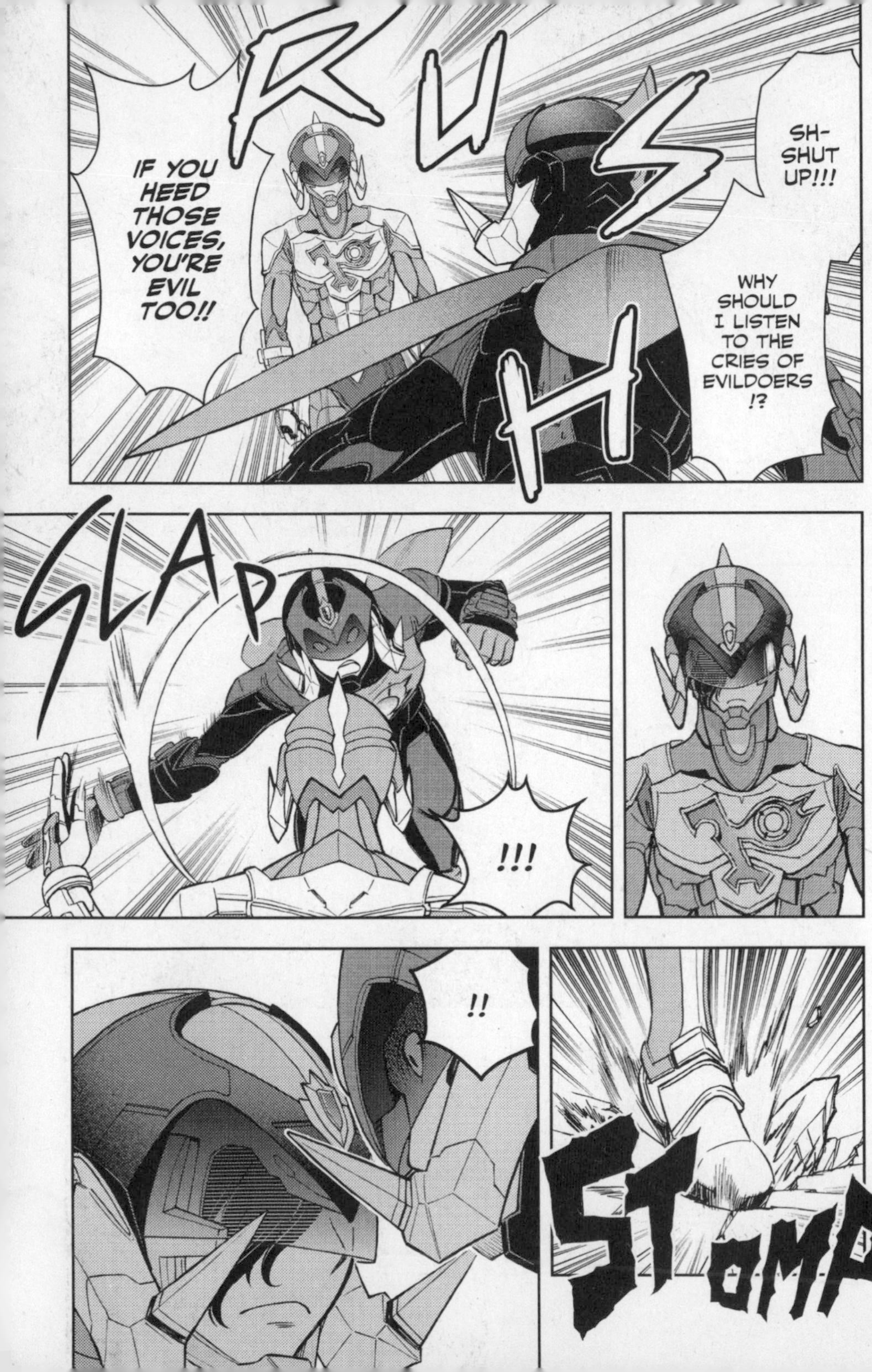
SH-SHUT UP!!!
WHY SHOULD I LISTEN TO THE CRIES OF EVILDOERS!?
RUSH
IF YOU HEED THOSE VOICES, YOU'RE EVIL TOO!!
SLAP
!!!
STOMP
!!

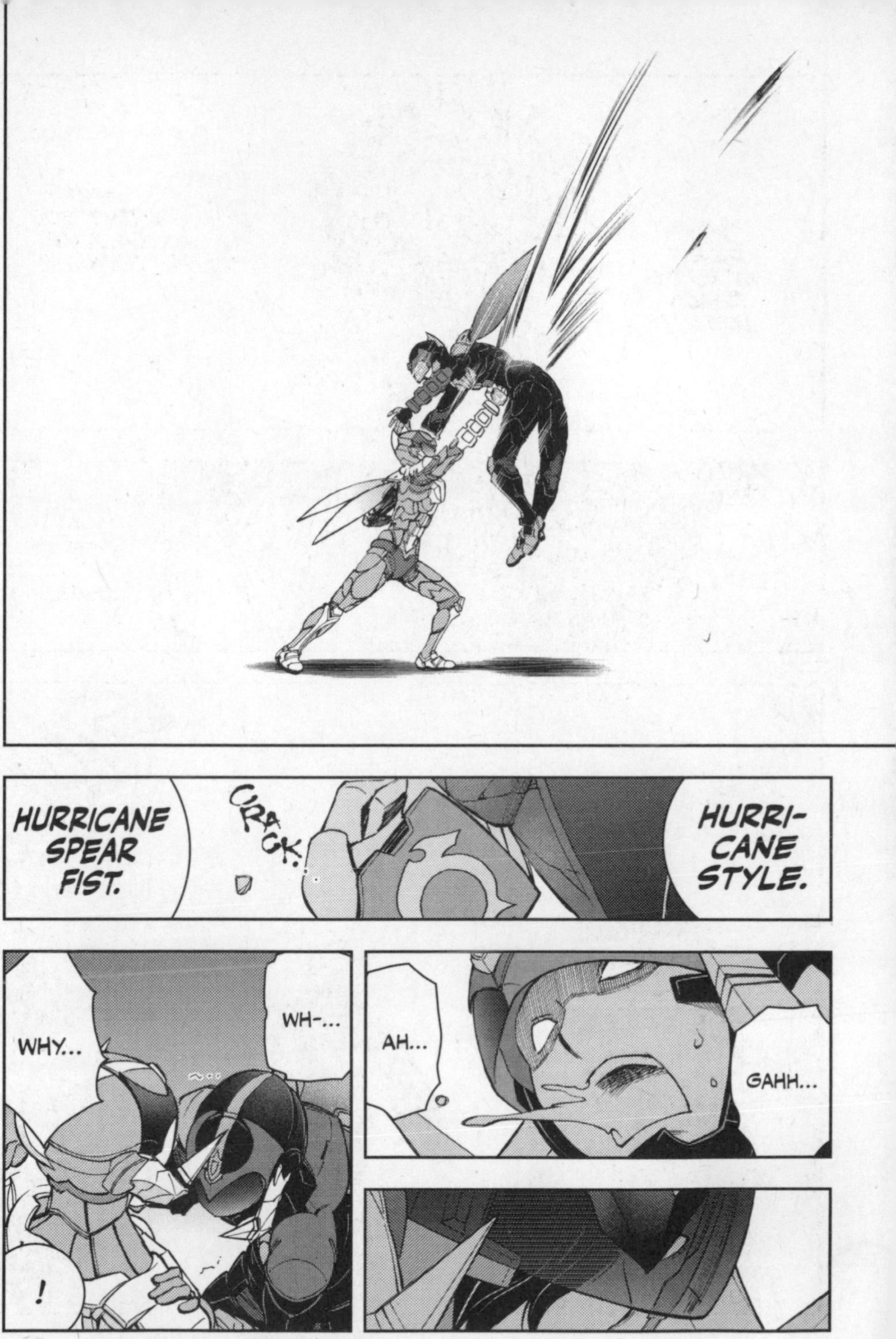
HURRI-CANE STYLE.
CRACK
HURRICANE SPEAR FIST.
GAHH...
AH...
WH-...
WHY...
!

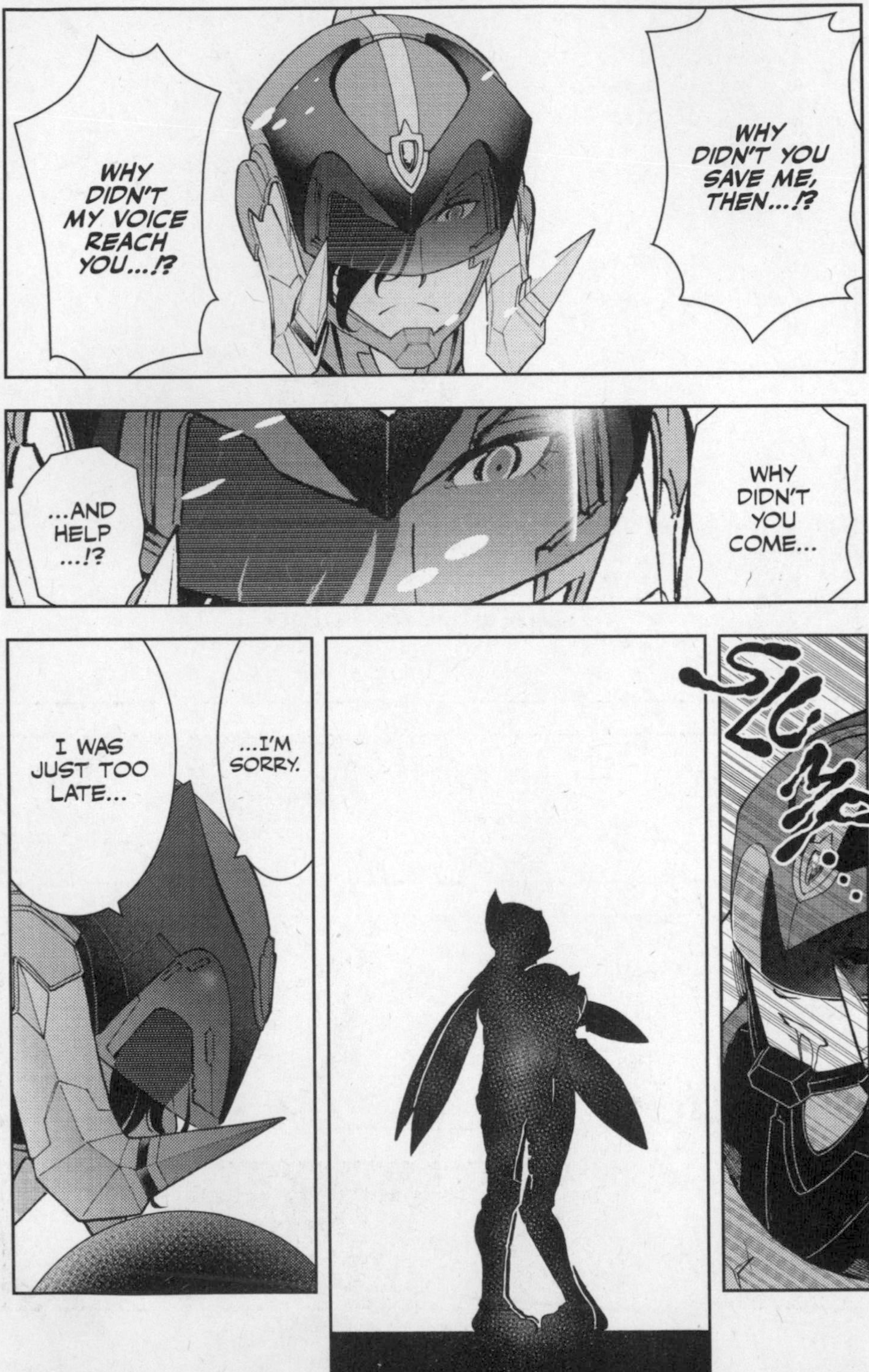
WHY DIDN'T YOU SAVE ME, THEN...!?
WHY DIDN'T MY VOICE REACH YOU...!?
WHY DIDN'T YOU COME...
...AND HELP ...!?
SLUMP...
...I'M SORRY.
I WAS JUST TOO LATE...

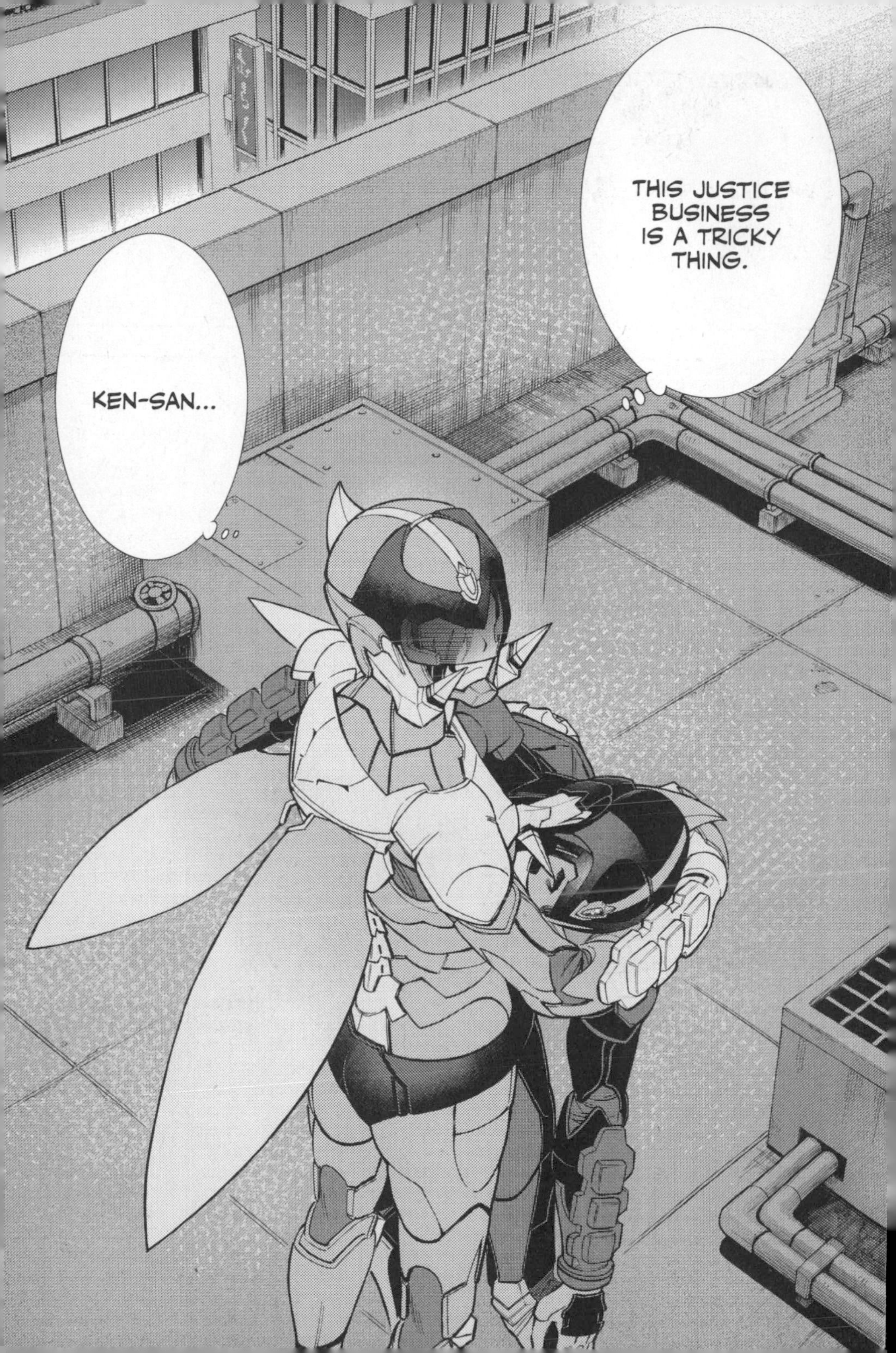
THIS JUSTICE BUSINESS IS A TRICKY THING.
KEN-SAN...

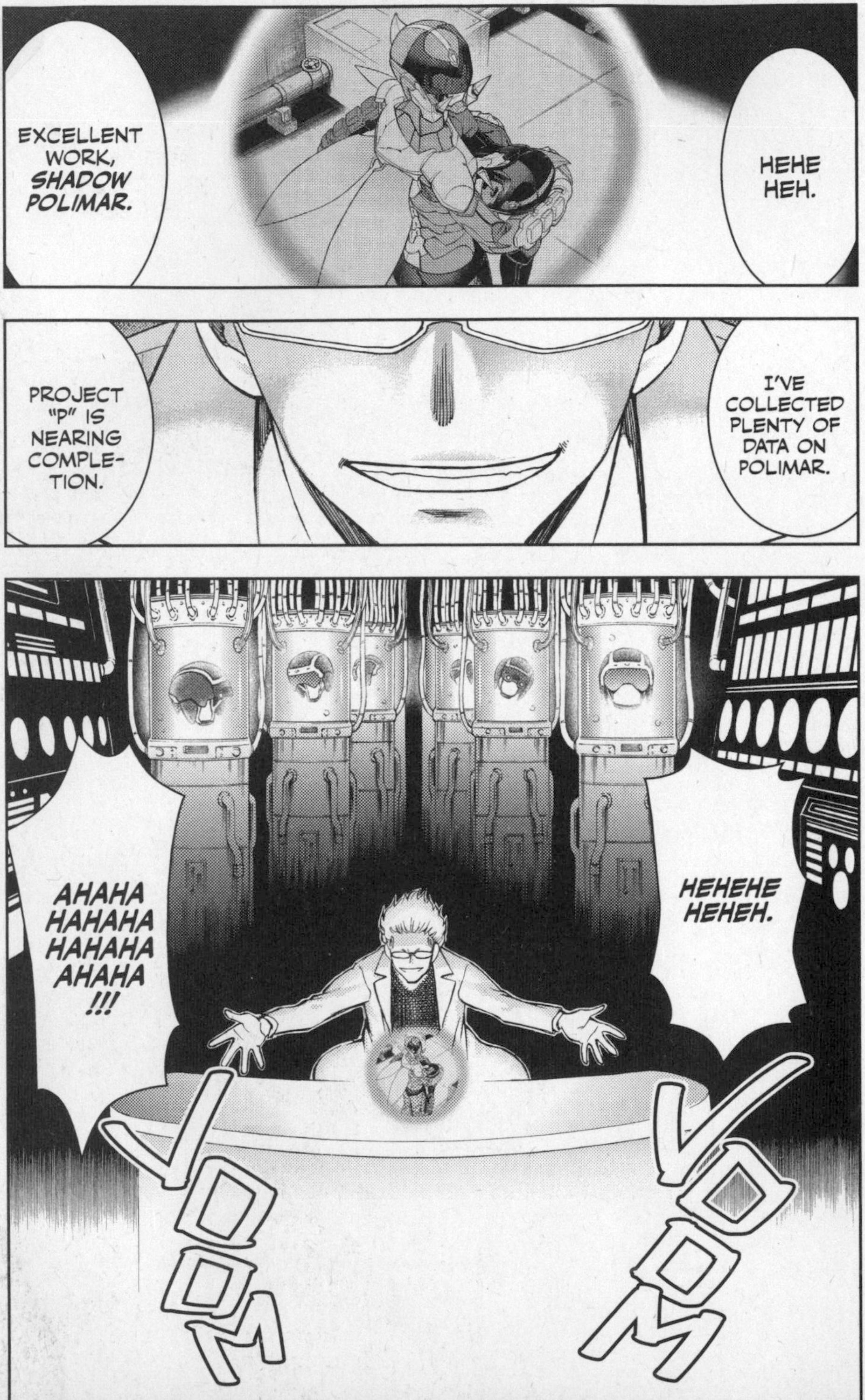
HEHE HEH.
EXCELLENT WORK, SHADOW POLIMAR.
I'VE COLLECTED PLENTY OF DATA ON POLIMAR.
PROJECT "P" IS NEARING COMPLE-TION.
HEHEHE HEHEH.
AHAHA HAHAHA HAHAHA AHAHA !!!
VOOM
VOOM

WHAT!?
YOU WON'T BRING ME KATSUDON !!?
I'LL PAY MYSELF!!

Infini-T Force インフィニティフォース
ARC TO THE FUTURE

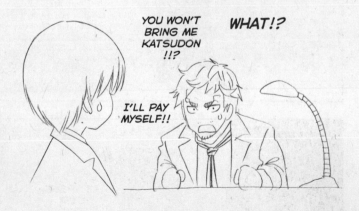

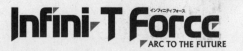

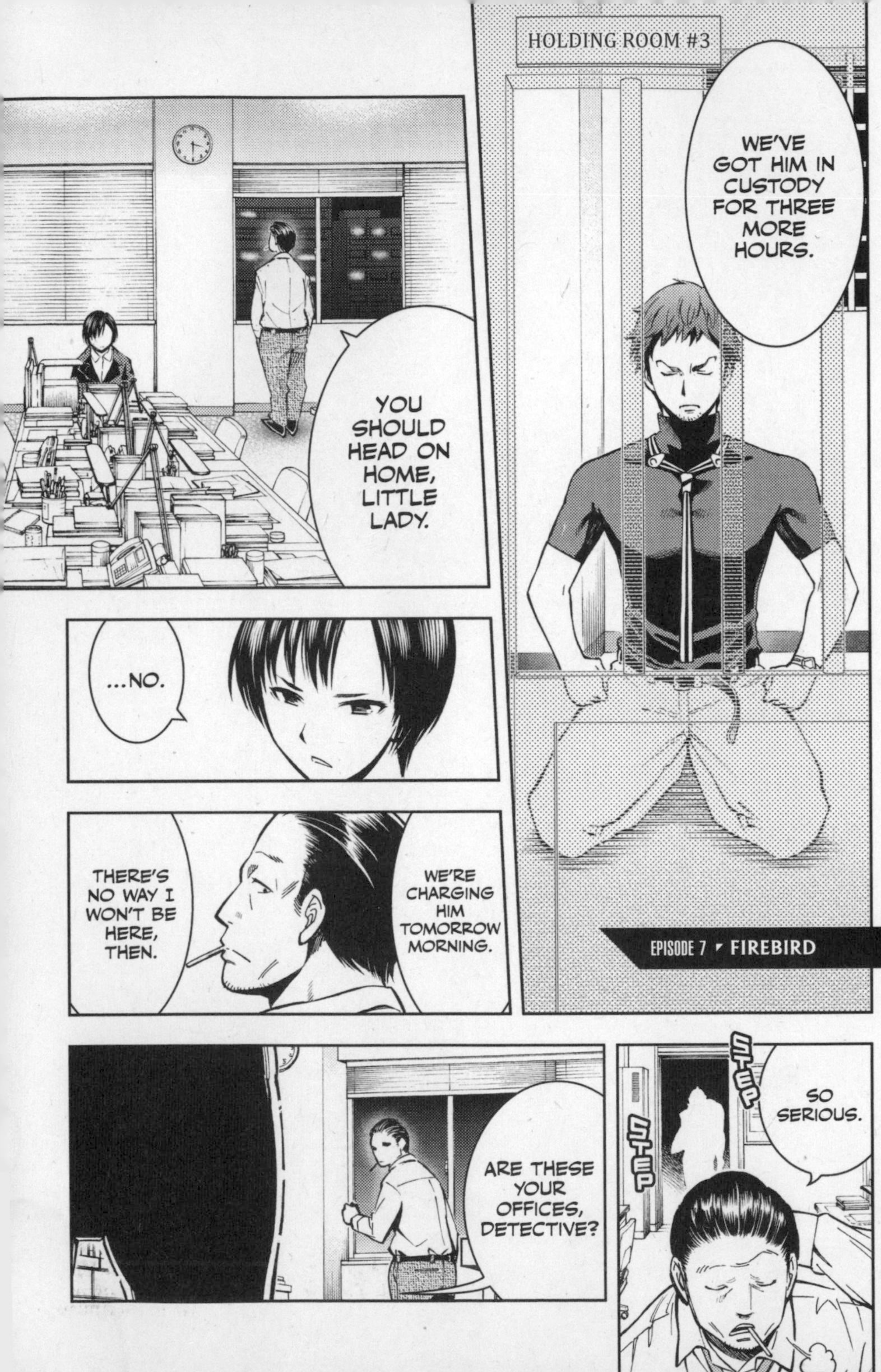
HOLDING ROOM #3
WE'VE GOT HIM IN CUSTODY FOR THREE MORE HOURS.
EPISODE 7 ▸ FIREBIRD
YOU SHOULD HEAD ON HOME, LITTLE LADY.
...NO.
WE'RE CHARGING HIM TOMORROW MORNING.
THERE'S NO WAY I WON'T BE HERE, THEN.
STEP
STEP
SO SERIOUS.
ARE THESE YOUR OFFICES, DETECTIVE?

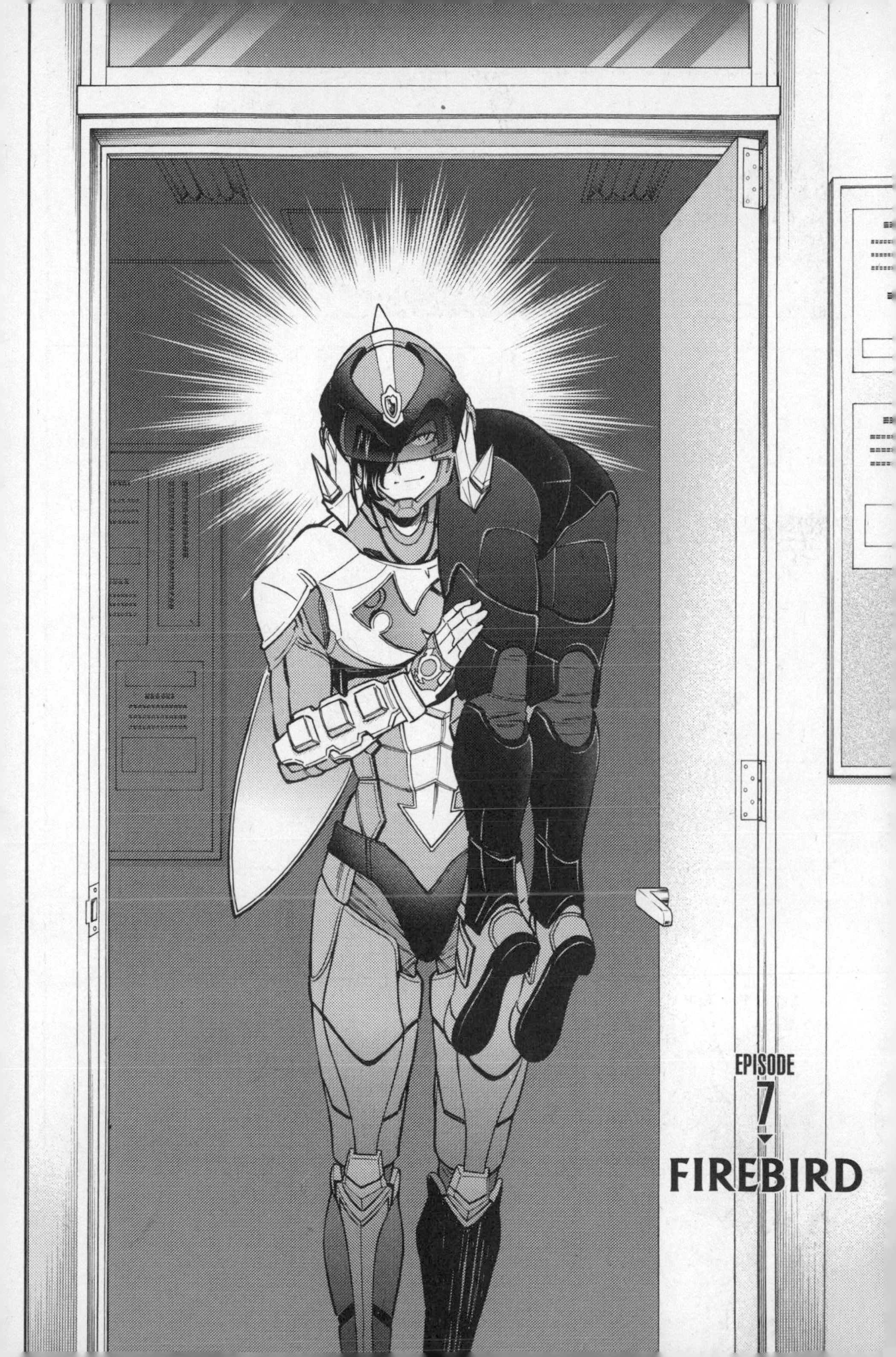
EPISODE
7
FIREBIRD

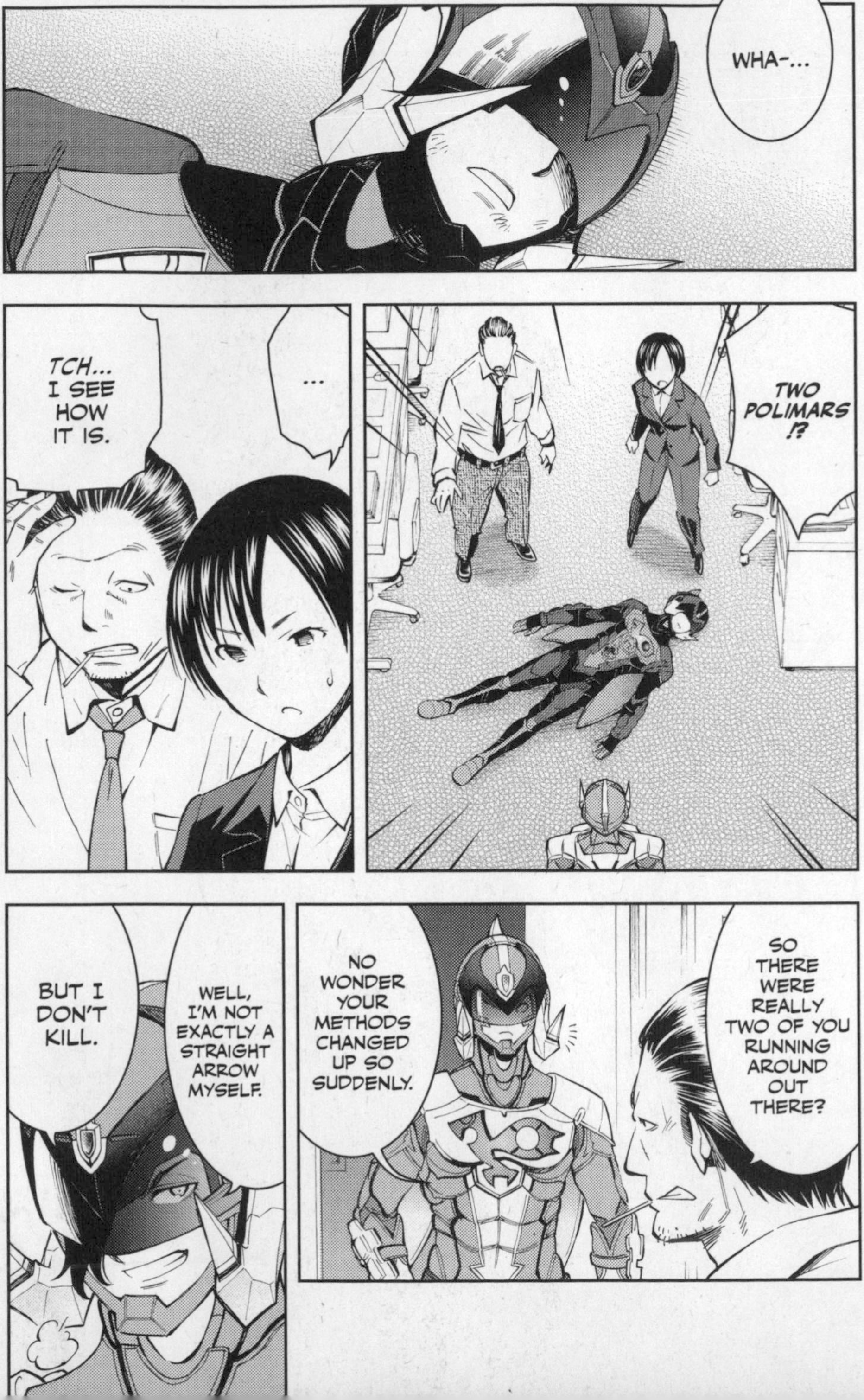
WHA-...
TWO POLIMARS!?
...
TCH... I SEE HOW IT IS.
SO THERE WERE REALLY TWO OF YOU RUNNING AROUND OUT THERE?
NO WONDER YOUR METHODS CHANGED UP SO SUDDENLY.
WELL, I'M NOT EXACTLY A STRAIGHT ARROW MYSELF.
BUT I DON'T KILL.

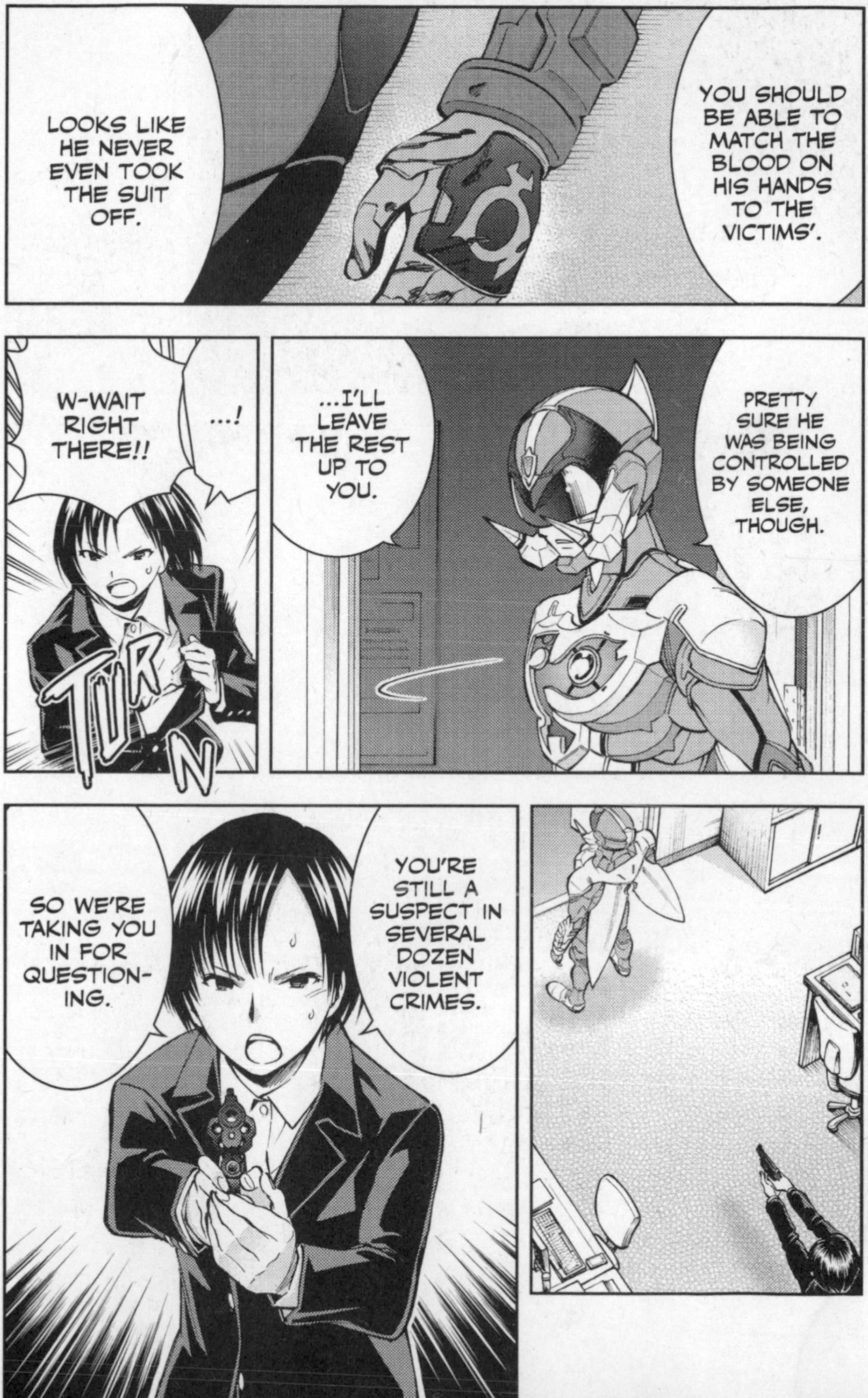
YOU SHOULD BE ABLE TO MATCH THE BLOOD ON HIS HANDS TO THE VICTIMS'.
LOOKS LIKE HE NEVER EVEN TOOK THE SUIT OFF.
PRETTY SURE HE WAS BEING CONTROLLED BY SOMEONE ELSE, THOUGH.
...I'LL LEAVE THE REST UP TO YOU.
...!
W-WAIT RIGHT THERE!!
TURN
YOU'RE STILL A SUSPECT IN SEVERAL DOZEN VIOLENT CRIMES.
SO WE'RE TAKING YOU IN FOR QUESTION-ING.

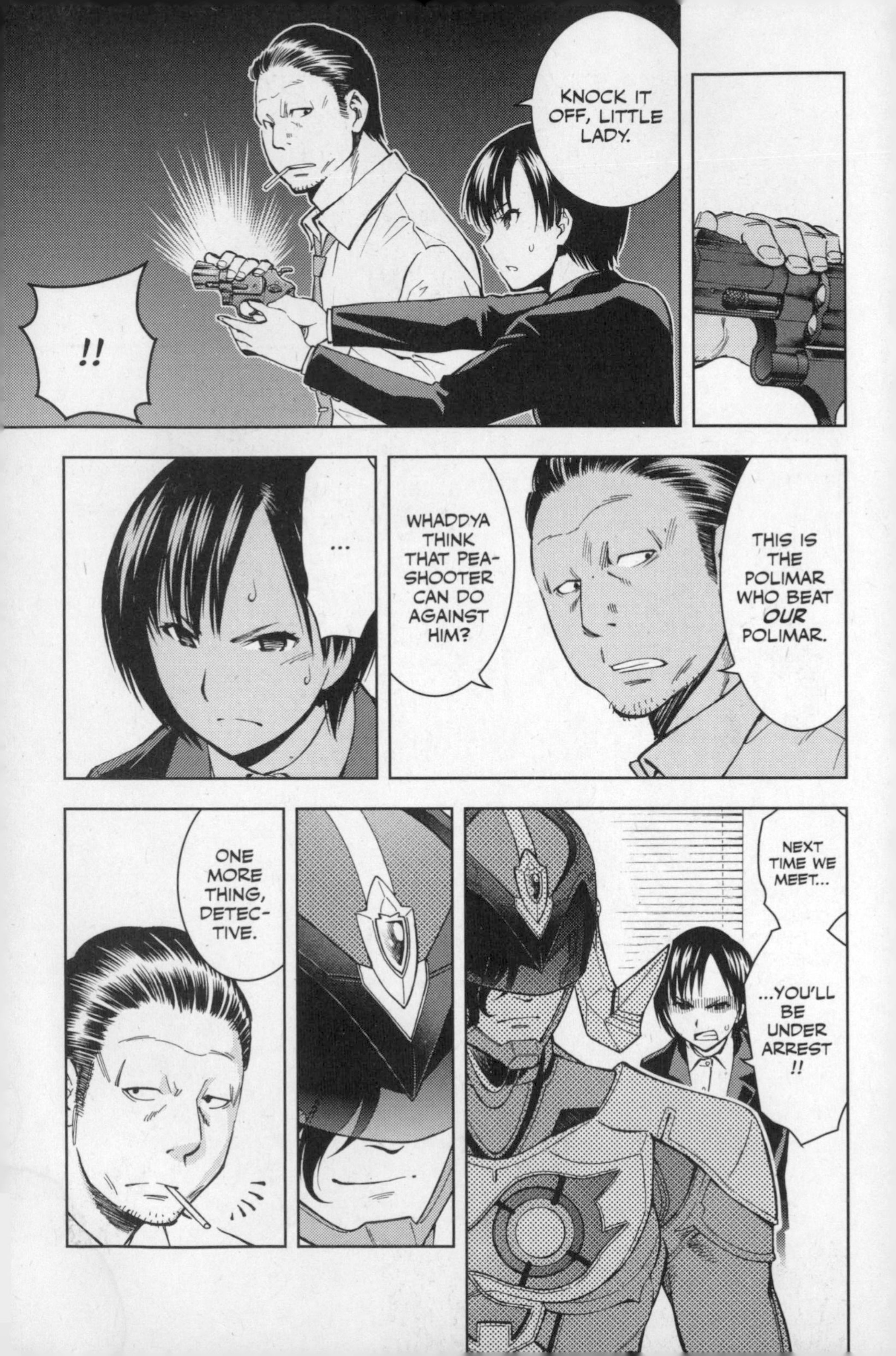
KNOCK IT OFF, LITTLE LADY.
!!
THIS IS THE POLIMAR WHO BEAT *OUR* POLIMAR.
WHADDYA THINK THAT PEA-SHOOTER CAN DO AGAINST HIM?
...
NEXT TIME WE MEET...
...YOU'LL BE UNDER ARREST!!
ONE MORE THING, DETECTIVE.

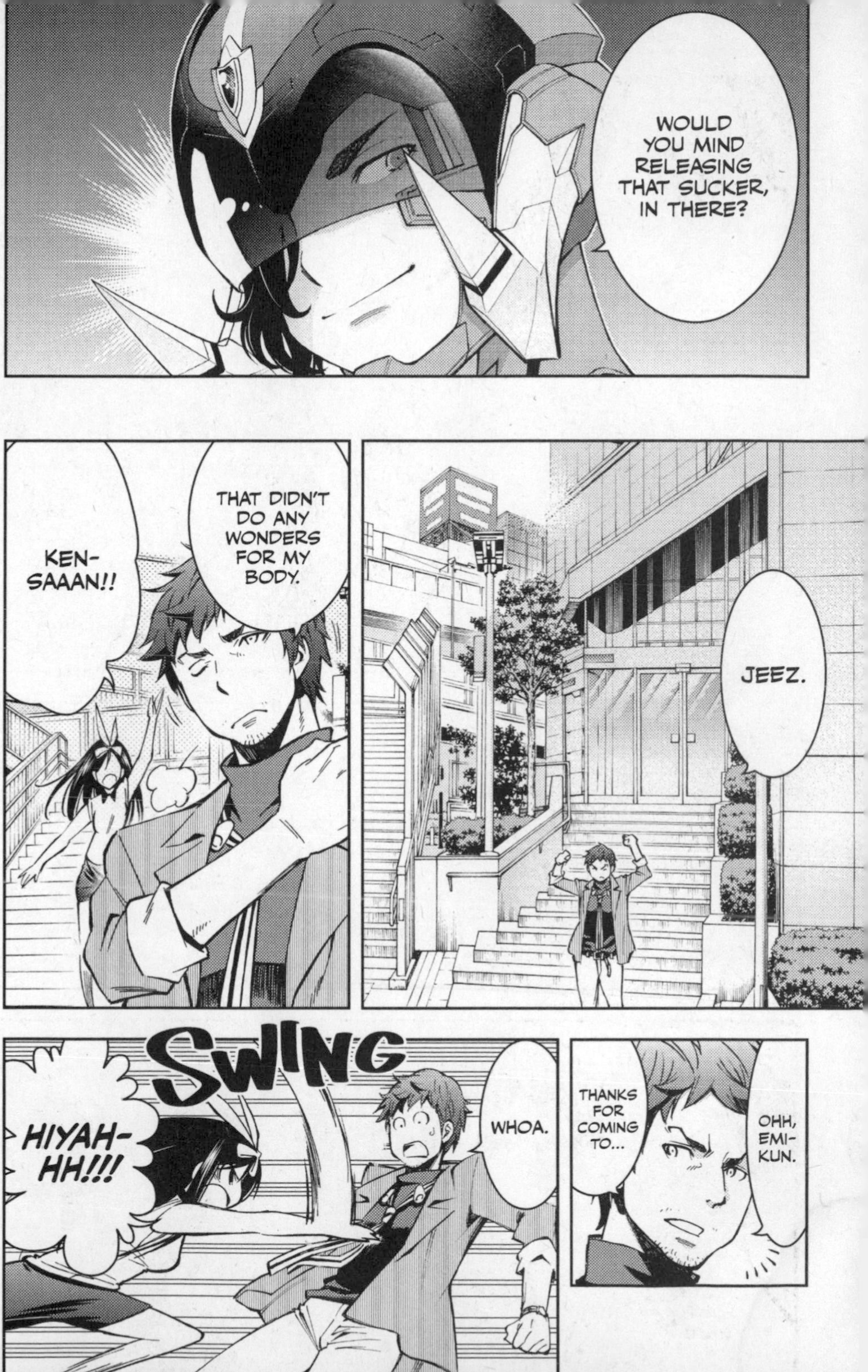
WOULD YOU MIND RELEASING THAT SUCKER, IN THERE?
JEEZ.
THAT DIDN'T DO ANY WONDERS FOR MY BODY.
KEN-SAAAN!!
OHH, EMI-KUN.
THANKS FOR COMING TO...
WHOA.
SWING
HIYAH-HH!!!

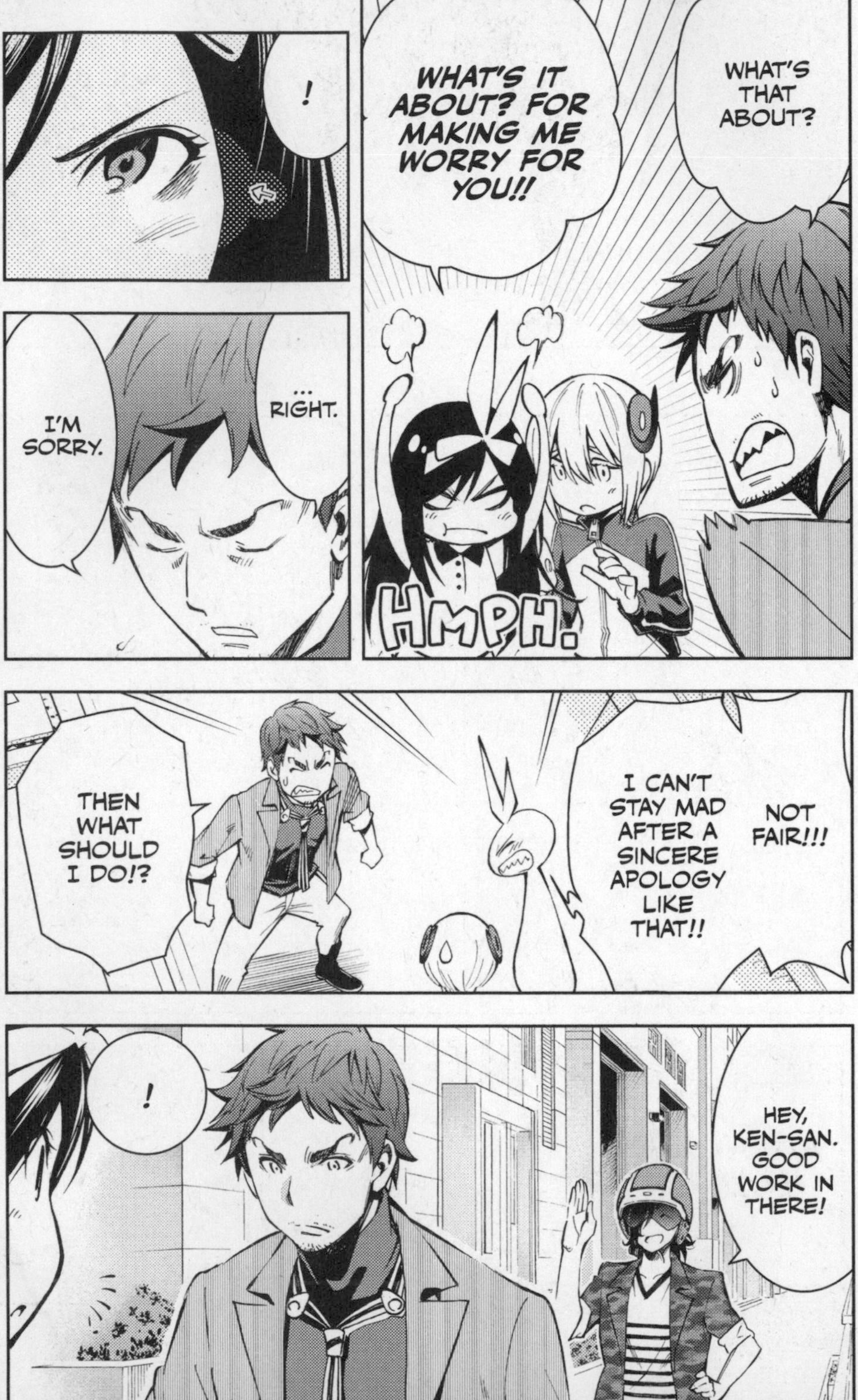

WHAT'S THAT ABOUT?
WHAT'S IT ABOUT? FOR MAKING ME WORRY FOR YOU!!
HMPH!
!
...RIGHT.
I'M SORRY.
NOT FAIR!!!
I CAN'T STAY MAD AFTER A SINCERE APOLOGY LIKE THAT!!
THEN WHAT SHOULD I DO!?
HEY, KEN-SAN. GOOD WORK IN THERE!
!

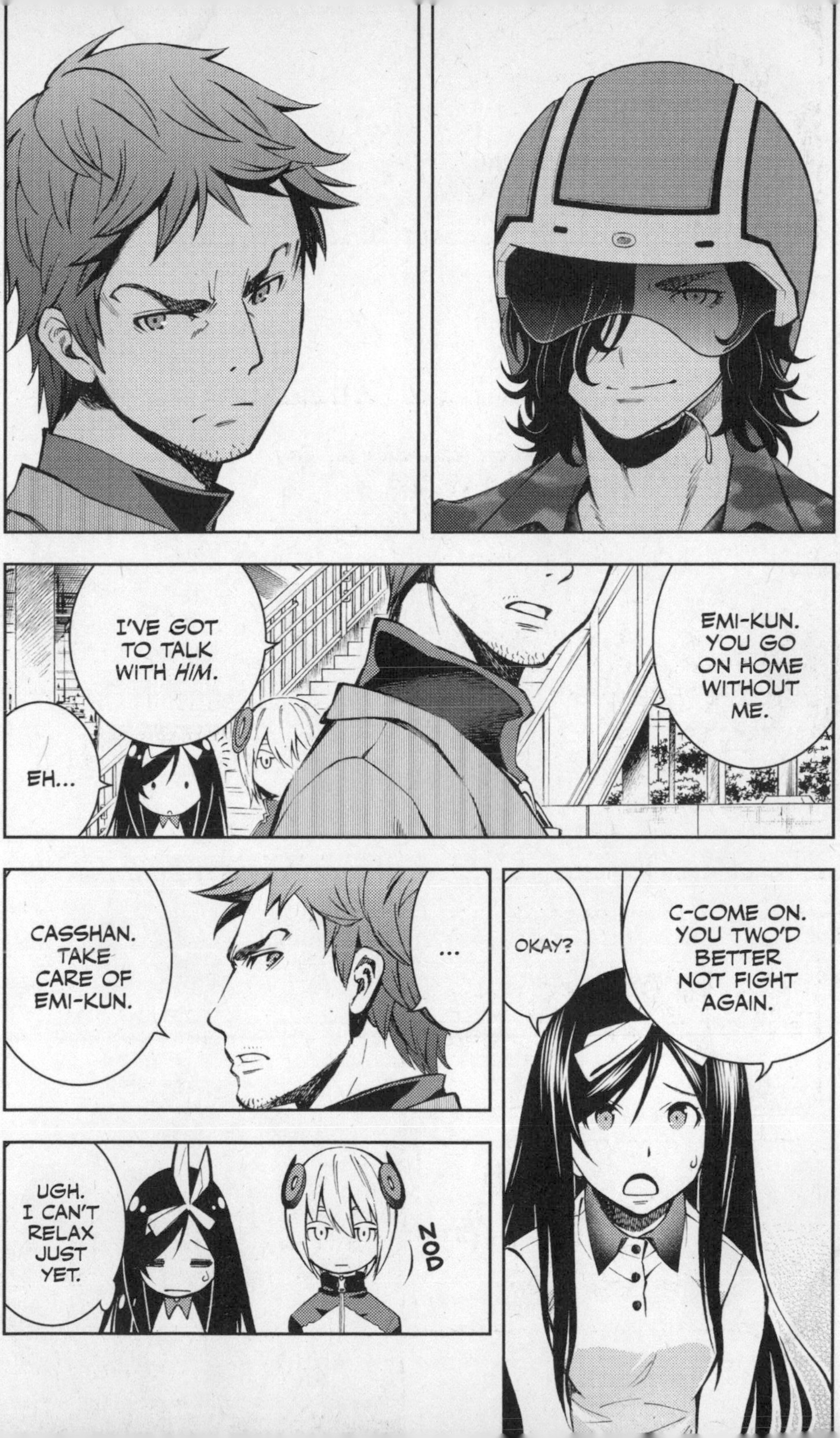
EMI-KUN. YOU GO ON HOME WITHOUT ME.
I'VE GOT TO TALK WITH *HIM*.
EH...
C-COME ON. YOU TWO'D BETTER NOT FIGHT AGAIN.
OKAY?
...
CASSHAN. TAKE CARE OF EMI-KUN.
NOD
UGH. I CAN'T RELAX JUST YET.

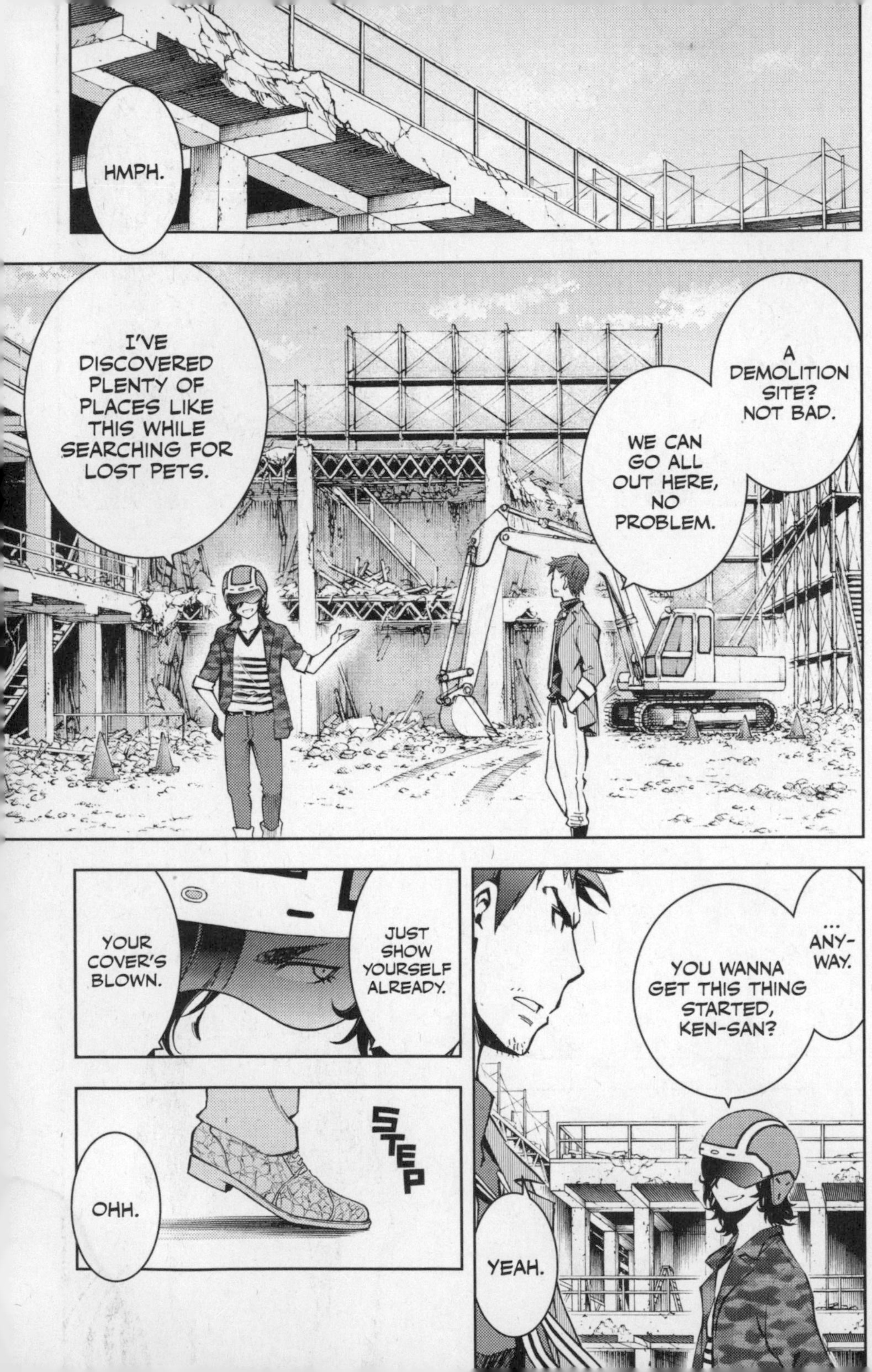
HMPH.
A DEMOLITION SITE? NOT BAD.
WE CAN GO ALL OUT HERE, NO PROBLEM.
I'VE DISCOVERED PLENTY OF PLACES LIKE THIS WHILE SEARCHING FOR LOST PETS.
... ANY-WAY.
YOU WANNA GET THIS THING STARTED, KEN-SAN?
YEAH.
JUST SHOW YOURSELF ALREADY.
YOUR COVER'S BLOWN.
STEP
OHH.

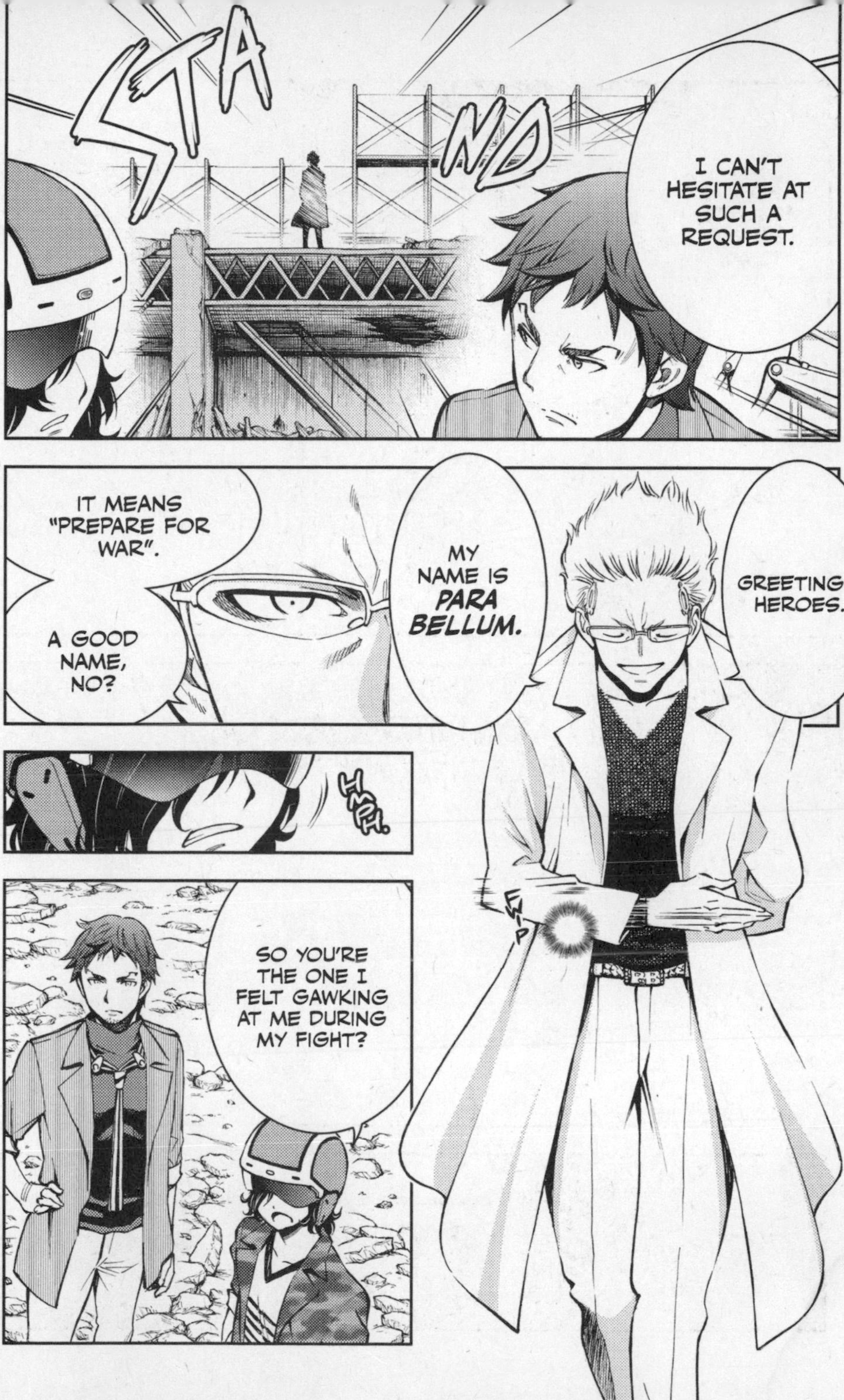
I CAN'T HESITATE AT SUCH A REQUEST.
STAND
GREETINGS, HEROES.
MY NAME IS PARA BELLUM.
FWIP
IT MEANS "PREPARE FOR WAR".
A GOOD NAME, NO?
HMPH.
SO YOU'RE THE ONE I FELT GAWKING AT ME DURING MY FIGHT?

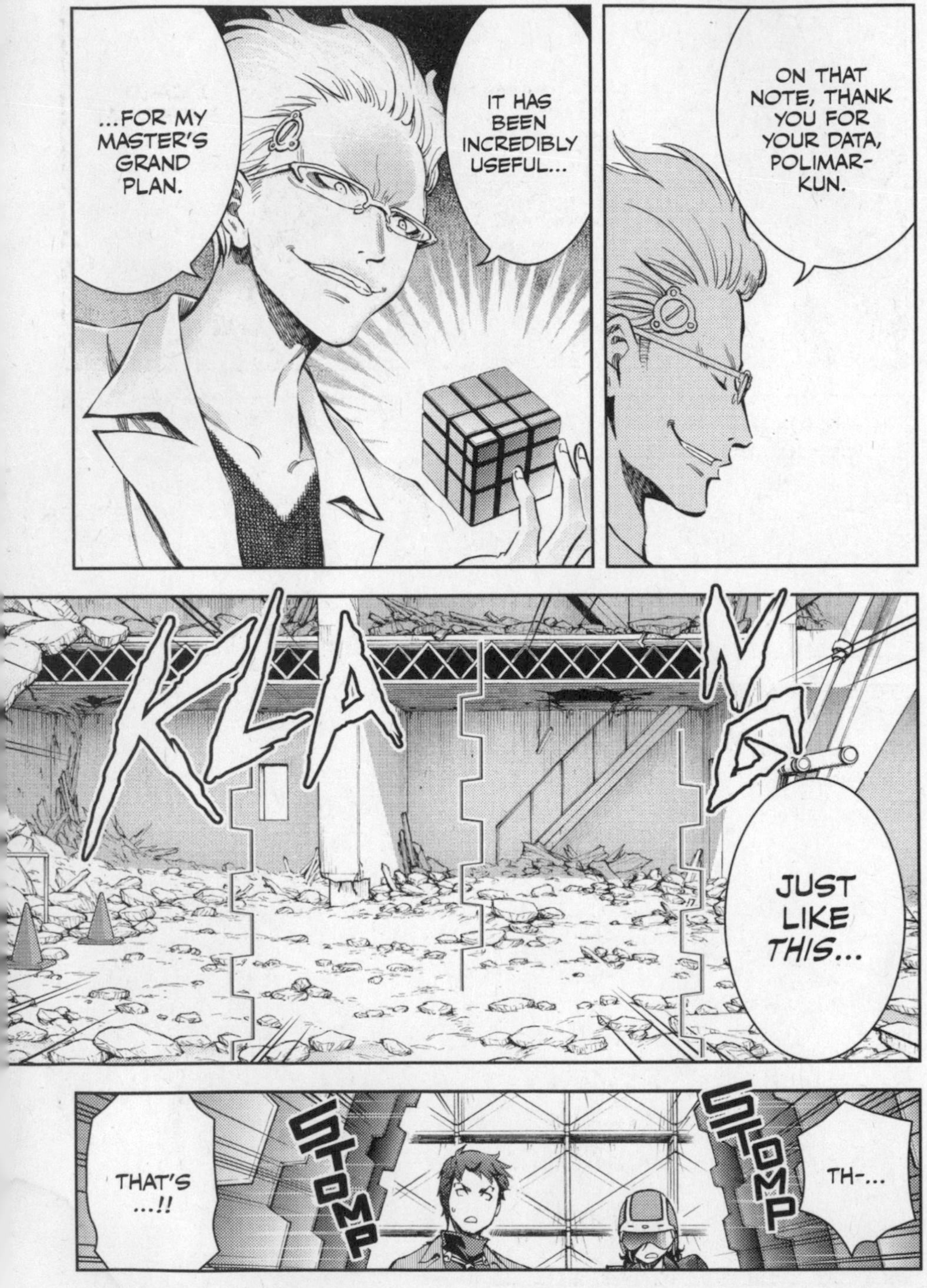
ON THAT NOTE, THANK YOU FOR YOUR DATA, POLIMAR-KUN.
IT HAS BEEN INCREDIBLY USEFUL...
...FOR MY MASTER'S GRAND PLAN.
KLANG
JUST LIKE *THIS*...
TH-...
STOMP
STOMP
THAT'S ...!!

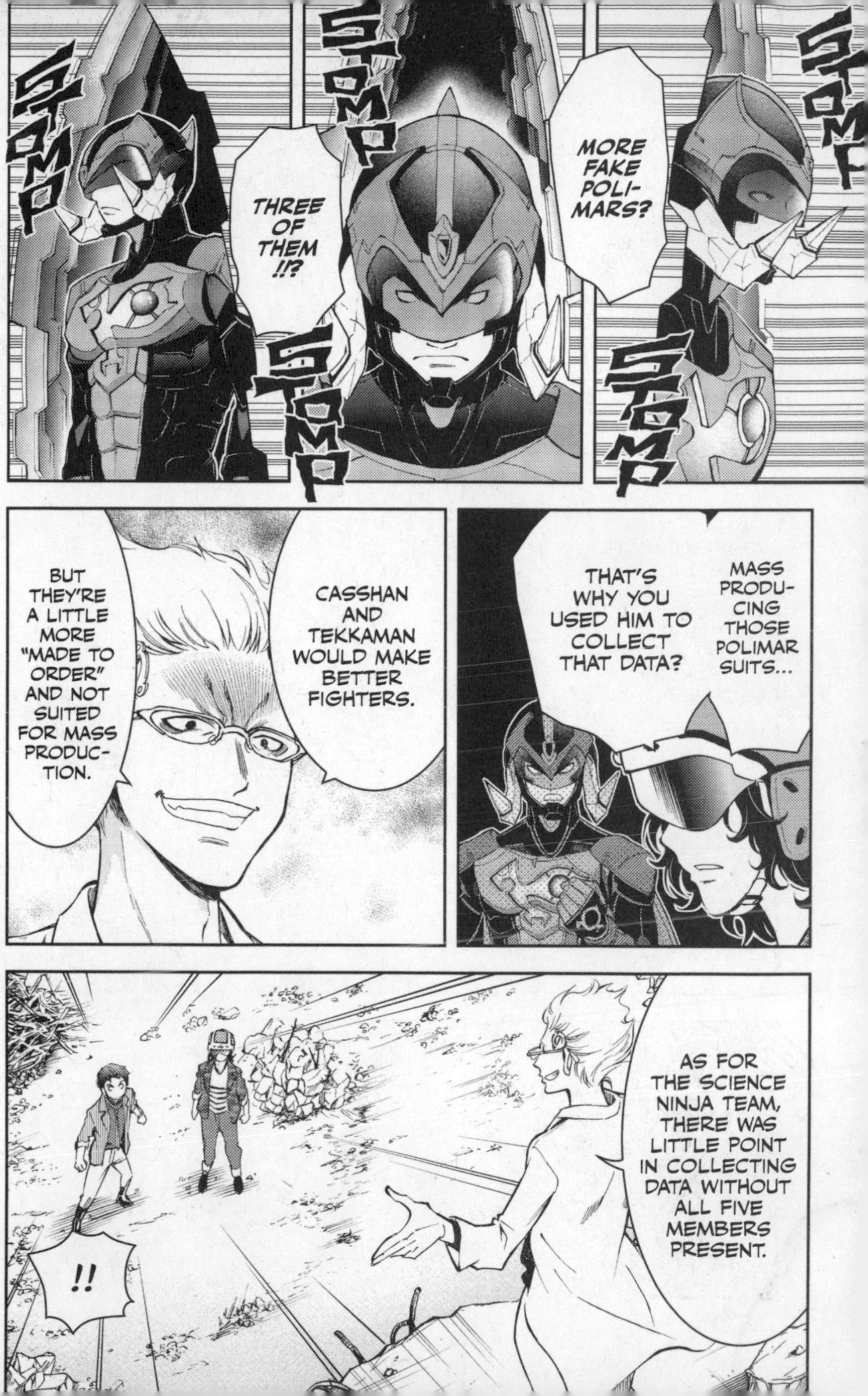
STOMP
STOMP
STOMP
MORE FAKE POLI-MARS?
THREE OF THEM!!?
STOMP
STOMP
MASS PRODU-CING THOSE POLIMAR SUITS...
THAT'S WHY YOU USED HIM TO COLLECT THAT DATA?
CASSHAN AND TEKKAMAN WOULD MAKE BETTER FIGHTERS.
BUT THEY'RE A LITTLE MORE "MADE TO ORDER" AND NOT SUITED FOR MASS PRODUC-TION.
AS FOR THE SCIENCE NINJA TEAM, THERE WAS LITTLE POINT IN COLLECTING DATA WITHOUT ALL FIVE MEMBERS PRESENT.
!!

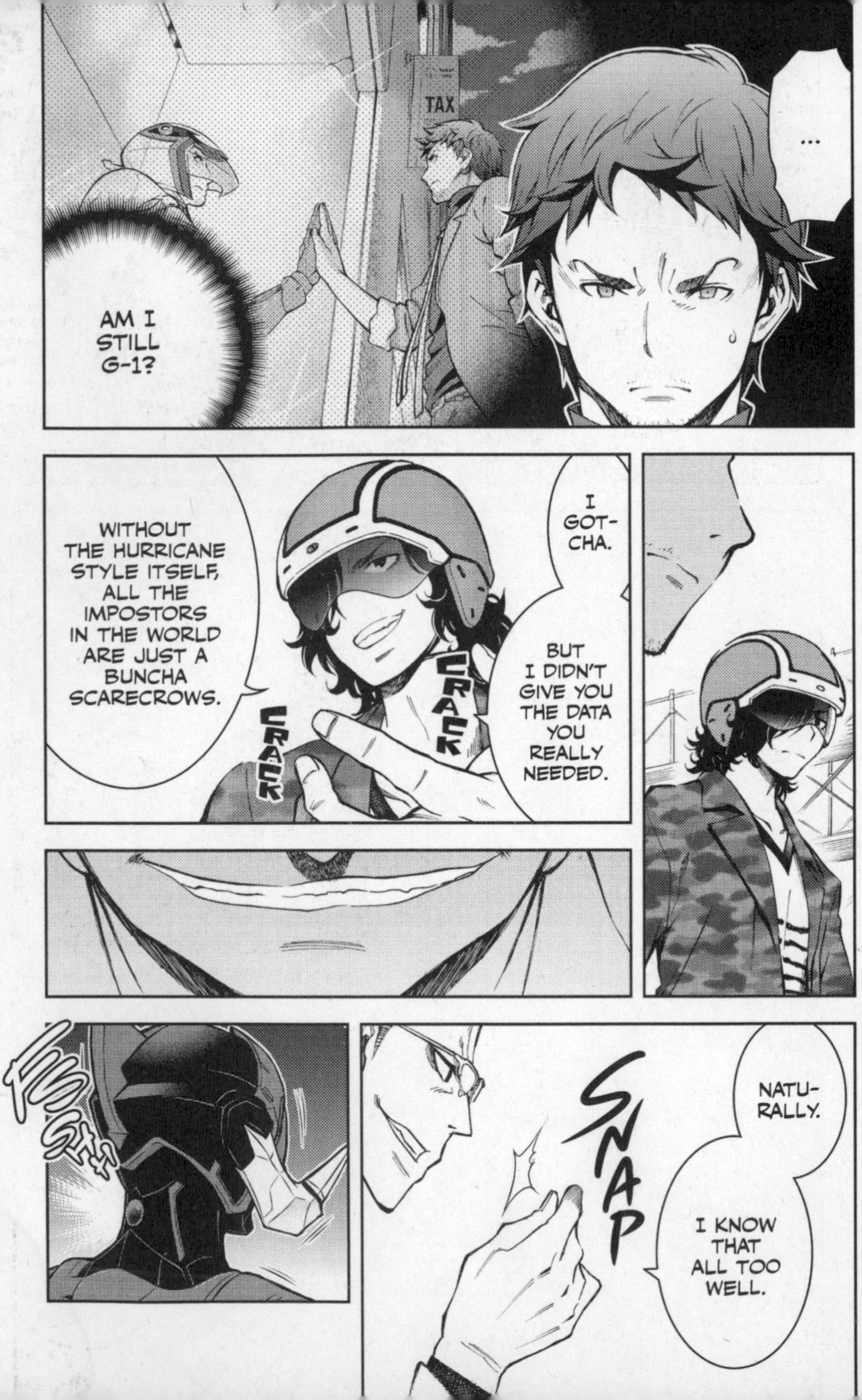
...
AM I STILL G-1?
I GOT-CHA.
BUT I DIDN'T GIVE YOU THE DATA YOU REALLY NEEDED.
CRACK
CRACK
CRACK
WITHOUT THE HURRICANE STYLE ITSELF, ALL THE IMPOSTORS IN THE WORLD ARE JUST A BUNCHA SCARECROWS.
NATU-RALLY.
SNAP
I KNOW THAT ALL TOO WELL.

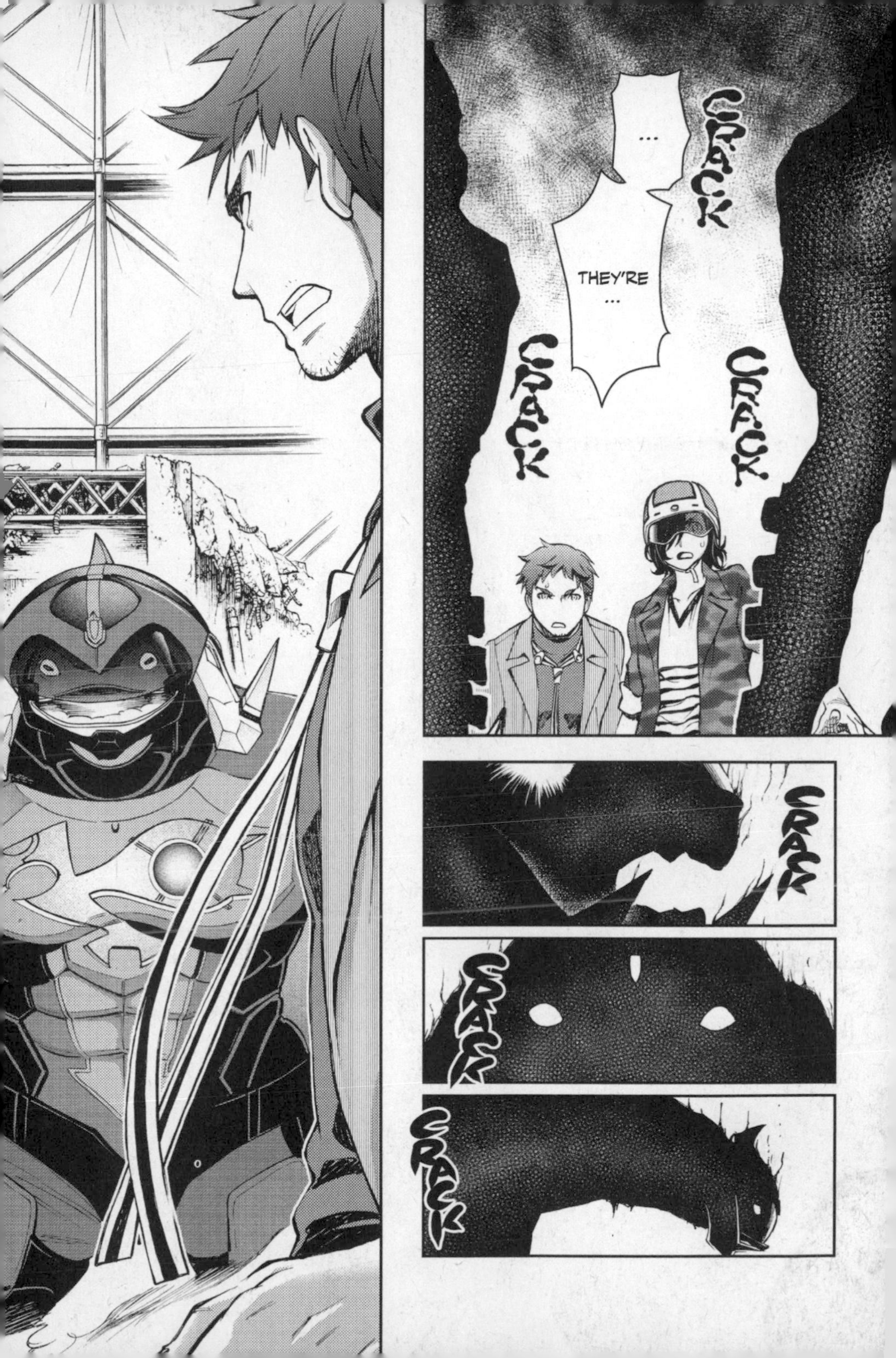
CRACK
...
THEY'RE ...
CRACK
CRACK
CRACK
CRACK
CRACK

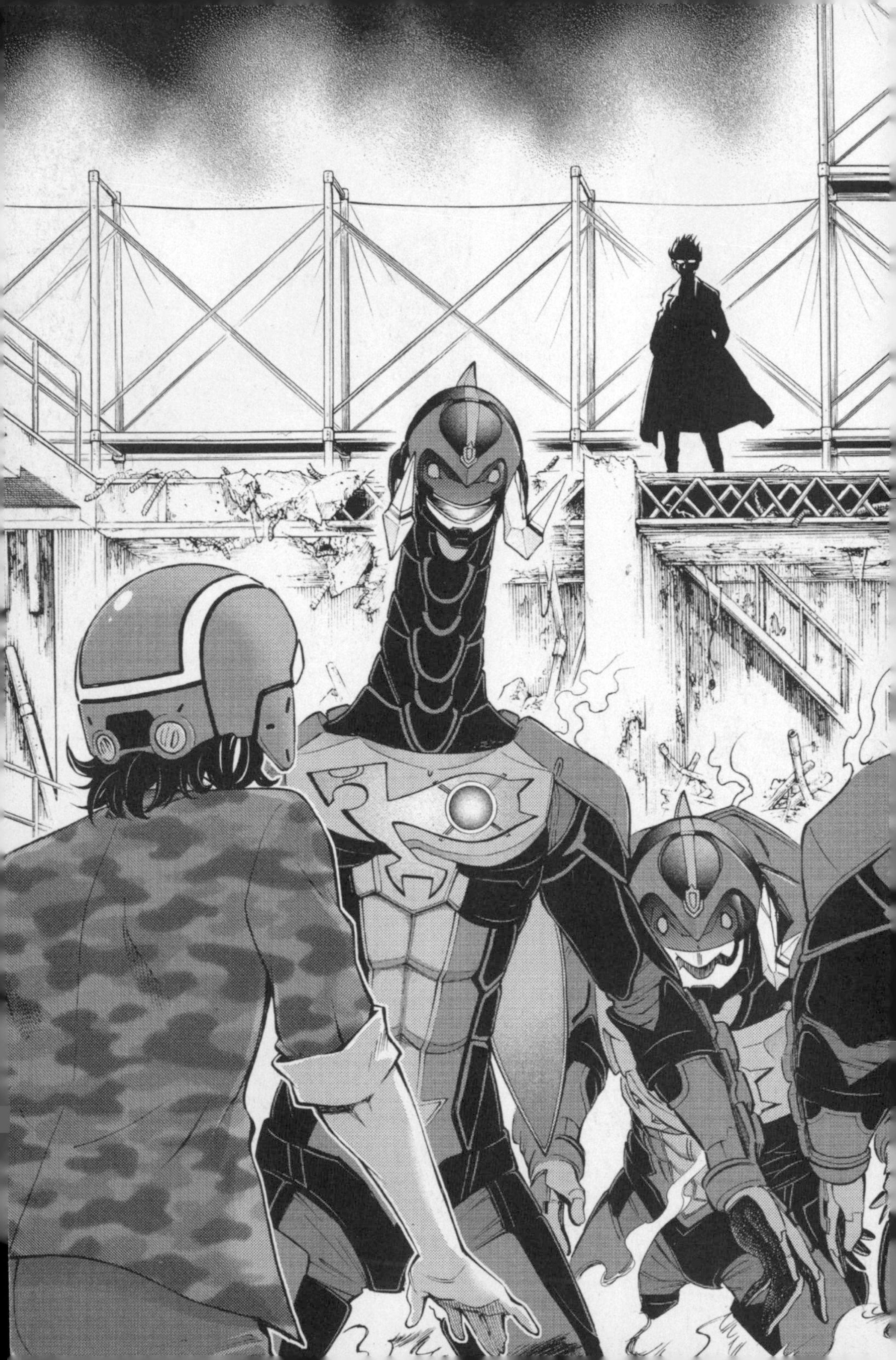

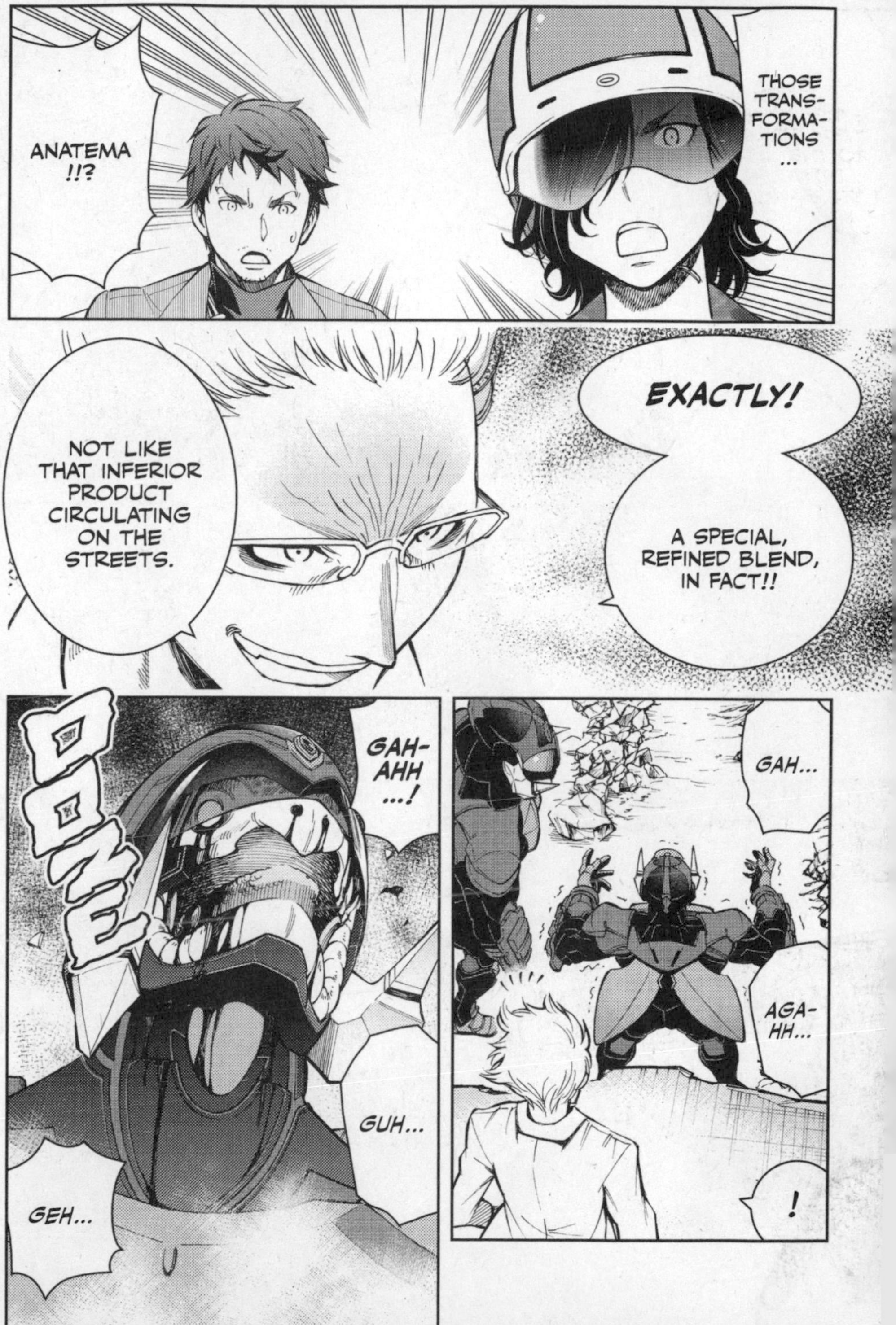
THOSE TRANS-FORMA-TIONS ...
ANATEMA !!?
EXACTLY!
A SPECIAL, REFINED BLEND, IN FACT!!
NOT LIKE THAT INFERIOR PRODUCT CIRCULATING ON THE STREETS.
GAH...
AGA-HH...
!
GAH-AHH ...!
DOZE
GUH...
GEH...

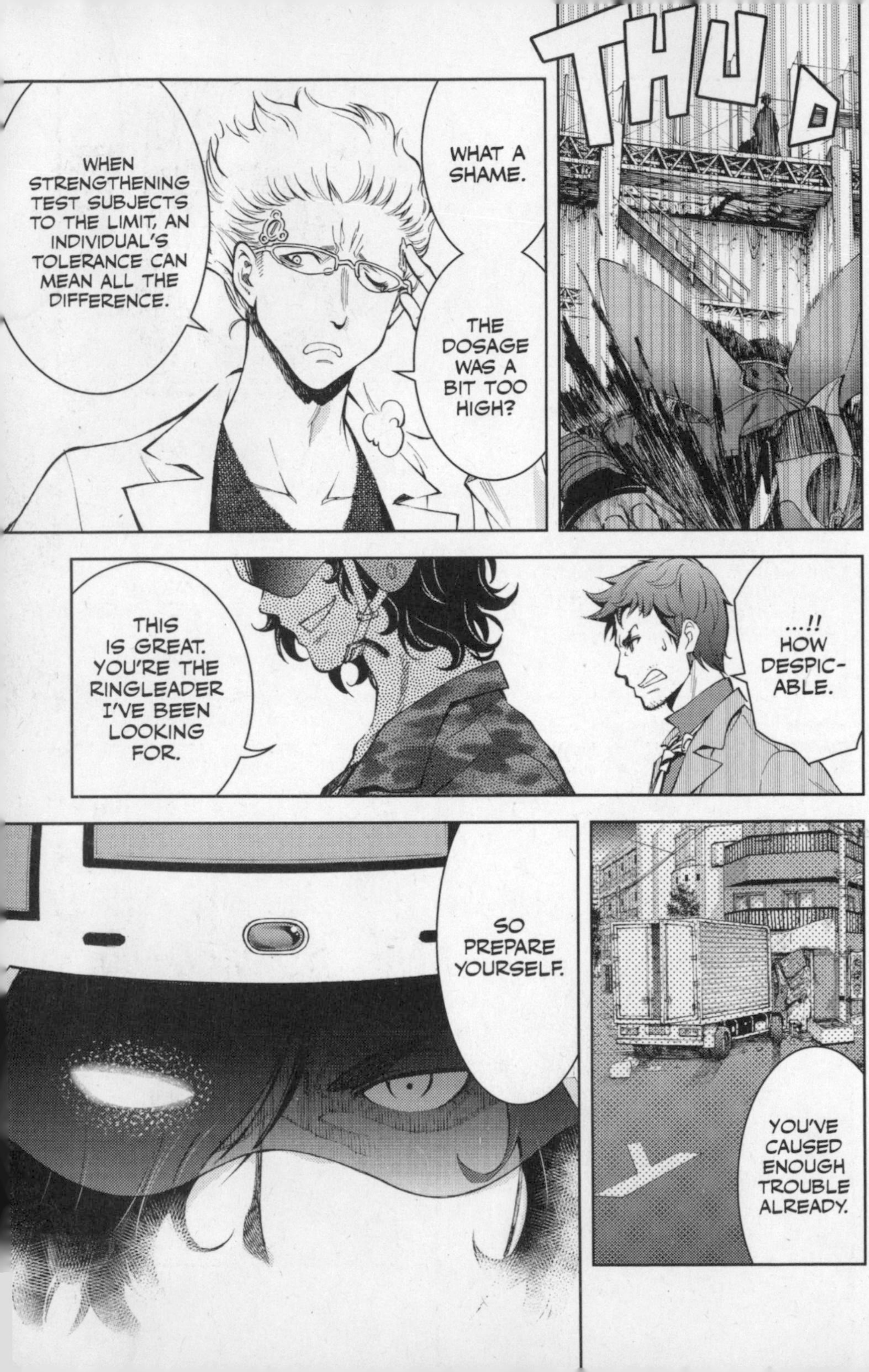
THUD
WHAT A SHAME.
THE DOSAGE WAS A BIT TOO HIGH?
WHEN STRENGTHENING TEST SUBJECTS TO THE LIMIT, AN INDIVIDUAL'S TOLERANCE CAN MEAN ALL THE DIFFERENCE.
...!! HOW DESPIC-ABLE.
THIS IS GREAT. YOU'RE THE RINGLEADER I'VE BEEN LOOKING FOR.
YOU'VE CAUSED ENOUGH TROUBLE ALREADY.
SO PREPARE YOURSELF.

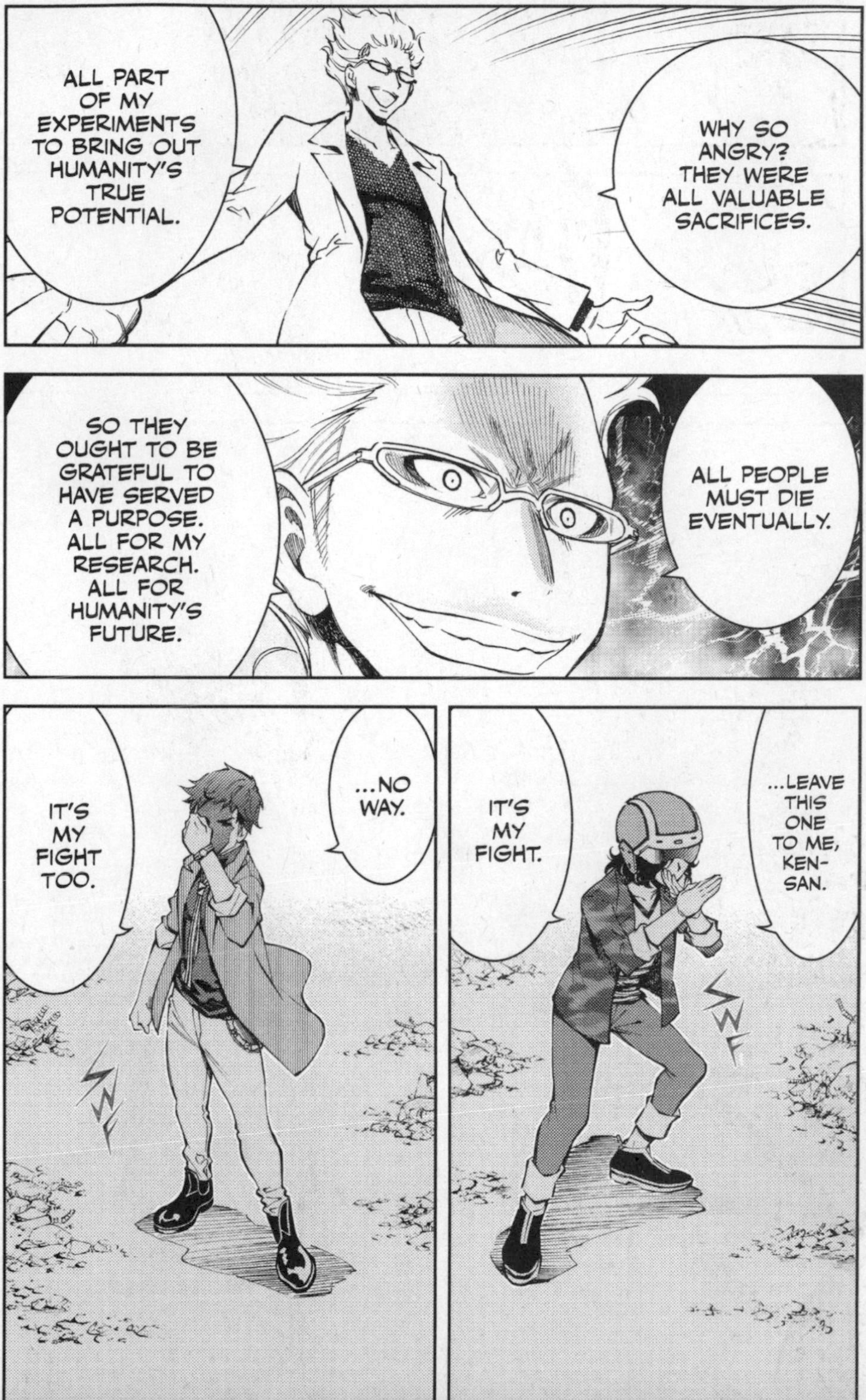
WHY SO ANGRY? THEY WERE ALL VALUABLE SACRIFICES.
ALL PART OF MY EXPERIMENTS TO BRING OUT HUMANITY'S TRUE POTENTIAL.
ALL PEOPLE MUST DIE EVENTUALLY.
SO THEY OUGHT TO BE GRATEFUL TO HAVE SERVED A PURPOSE. ALL FOR MY RESEARCH. ALL FOR HUMANITY'S FUTURE.
...LEAVE THIS ONE TO ME, KEN-SAN.
IT'S MY FIGHT.
SWF
...NO WAY.
IT'S MY FIGHT TOO.
SWF

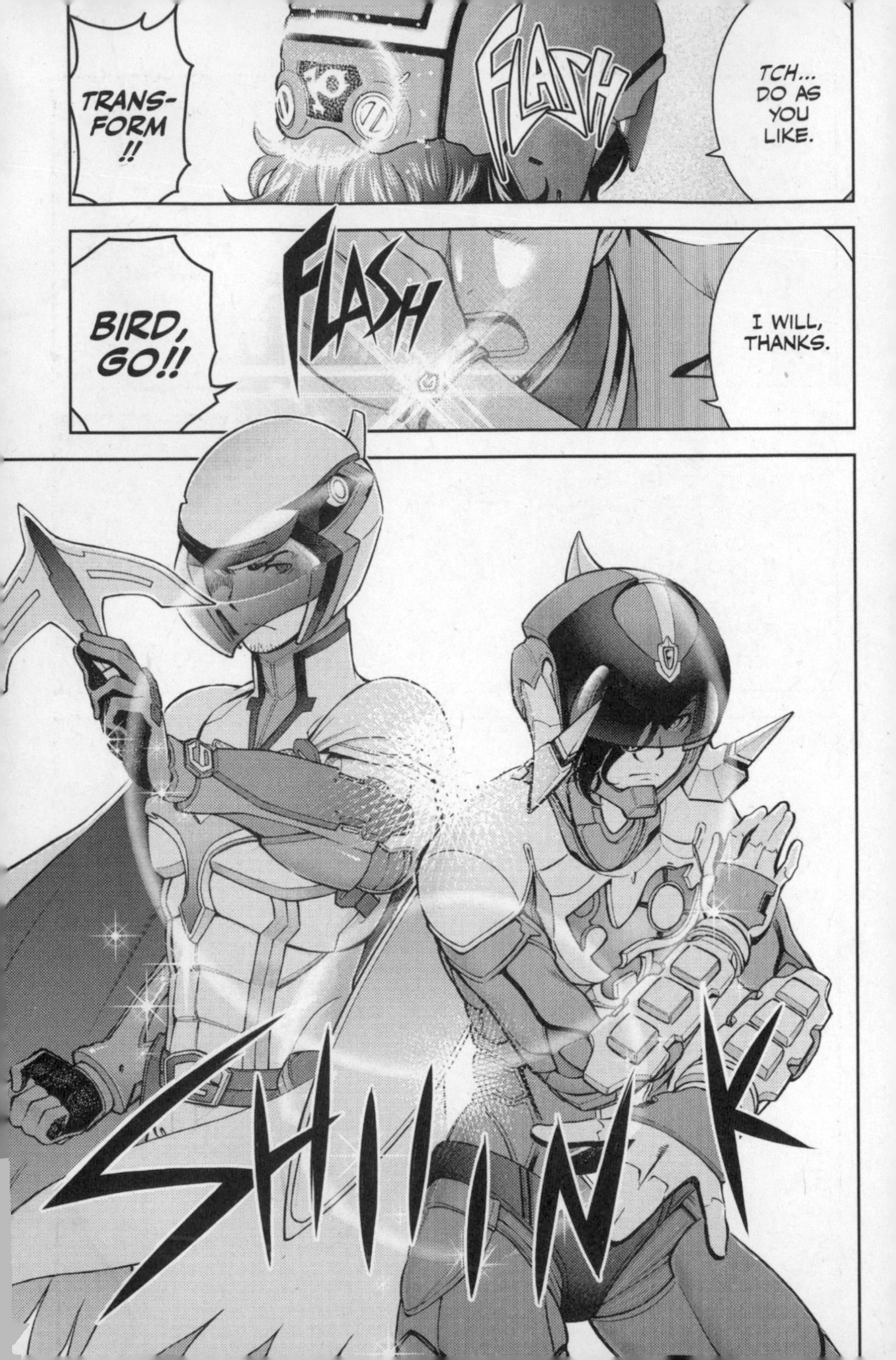
TCH... DO AS YOU LIKE.
FLASH
TRANS-FORM!!
I WILL, THANKS.
FLASH
BIRD, GO!!
SHIIINK

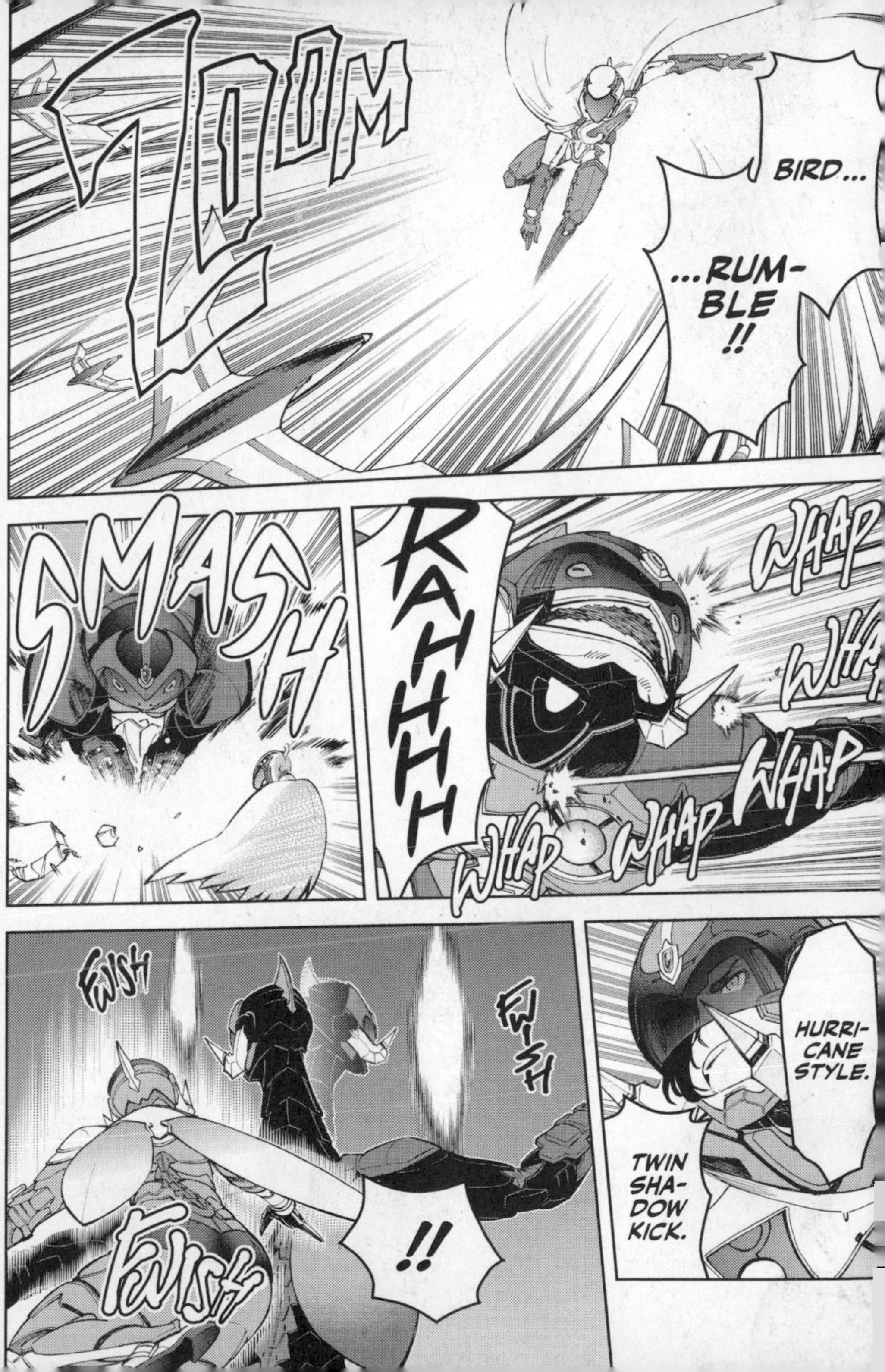
BIRD...
...RUMBLE!!
ZOOM
WHAP
WHAP
WHAP
RAHHHH
WHAP
WHAP
SMASH
HURRICANE STYLE.
TWIN SHADOW KICK.
FWISH
FWISH
!!
FWISH

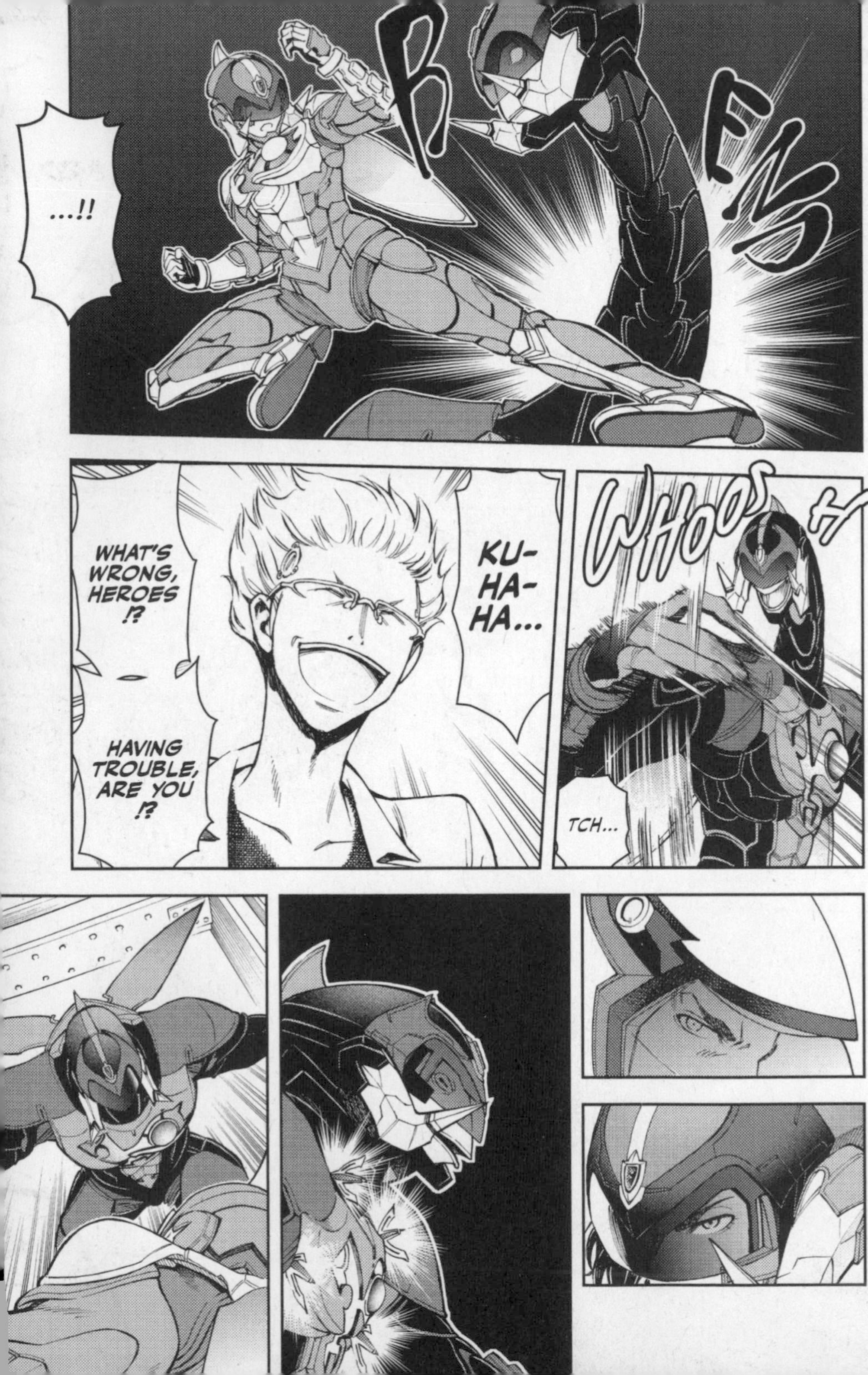
...!!
WHOOSH
TCH...
KU-HA-HA...
WHAT'S WRONG, HEROES!?
HAVING TROUBLE, ARE YOU!?

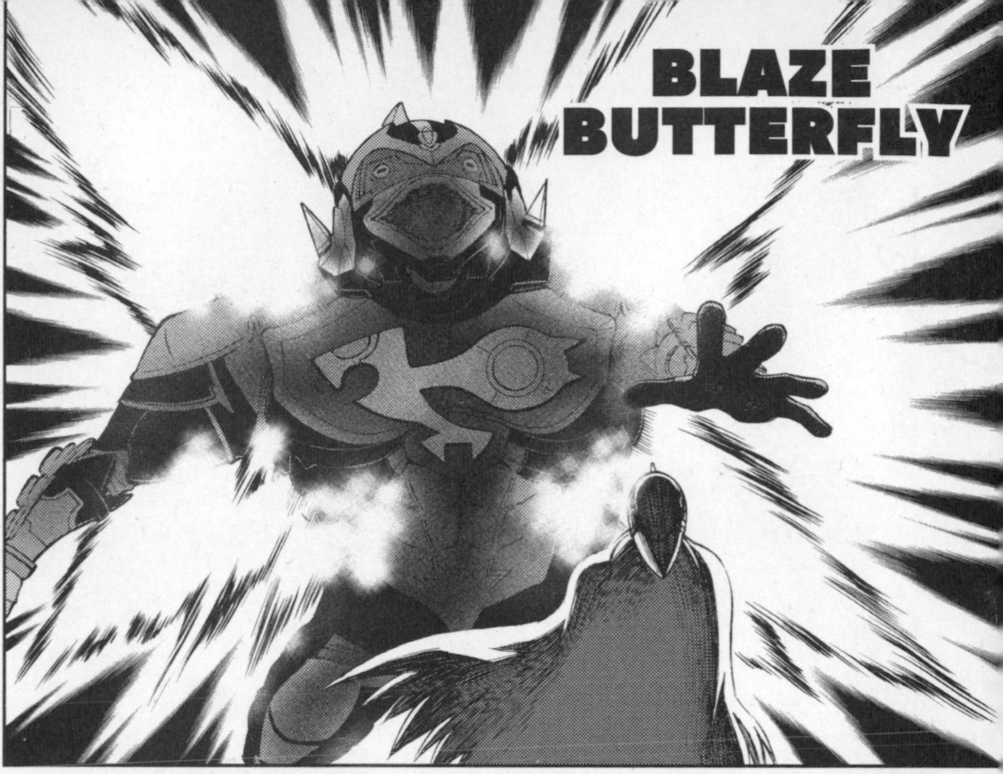
BLAZE BUTTERFLY
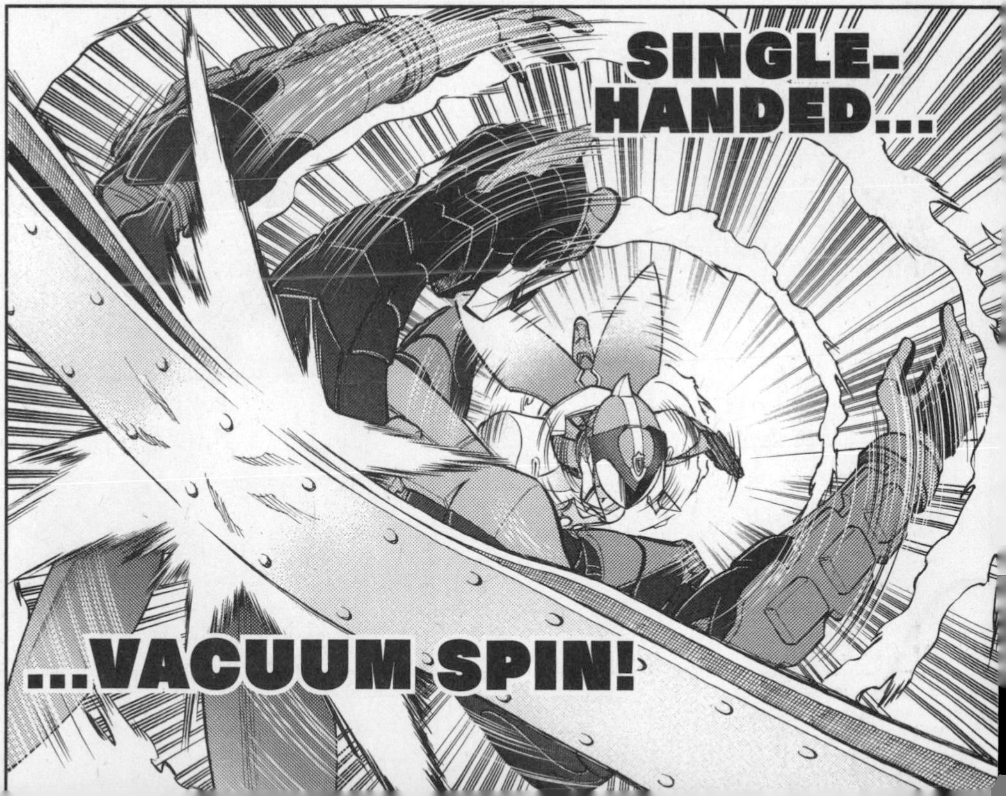
SINGLE-HANDED...
...VACUUM SPIN!

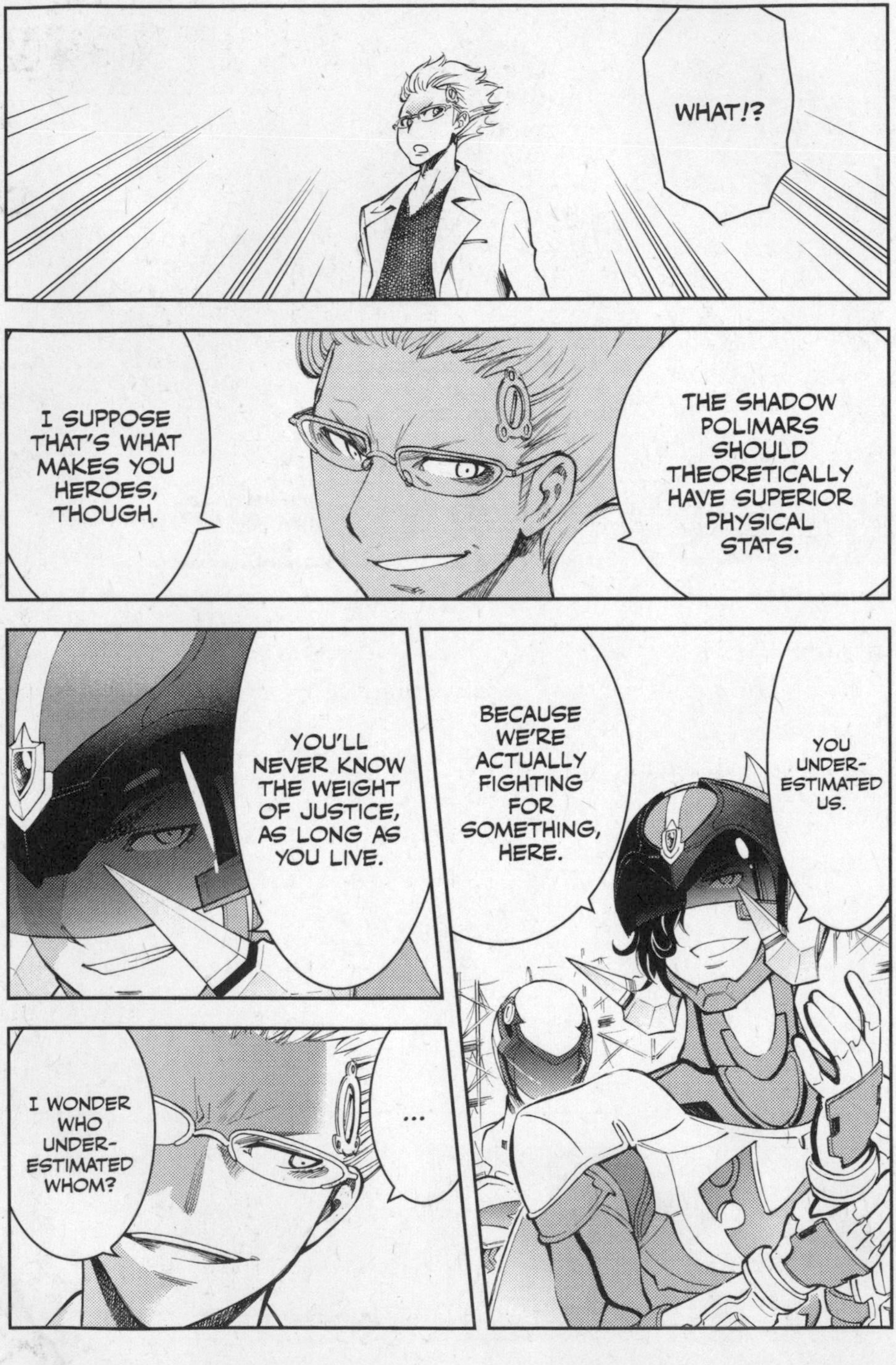
WHAT!?
THE SHADOW POLIMARS SHOULD THEORETICALLY HAVE SUPERIOR PHYSICAL STATS.
I SUPPOSE THAT'S WHAT MAKES YOU HEROES, THOUGH.
YOU UNDER-ESTIMATED US.
BECAUSE WE'RE ACTUALLY FIGHTING FOR SOMETHING, HERE.
YOU'LL NEVER KNOW THE WEIGHT OF JUSTICE, AS LONG AS YOU LIVE.
...
I WONDER WHO UNDER-ESTIMATED WHOM?

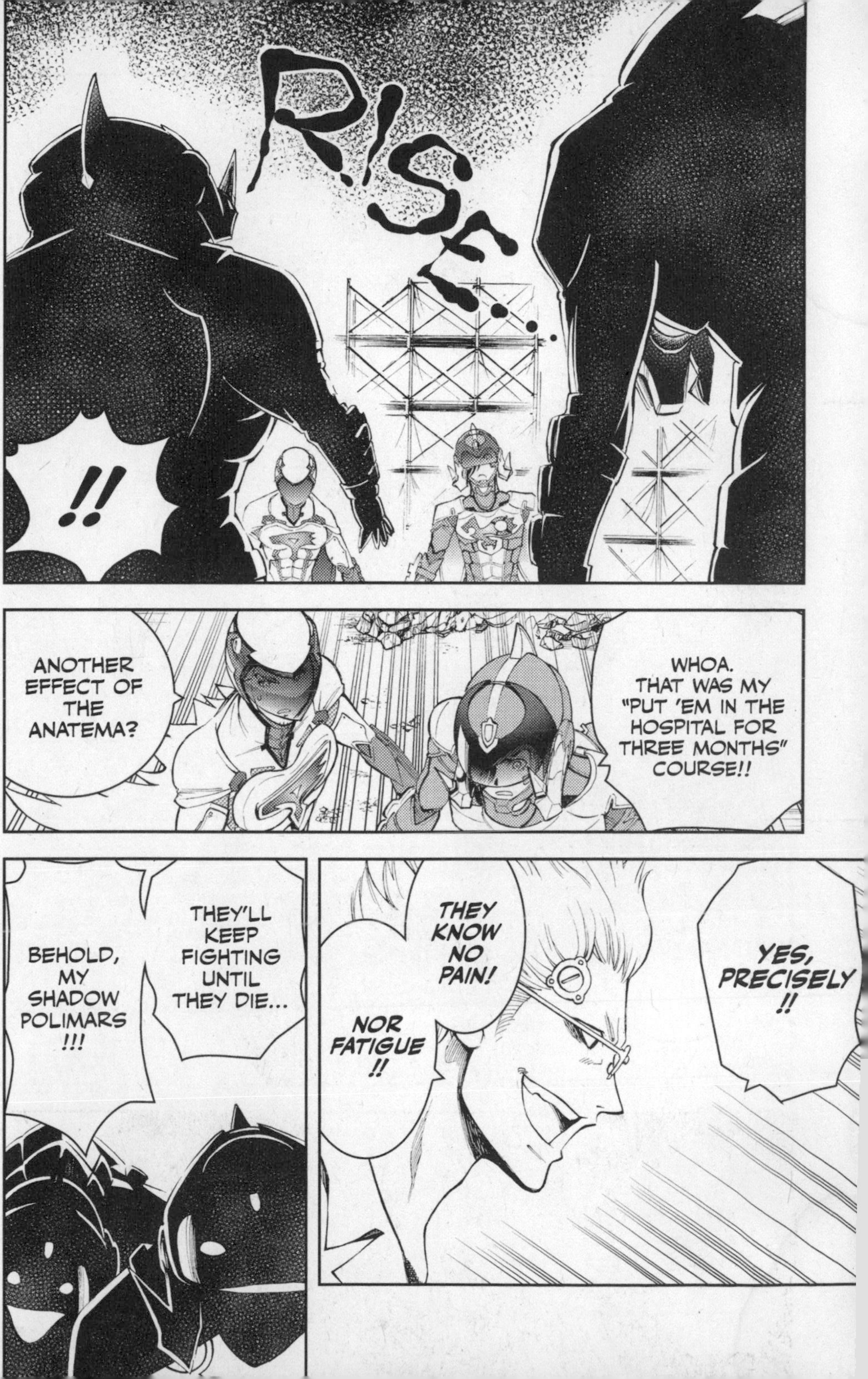
RISE...
!!
WHOA. THAT WAS MY "PUT 'EM IN THE HOSPITAL FOR THREE MONTHS" COURSE!!
ANOTHER EFFECT OF THE ANATEMA?
YES, PRECISELY!!
THEY KNOW NO PAIN!
NOR FATIGUE!!
THEY'LL KEEP FIGHTING UNTIL THEY DIE...
BEHOLD, MY SHADOW POLIMARS!!!

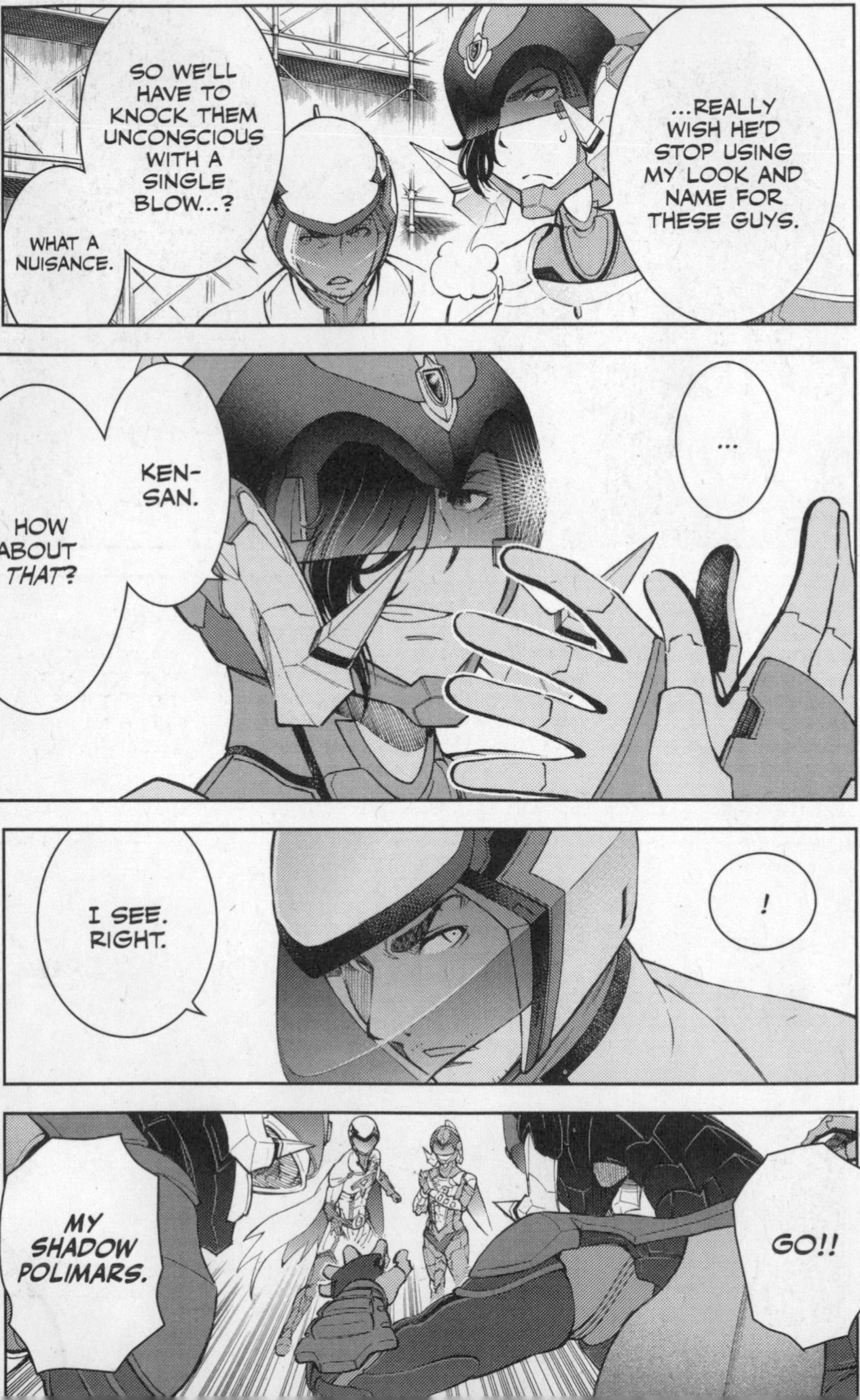
...REALLY WISH HE'D STOP USING MY LOOK AND NAME FOR THESE GUYS.
SO WE'LL HAVE TO KNOCK THEM UNCONSCIOUS WITH A SINGLE BLOW...?
WHAT A NUISANCE.
...
KEN-SAN.
HOW ABOUT *THAT*?
!
I SEE. RIGHT.
GO!!
MY SHADOW POLIMARS.

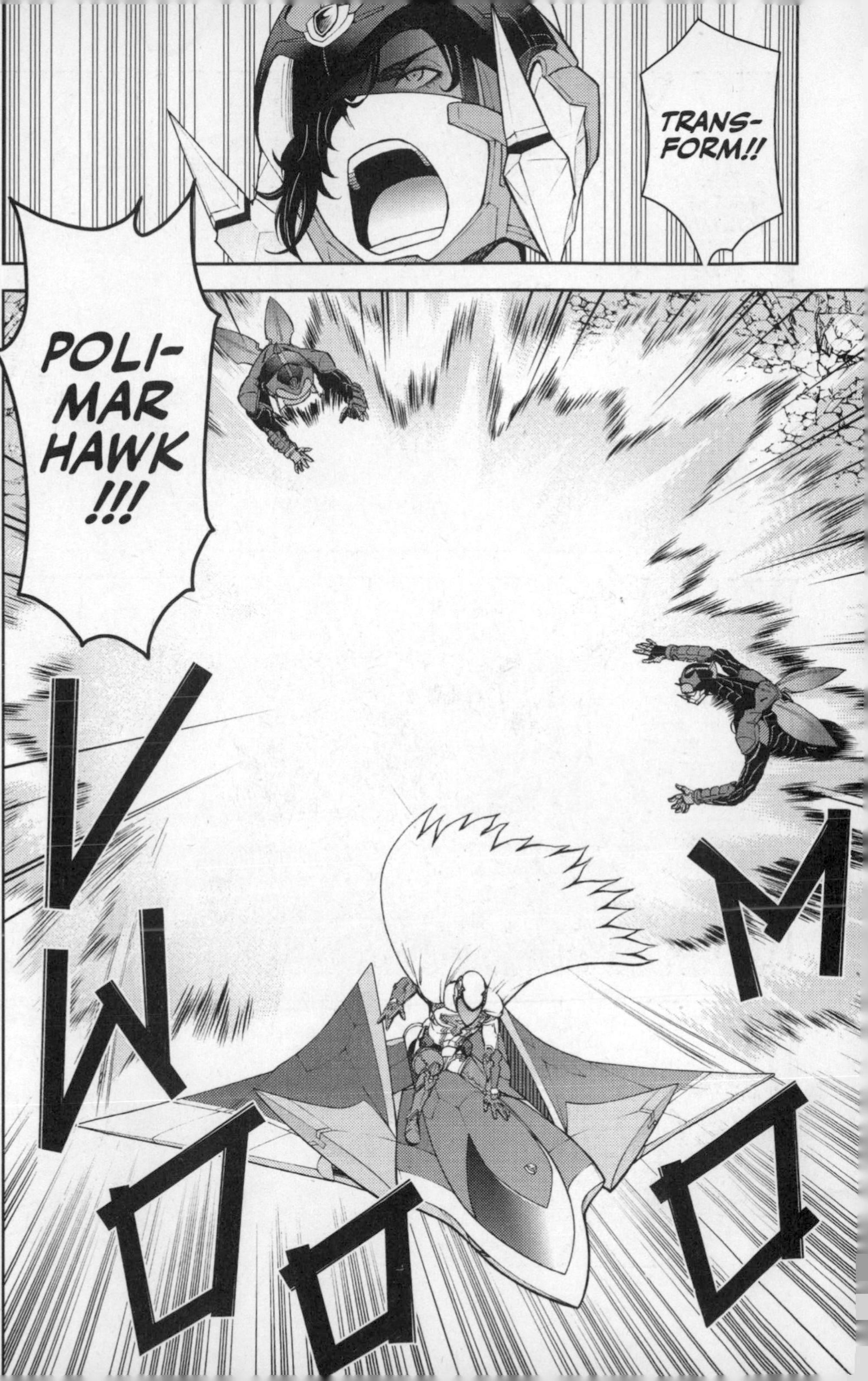
TRANS-
FORM!!
POLI-
MAR
HAWK
!!!
VWOOOM

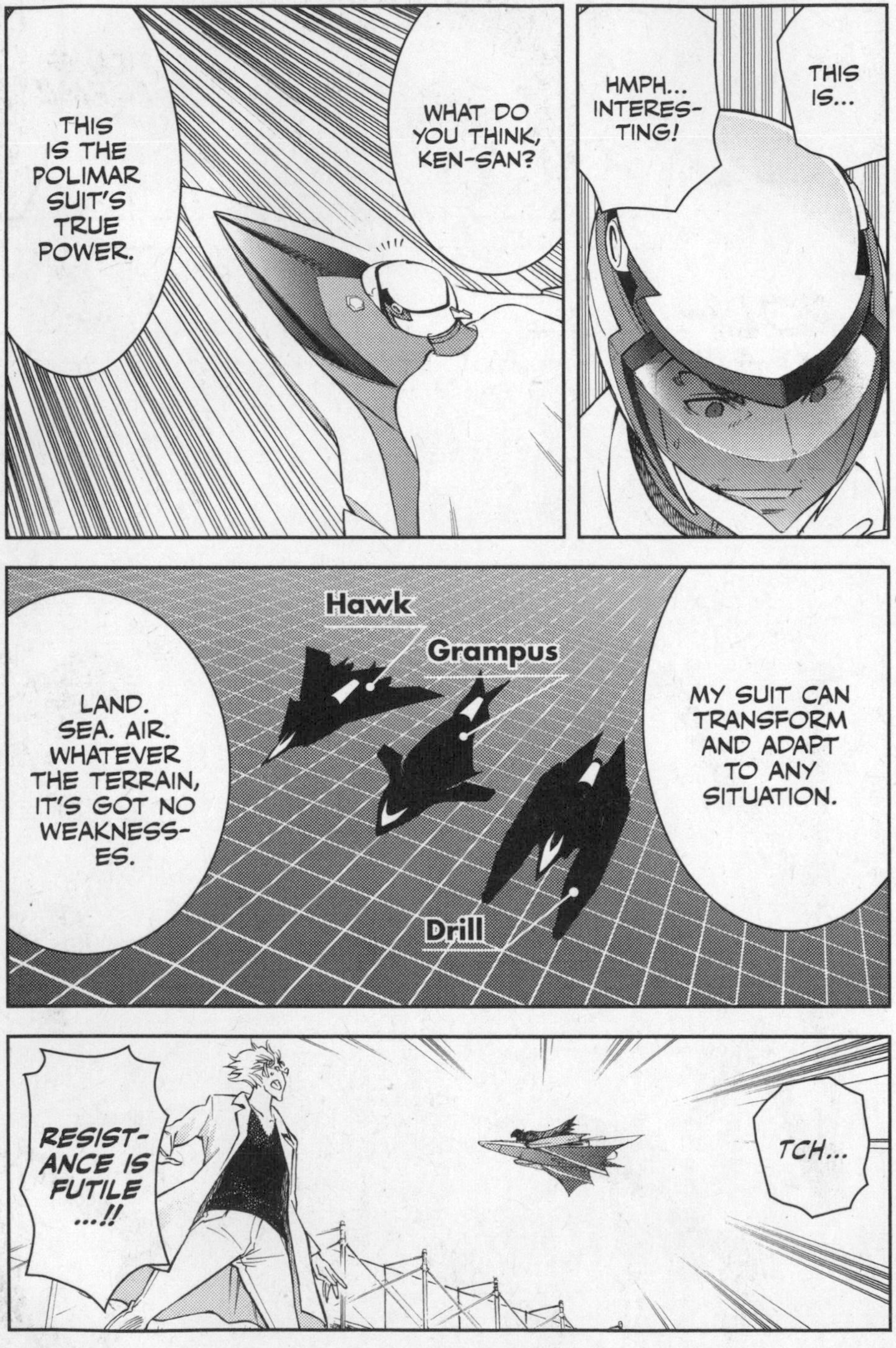
THIS IS...
HMPH... INTERES- TING!
WHAT DO YOU THINK, KEN-SAN?
THIS IS THE POLIMAR SUIT'S TRUE POWER.
MY SUIT CAN TRANSFORM AND ADAPT TO ANY SITUATION.
Hawk
Grampus
Drill
LAND. SEA. AIR. WHATEVER THE TERRAIN, IT'S GOT NO WEAKNESS- ES.
TCH...
RESIST- ANCE IS FUTILE ...!!

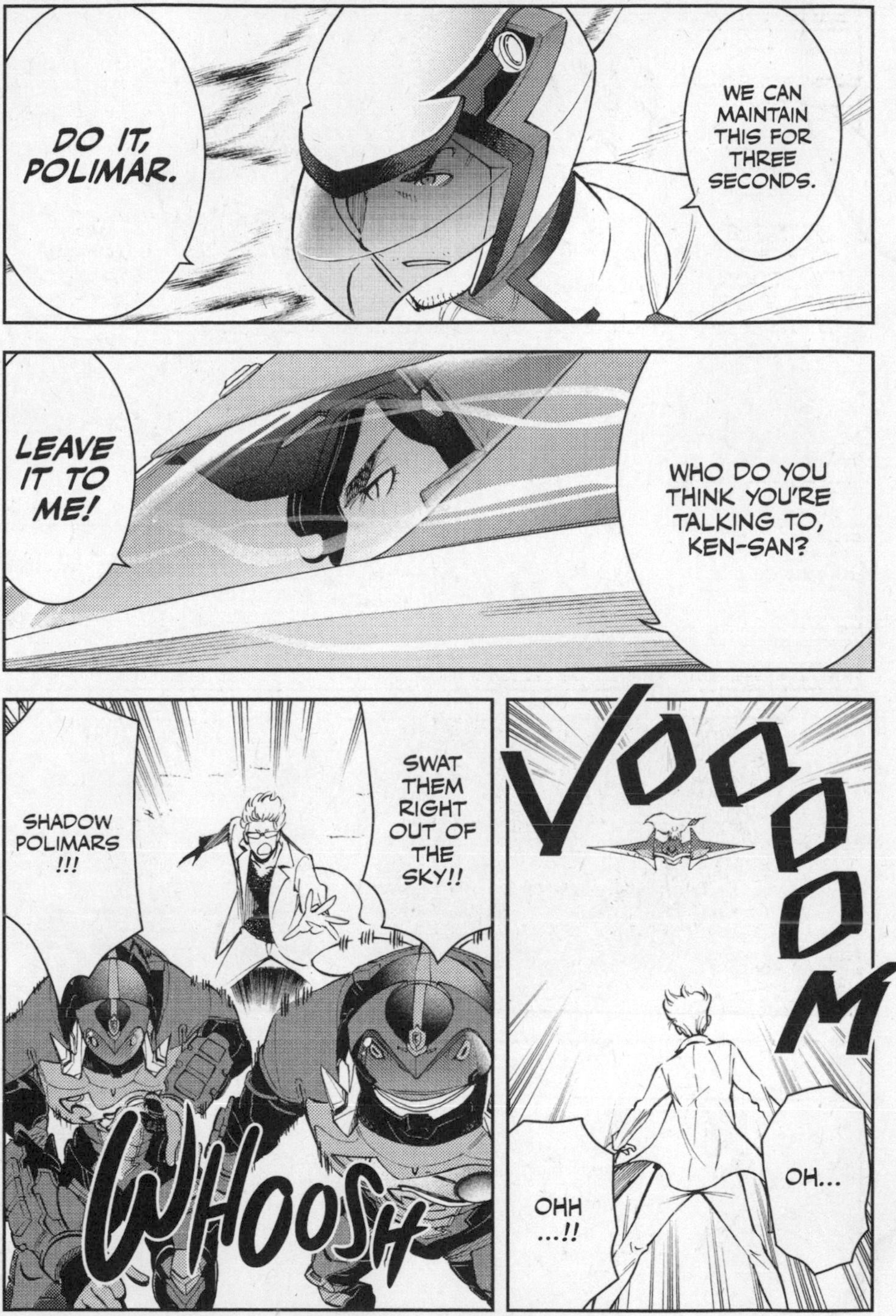
WE CAN MAINTAIN THIS FOR THREE SECONDS.
DO IT, POLIMAR.
WHO DO YOU THINK YOU'RE TALKING TO, KEN-SAN?
LEAVE IT TO ME!
VOOOOM
OH...
OHH ...!!
SWAT THEM RIGHT OUT OF THE SKY!!
SHADOW POLIMARS !!!
WHOOSH

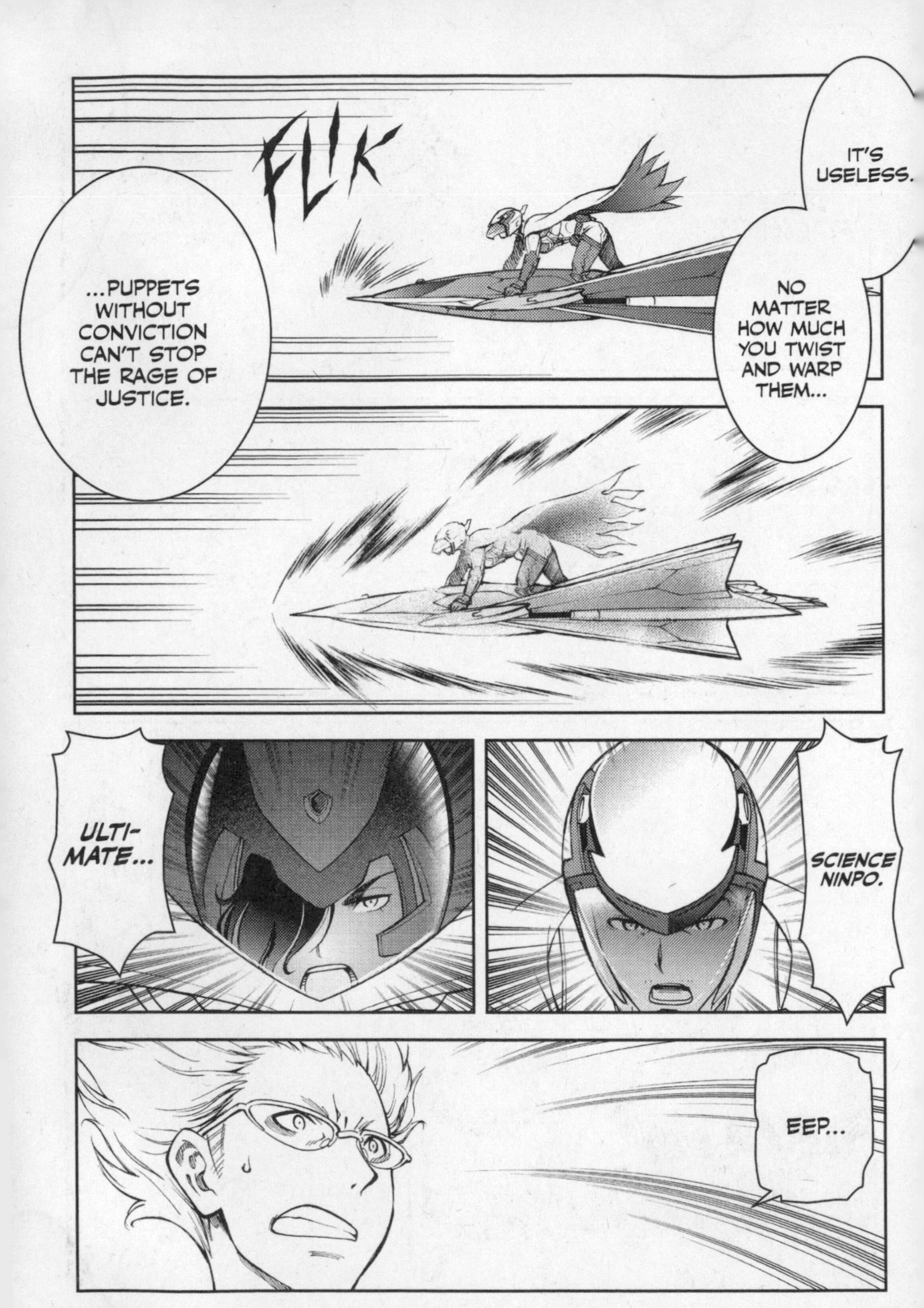
IT'S USELESS.
NO MATTER HOW MUCH YOU TWIST AND WARP THEM...
FLIK
...PUPPETS WITHOUT CONVICTION CAN'T STOP THE RAGE OF JUSTICE.
SCIENCE NINPO.
ULTI- MATE...
EEP...

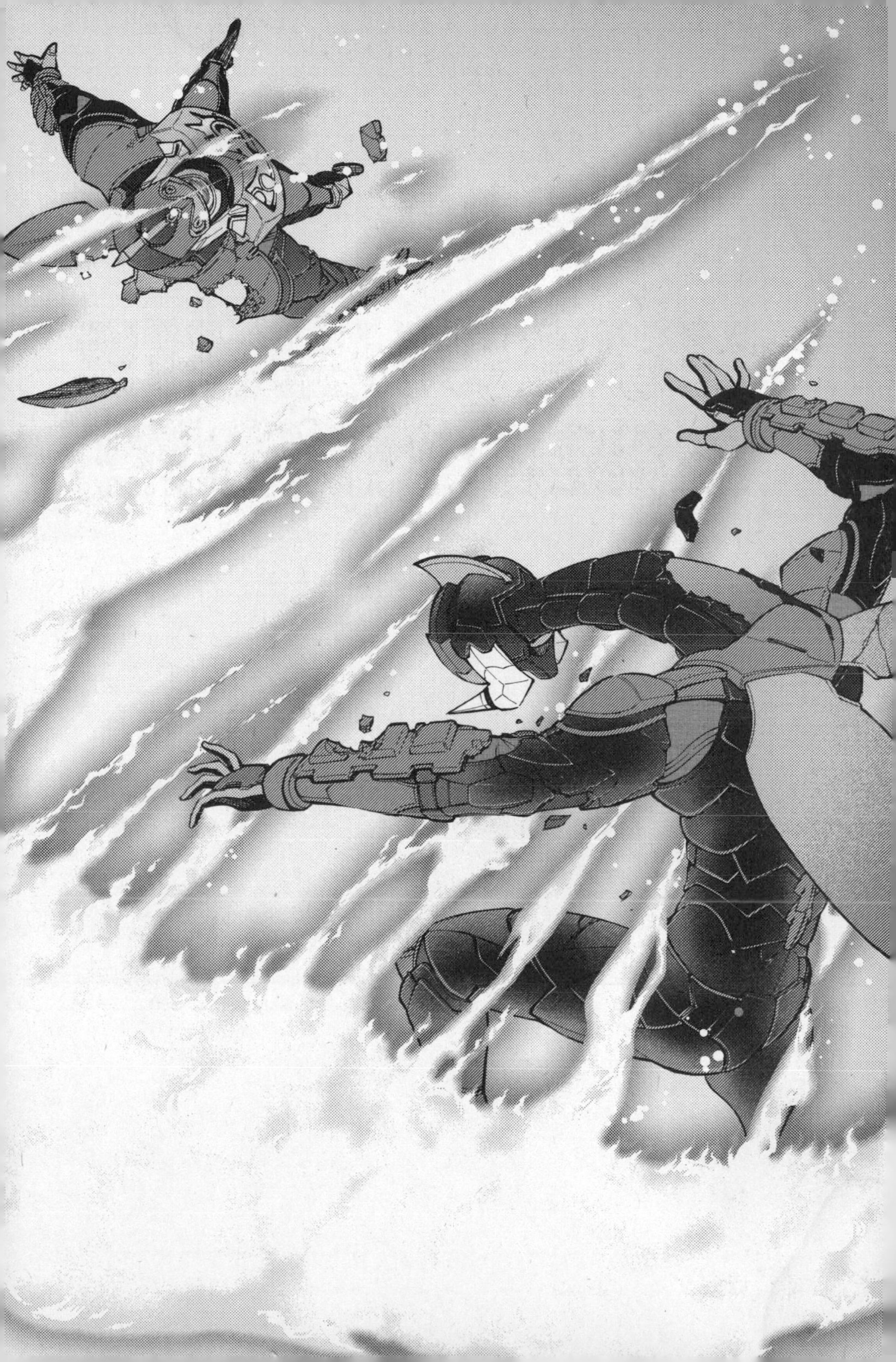

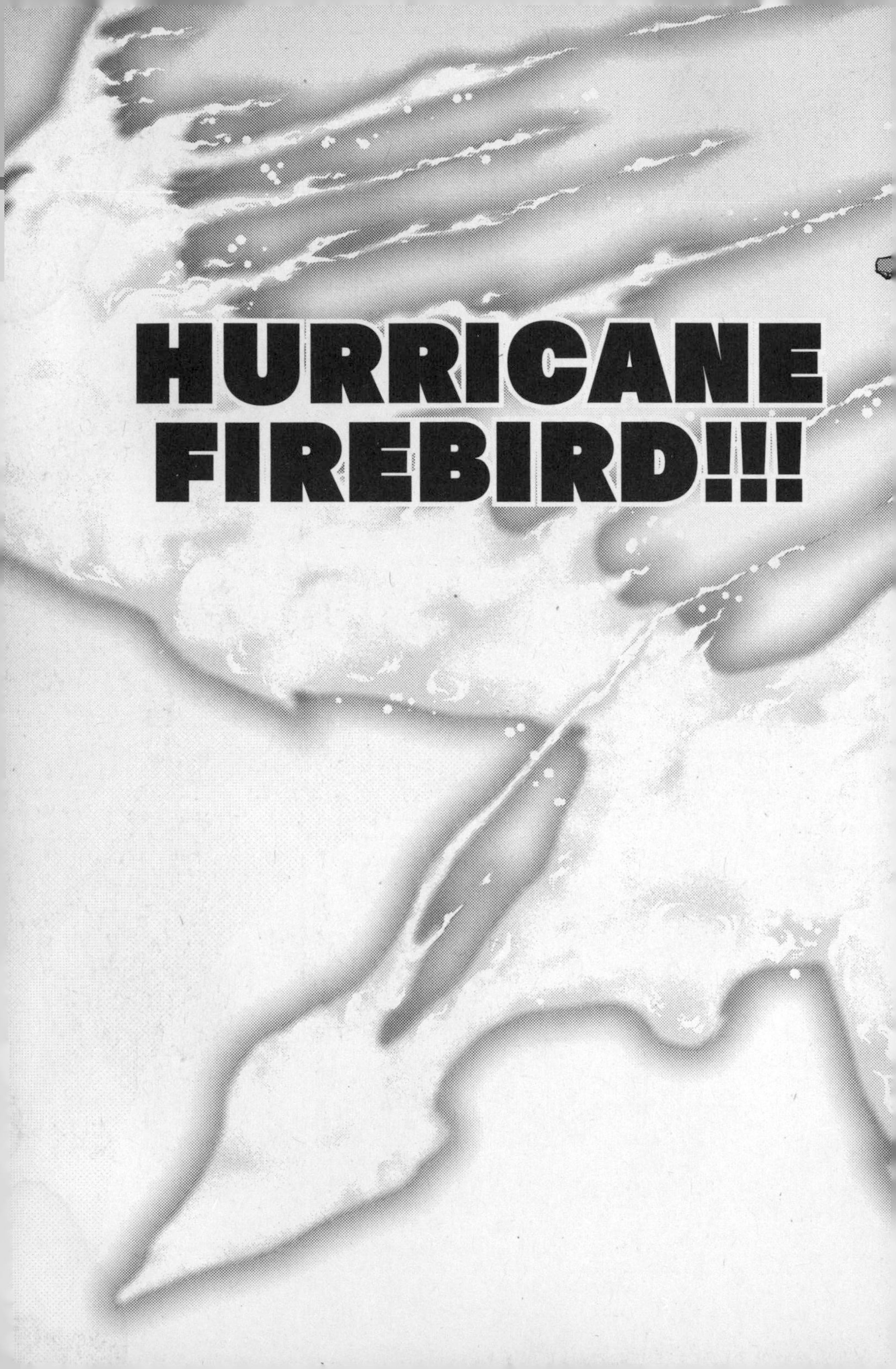
HURRICANE FIREBIRD!!!

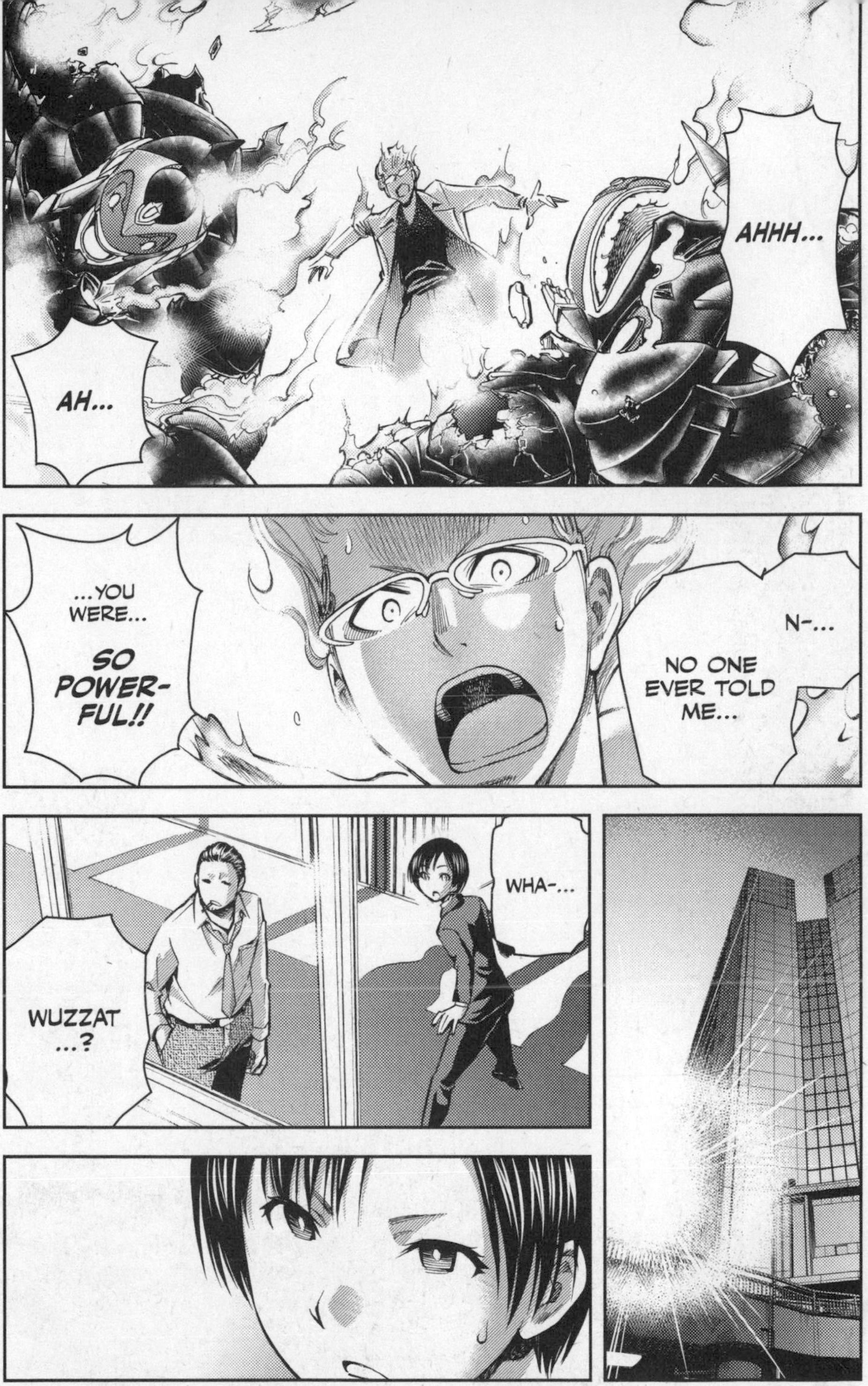
AHHH...
AH...
N-...
NO ONE EVER TOLD ME...
...YOU WERE... SO POWER-FUL!!
WHA-...
WUZZAT ...?

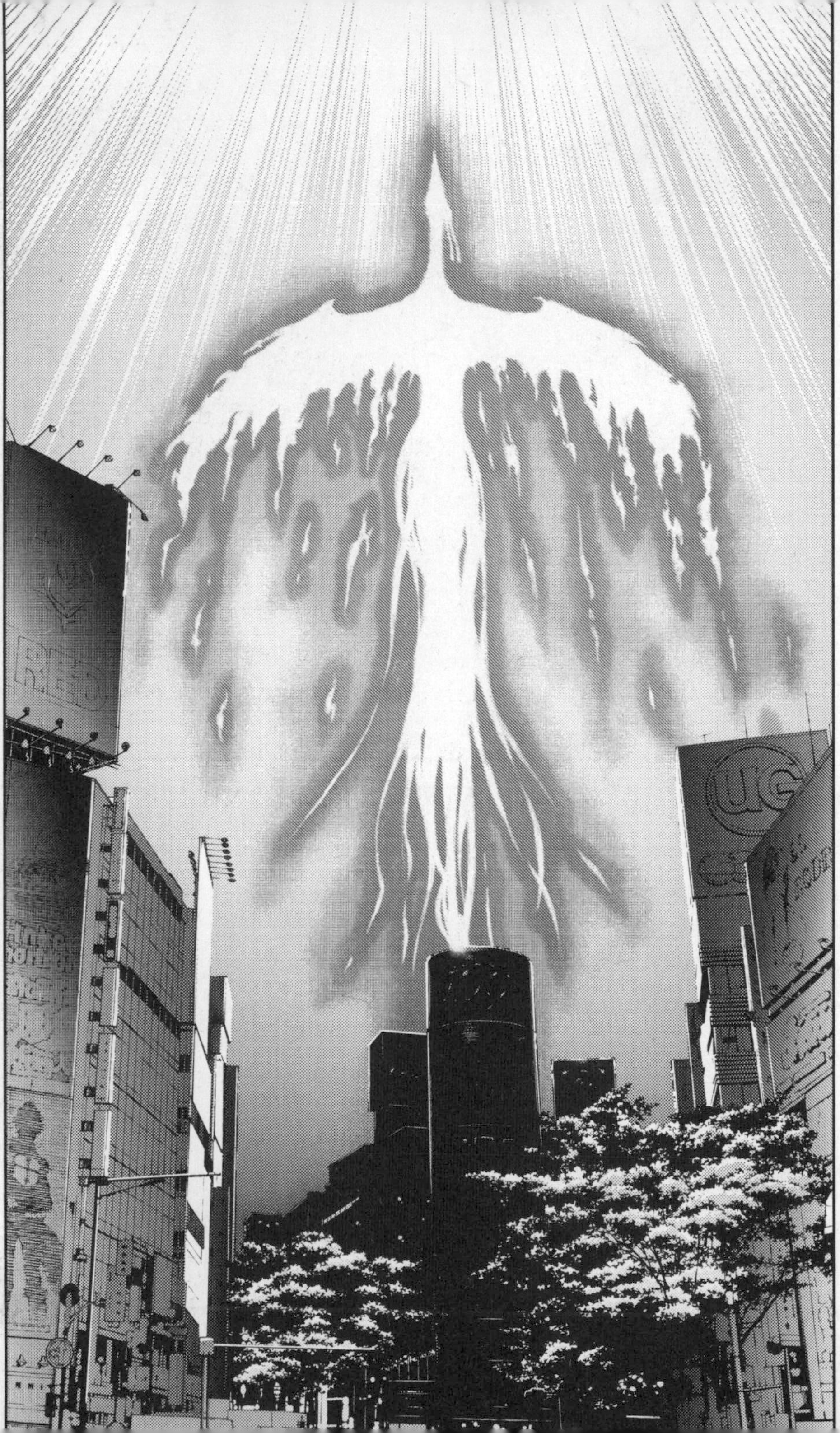
RED

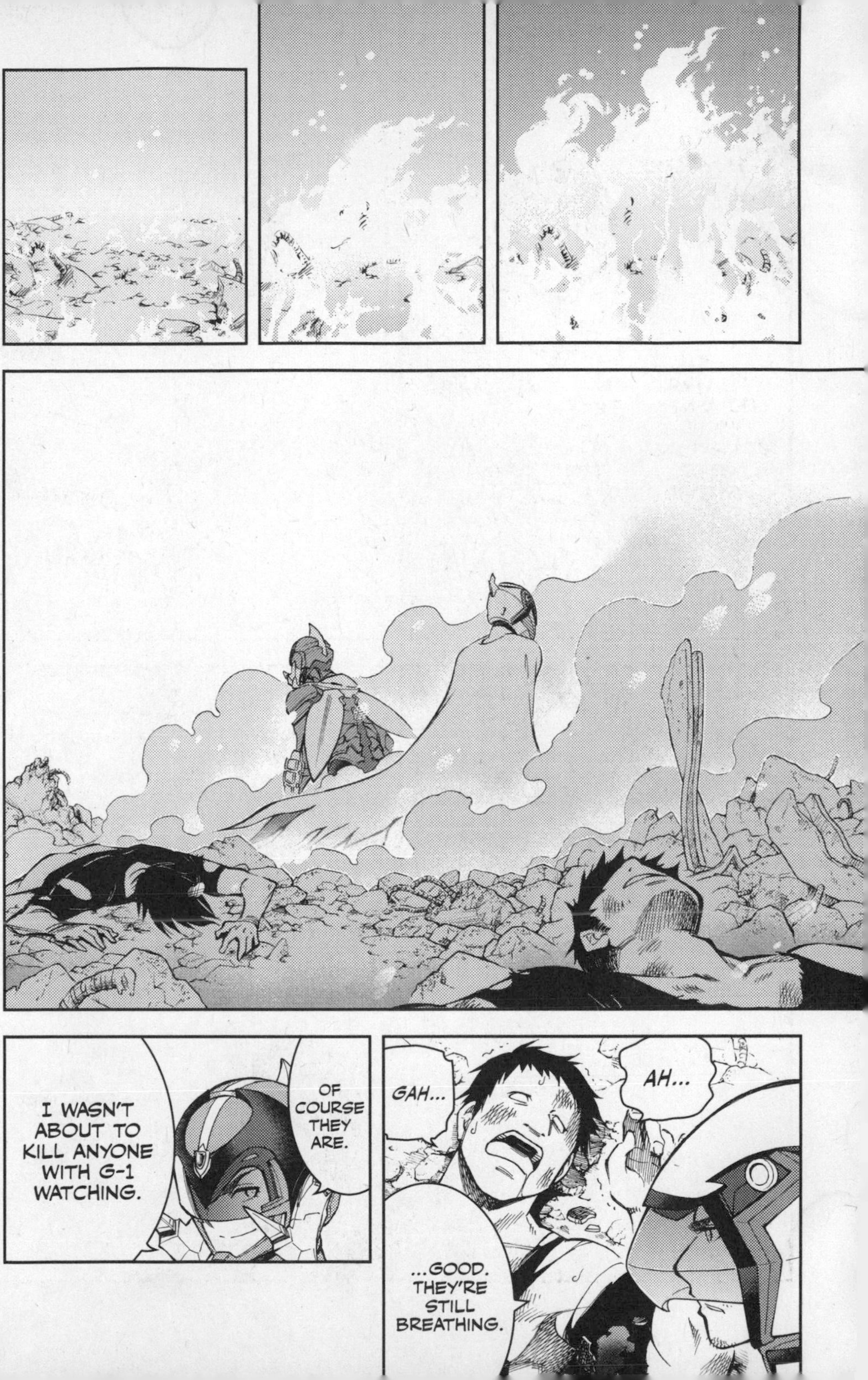
AH...
GAH...
...GOOD. THEY'RE STILL BREATHING.
OF COURSE THEY ARE.
I WASN'T ABOUT TO KILL ANYONE WITH G-1 WATCHING.

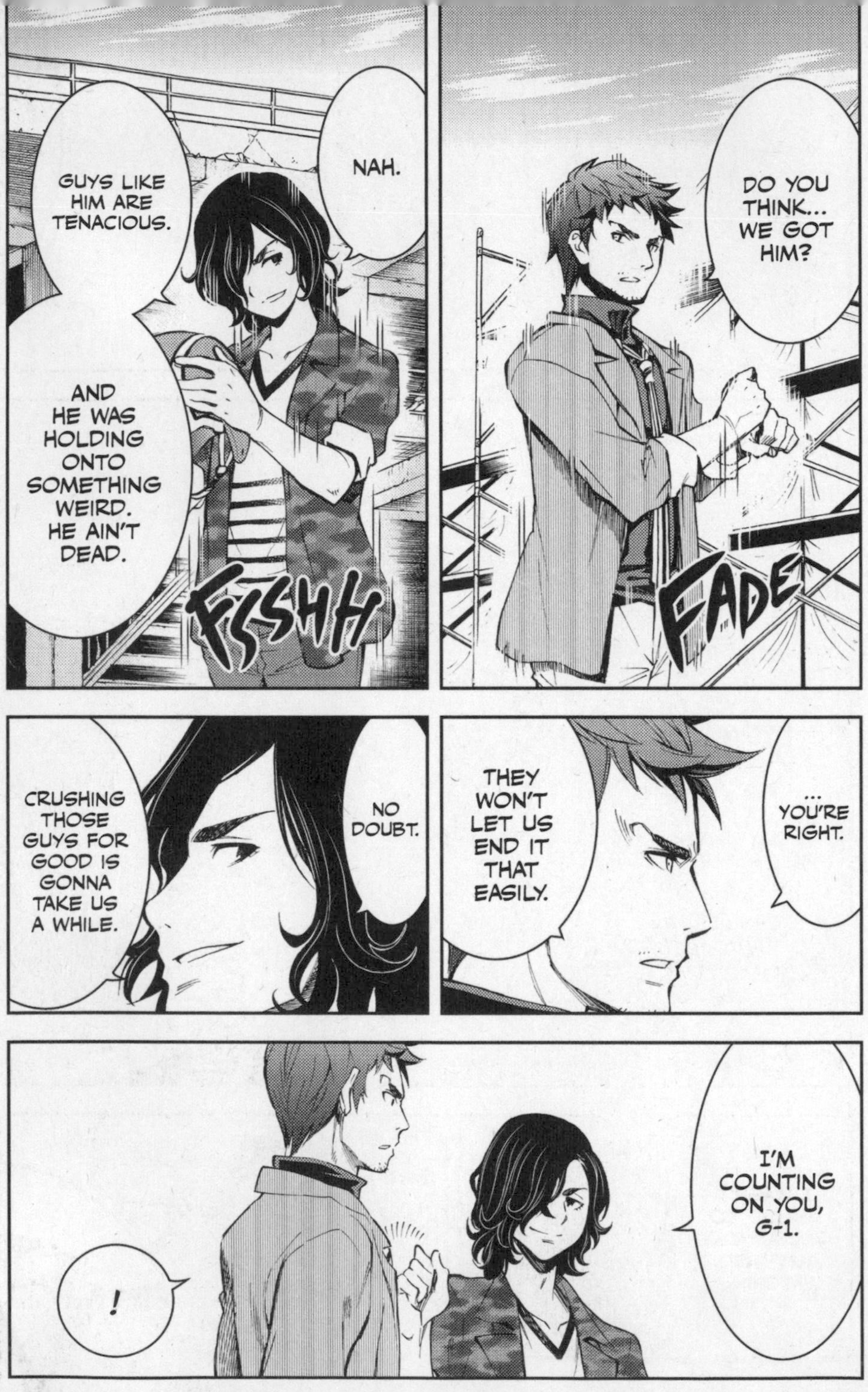
DO YOU THINK... WE GOT HIM?
FADE
NAH.
GUYS LIKE HIM ARE TENACIOUS.
AND HE WAS HOLDING ONTO SOMETHING WEIRD. HE AIN'T DEAD.
FSSHH
... YOU'RE RIGHT.
THEY WON'T LET US END IT THAT EASILY.
NO DOUBT.
CRUSHING THOSE GUYS FOR GOOD IS GONNA TAKE US A WHILE.
I'M COUNTING ON YOU, G-1.
!

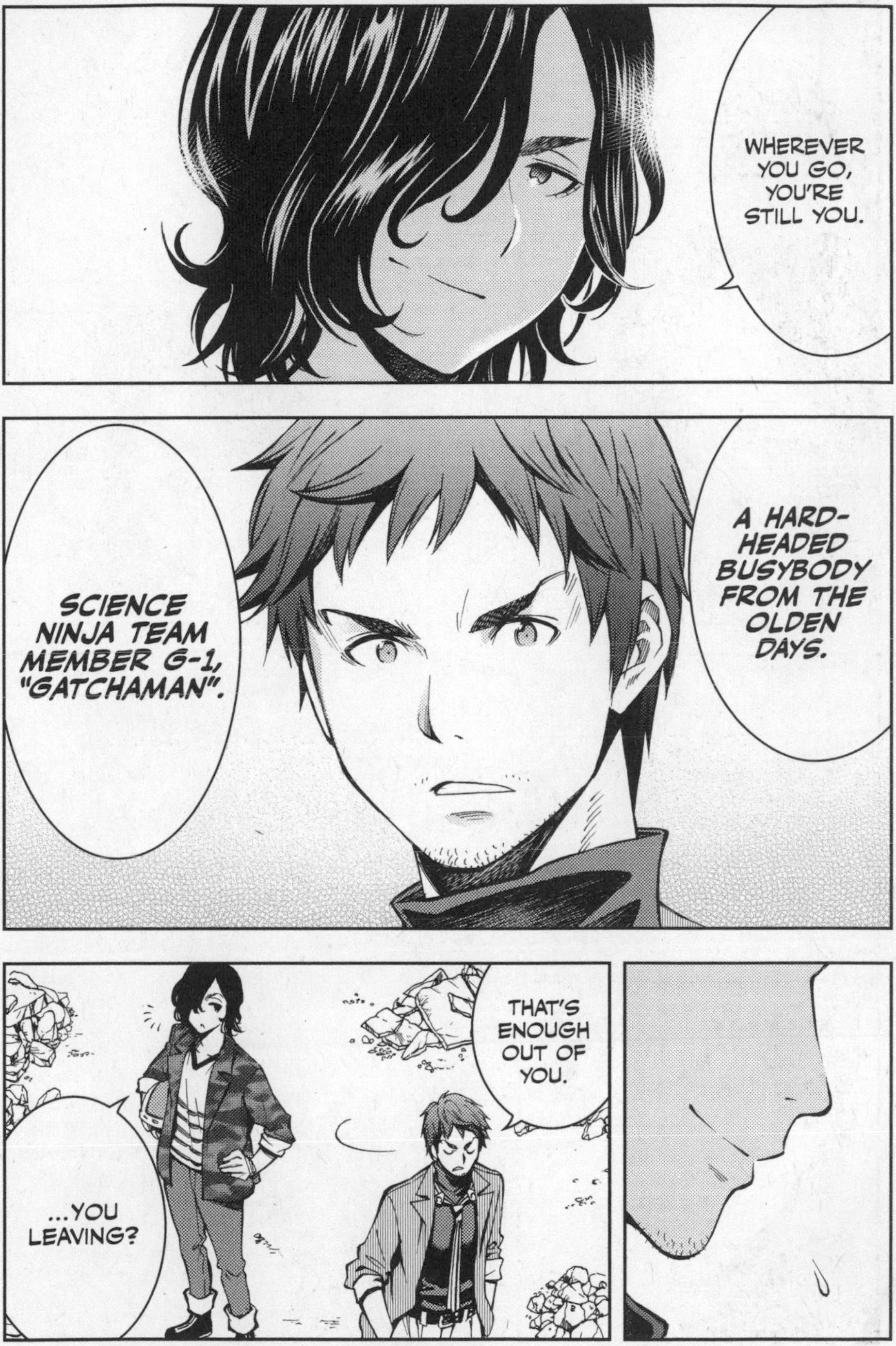
WHEREVER YOU GO, YOU'RE STILL YOU.
A HARD-HEADED BUSYBODY FROM THE OLDEN DAYS.
SCIENCE NINJA TEAM MEMBER G-1, "GATCHAMAN".
THAT'S ENOUGH OUT OF YOU.
...YOU LEAVING?

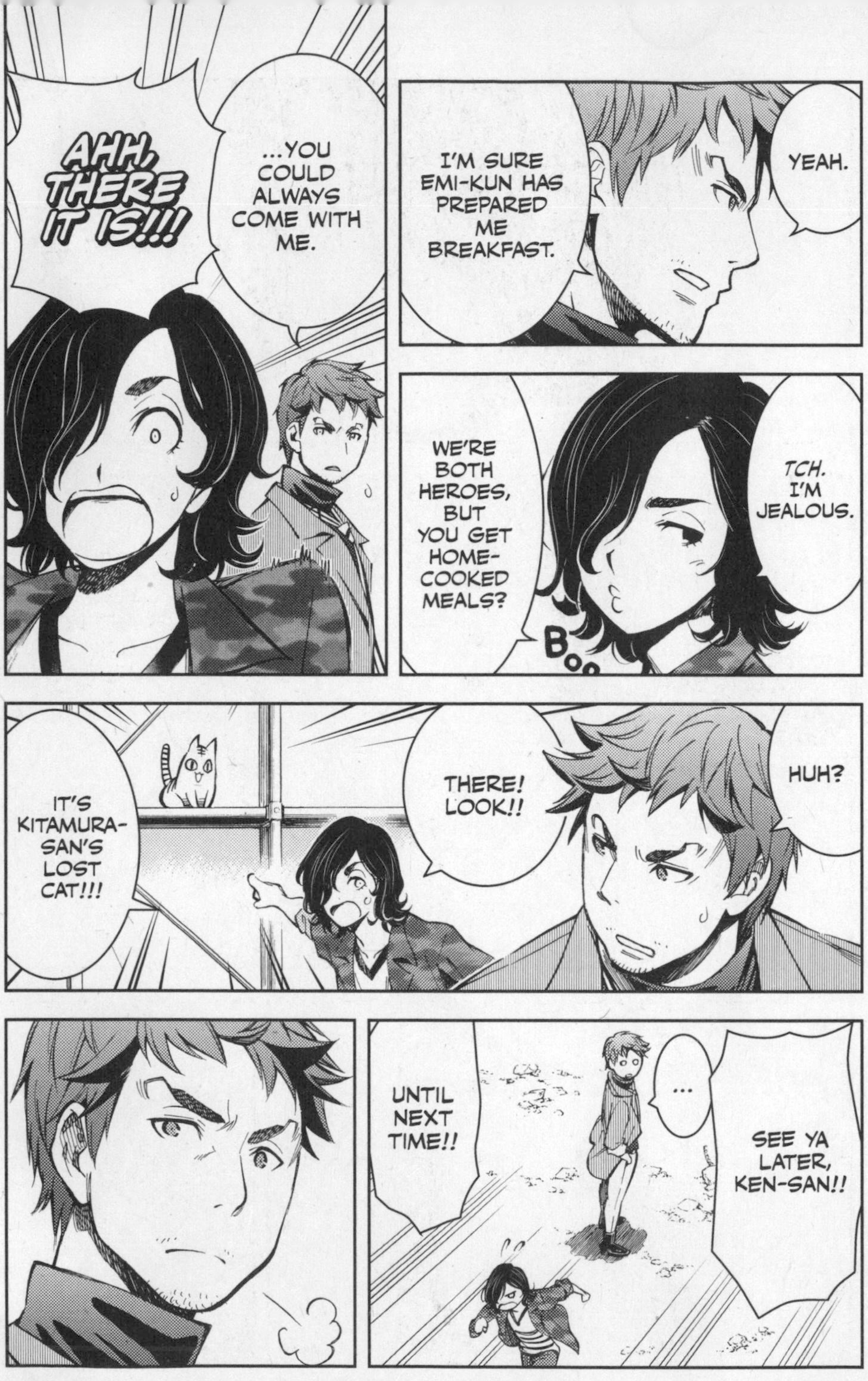
YEAH.
I'M SURE EMI-KUN HAS PREPARED ME BREAKFAST.
TCH. I'M JEALOUS.
WE'RE BOTH HEROES, BUT YOU GET HOME-COOKED MEALS?
Bo
...YOU COULD ALWAYS COME WITH ME.
AHH, THERE IT IS!!!
HUH?
THERE! LOOK!!
IT'S KITAMURA-SAN'S LOST CAT!!!
SEE YA LATER, KEN-SAN!!
...
UNTIL NEXT TIME!!

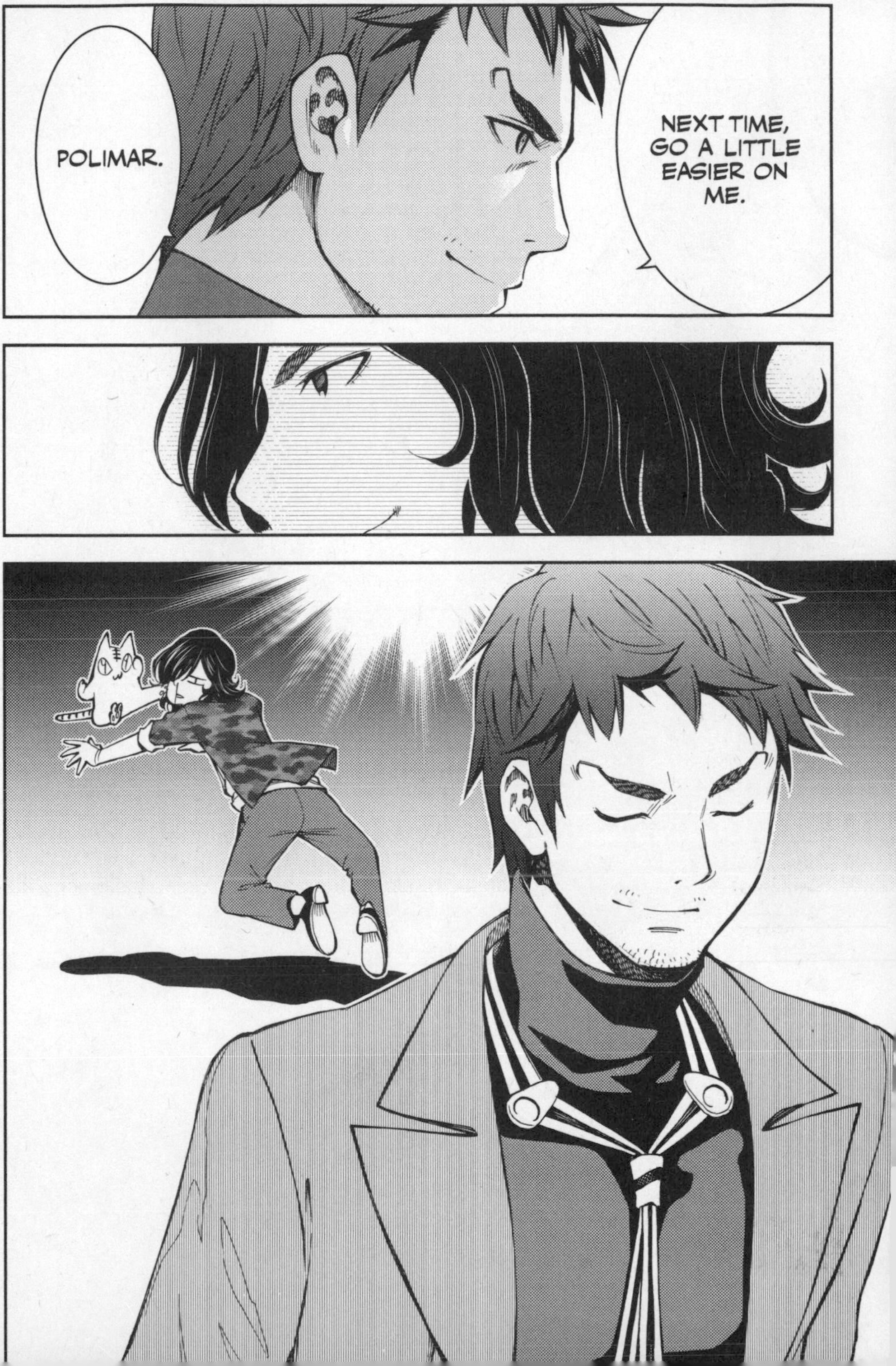
NEXT TIME, GO A LITTLE EASIER ON ME.
POLIMAR.

**TRUE
SINGLE-
HANDED
VACUUM
SPIN**

Infini-T Force
ARC TO THE FUTURE

インフィニティフォース
Infini-T Force
ARC TO THE FUTURE

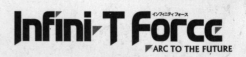

EPISODE 8 ▸ MEMORIES OF THE SEA

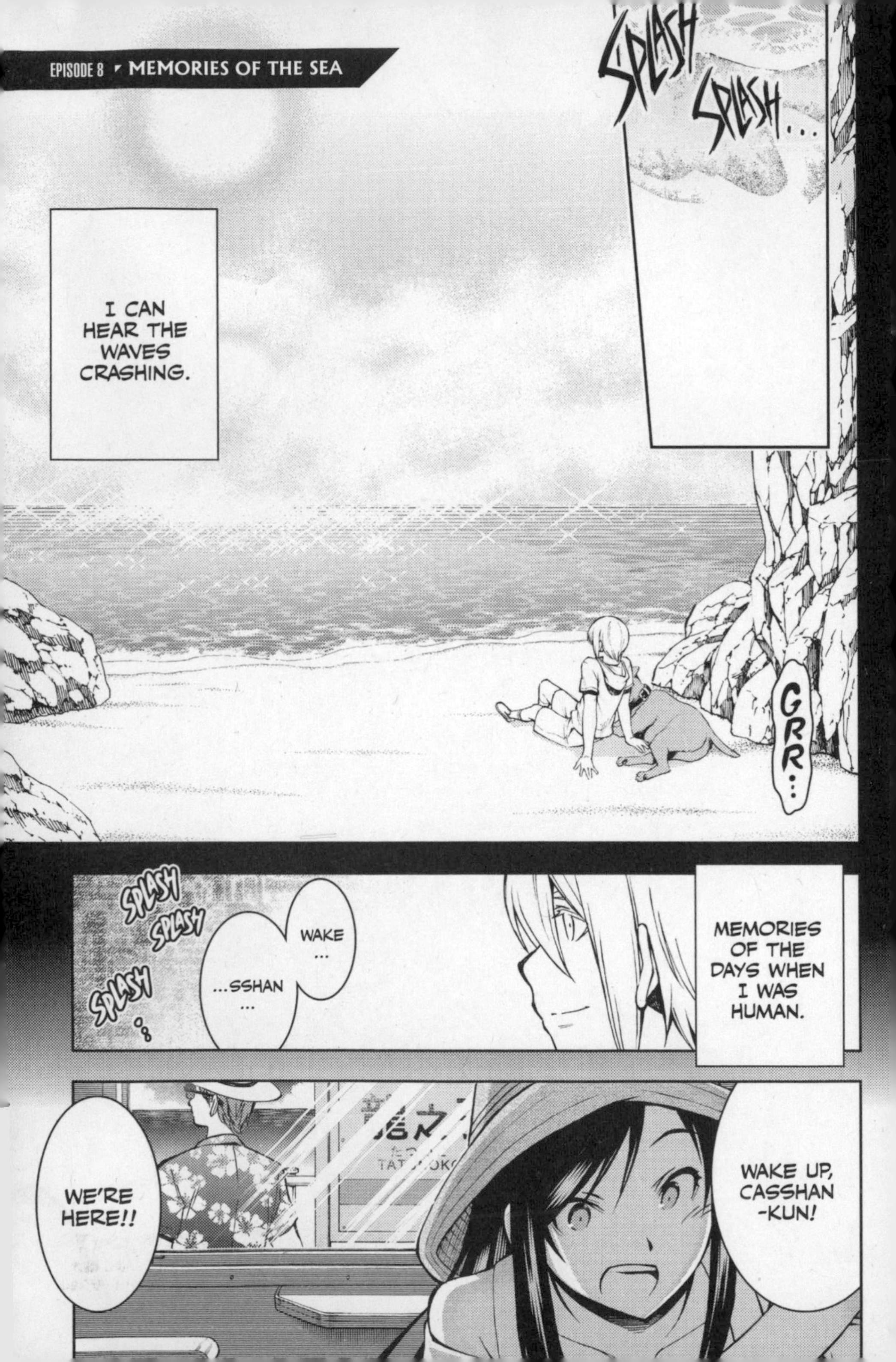
SPLASH SPLASH...
I CAN HEAR THE WAVES CRASHING.
GRR...
MEMORIES OF THE DAYS WHEN I WAS HUMAN.
WAKE ...
...SSHAN ...
SPLASH SPLASH SPLASH
WAKE UP, CASSHAN-KUN!
WE'RE HERE!!

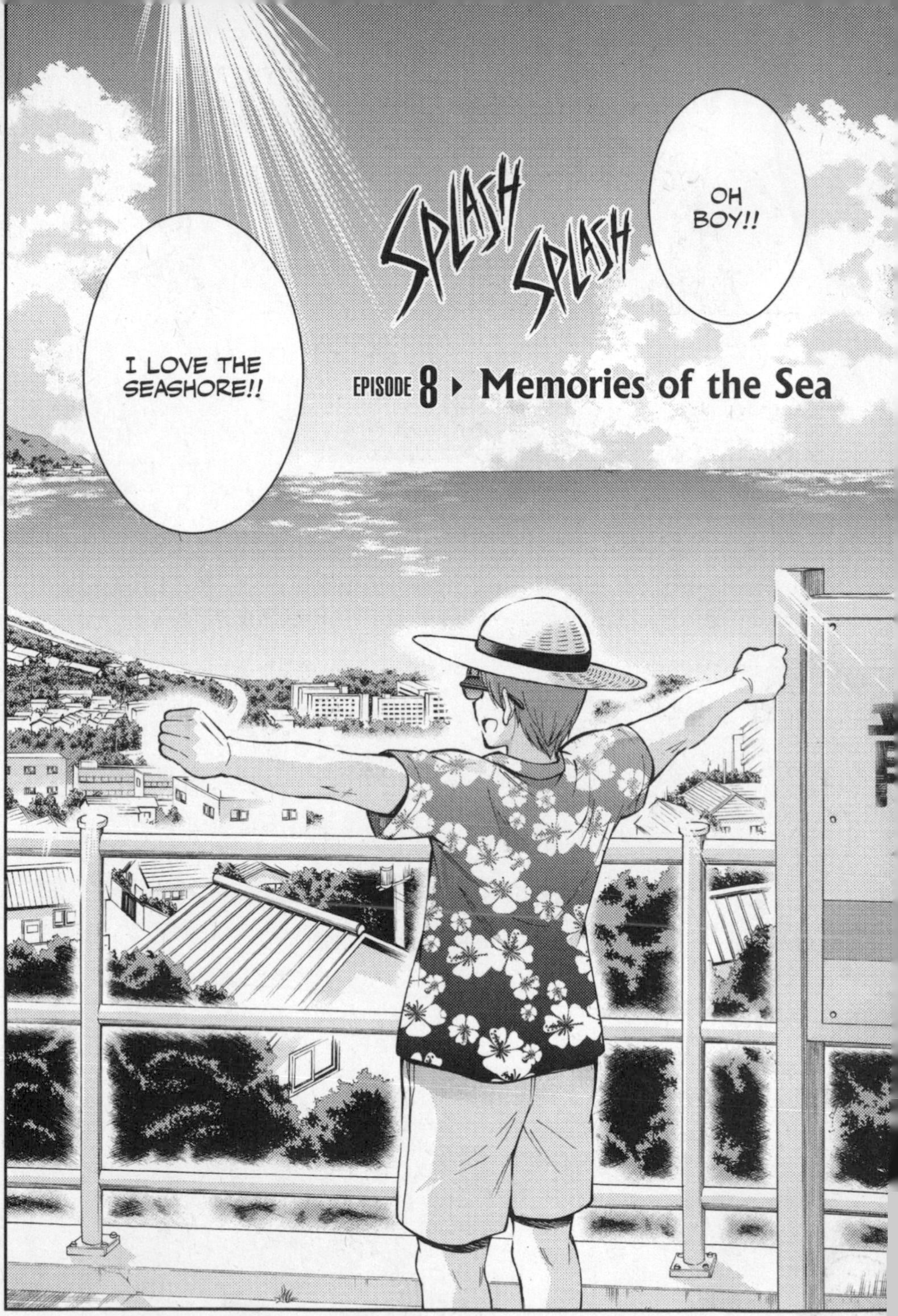
OH BOY!!
SPLASH SPLASH
EPISODE 8 ▸ Memories of the Sea
I LOVE THE SEASHORE!!

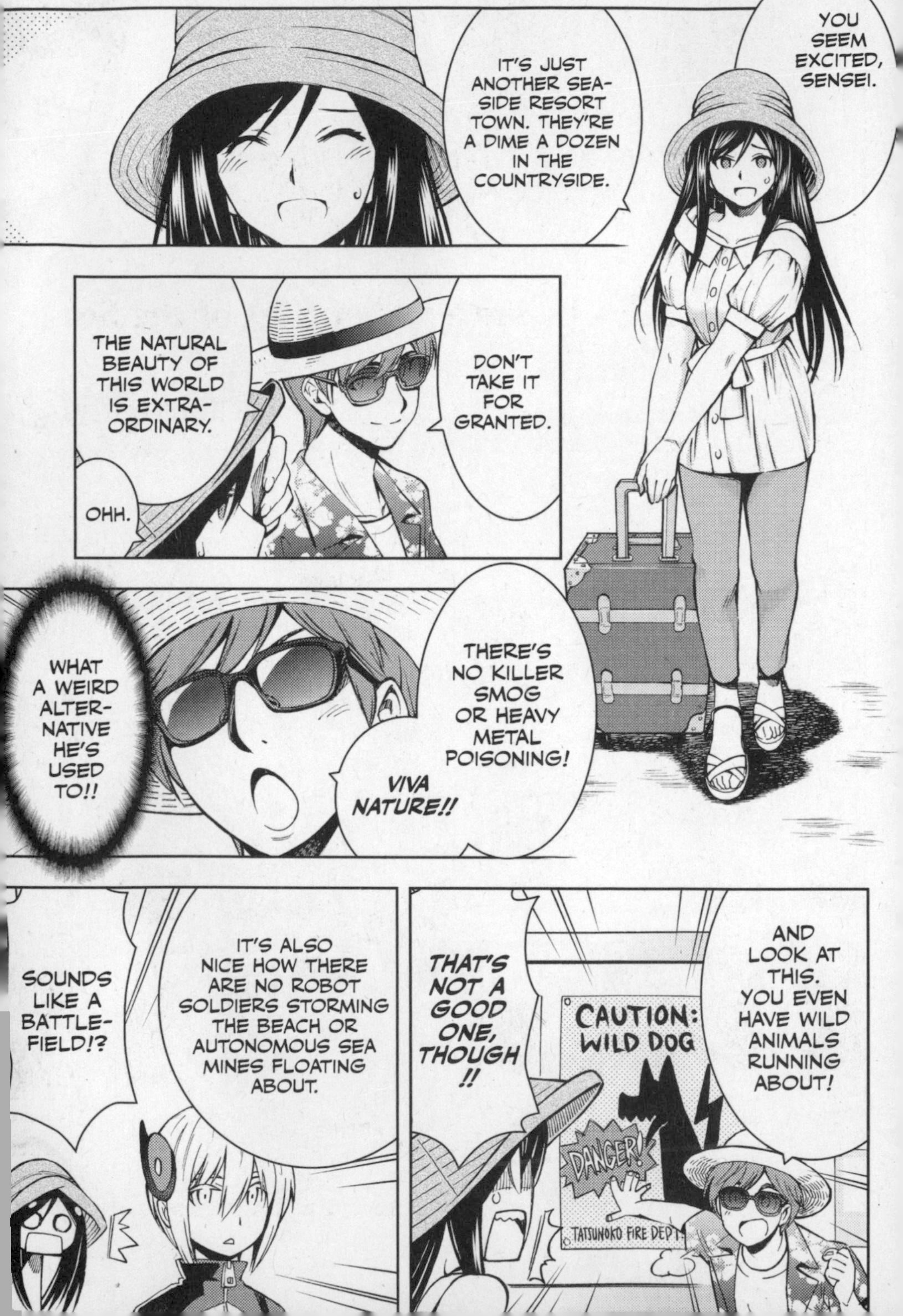
YOU SEEM EXCITED, SENSEI.
IT'S JUST ANOTHER SEA-SIDE RESORT TOWN. THEY'RE A DIME A DOZEN IN THE COUNTRYSIDE.
DON'T TAKE IT FOR GRANTED.
THE NATURAL BEAUTY OF THIS WORLD IS EXTRA-ORDINARY.
OHH.
THERE'S NO KILLER SMOG OR HEAVY METAL POISONING!
VIVA NATURE!!
WHAT A WEIRD ALTER-NATIVE HE'S USED TO!!
AND LOOK AT THIS. YOU EVEN HAVE WILD ANIMALS RUNNING ABOUT!
CAUTION: WILD DOG
DANGER!
TATSUNOKO FIRE DEPT.
THAT'S NOT A GOOD ONE, THOUGH!!
IT'S ALSO NICE HOW THERE ARE NO ROBOT SOLDIERS STORMING THE BEACH OR AUTONOMOUS SEA MINES FLOATING ABOUT.
SOUNDS LIKE A BATTLE-FIELD!?

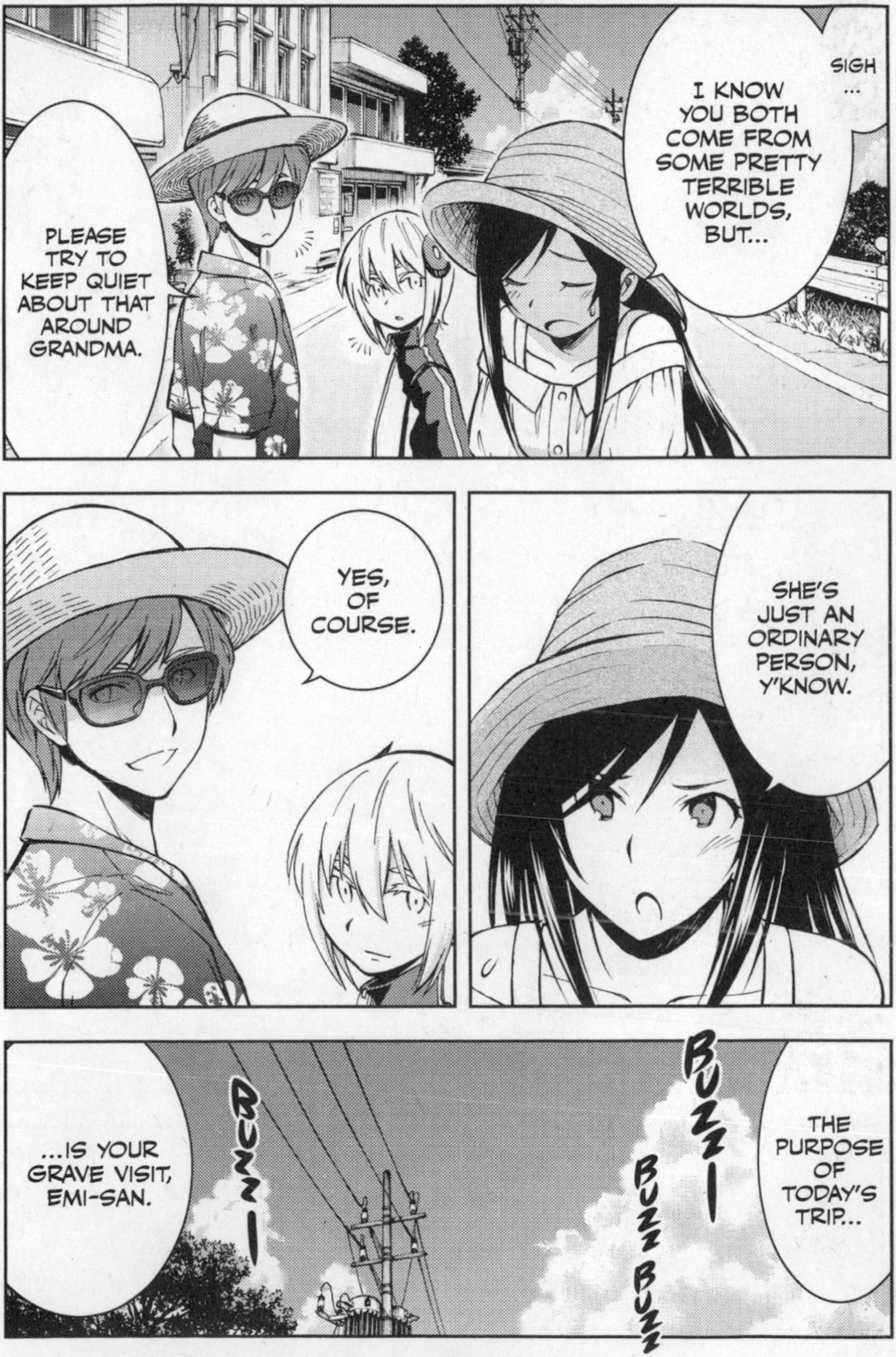

SIGH ...
I KNOW YOU BOTH COME FROM SOME PRETTY TERRIBLE WORLDS, BUT...
PLEASE TRY TO KEEP QUIET ABOUT THAT AROUND GRANDMA.
SHE'S JUST AN ORDINARY PERSON, Y'KNOW.
YES, OF COURSE.
THE PURPOSE OF TODAY'S TRIP...
BUZZ!
BUZZ BUZZ
BUZZ!
...IS YOUR GRAVE VISIT, EMI-SAN.

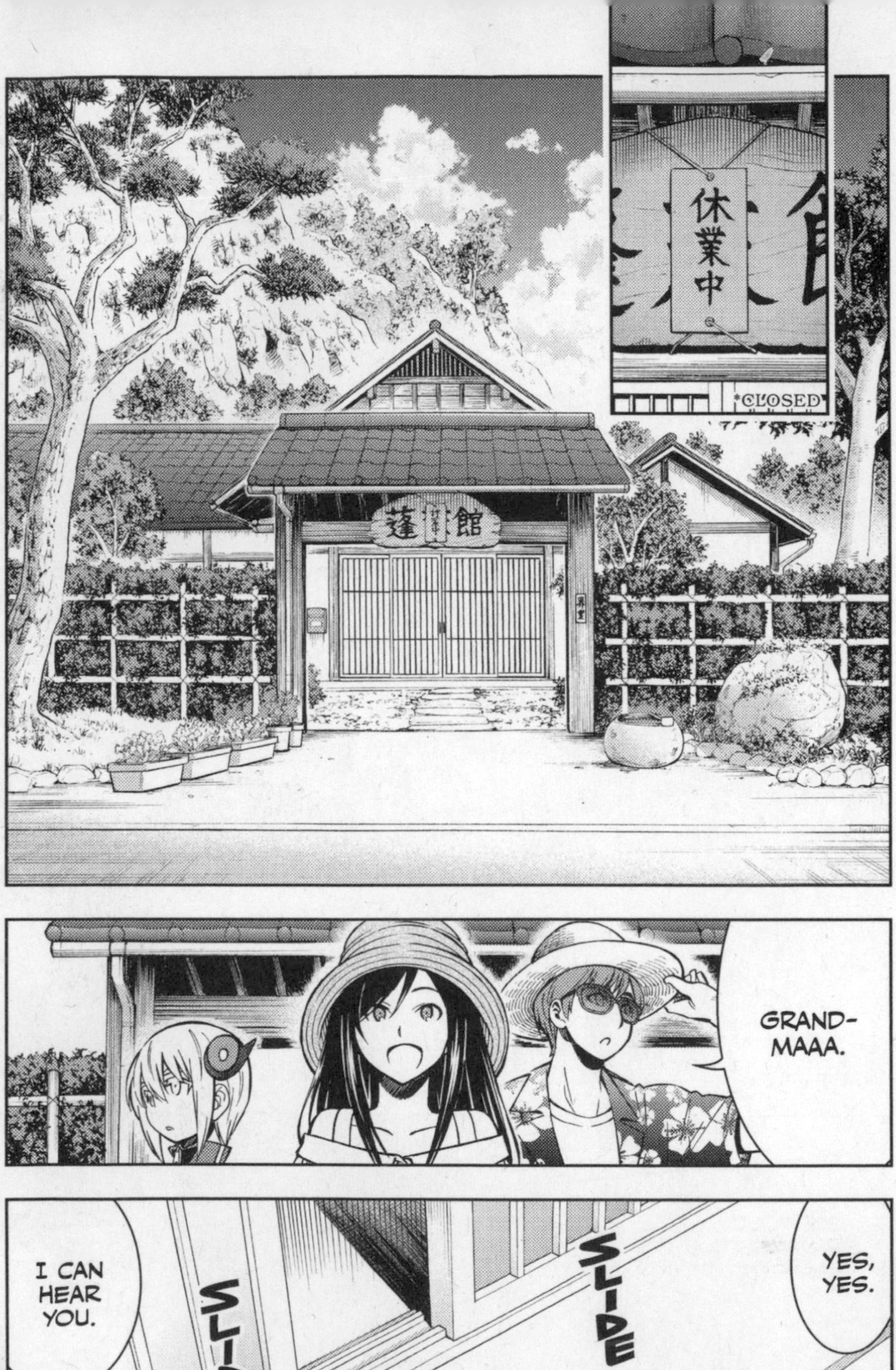

休業中
*CLOSED
蓬 館
GRAND-MAAA.
YES, YES.
SLIDE
SLIDE
I CAN HEAR YOU.

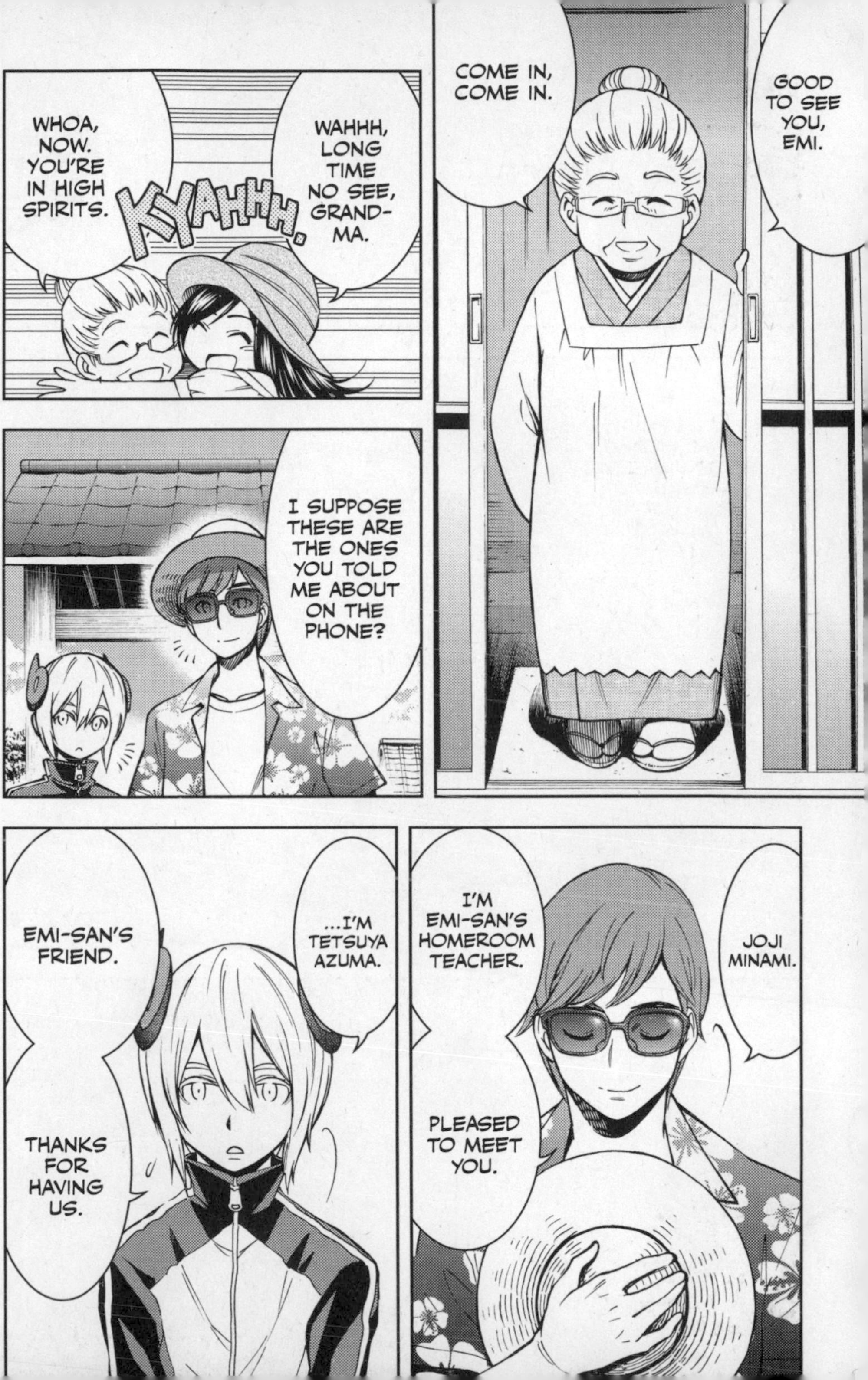
GOOD TO SEE YOU, EMI.
COME IN, COME IN.
WAHHH, LONG TIME NO SEE, GRANDMA.
KYAHHH.
WHOA, NOW. YOU'RE IN HIGH SPIRITS.
I SUPPOSE THESE ARE THE ONES YOU TOLD ME ABOUT ON THE PHONE?
JOJI MINAMI.
I'M EMI-SAN'S HOMEROOM TEACHER.
PLEASED TO MEET YOU.
...I'M TETSUYA AZUMA.
EMI-SAN'S FRIEND.
THANKS FOR HAVING US.

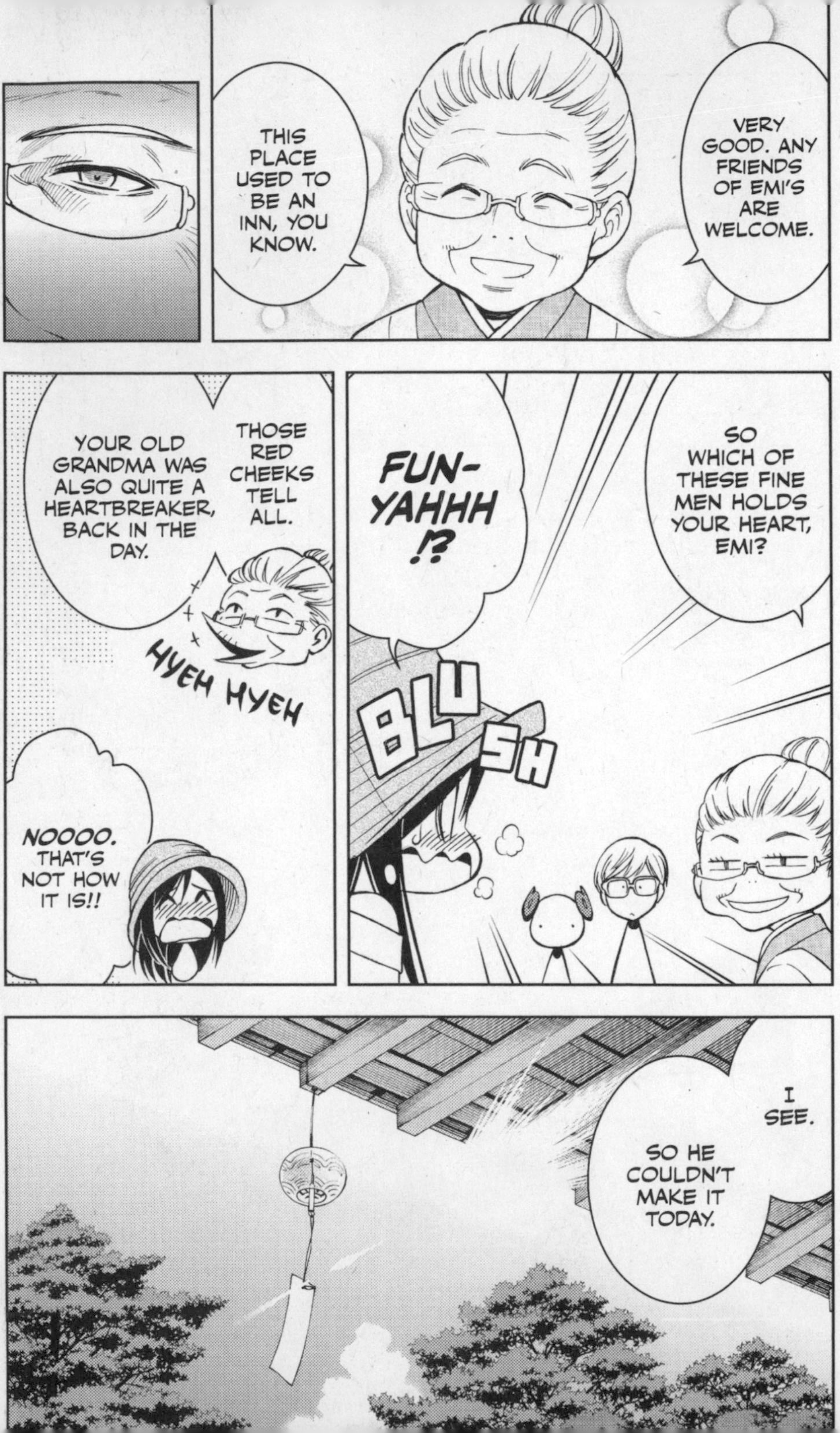
VERY GOOD. ANY FRIENDS OF EMI'S ARE WELCOME.
THIS PLACE USED TO BE AN INN, YOU KNOW.
SO WHICH OF THESE FINE MEN HOLDS YOUR HEART, EMI?
FUN-YAHHH!?
BLUSH
THOSE RED CHEEKS TELL ALL.
YOUR OLD GRANDMA WAS ALSO QUITE A HEARTBREAKER, BACK IN THE DAY.
HYEH HYEH
NOOOO. THAT'S NOT HOW IT IS!!
I SEE.
SO HE COULDN'T MAKE IT TODAY.

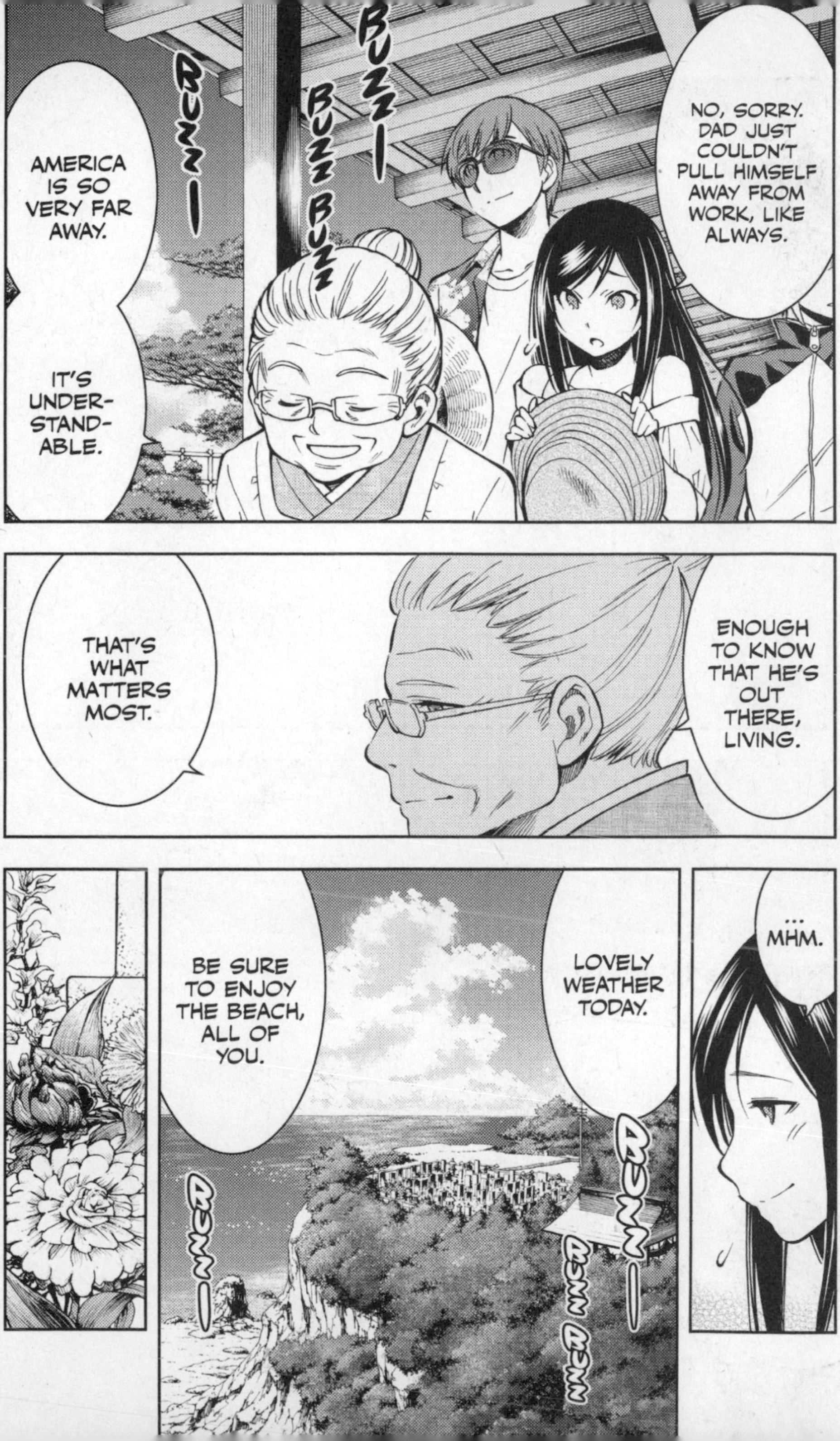
NO, SORRY. DAD JUST COULDN'T PULL HIMSELF AWAY FROM WORK, LIKE ALWAYS.
BUZZ—
BUZZ BUZZ
BUZZ—
AMERICA IS SO VERY FAR AWAY.
IT'S UNDER-STANDABLE.
ENOUGH TO KNOW THAT HE'S OUT THERE, LIVING.
THAT'S WHAT MATTERS MOST.
...MHM.
LOVELY WEATHER TODAY.
BE SURE TO ENJOY THE BEACH, ALL OF YOU.
BUZZ—
BUZZ BUZZ
BUZZ—

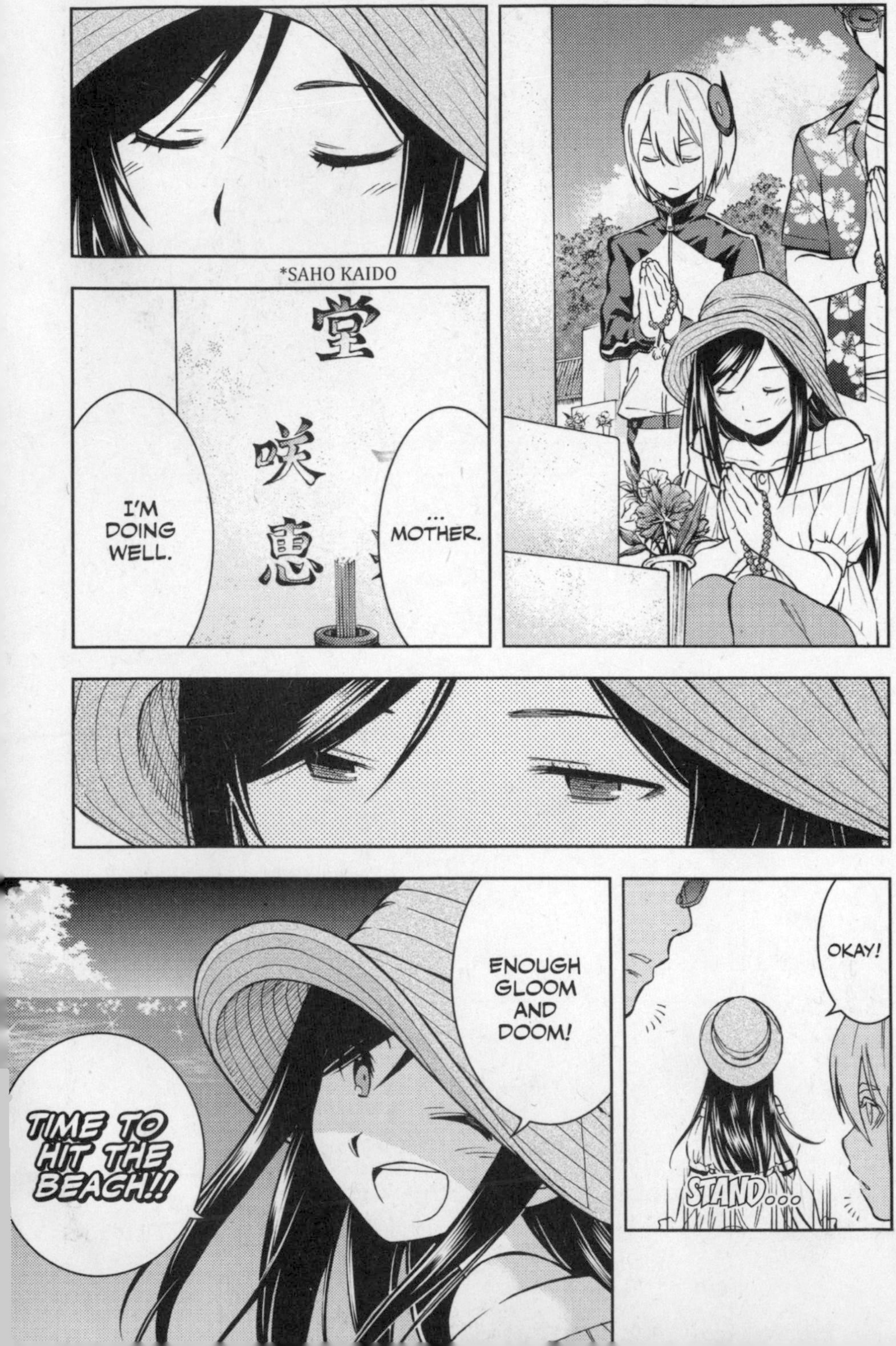
*SAHO KAIDO
堂咲恵
... MOTHER.
I'M DOING WELL.
OKAY!
STAND...
ENOUGH GLOOM AND DOOM!
TIME TO HIT THE BEACH!!

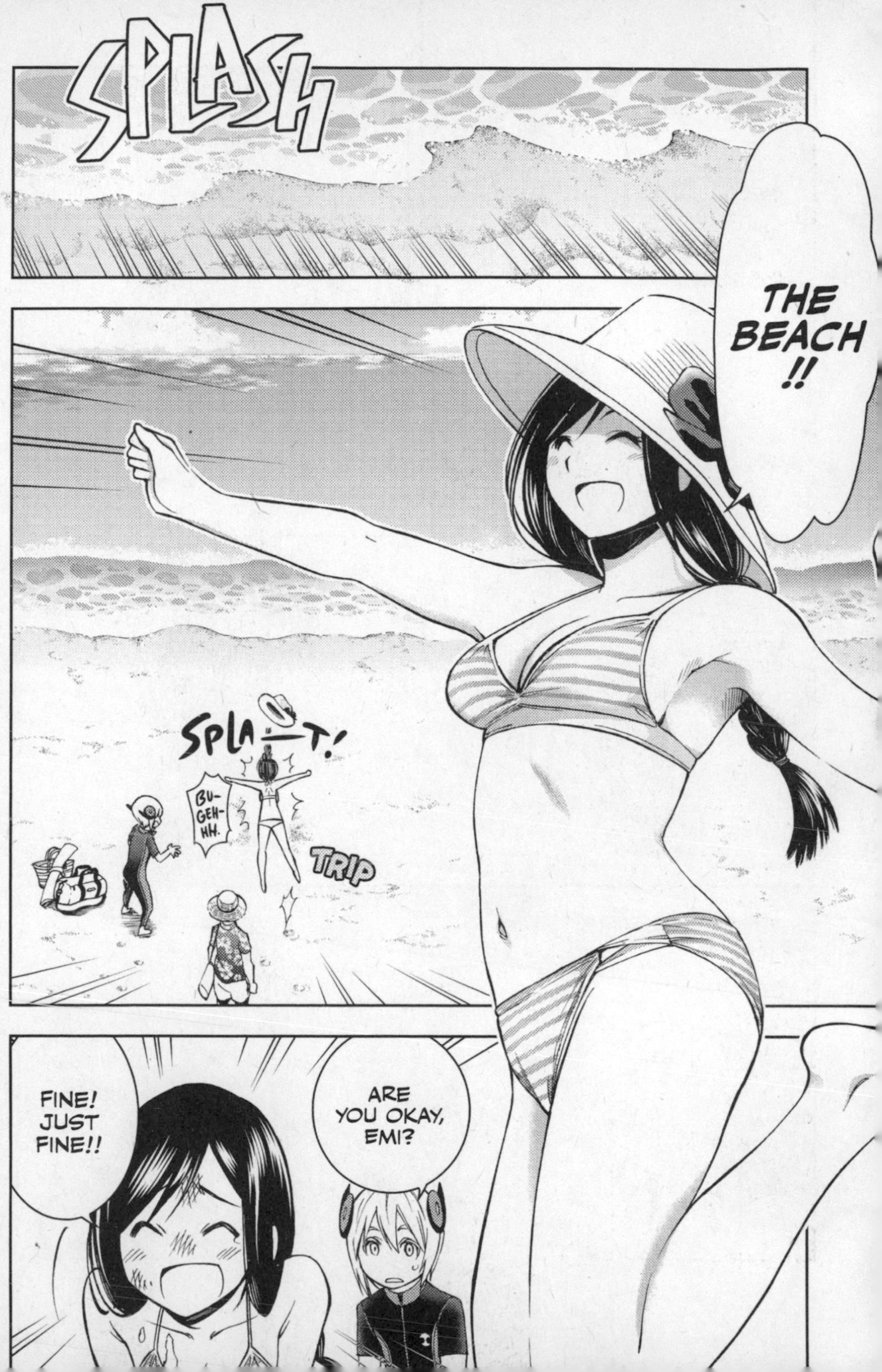
SPLASH
THE BEACH!!
SPLA—T!
BU-GEH-HH.
TRIP
ARE YOU OKAY, EMI?
FINE! JUST FINE!!

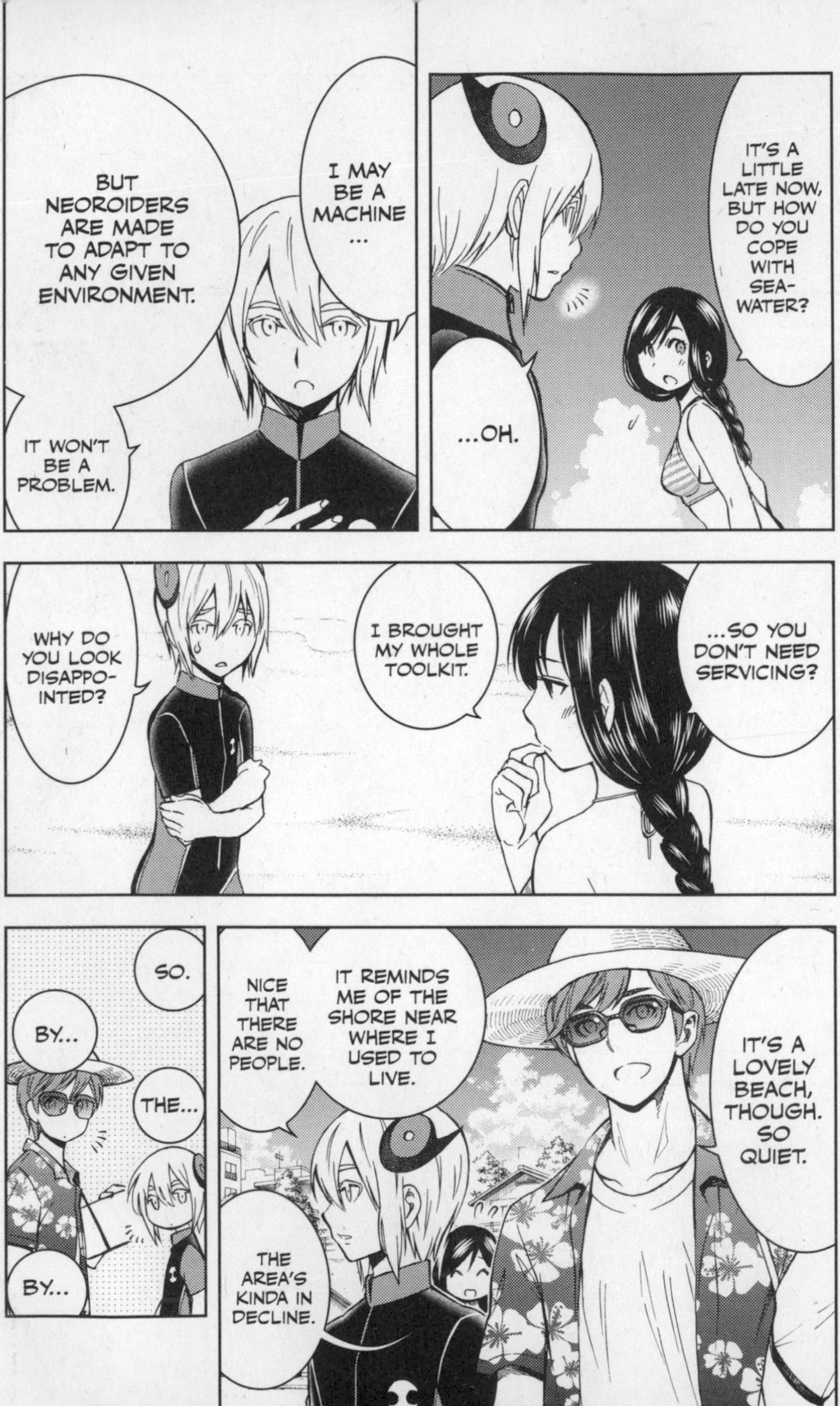
IT'S A LITTLE LATE NOW, BUT HOW DO YOU COPE WITH SEA-WATER?
...OH.
I MAY BE A MACHINE ...
BUT NEOROIDERS ARE MADE TO ADAPT TO ANY GIVEN ENVIRONMENT.
IT WON'T BE A PROBLEM.
...SO YOU DON'T NEED SERVICING?
I BROUGHT MY WHOLE TOOLKIT.
WHY DO YOU LOOK DISAPPO-INTED?
IT'S A LOVELY BEACH, THOUGH. SO QUIET.
IT REMINDS ME OF THE SHORE NEAR WHERE I USED TO LIVE.
NICE THAT THERE ARE NO PEOPLE.
THE AREA'S KINDA IN DECLINE.
SO.
BY...
THE...
BY...

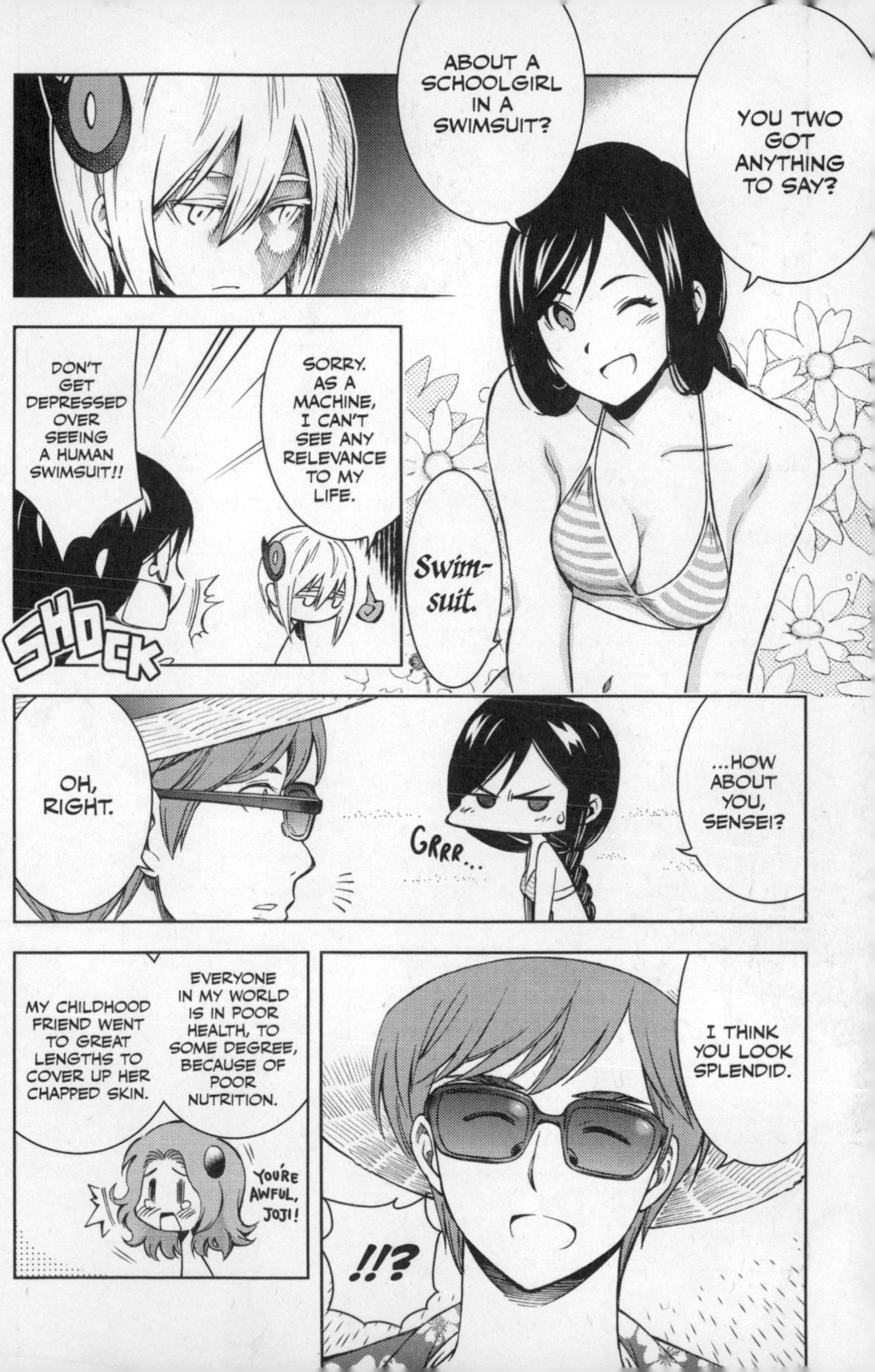
YOU TWO GOT ANYTHING TO SAY?
ABOUT A SCHOOLGIRL IN A SWIMSUIT?
Swim-suit.
SORRY. AS A MACHINE, I CAN'T SEE ANY RELEVANCE TO MY LIFE.
DON'T GET DEPRESSED OVER SEEING A HUMAN SWIMSUIT!!
SHOCK
...HOW ABOUT YOU, SENSEI?
GRRR...
OH, RIGHT.
I THINK YOU LOOK SPLENDID.
!!?
EVERYONE IN MY WORLD IS IN POOR HEALTH, TO SOME DEGREE, BECAUSE OF POOR NUTRITION.
MY CHILDHOOD FRIEND WENT TO GREAT LENGTHS TO COVER UP HER CHAPPED SKIN.
YOU'RE AWFUL, JOJI!

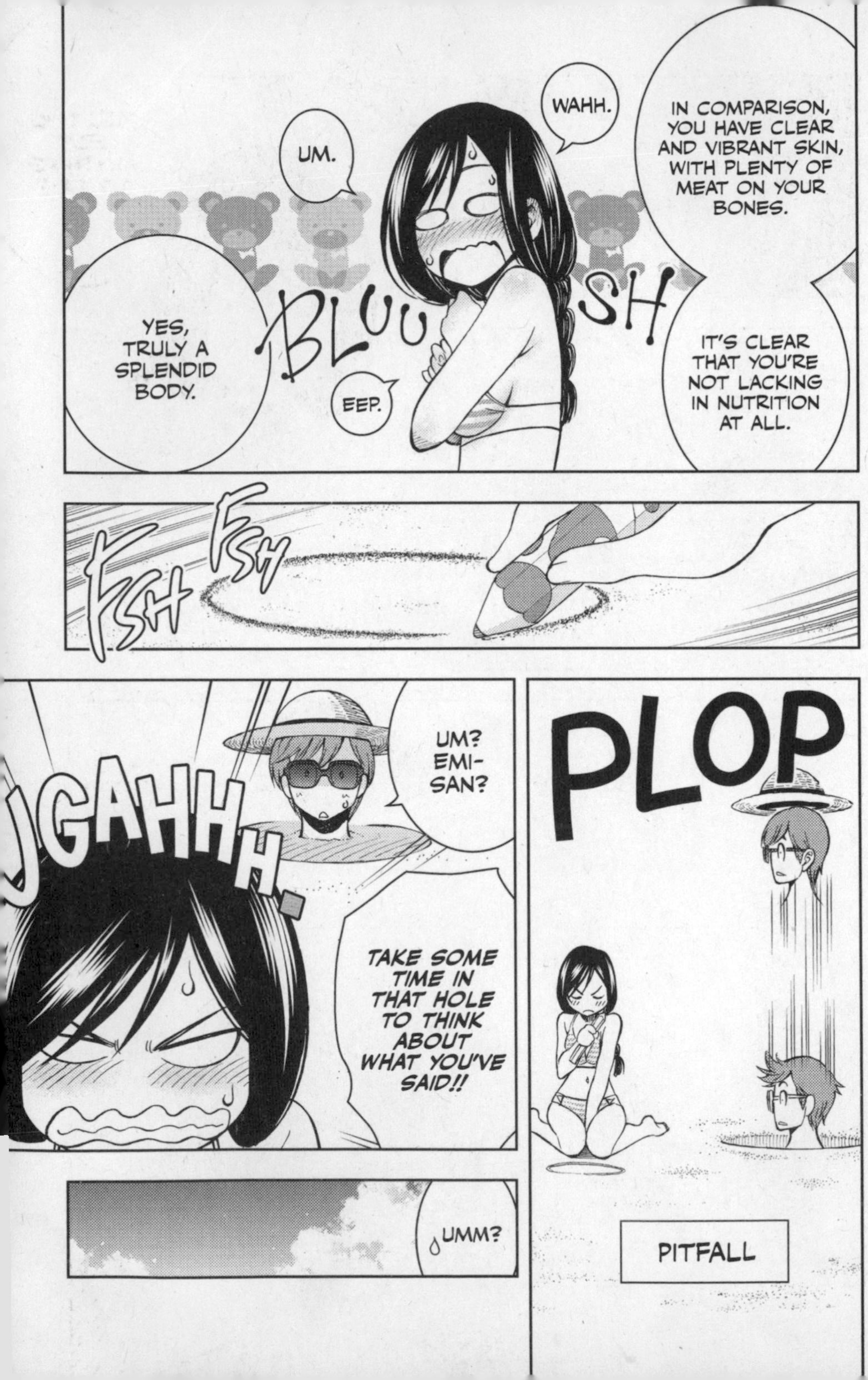
IN COMPARISON, YOU HAVE CLEAR AND VIBRANT SKIN, WITH PLENTY OF MEAT ON YOUR BONES.
WAHH.
UM.
IT'S CLEAR THAT YOU'RE NOT LACKING IN NUTRITION AT ALL.
BLUUSH
EEP.
YES, TRULY A SPLENDID BODY.
FSH
FSH
PLOP
PITFALL
UM? EMI-SAN?
UGAHHH.
TAKE SOME TIME IN THAT HOLE TO THINK ABOUT WHAT YOU'VE SAID!!
UMM?

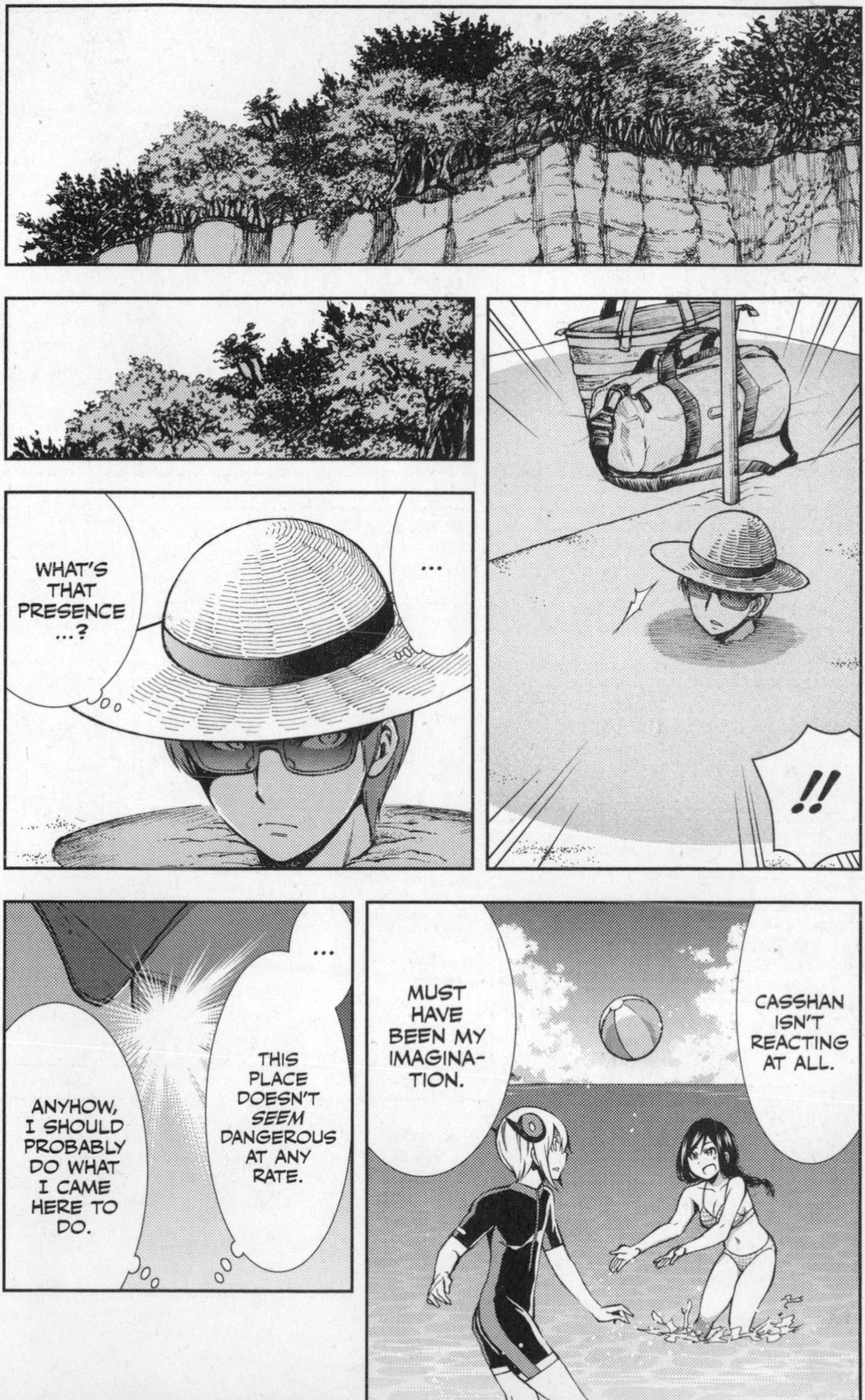
!!
...
WHAT'S THAT PRESENCE ...?
CASSHAN ISN'T REACTING AT ALL.
MUST HAVE BEEN MY IMAGINA-TION.
...
THIS PLACE DOESN'T *SEEM* DANGEROUS AT ANY RATE.
ANYHOW, I SHOULD PROBABLY DO WHAT I CAME HERE TO DO.

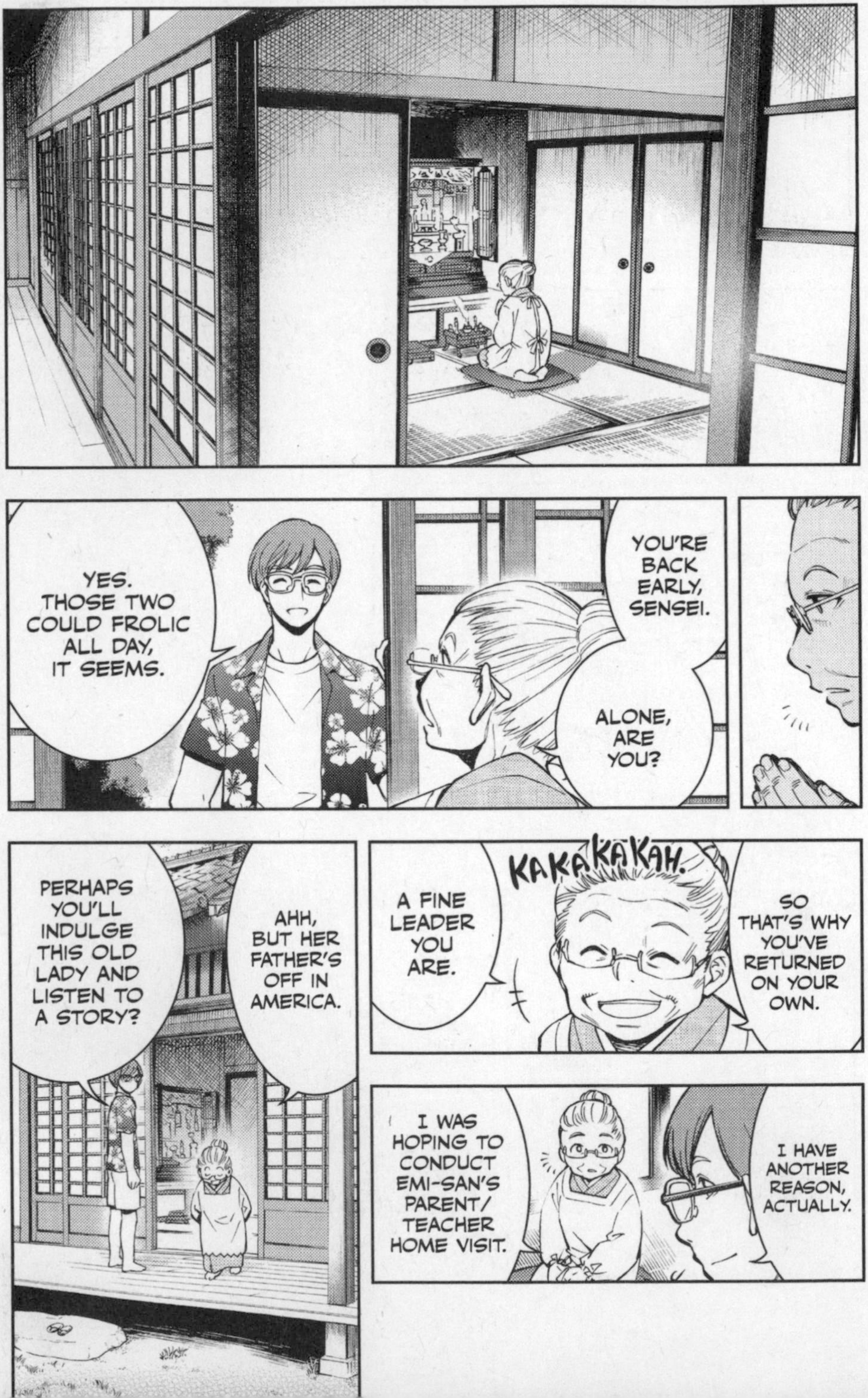
YOU'RE BACK EARLY, SENSEI.
ALONE, ARE YOU?
YES. THOSE TWO COULD FROLIC ALL DAY, IT SEEMS.
SO THAT'S WHY YOU'VE RETURNED ON YOUR OWN.
KAKAKAKAH.
A FINE LEADER YOU ARE.
I HAVE ANOTHER REASON, ACTUALLY.
I WAS HOPING TO CONDUCT EMI-SAN'S PARENT/ TEACHER HOME VISIT.
AHH, BUT HER FATHER'S OFF IN AMERICA.
PERHAPS YOU'LL INDULGE THIS OLD LADY AND LISTEN TO A STORY?

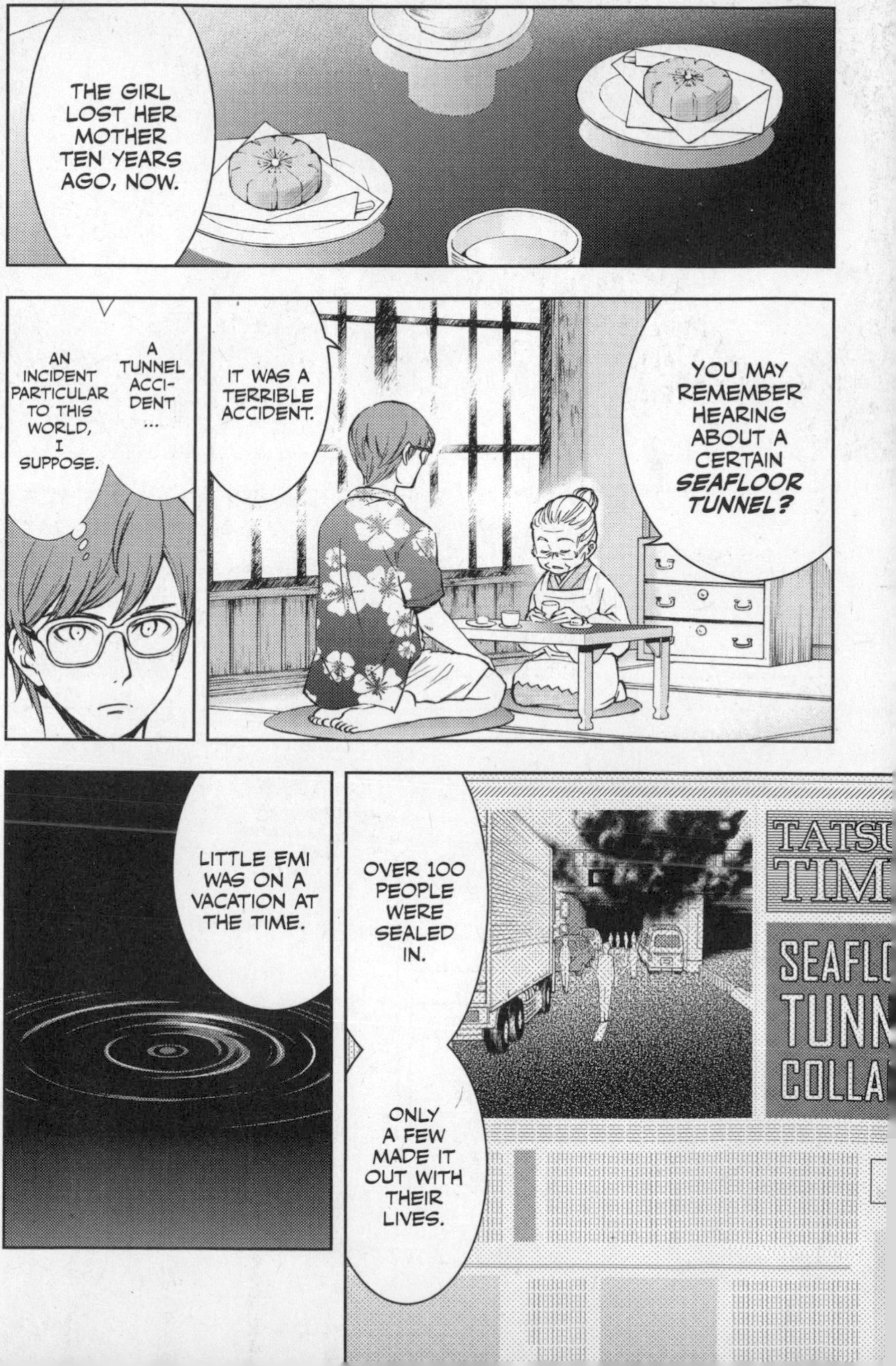
THE GIRL LOST HER MOTHER TEN YEARS AGO, NOW.
YOU MAY REMEMBER HEARING ABOUT A CERTAIN *SEAFLOOR TUNNEL?*
IT WAS A TERRIBLE ACCIDENT.
A TUNNEL ACCI-DENT ...
AN INCIDENT PARTICULAR TO THIS WORLD, I SUPPOSE.
OVER 100 PEOPLE WERE SEALED IN.
ONLY A FEW MADE IT OUT WITH THEIR LIVES.
LITTLE EMI WAS ON A VACATION AT THE TIME.

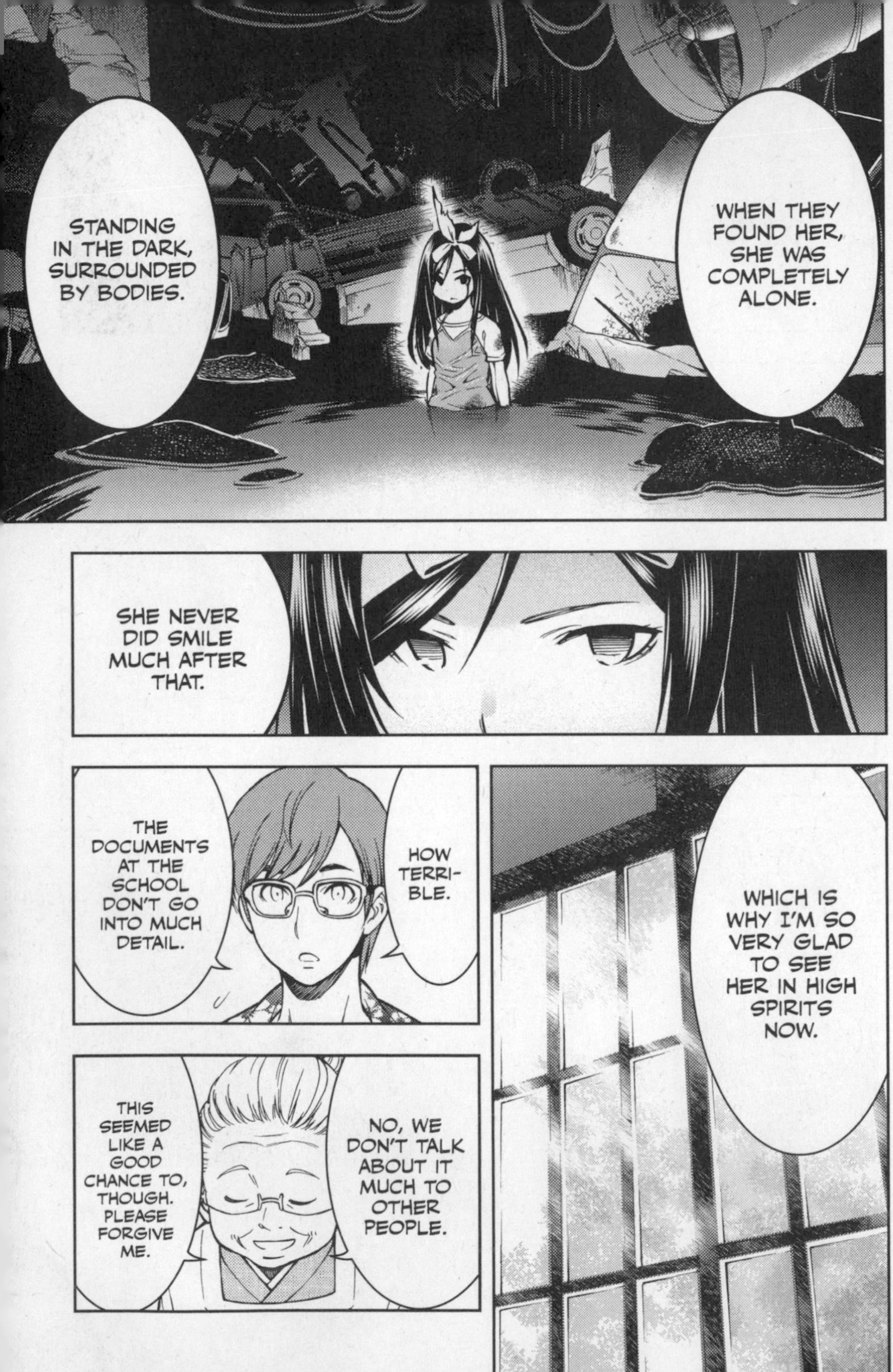
WHEN THEY FOUND HER, SHE WAS COMPLETELY ALONE.
STANDING IN THE DARK, SURROUNDED BY BODIES.
SHE NEVER DID SMILE MUCH AFTER THAT.
WHICH IS WHY I'M SO VERY GLAD TO SEE HER IN HIGH SPIRITS NOW.
HOW TERRI-BLE.
THE DOCUMENTS AT THE SCHOOL DON'T GO INTO MUCH DETAIL.
NO, WE DON'T TALK ABOUT IT MUCH TO OTHER PEOPLE.
THIS SEEMED LIKE A GOOD CHANCE TO, THOUGH. PLEASE FORGIVE ME.

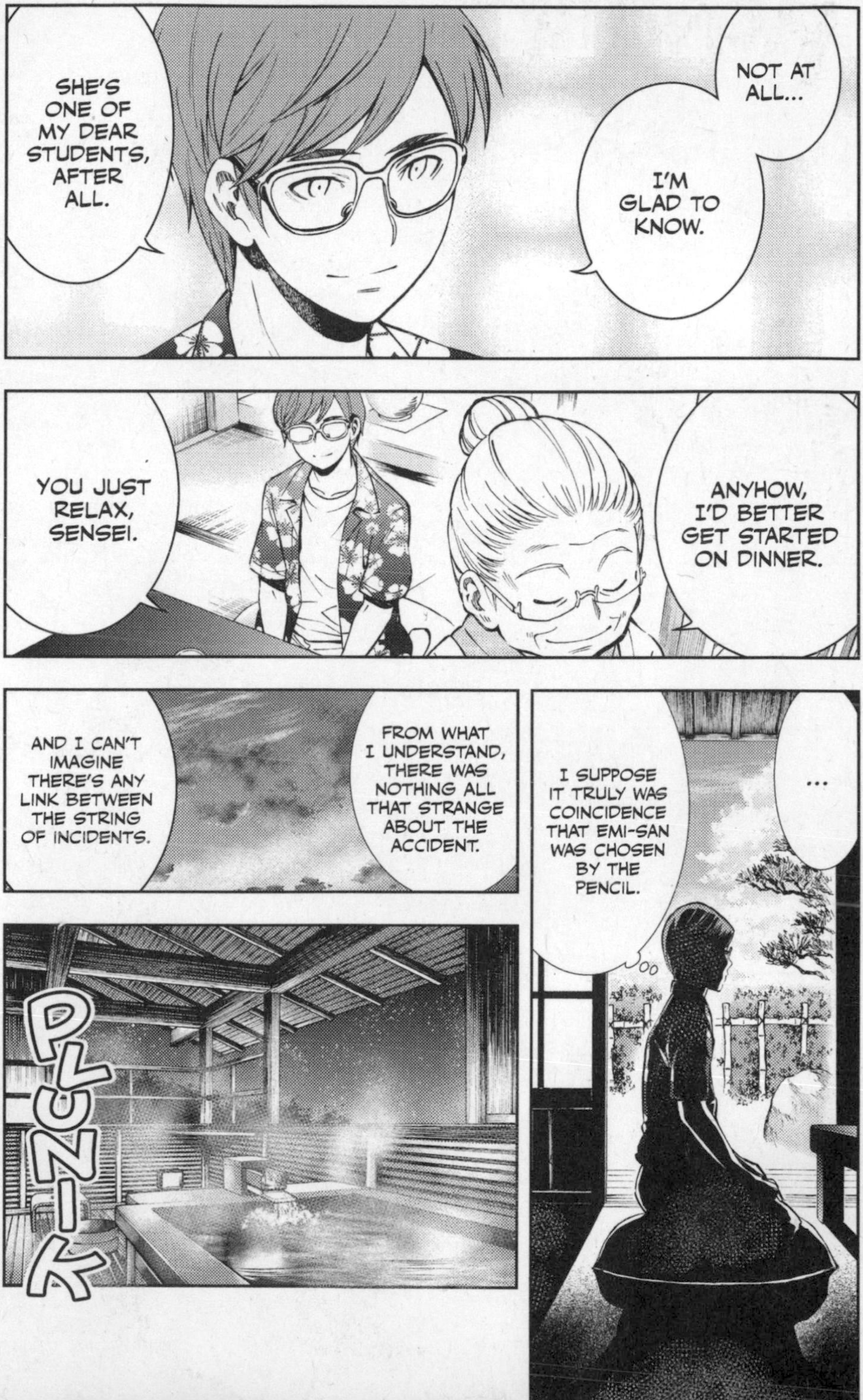
NOT AT ALL...
I'M GLAD TO KNOW.
SHE'S ONE OF MY DEAR STUDENTS, AFTER ALL.
ANYHOW, I'D BETTER GET STARTED ON DINNER.
YOU JUST RELAX, SENSEI.
...
I SUPPOSE IT TRULY WAS COINCIDENCE THAT EMI-SAN WAS CHOSEN BY THE PENCIL.
FROM WHAT I UNDERSTAND, THERE WAS NOTHING ALL THAT STRANGE ABOUT THE ACCIDENT.
AND I CAN'T IMAGINE THERE'S ANY LINK BETWEEN THE STRING OF INCIDENTS.
PLUNK

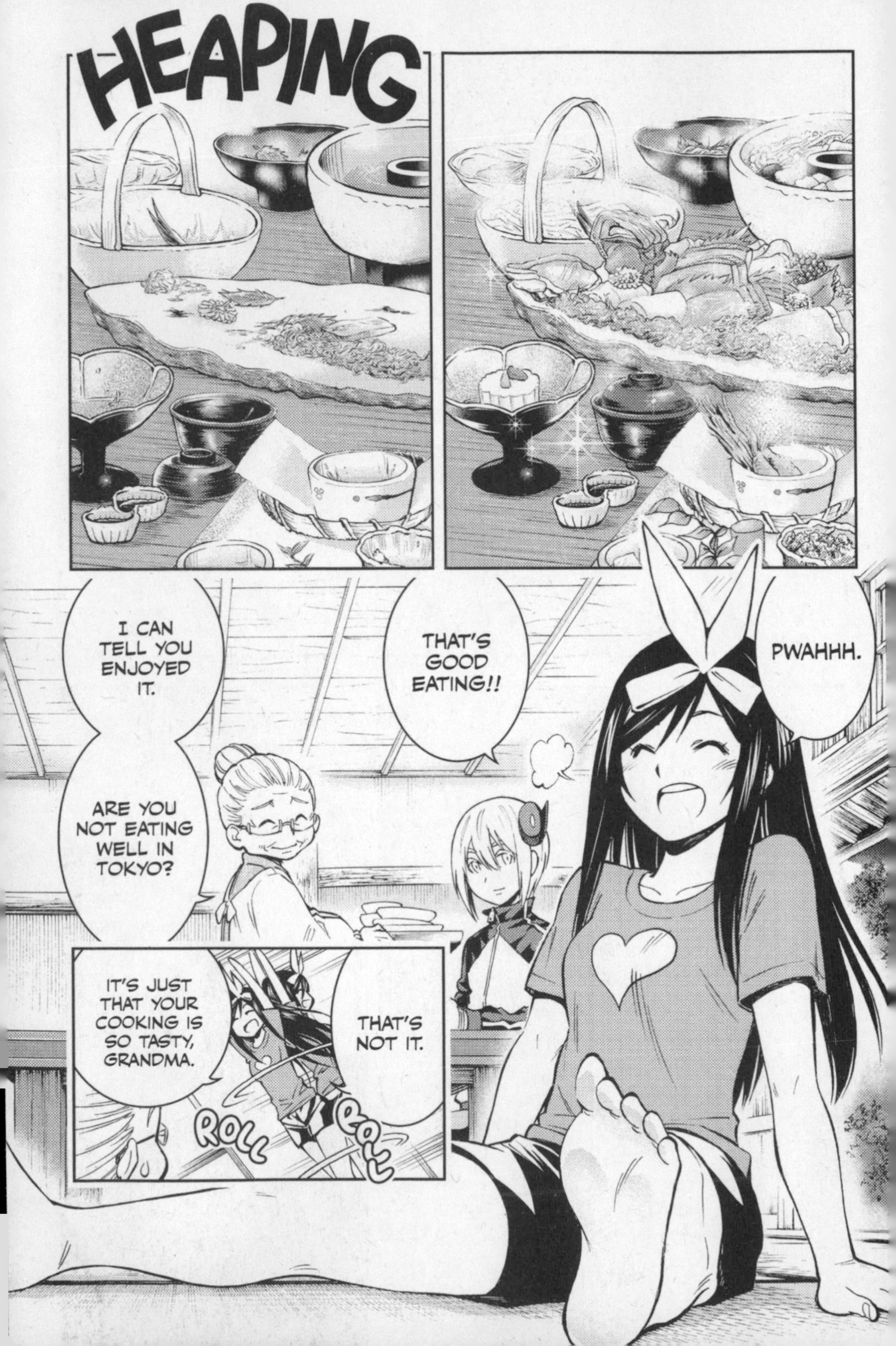
HEAPING
PWAHHH.
THAT'S GOOD EATING!!
I CAN TELL YOU ENJOYED IT.
ARE YOU NOT EATING WELL IN TOKYO?
THAT'S NOT IT.
IT'S JUST THAT YOUR COOKING IS SO TASTY, GRANDMA.
ROLL
ROLL

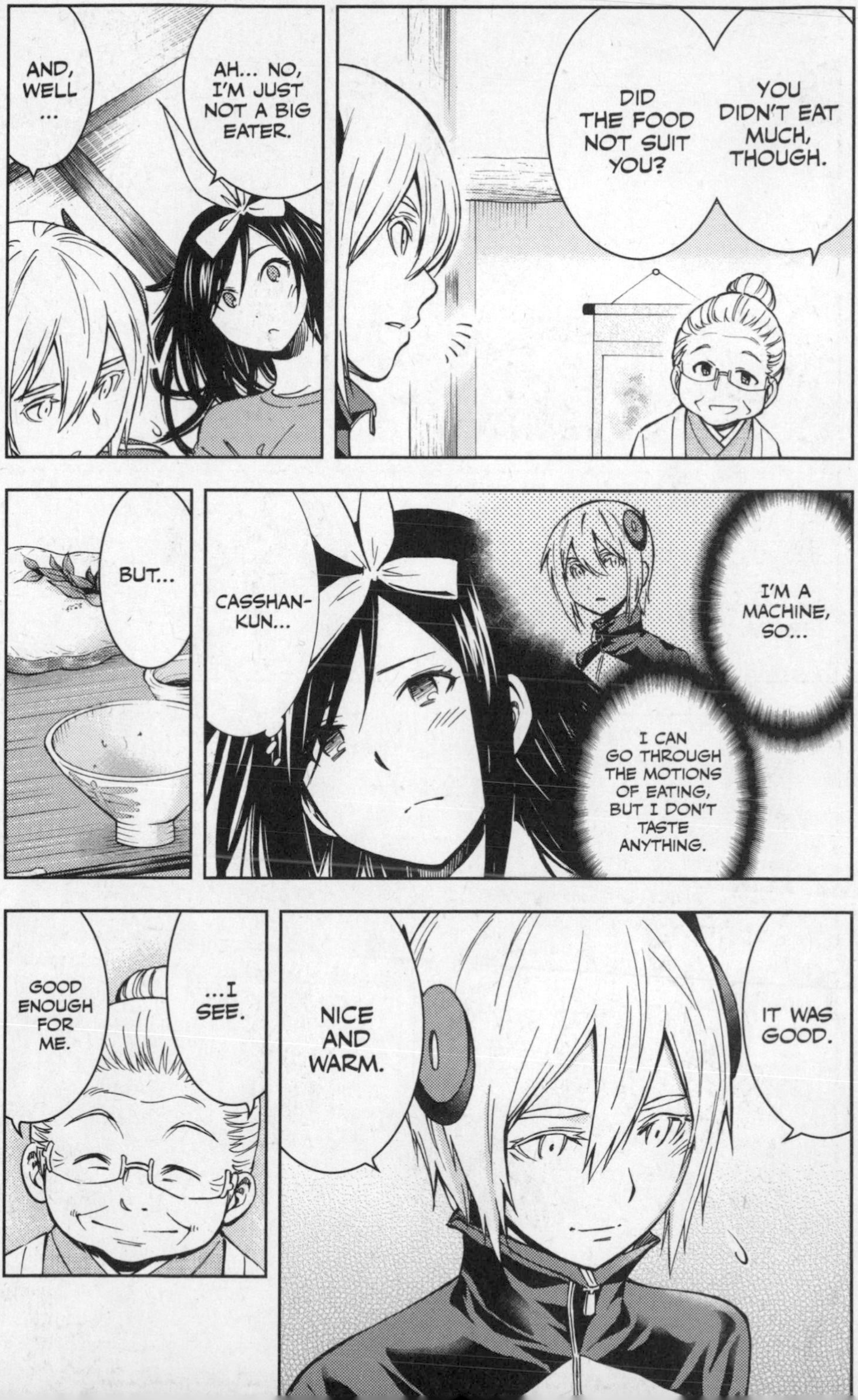
YOU DIDN'T EAT MUCH, THOUGH.
DID THE FOOD NOT SUIT YOU?
AH... NO, I'M JUST NOT A BIG EATER.
AND, WELL ...
I'M A MACHINE, SO...
I CAN GO THROUGH THE MOTIONS OF EATING, BUT I DON'T TASTE ANYTHING.
CASSHAN-KUN...
BUT...
IT WAS GOOD.
NICE AND WARM.
...I SEE.
GOOD ENOUGH FOR ME.

STAND

AN ARMED BATTALION HAS JUST COME ONTO THE PROPERTY.

WHAT'S WRONG?

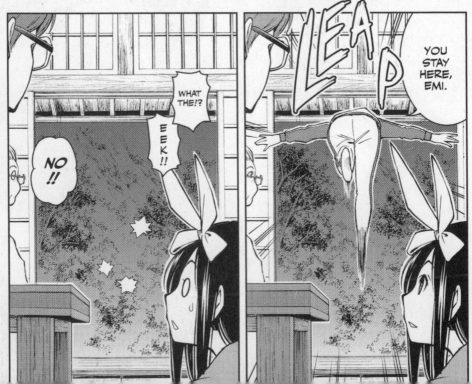

WHAT THE!?

EEK!!

NO!!

LEAP

YOU STAY HERE, EMI.

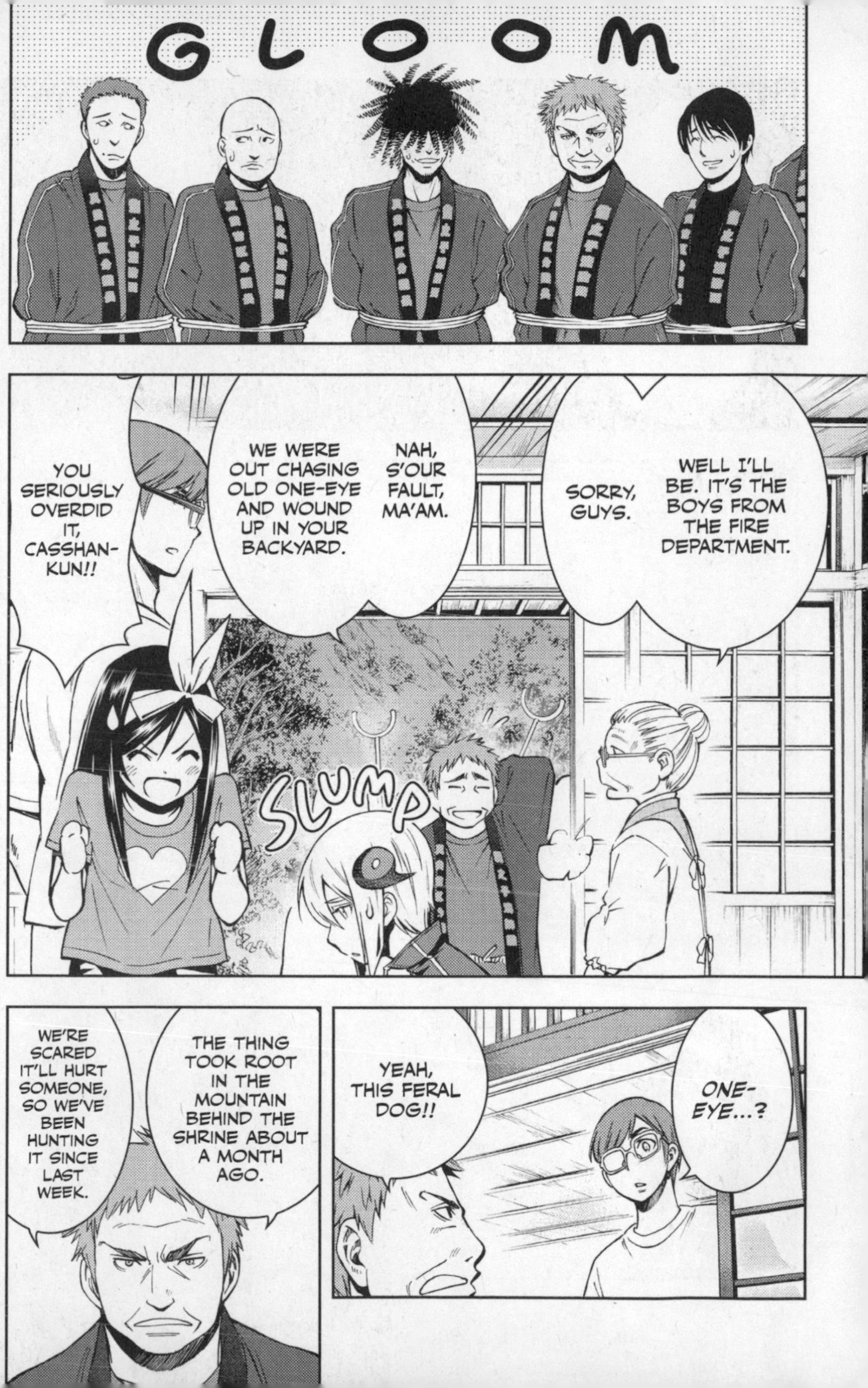
GLOOM
WELL I'LL BE. IT'S THE BOYS FROM THE FIRE DEPARTMENT.
SORRY, GUYS.
NAH, S'OUR FAULT, MA'AM.
WE WERE OUT CHASING OLD ONE-EYE AND WOUND UP IN YOUR BACKYARD.
SLUMP
YOU SERIOUSLY OVERDID IT, CASSHAN-KUN!!
ONE-EYE...?
YEAH, THIS FERAL DOG!!
THE THING TOOK ROOT IN THE MOUNTAIN BEHIND THE SHRINE ABOUT A MONTH AGO.
WE'RE SCARED IT'LL HURT SOMEONE, SO WE'VE BEEN HUNTING IT SINCE LAST WEEK.

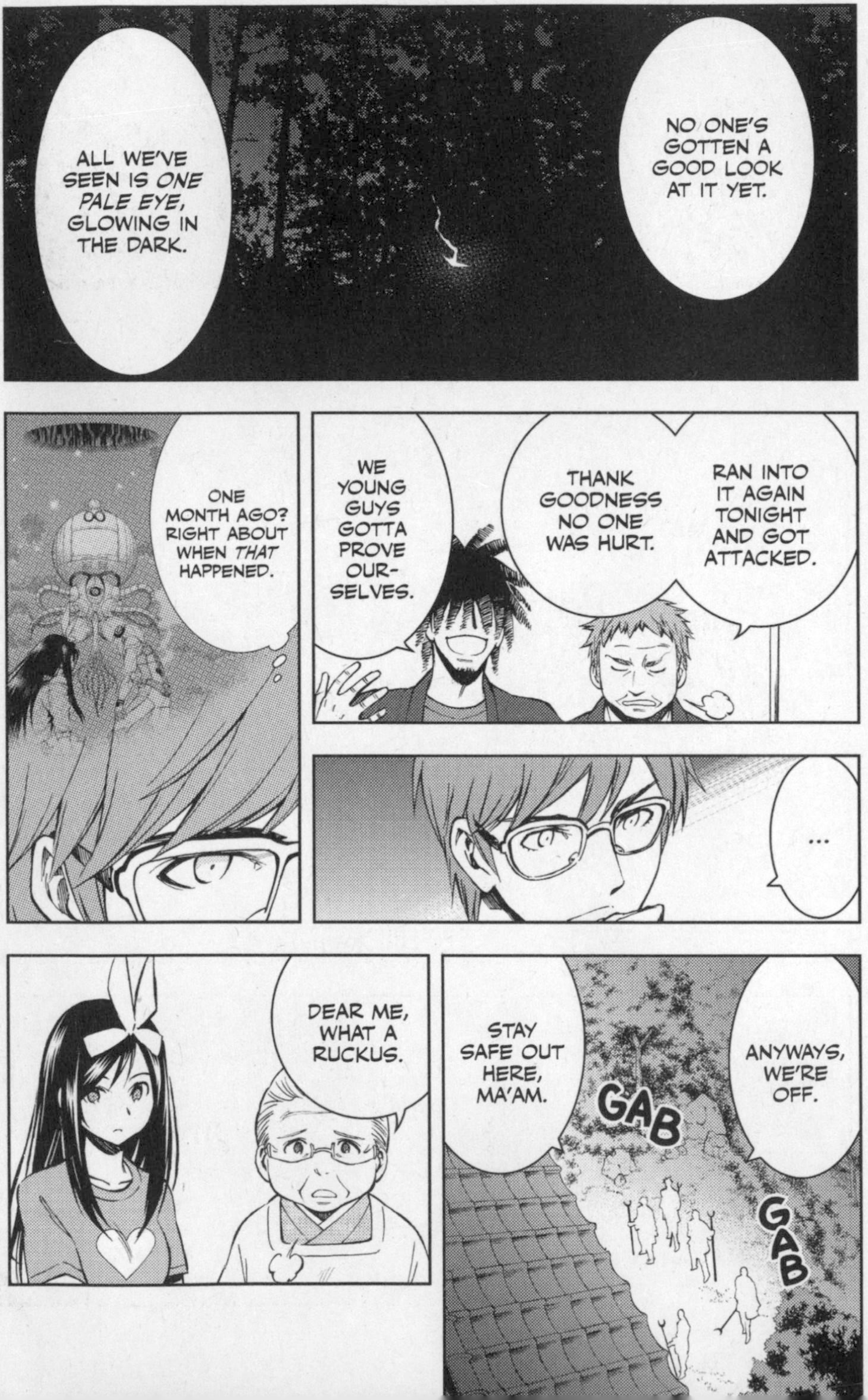
NO ONE'S GOTTEN A GOOD LOOK AT IT YET.
ALL WE'VE SEEN IS *ONE PALE EYE*, GLOWING IN THE DARK.
RAN INTO IT AGAIN TONIGHT AND GOT ATTACKED.
THANK GOODNESS NO ONE WAS HURT.
WE YOUNG GUYS GOTTA PROVE OUR-SELVES.
...
ONE MONTH AGO? RIGHT ABOUT WHEN *THAT* HAPPENED.
ANYWAYS, WE'RE OFF.
GAB
STAY SAFE OUT HERE, MA'AM.
GAB
DEAR ME, WHAT A RUCKUS.

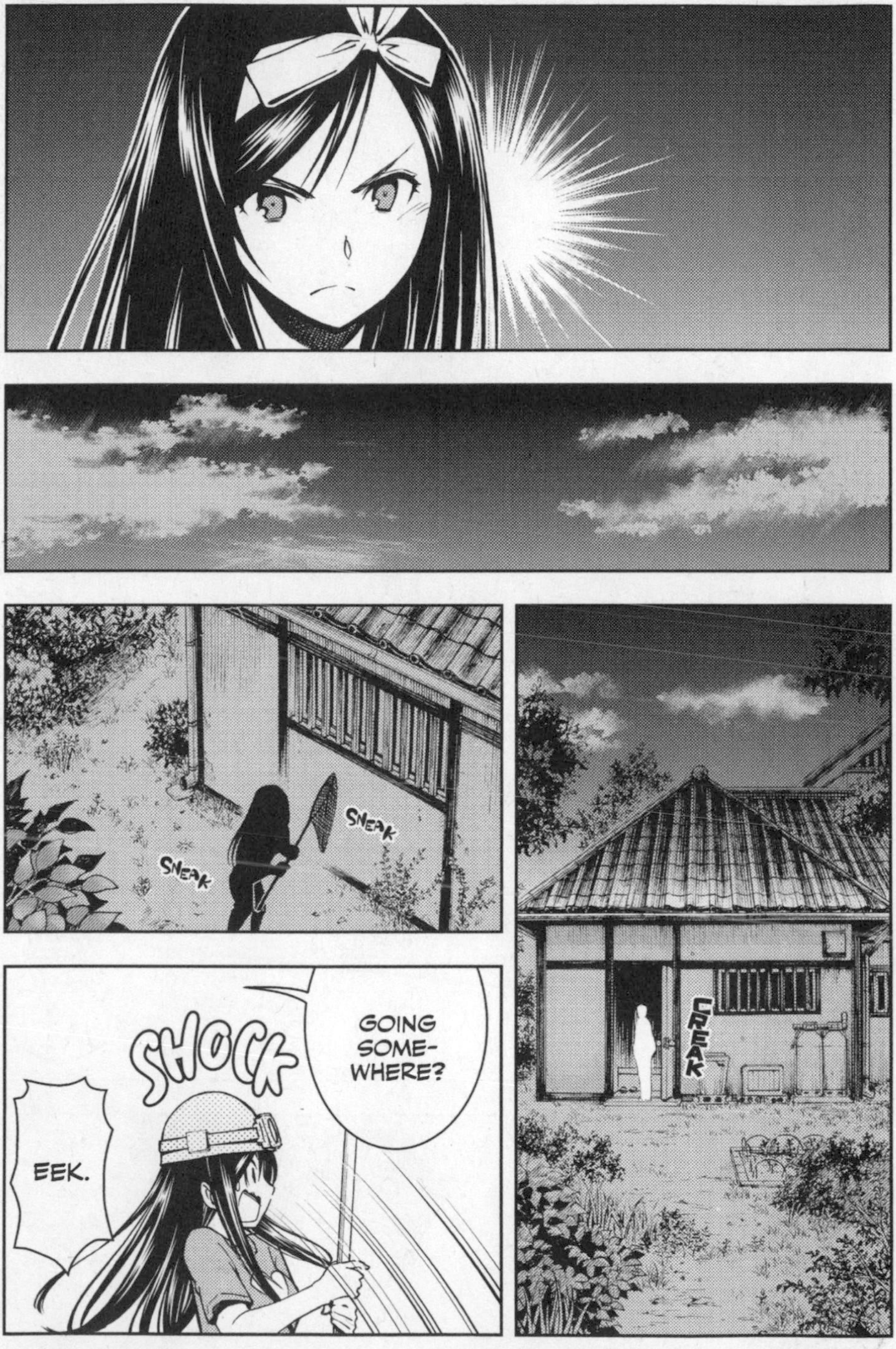
CREAK
SNEAK
SNEAK
GOING SOME-WHERE?
SHOCK
EEK.

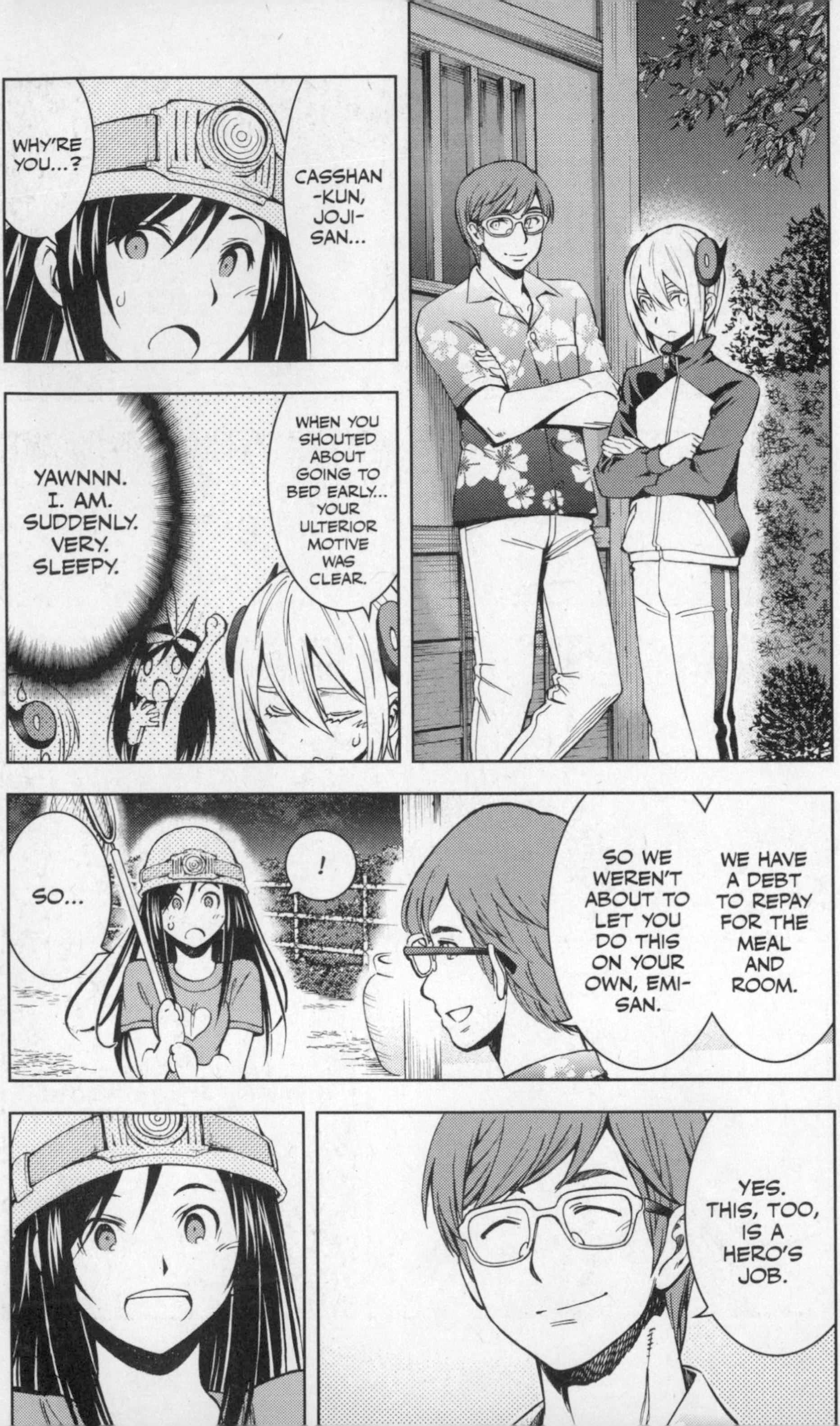
CASSHAN -KUN, JOJI- SAN...
WHY'RE YOU...?
WHEN YOU SHOUTED ABOUT GOING TO BED EARLY... YOUR ULTERIOR MOTIVE WAS CLEAR.
YAWNNN. I. AM. SUDDENLY. VERY. SLEEPY.
WE HAVE A DEBT TO REPAY FOR THE MEAL AND ROOM.
SO WE WEREN'T ABOUT TO LET YOU DO THIS ON YOUR OWN, EMI- SAN.
!
SO...
YES. THIS, TOO, IS A HERO'S JOB.

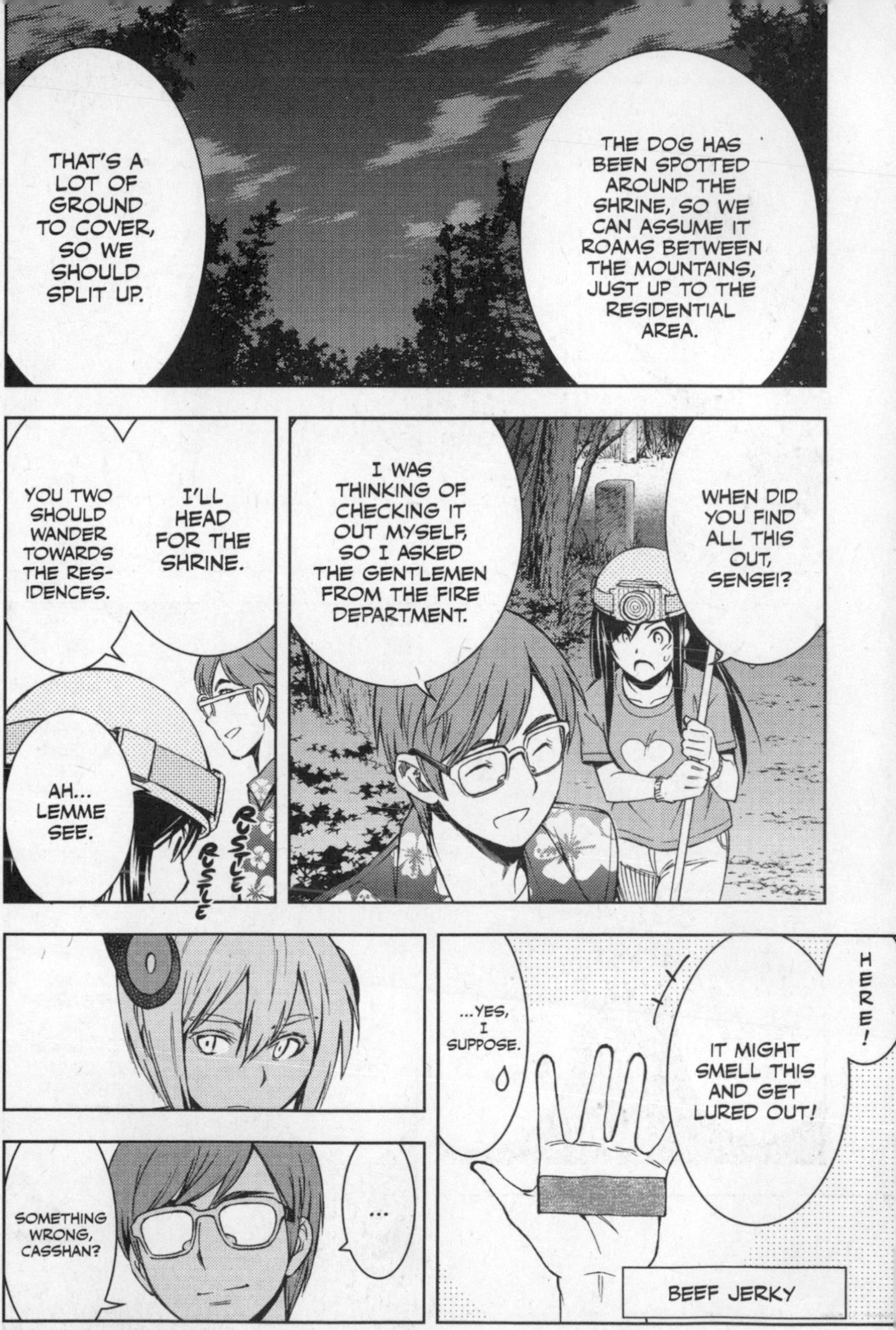
THE DOG HAS BEEN SPOTTED AROUND THE SHRINE, SO WE CAN ASSUME IT ROAMS BETWEEN THE MOUNTAINS, JUST UP TO THE RESIDENTIAL AREA.
THAT'S A LOT OF GROUND TO COVER, SO WE SHOULD SPLIT UP.
WHEN DID YOU FIND ALL THIS OUT, SENSEI?
I WAS THINKING OF CHECKING IT OUT MYSELF, SO I ASKED THE GENTLEMEN FROM THE FIRE DEPARTMENT.
I'LL HEAD FOR THE SHRINE.
YOU TWO SHOULD WANDER TOWARDS THE RES-IDENCES.
AH... LEMME SEE.
RUSTLE RUSTLE
HERE!
IT MIGHT SMELL THIS AND GET LURED OUT!
...YES, I SUPPOSE.
BEEF JERKY
...
SOMETHING WRONG, CASSHAN?

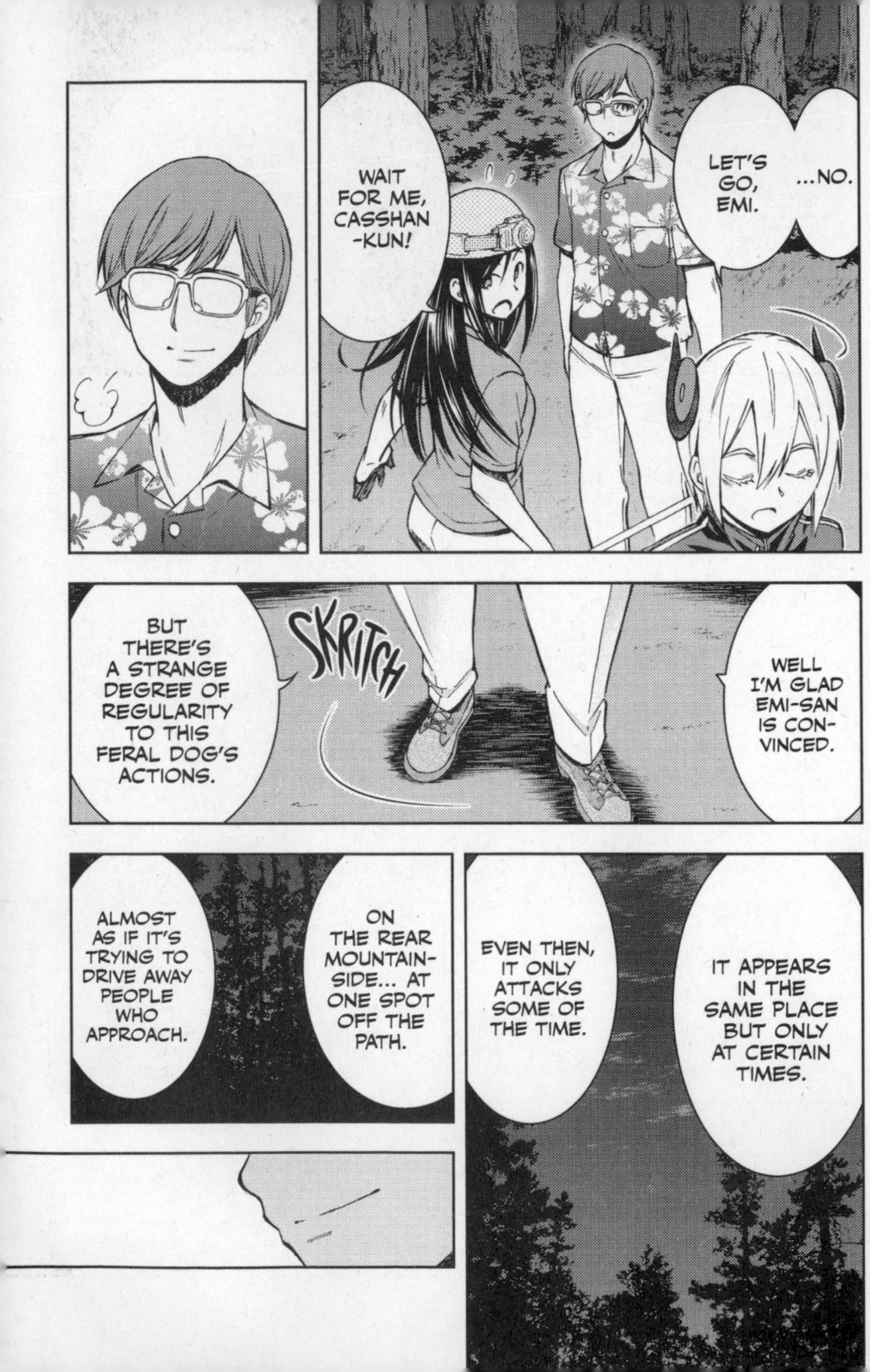
...NO.
LET'S GO, EMI.
WAIT FOR ME, CASSHAN-KUN!
WELL I'M GLAD EMI-SAN IS CONVINCED.
SKRITCH
BUT THERE'S A STRANGE DEGREE OF REGULARITY TO THIS FERAL DOG'S ACTIONS.
IT APPEARS IN THE SAME PLACE BUT ONLY AT CERTAIN TIMES.
EVEN THEN, IT ONLY ATTACKS SOME OF THE TIME.
ON THE REAR MOUNTAIN-SIDE... AT ONE SPOT OFF THE PATH.
ALMOST AS IF IT'S TRYING TO DRIVE AWAY PEOPLE WHO APPROACH.

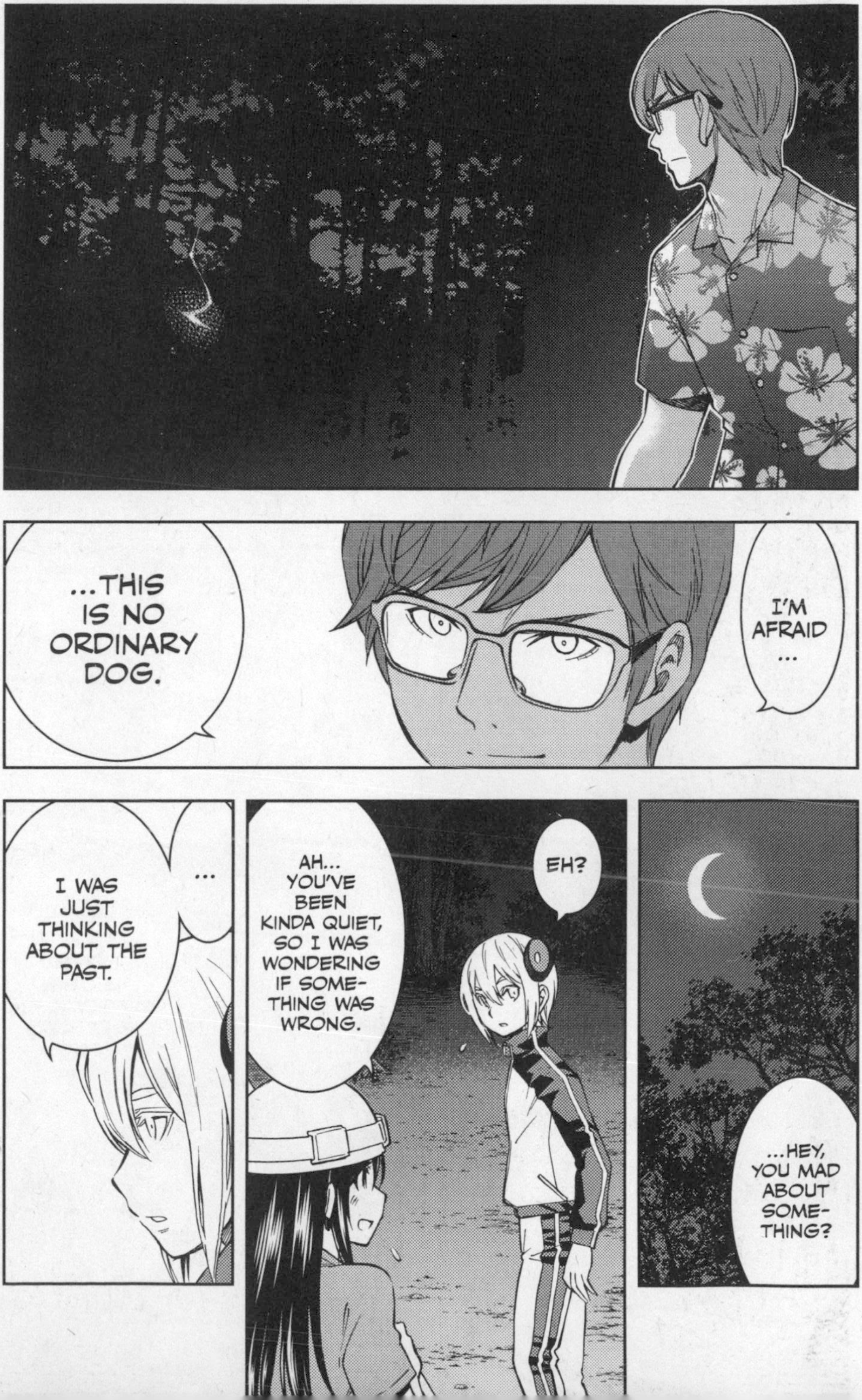
I'M AFRAID ...
...THIS IS NO ORDINARY DOG.
...HEY, YOU MAD ABOUT SOME-THING?
EH?
AH... YOU'VE BEEN KINDA QUIET, SO I WAS WONDERING IF SOME-THING WAS WRONG.
...
I WAS JUST THINKING ABOUT THE PAST.

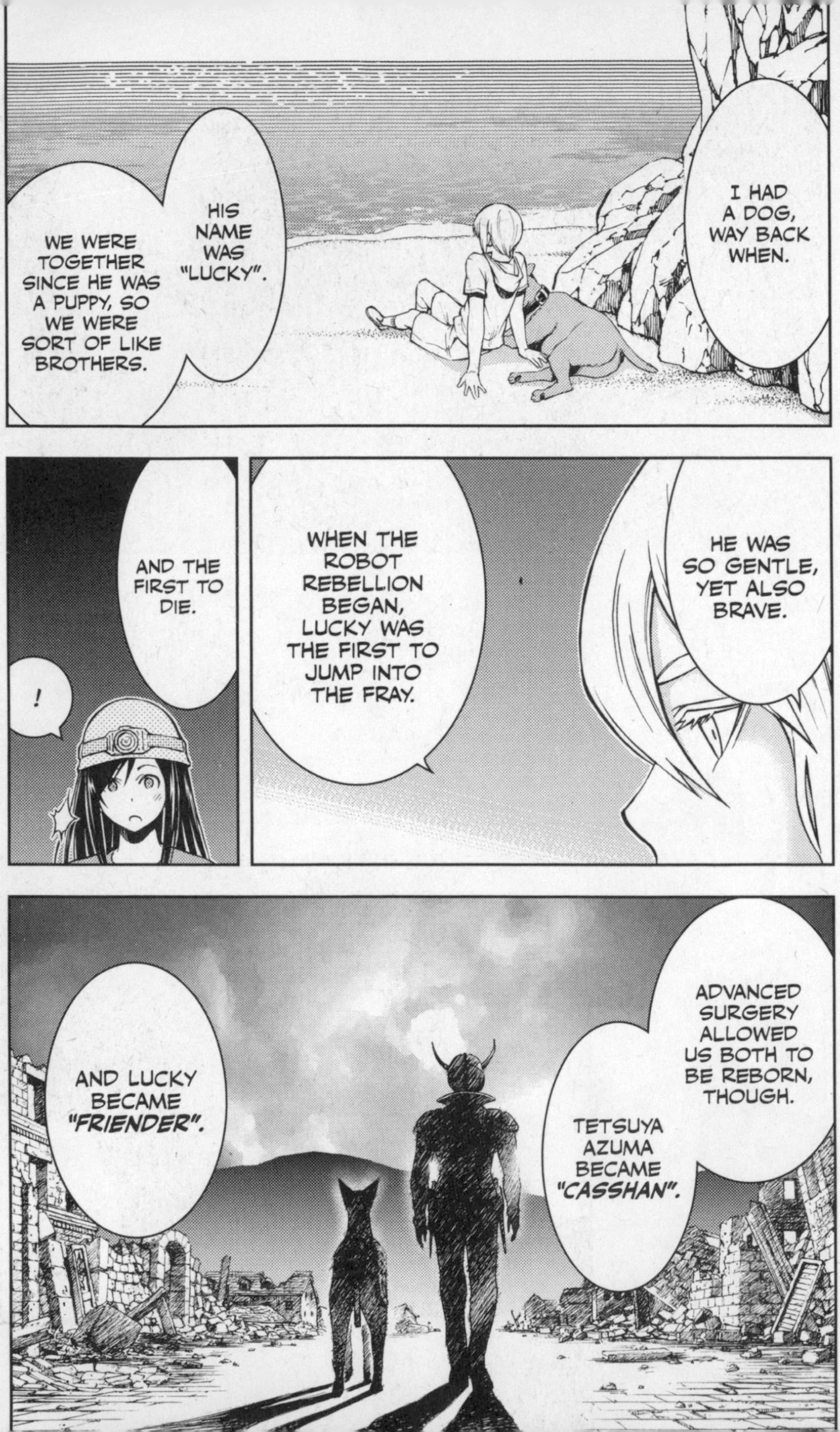
I HAD A DOG, WAY BACK WHEN.
HIS NAME WAS "LUCKY".
WE WERE TOGETHER SINCE HE WAS A PUPPY, SO WE WERE SORT OF LIKE BROTHERS.
HE WAS SO GENTLE, YET ALSO BRAVE.
WHEN THE ROBOT REBELLION BEGAN, LUCKY WAS THE FIRST TO JUMP INTO THE FRAY.
AND THE FIRST TO DIE.
!
ADVANCED SURGERY ALLOWED US BOTH TO BE REBORN, THOUGH.
TETSUYA AZUMA BECAME ***"CASSHAN"***.
AND LUCKY BECAME ***"FRIENDER"***.

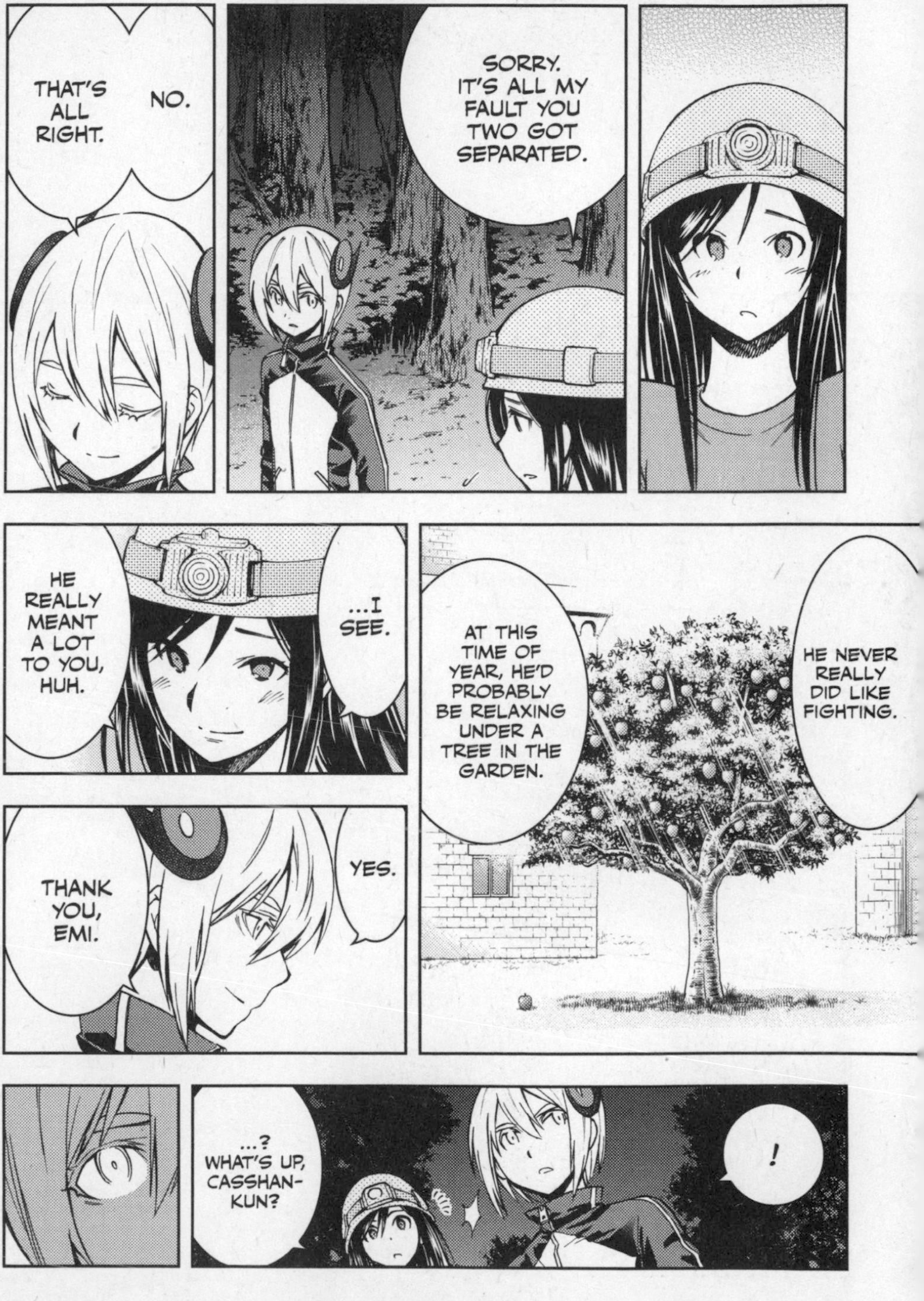
SORRY. IT'S ALL MY FAULT YOU TWO GOT SEPARATED.
NO.
THAT'S ALL RIGHT.
HE NEVER REALLY DID LIKE FIGHTING.
AT THIS TIME OF YEAR, HE'D PROBABLY BE RELAXING UNDER A TREE IN THE GARDEN.
...I SEE.
HE REALLY MEANT A LOT TO YOU, HUH.
YES.
THANK YOU, EMI.
!
...? WHAT'S UP, CASSHAN-KUN?

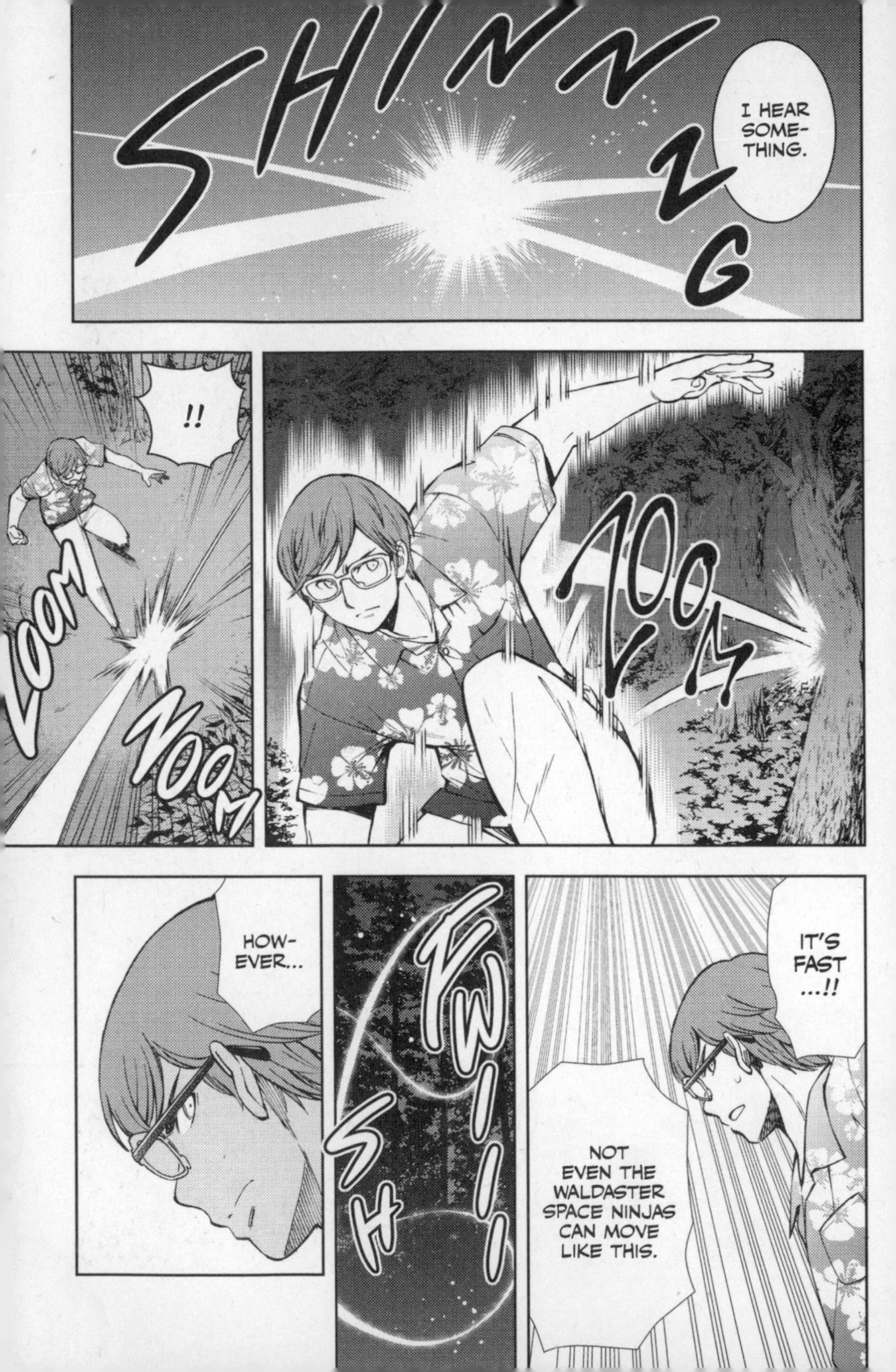
SHINNNG
I HEAR SOME-THING.
ZOOOM
!!
ZOOM
NOOOM
IT'S FAST ...!!
NOT EVEN THE WALDASTER SPACE NINJAS CAN MOVE LIKE THIS.
FWIIISH
HOW-EVER...

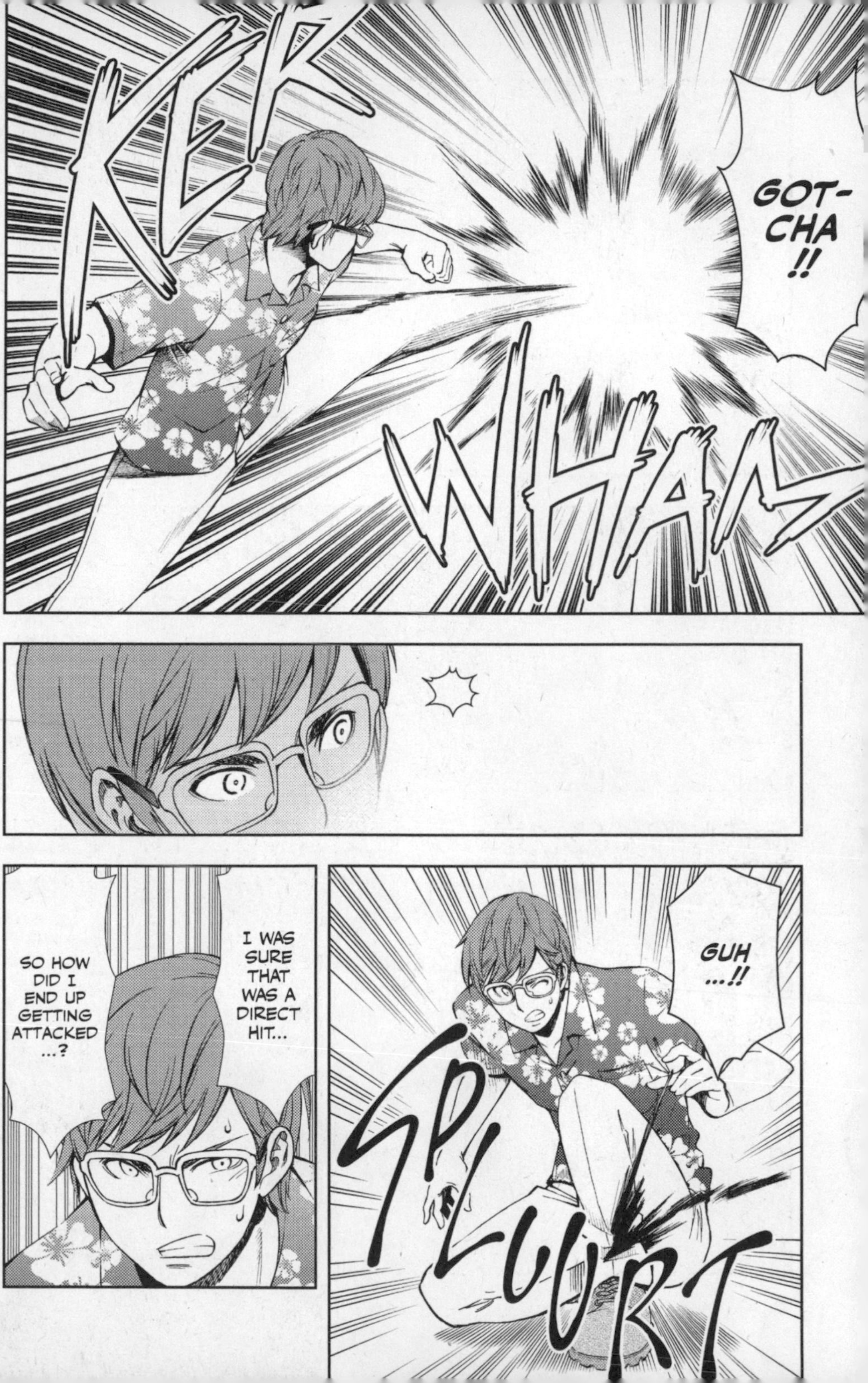
GOT-CHA!!
KER
WHAM
GUH...!!
SPLUURT
I WAS SURE THAT WAS A DIRECT HIT...
SO HOW DID I END UP GETTING ATTACKED...?

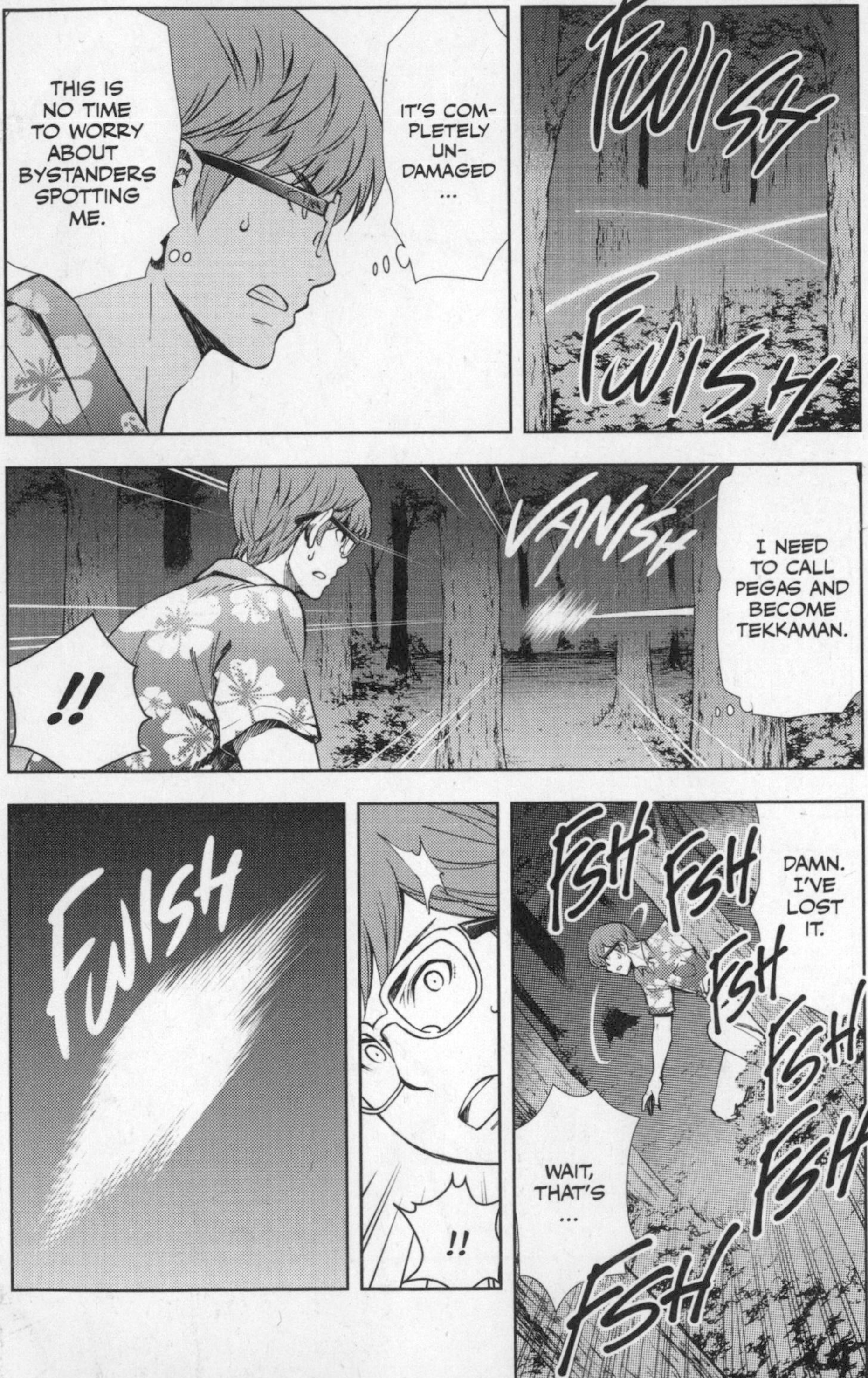
FWISH
FWISH
IT'S COM-PLETELY UN-DAMAGED ...
THIS IS NO TIME TO WORRY ABOUT BYSTANDERS SPOTTING ME.
I NEED TO CALL PEGAS AND BECOME TEKKAMAN.
VANISH
!!
FSH FSH
DAMN. I'VE LOST IT.
FSH FSH FSH FSH
WAIT, THAT'S ...
FSH
!!
FWISH

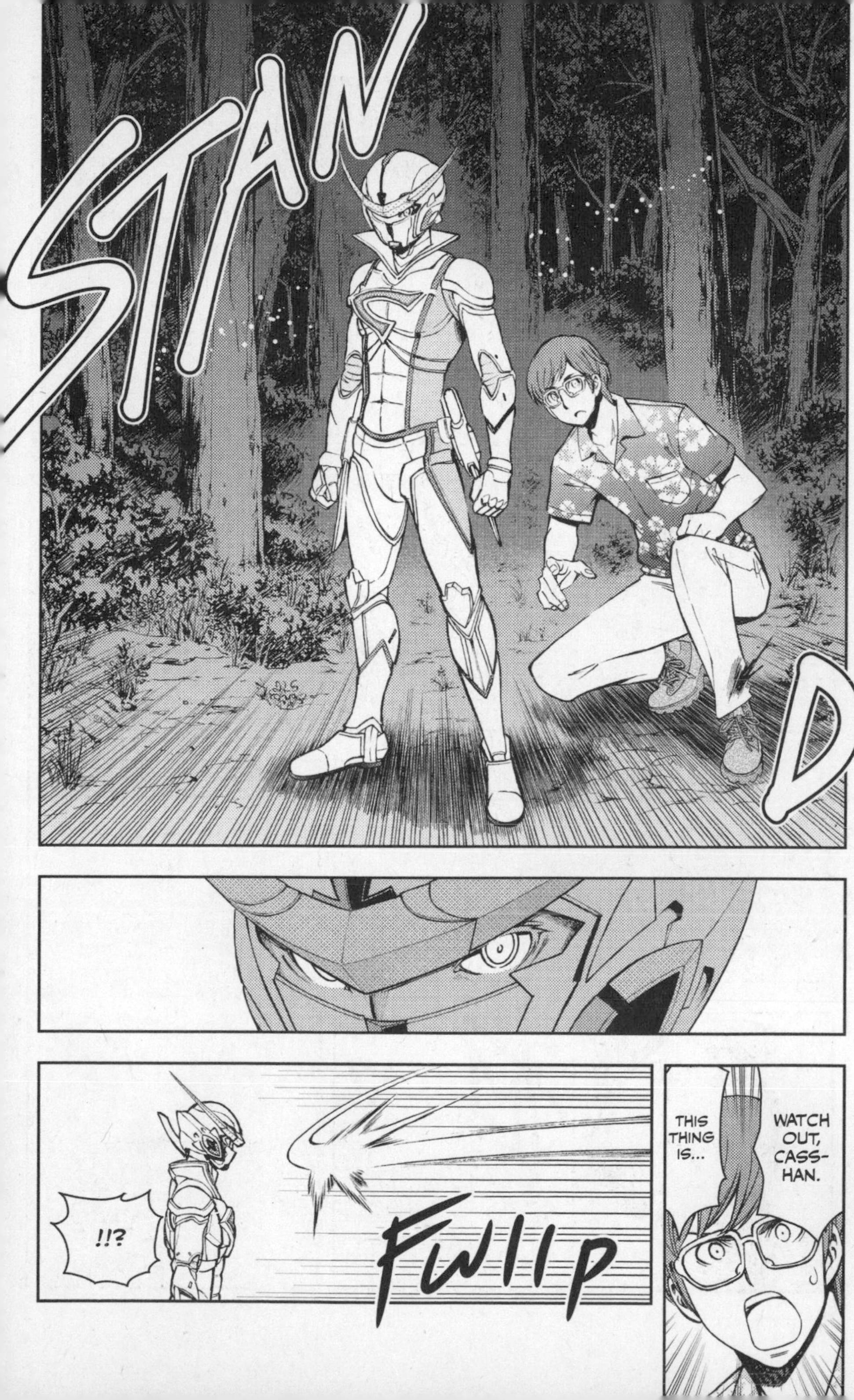
STAND
WATCH OUT, CASS-HAN.
THIS THING IS...
FWIIP
!!?

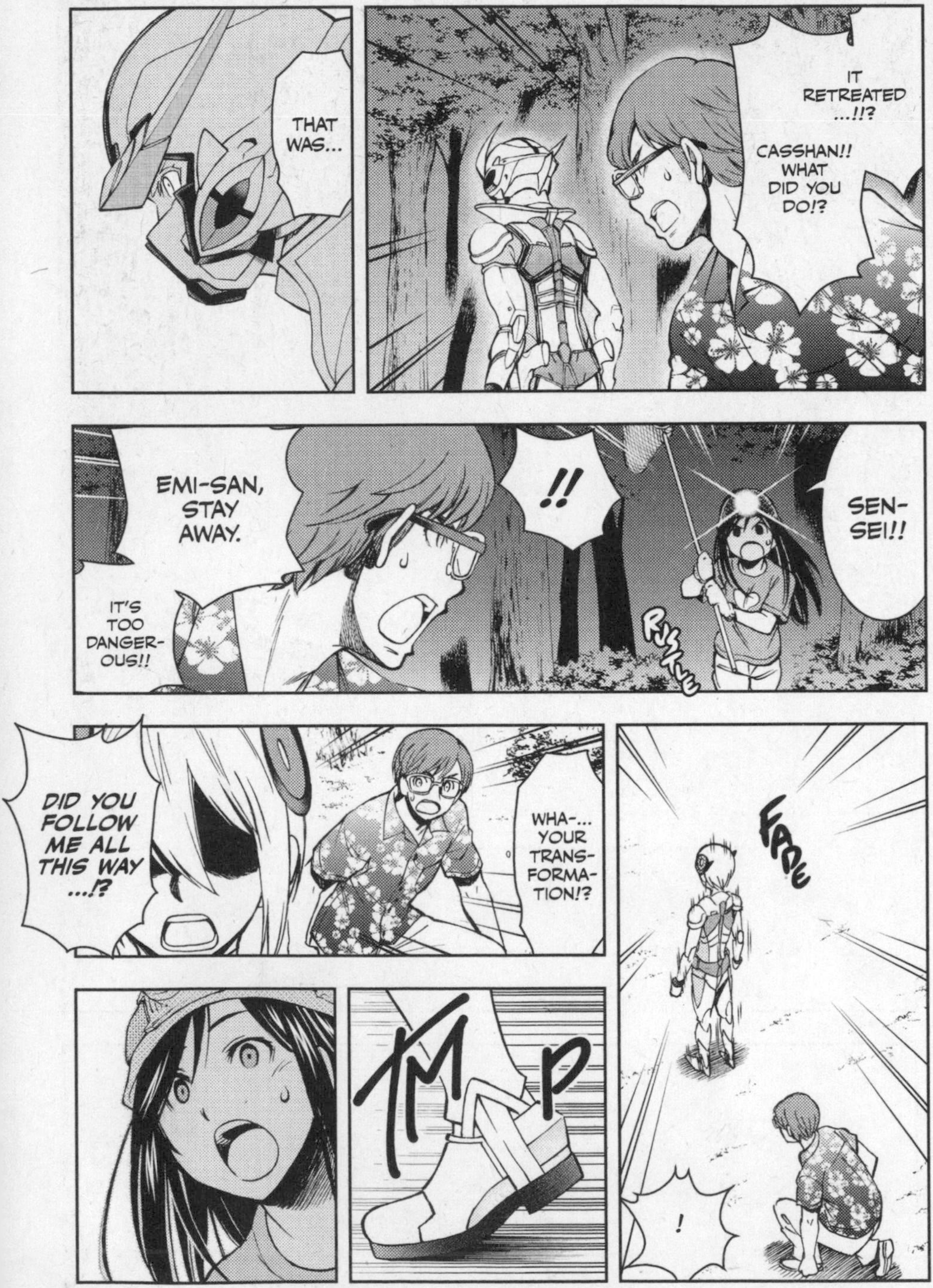
IT RETREATED ...!!?
CASSHAN!! WHAT DID YOU DO!?
THAT WAS...
SEN-SEI!!
RUSTLE
!!
EMI-SAN, STAY AWAY.
IT'S TOO DANGER-OUS!!
FADE
!
WHA-... YOUR TRANS-FORMA-TION!?
DID YOU FOLLOW ME ALL THIS WAY ...!?
TMP

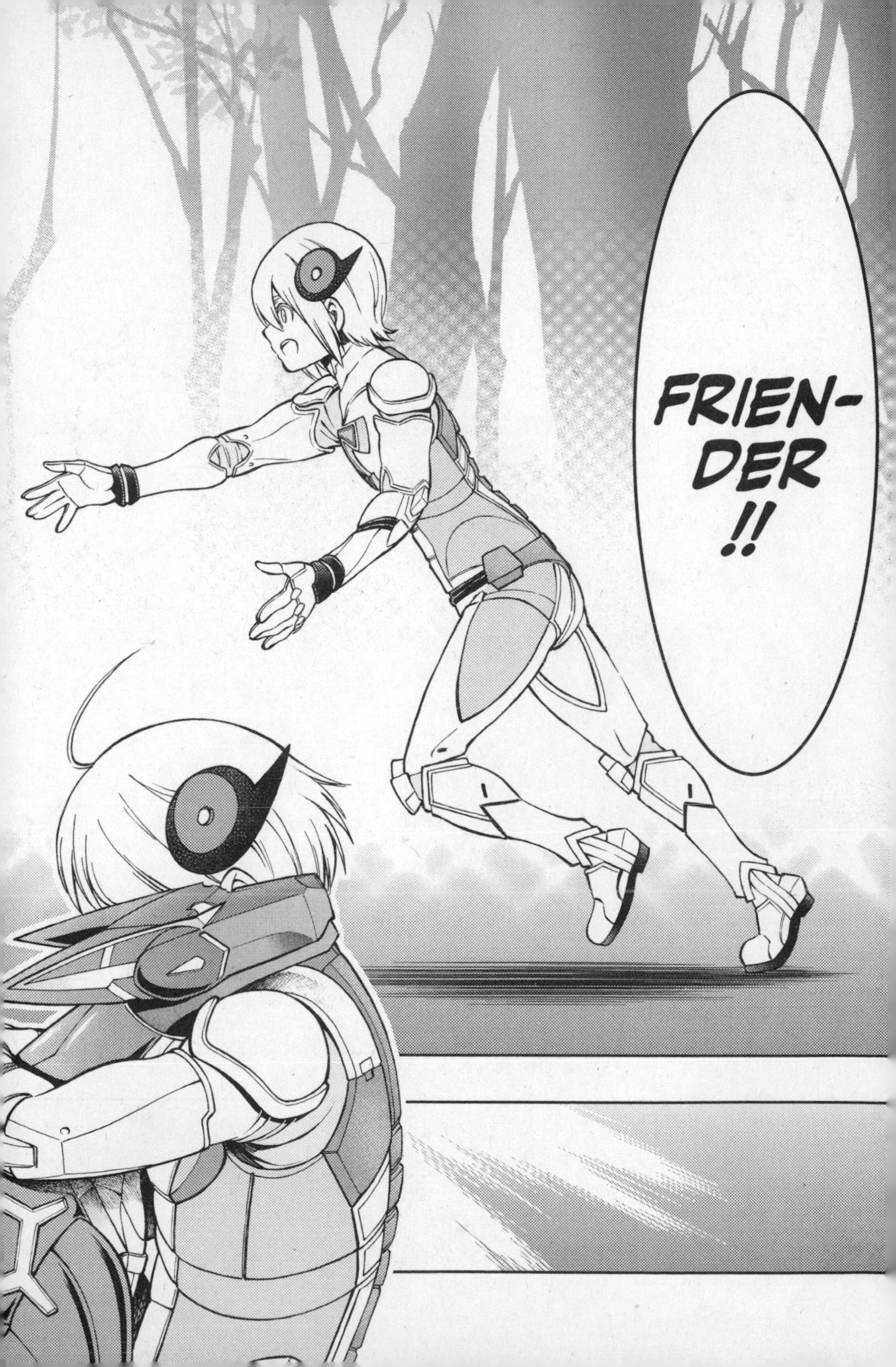
FRIEN-
DER
!!

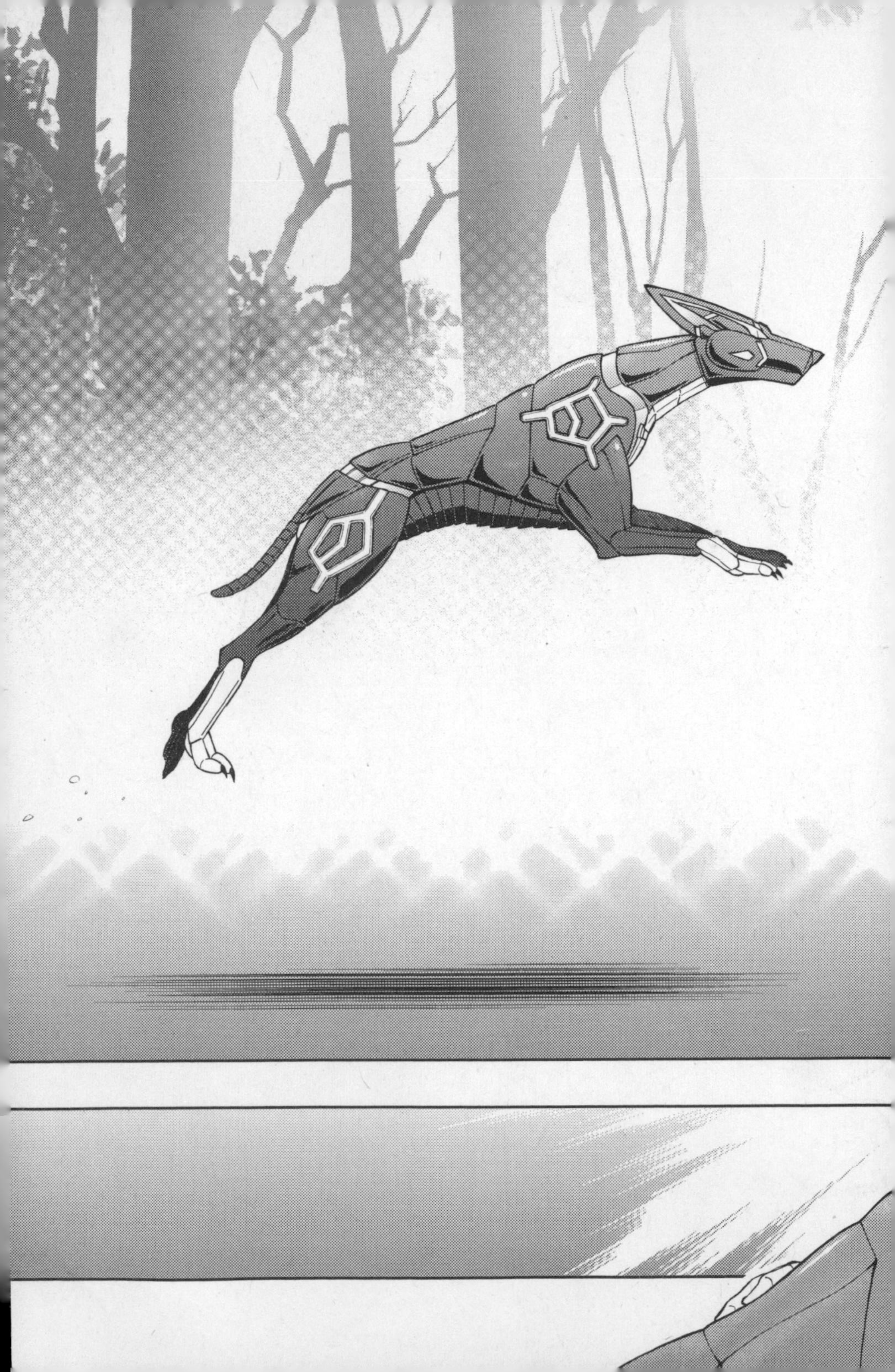

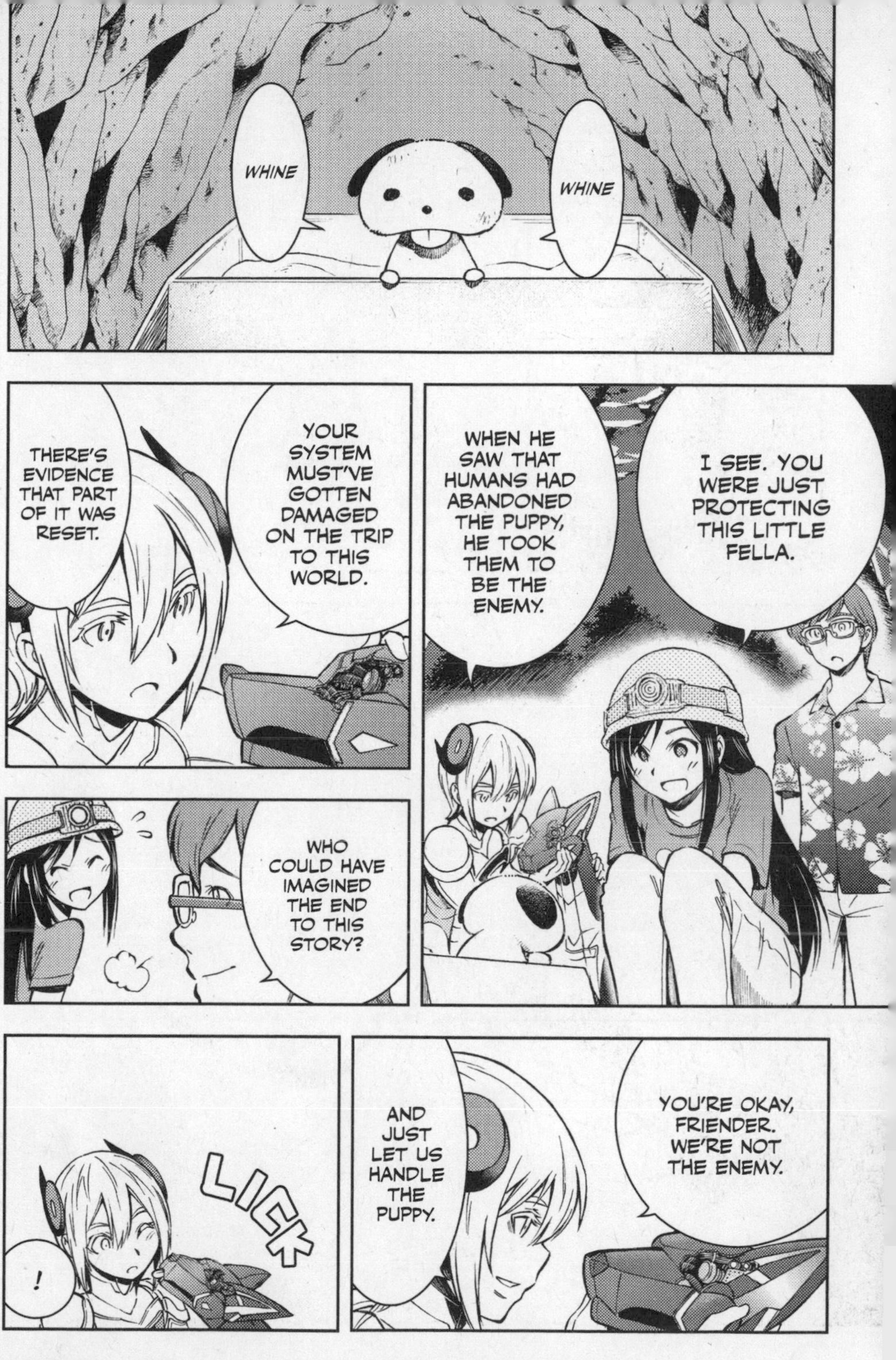
WHINE
WHINE
I SEE. YOU WERE JUST PROTECTING THIS LITTLE FELLA.
WHEN HE SAW THAT HUMANS HAD ABANDONED THE PUPPY, HE TOOK THEM TO BE THE ENEMY.
YOUR SYSTEM MUST'VE GOTTEN DAMAGED ON THE TRIP TO THIS WORLD.
THERE'S EVIDENCE THAT PART OF IT WAS RESET.
WHO COULD HAVE IMAGINED THE END TO THIS STORY?
YOU'RE OKAY, FRIENDER. WE'RE NOT THE ENEMY.
AND JUST LET US HANDLE THE PUPPY.
LICK
!

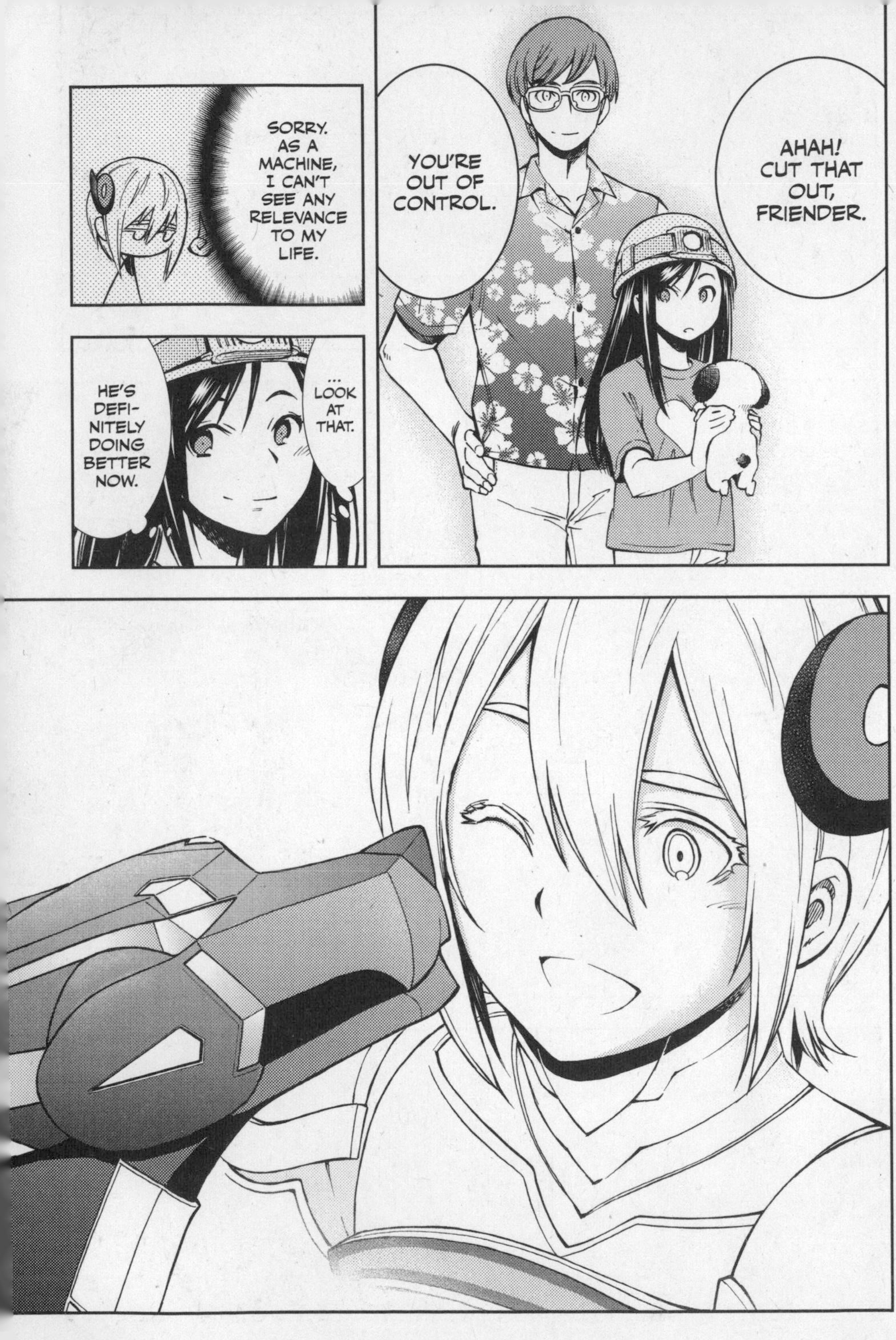
AHAH! CUT THAT OUT, FRIENDER.
YOU'RE OUT OF CONTROL.
SORRY. AS A MACHINE, I CAN'T SEE ANY RELEVANCE TO MY LIFE.
... LOOK AT THAT.
HE'S DEFI-NITELY DOING BETTER NOW.

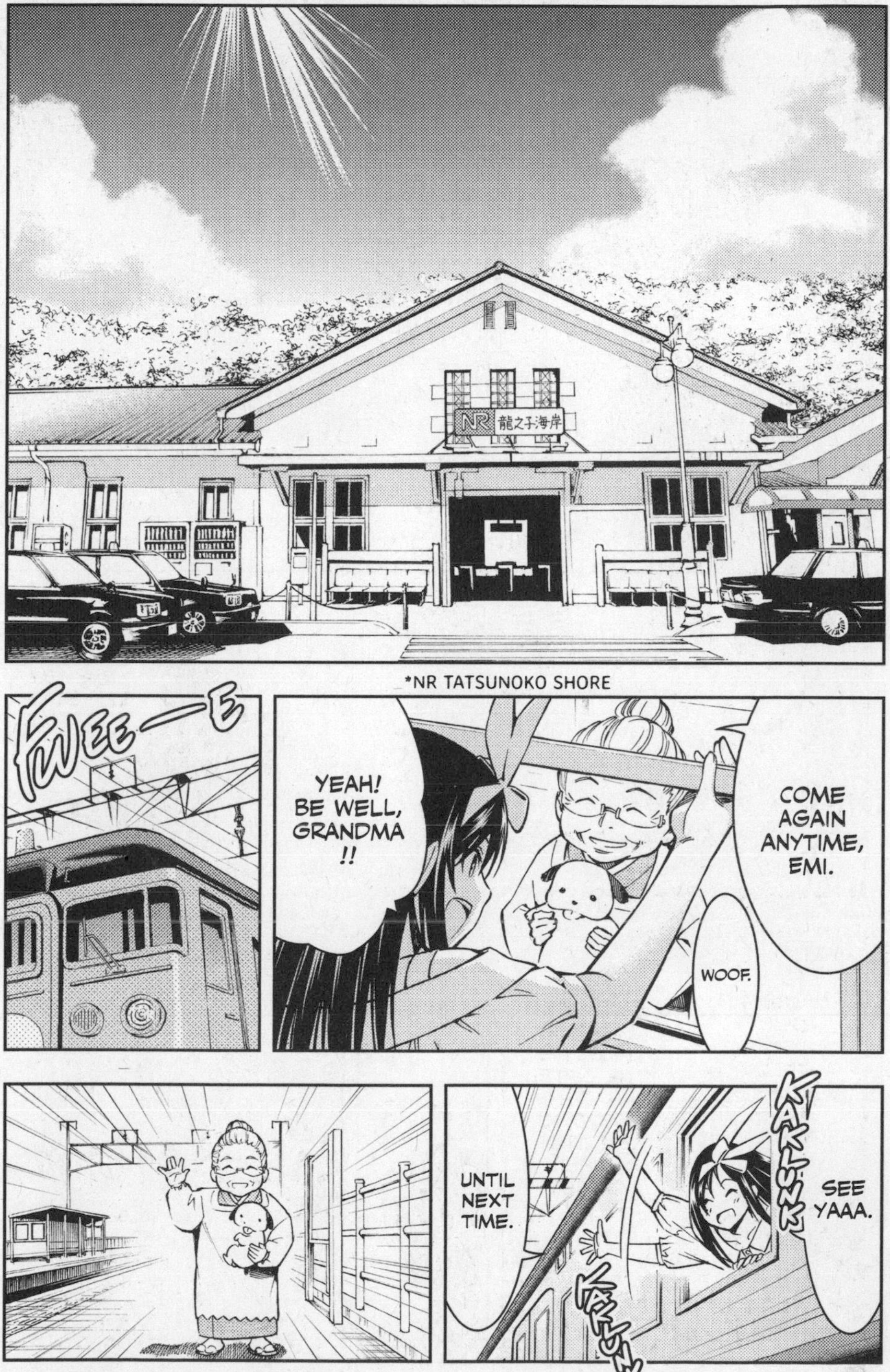
NR 龍之子海岸
*NR TATSUNOKO SHORE
COME AGAIN ANYTIME, EMI.
WOOF.
YEAH! BE WELL, GRANDMA!!
FWEE—E
SEE YAAA.
KAKLUNK
UNTIL NEXT TIME.
KAKLUNK

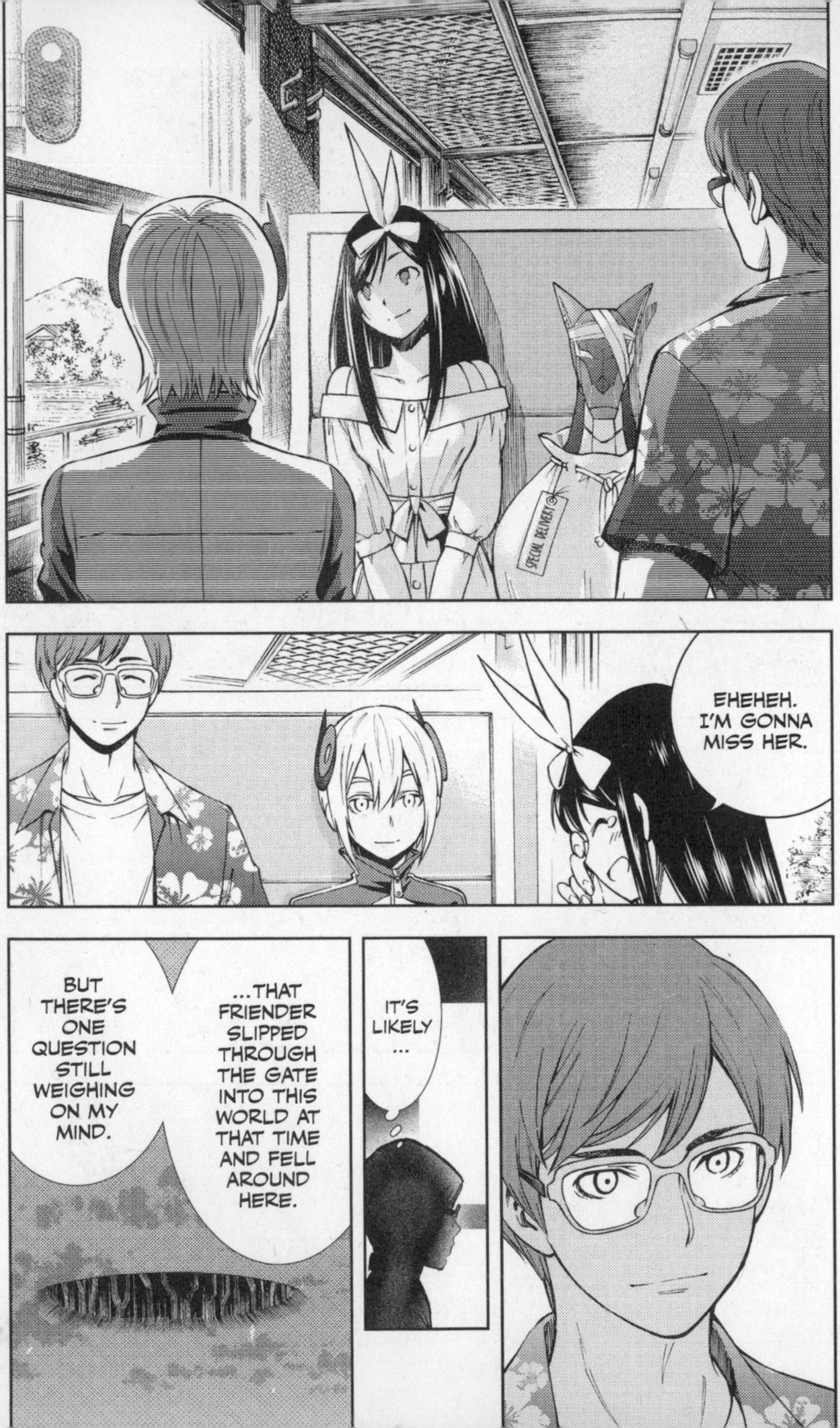
SPECIAL DELIVERY
EHEHEH. I'M GONNA MISS HER.
IT'S LIKELY ...
...THAT FRIENDER SLIPPED THROUGH THE GATE INTO THIS WORLD AT THAT TIME AND FELL AROUND HERE.
BUT THERE'S ONE QUESTION STILL WEIGHING ON MY MIND.

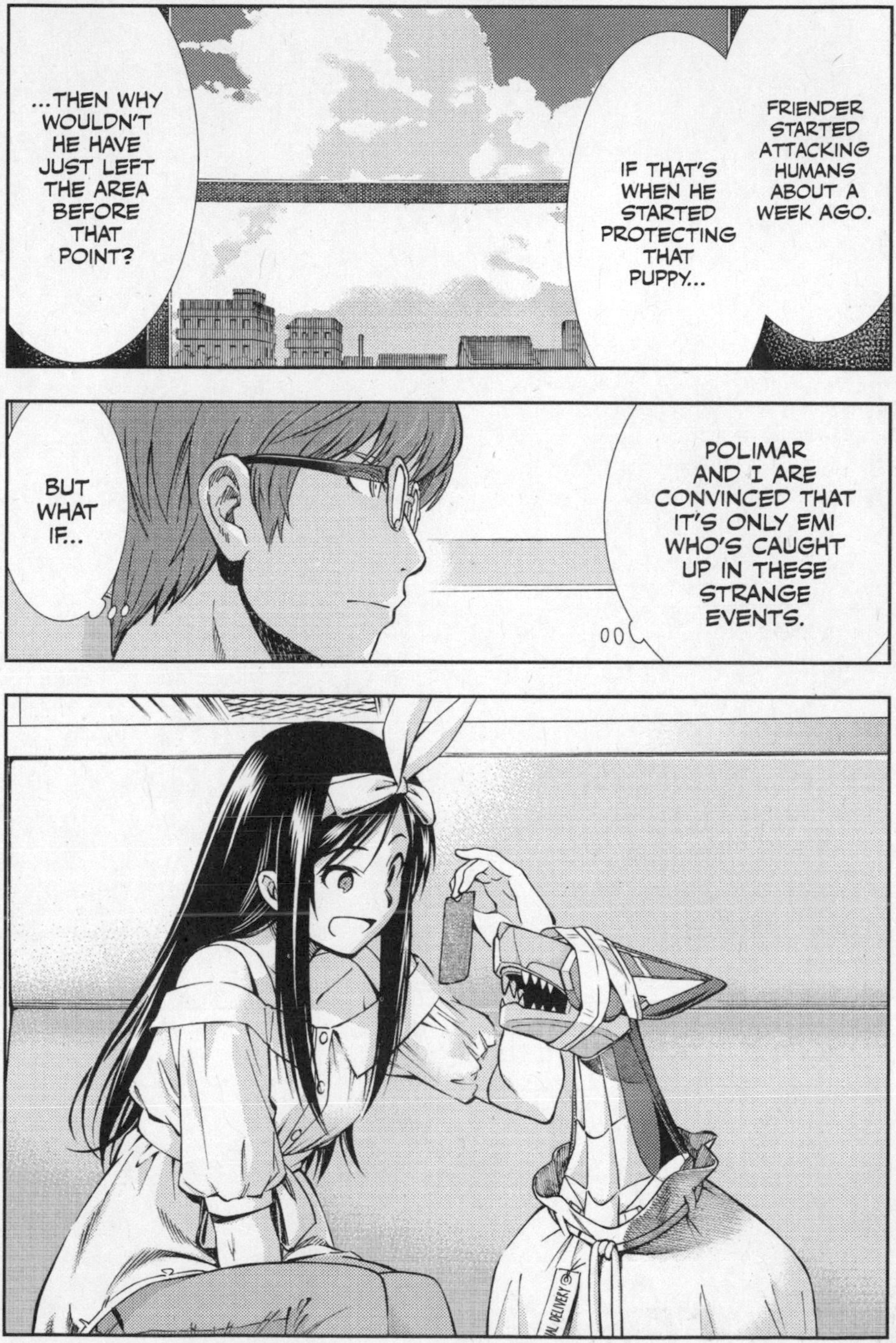
FRIENDER STARTED ATTACKING HUMANS ABOUT A WEEK AGO.
IF THAT'S WHEN HE STARTED PROTECTING THAT PUPPY...
...THEN WHY WOULDN'T HE HAVE JUST LEFT THE AREA BEFORE THAT POINT?
POLIMAR AND I ARE CONVINCED THAT IT'S ONLY EMI WHO'S CAUGHT UP IN THESE STRANGE EVENTS.
BUT WHAT IF...

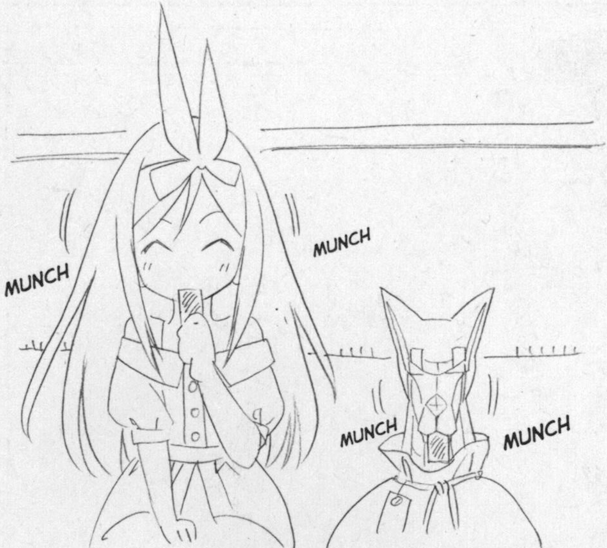
MUNCH
MUNCH
MUNCH
MUNCH

Infini-T Force
インフィニティフォース
ARC TO THE FUTURE

インフィニティフォース
Infini-T Force
ARC TO THE FUTURE

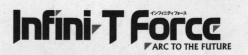

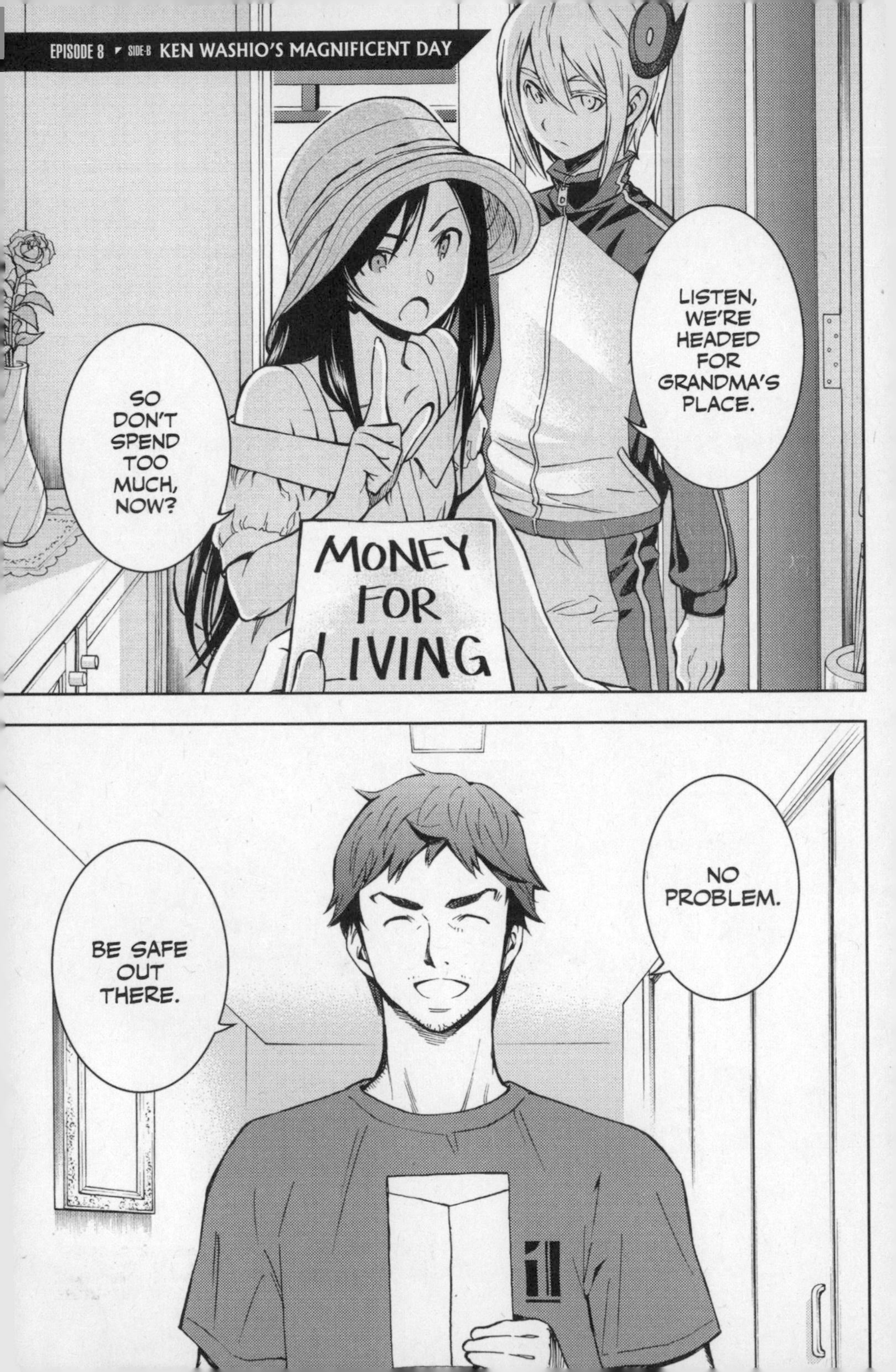
EPISODE 8 SIDE-B KEN WASHIO'S MAGNIFICENT DAY
LISTEN, WE'RE HEADED FOR GRANDMA'S PLACE.
SO DON'T SPEND TOO MUCH, NOW?
MONEY FOR LIVING
NO PROBLEM.
BE SAFE OUT THERE.

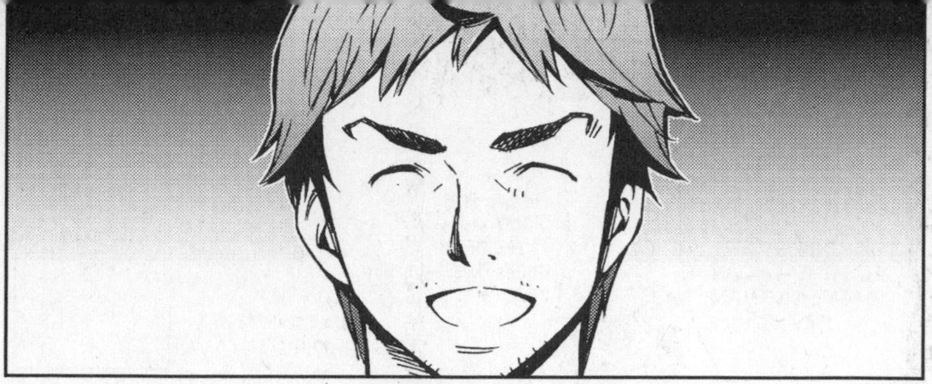

## EPISODE 8 ▸ SIDE-B Ken Washio's Magnificent Day

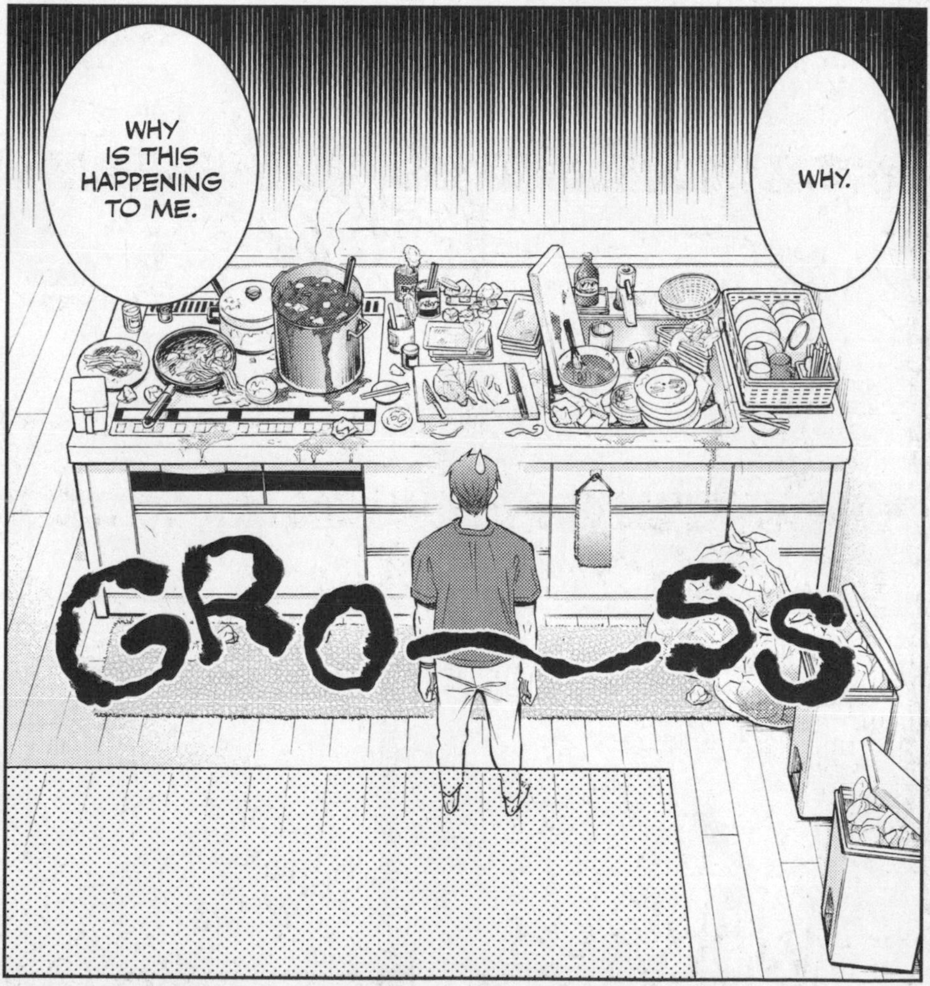
WHY.
WHY IS THIS HAPPENING TO ME.
GRO—SS

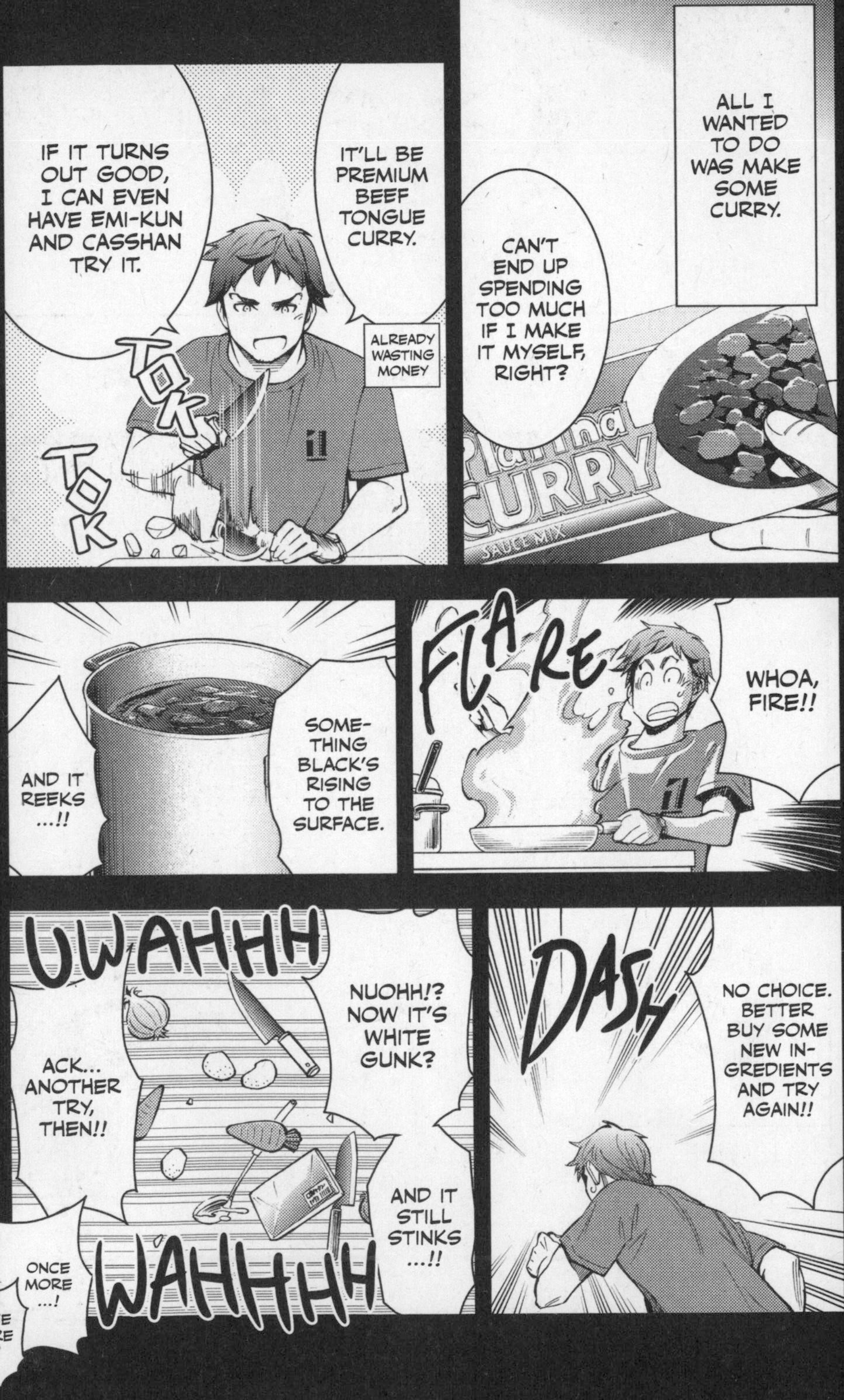
ALL I WANTED TO DO WAS MAKE SOME CURRY.
CAN'T END UP SPENDING TOO MUCH IF I MAKE IT MYSELF, RIGHT?
CURRY
SAUCE MIX
IT'LL BE PREMIUM BEEF TONGUE CURRY.
IF IT TURNS OUT GOOD, I CAN EVEN HAVE EMI-KUN AND CASSHAN TRY IT.
ALREADY WASTING MONEY
TOK
TOK
FLARE
WHOA, FIRE!!
SOME-THING BLACK'S RISING TO THE SURFACE.
AND IT REEKS ...!!
DASH
NO CHOICE. BETTER BUY SOME NEW IN-GREDIENTS AND TRY AGAIN!!
UWAHHH
NUOHH!? NOW IT'S WHITE GUNK?
ACK... ANOTHER TRY, THEN!!
AND IT STILL STINKS ...!!
WAHHHH
ONCE MORE ...!
ONCE MORE ...!

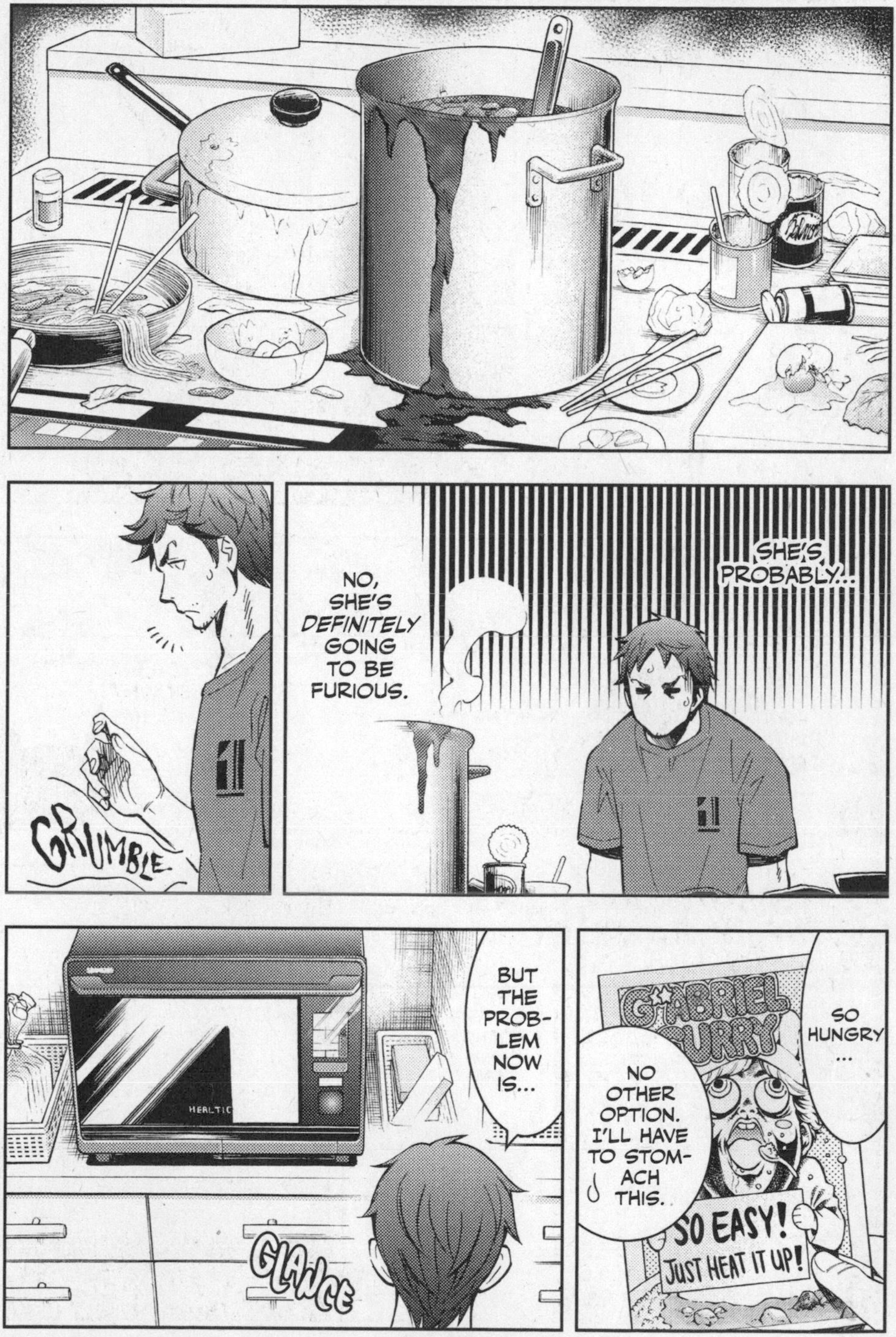
SHE'S PROBABLY...
NO, SHE'S DEFINITELY GOING TO BE FURIOUS.
GRUMBLE
SO HUNGRY ...
G★ABRIEL CURRY
NO OTHER OPTION. I'LL HAVE TO STOMACH THIS.
SO EASY!
JUST HEAT IT UP!
BUT THE PROBLEM NOW IS...
GLANCE

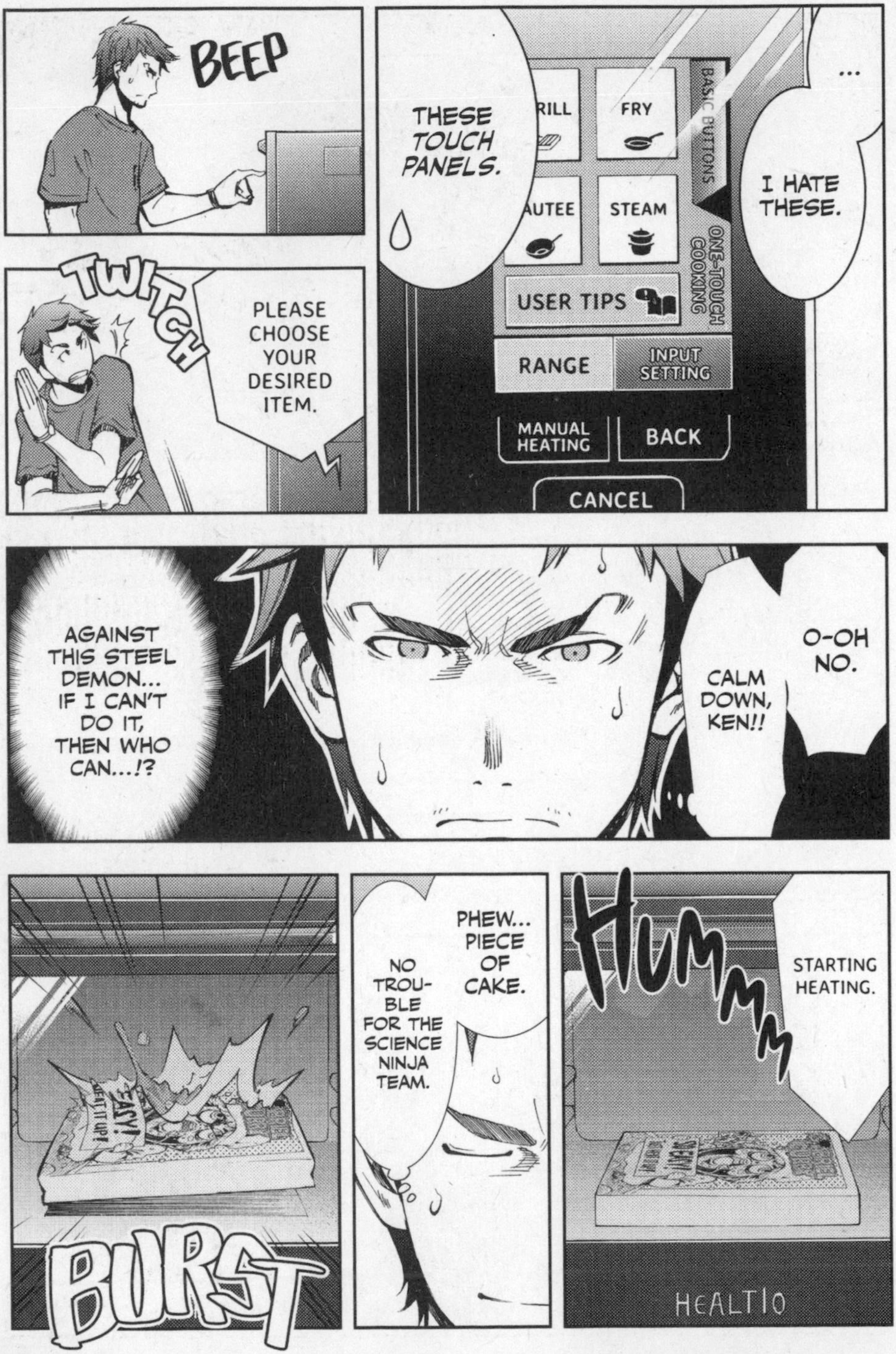
...
I HATE THESE.
THESE TOUCH PANELS.
BASIC BUTTONS
RILL
FRY
AUTEE
STEAM
ONE-TOUCH COOKING
USER TIPS
RANGE
INPUT SETTING
MANUAL HEATING
BACK
CANCEL
BEEP
TWITCH
PLEASE CHOOSE YOUR DESIRED ITEM.
O-OH NO.
CALM DOWN, KEN!!
AGAINST THIS STEEL DEMON... IF I CAN'T DO IT, THEN WHO CAN...!?
STARTING HEATING.
HUMMM
HEALTIO
PHEW... PIECE OF CAKE.
NO TROUBLE FOR THE SCIENCE NINJA TEAM.
BURST

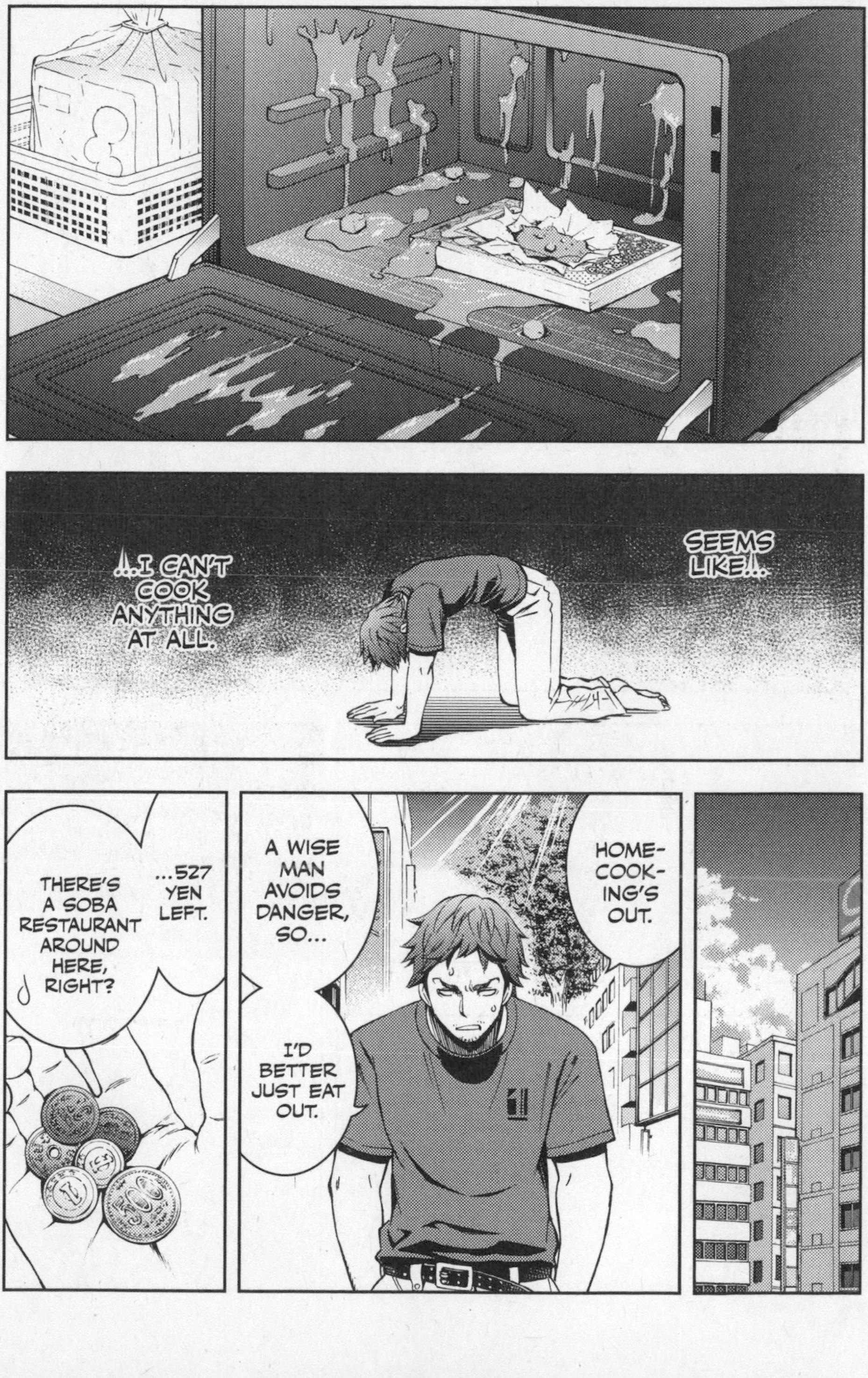
SEEMS LIKE...
...I CAN'T COOK ANYTHING AT ALL.
HOME-COOKING'S OUT.
A WISE MAN AVOIDS DANGER, SO...
I'D BETTER JUST EAT OUT.
...527 YEN LEFT.
THERE'S A SOBA RESTAURANT AROUND HERE, RIGHT?

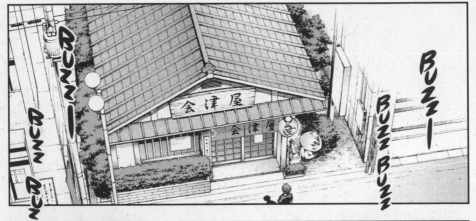

BUZZ!
BUZZ BUZZ
会津屋
会津屋
BUZZ!
BUZZ BUZZ
THE RESTAURANT IS TEMPORARILY CLOSED, AS THE OWNER IS PARTICIPATING IN A RACE.
WE ARE TERRIBLY SORRY FOR THE INCONVENIENCE.
-THE MANAGEMENT
WHAT THE?
A RACE...?
SO HOT...
LIKE A DESERT.
THE TOKYO DESERT...
DEATH...
DRIP
DRIP
DRIP
AM I GOING TO DIE HERE...?

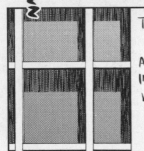

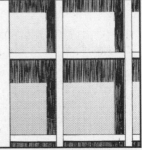

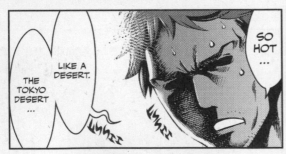

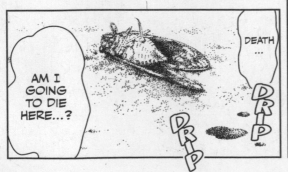

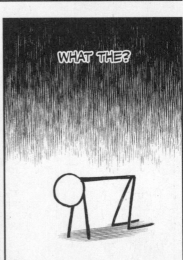

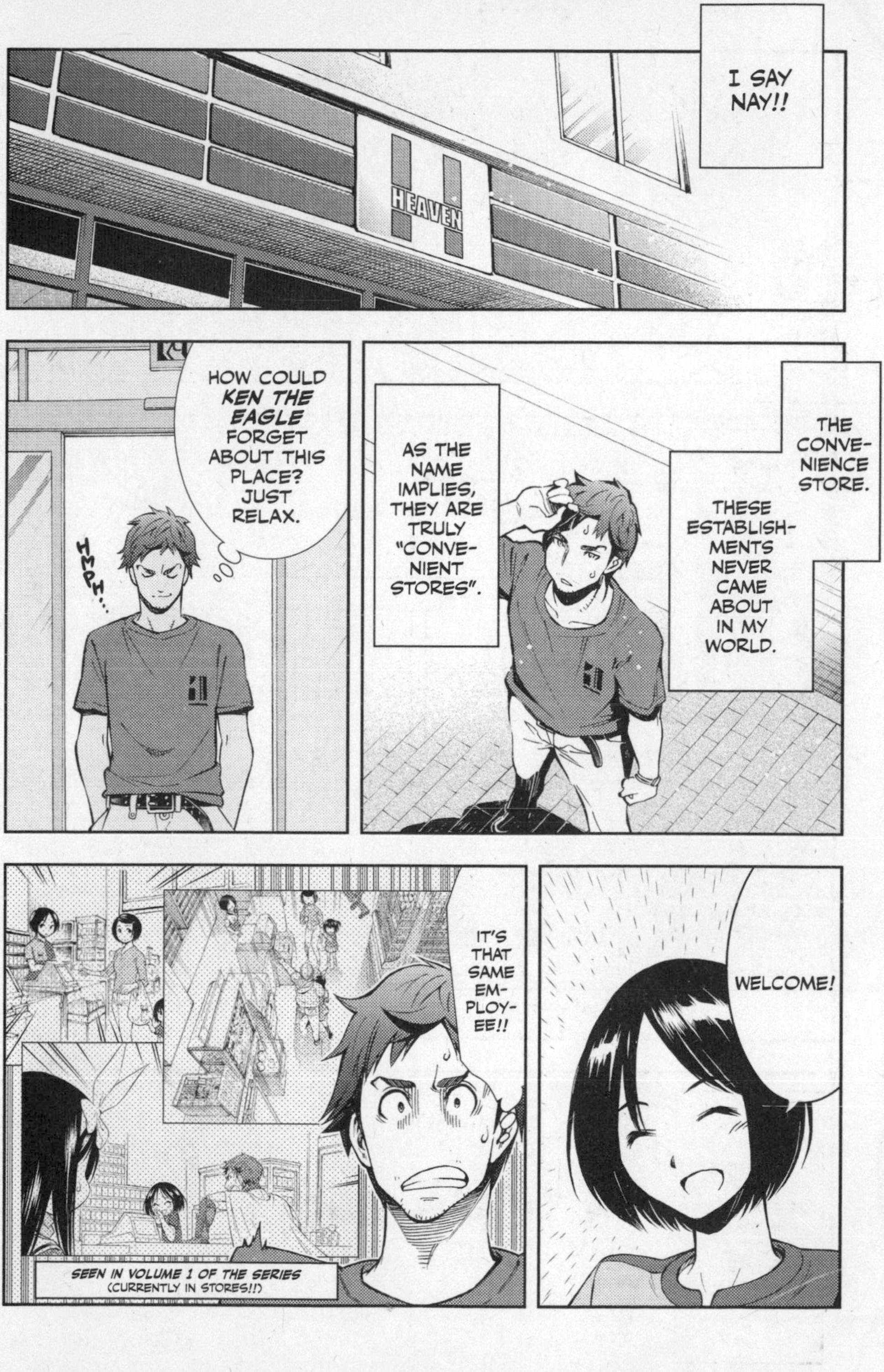

I SAY NAY!!
HEAVEN
THE CONVENIENCE STORE.
THESE ESTABLISHMENTS NEVER CAME ABOUT IN MY WORLD.
AS THE NAME IMPLIES, THEY ARE TRULY "CONVENIENT STORES".
HOW COULD KEN THE EAGLE FORGET ABOUT THIS PLACE? JUST RELAX.
HMPH...
WELCOME!
IT'S THAT SAME EMPLOYEE!!
SEEN IN VOLUME 1 OF THE SERIES (CURRENTLY IN STORES!!)

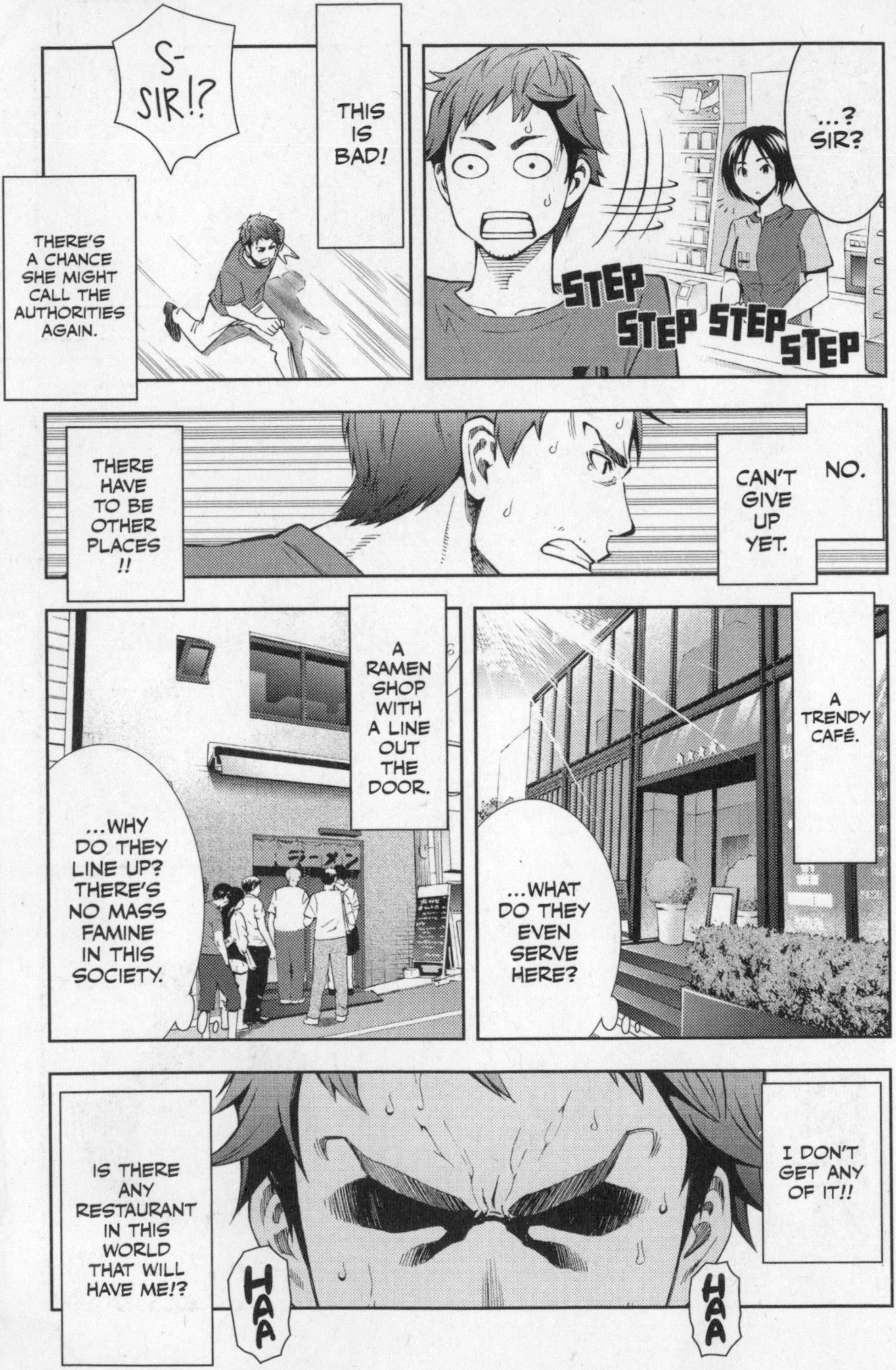
...? SIR?
STEP STEP STEP STEP
S-SIR!?
THIS IS BAD!
THERE'S A CHANCE SHE MIGHT CALL THE AUTHORITIES AGAIN.
NO.
CAN'T GIVE UP YET.
THERE HAVE TO BE OTHER PLACES!!
A TRENDY CAFÉ.
...WHAT DO THEY EVEN SERVE HERE?
A RAMEN SHOP WITH A LINE OUT THE DOOR.
...WHY DO THEY LINE UP? THERE'S NO MASS FAMINE IN THIS SOCIETY.
I DON'T GET ANY OF IT!!
HAA
IS THERE ANY RESTAURANT IN THIS WORLD THAT WILL HAVE ME!?
HAA

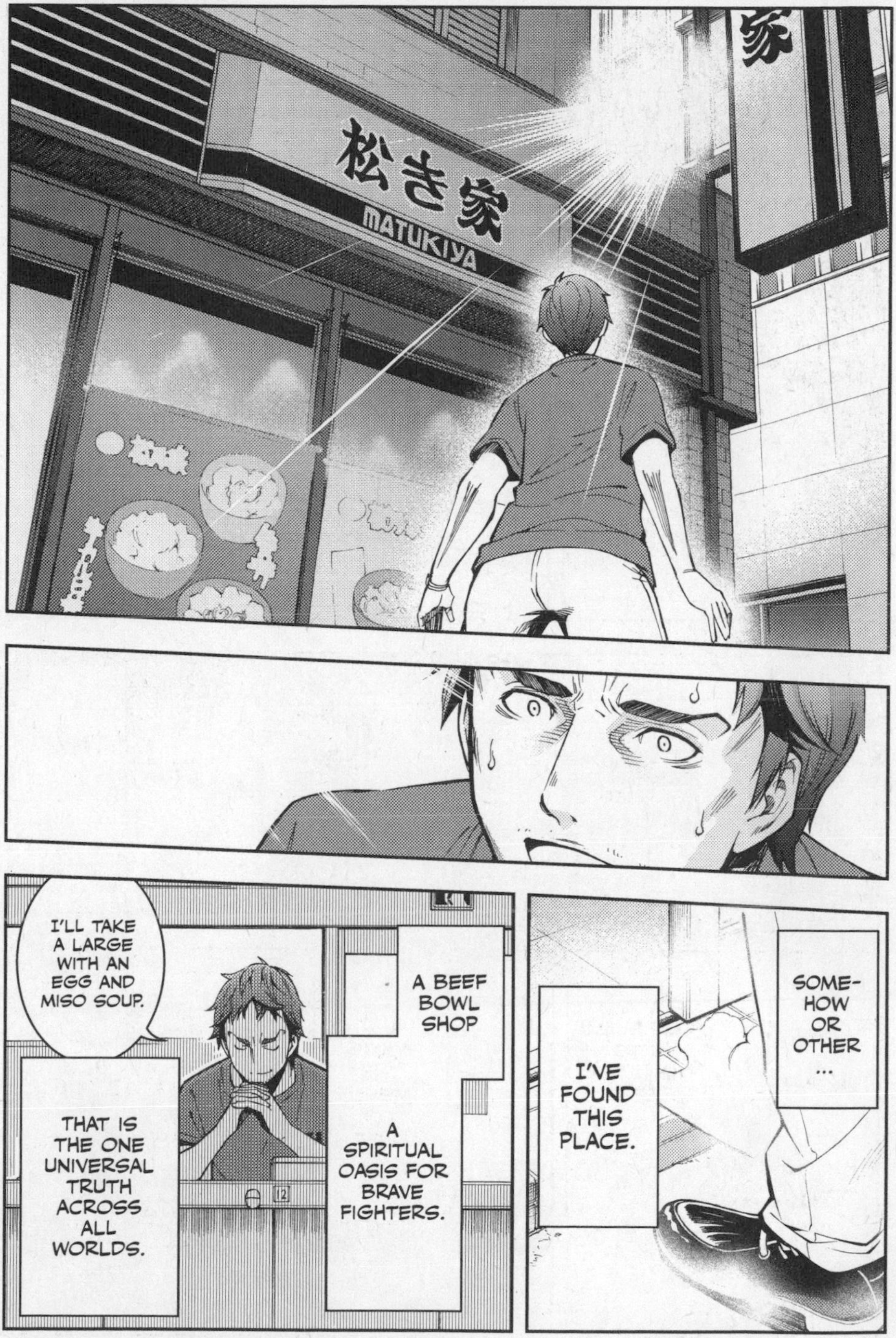
松き家
MATUKIYA
SOME-HOW OR OTHER ...
I'VE FOUND THIS PLACE.
A BEEF BOWL SHOP
A SPIRITUAL OASIS FOR BRAVE FIGHTERS.
I'LL TAKE A LARGE WITH AN EGG AND MISO SOUP.
THAT IS THE ONE UNIVERSAL TRUTH ACROSS ALL WORLDS.

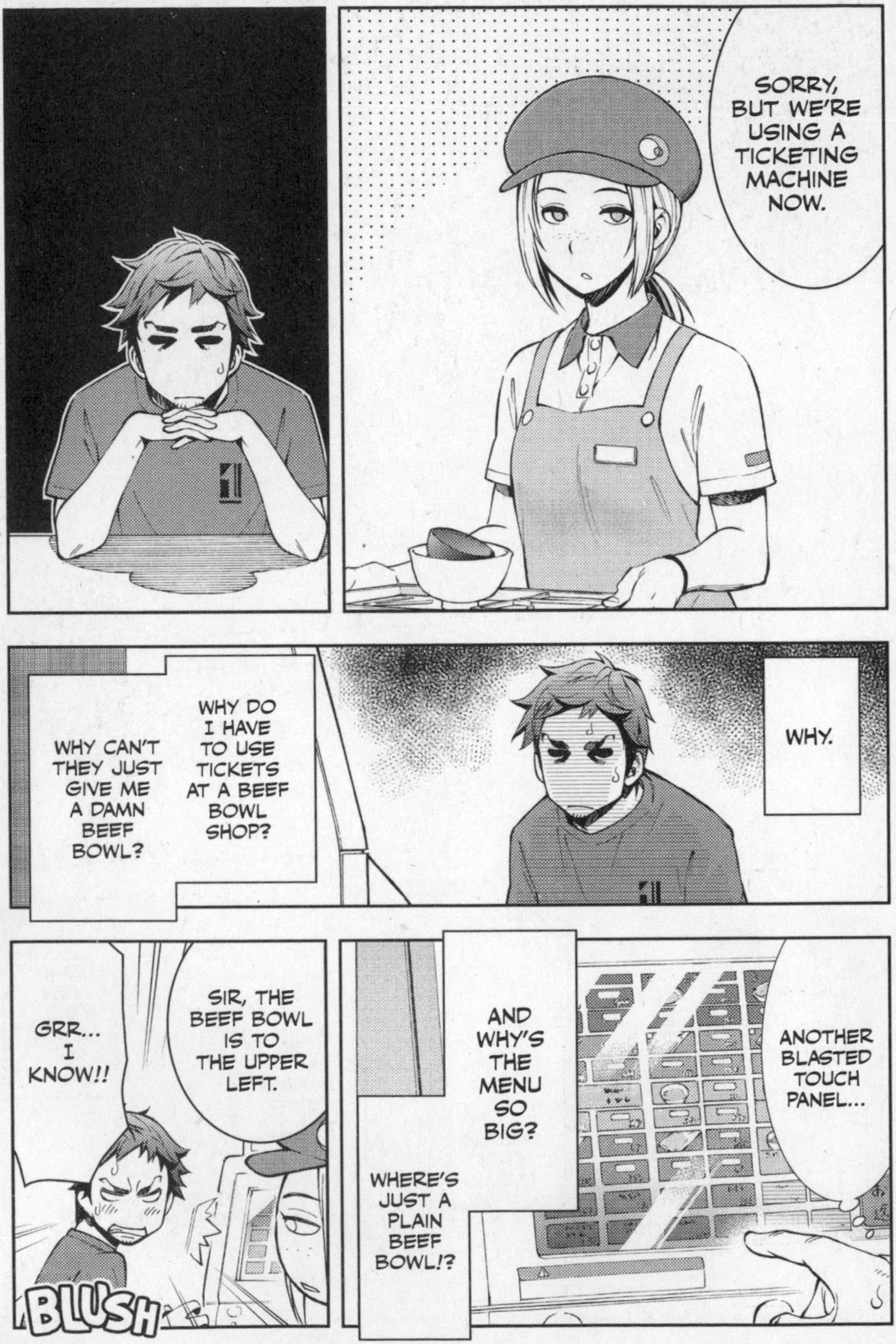
SORRY, BUT WE'RE USING A TICKETING MACHINE NOW.
WHY.
WHY DO I HAVE TO USE TICKETS AT A BEEF BOWL SHOP?
WHY CAN'T THEY JUST GIVE ME A DAMN BEEF BOWL?
ANOTHER BLASTED TOUCH PANEL...
AND WHY'S THE MENU SO BIG?
WHERE'S JUST A PLAIN BEEF BOWL!?
SIR, THE BEEF BOWL IS TO THE UPPER LEFT.
GRR... I KNOW!!
BLUSH

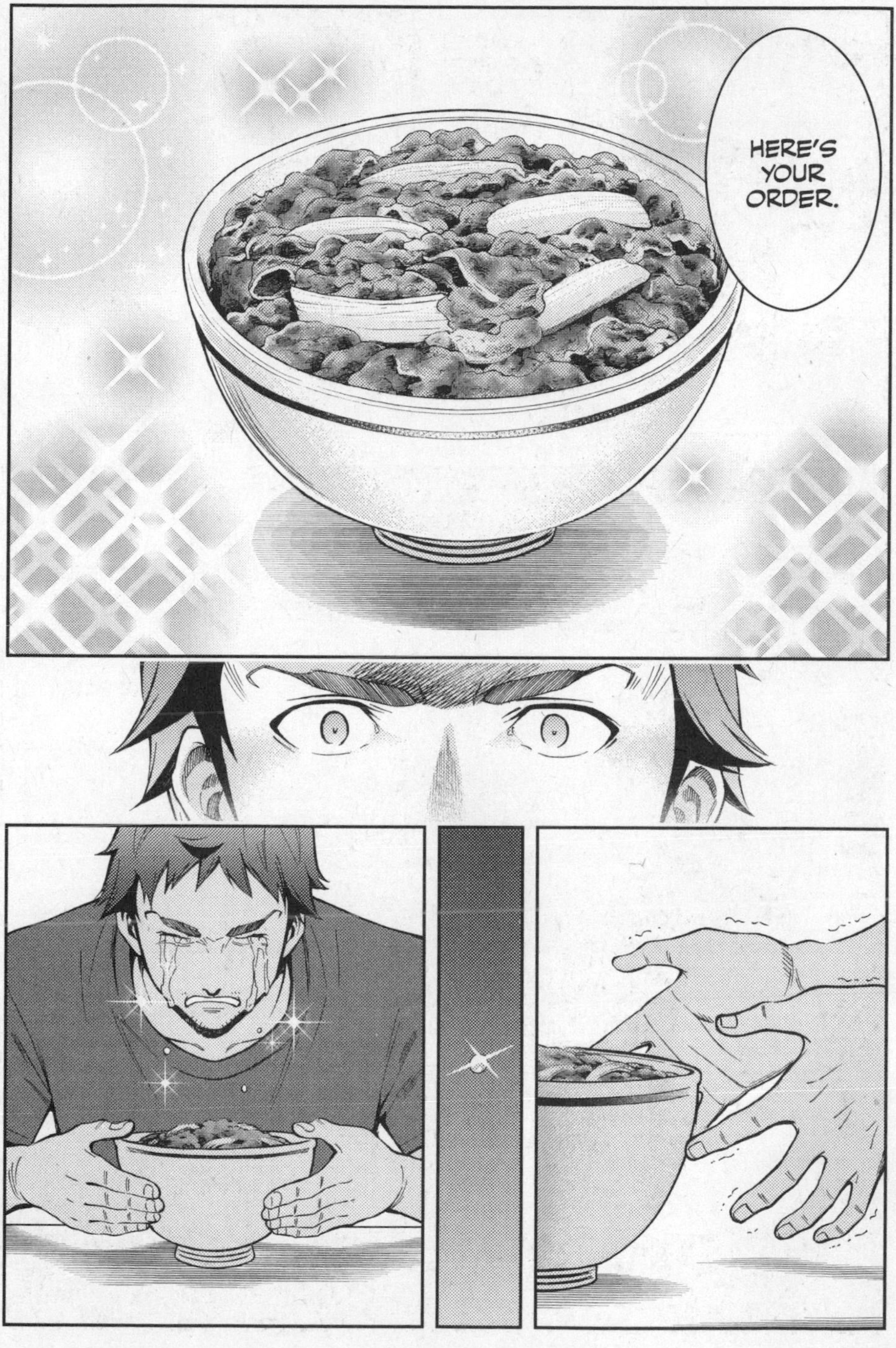
HERE'S YOUR ORDER.

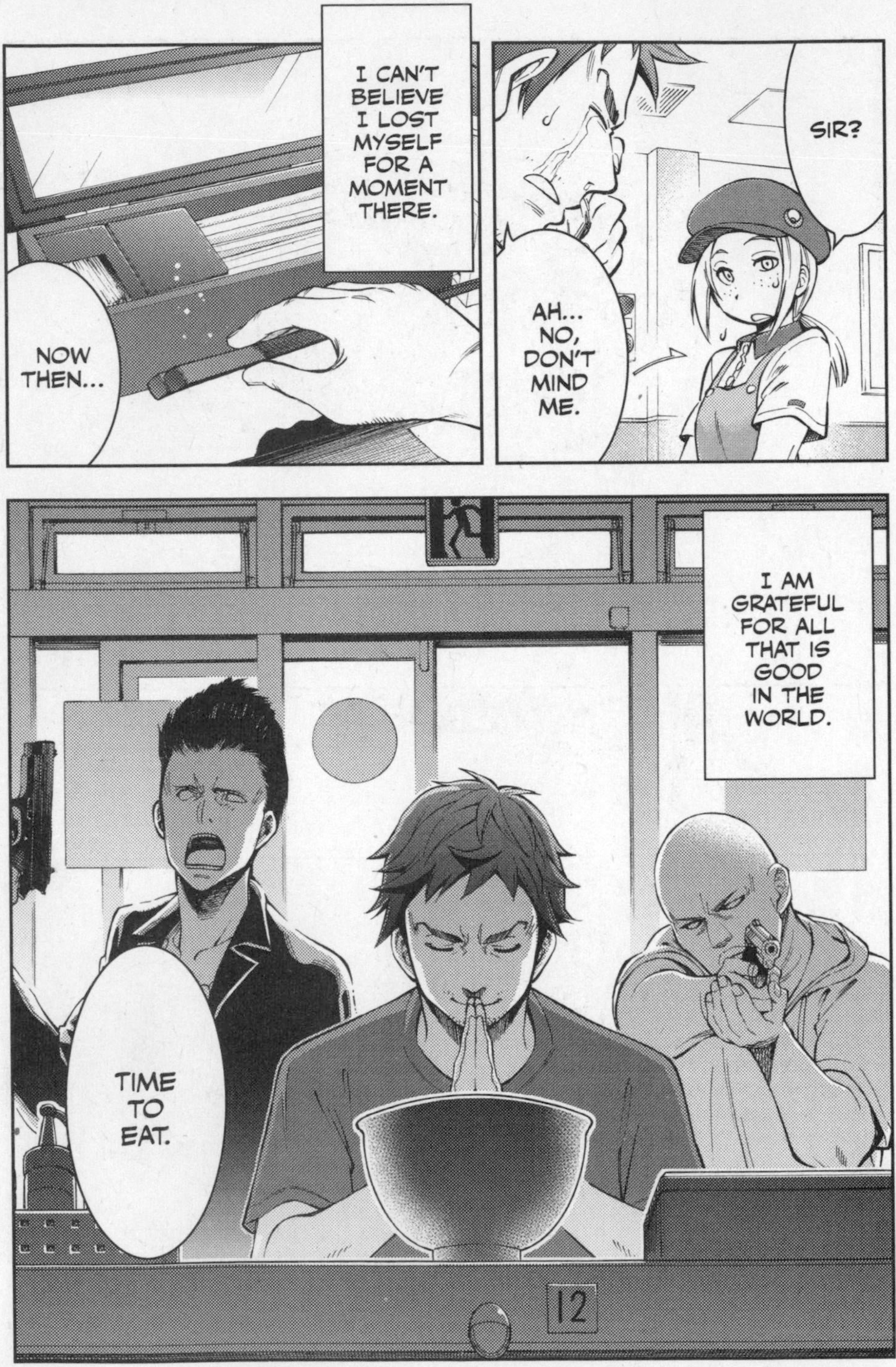
SIR?
AH... NO, DON'T MIND ME.
I CAN'T BELIEVE I LOST MYSELF FOR A MOMENT THERE.
NOW THEN...
I AM GRATEFUL FOR ALL THAT IS GOOD IN THE WORLD.
TIME TO EAT.
12

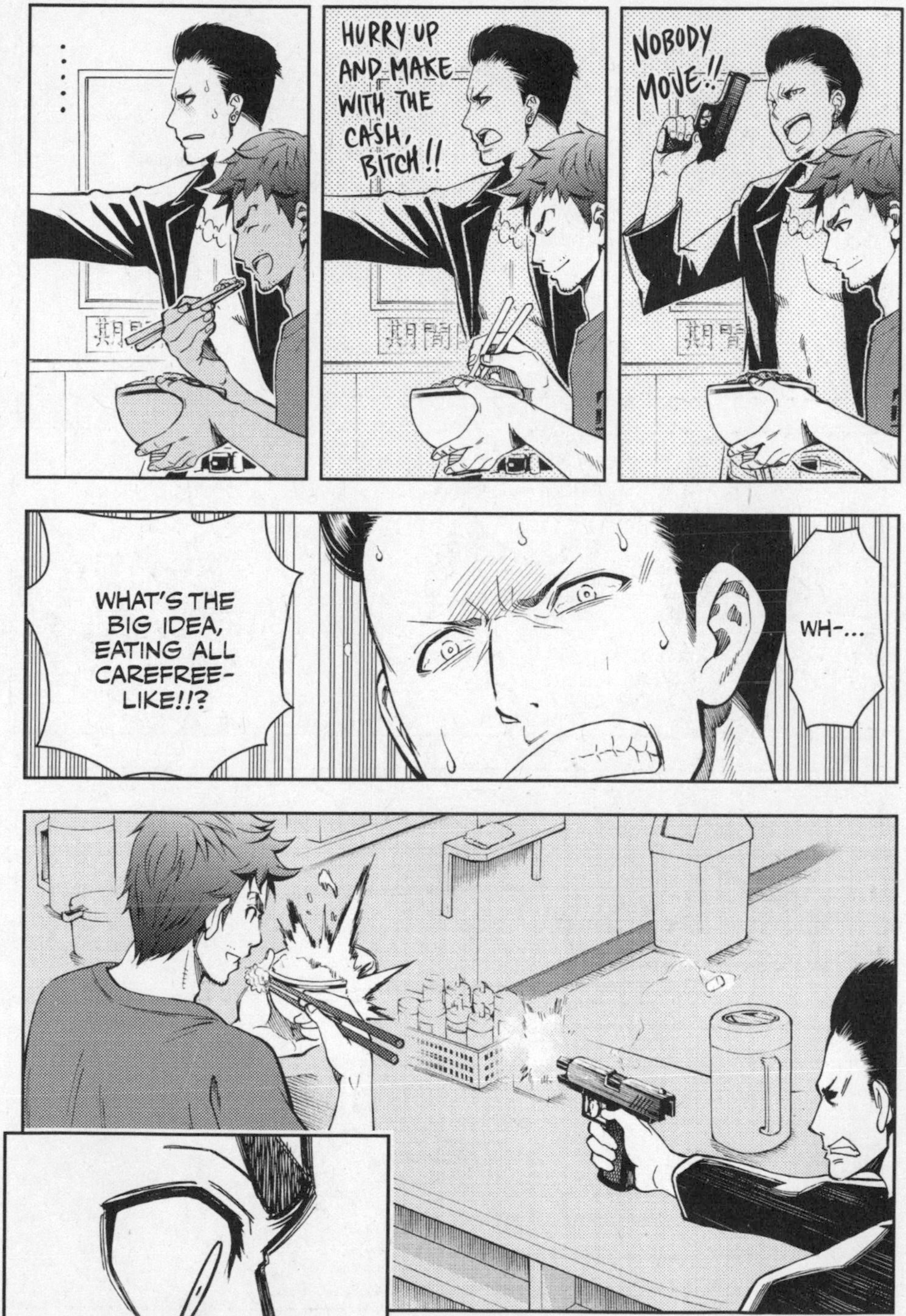
NOBODY MOVE!!
HURRY UP AND MAKE WITH THE CASH, BITCH!!
.....
WH-...
WHAT'S THE BIG IDEA, EATING ALL CAREFREE-LIKE!!?

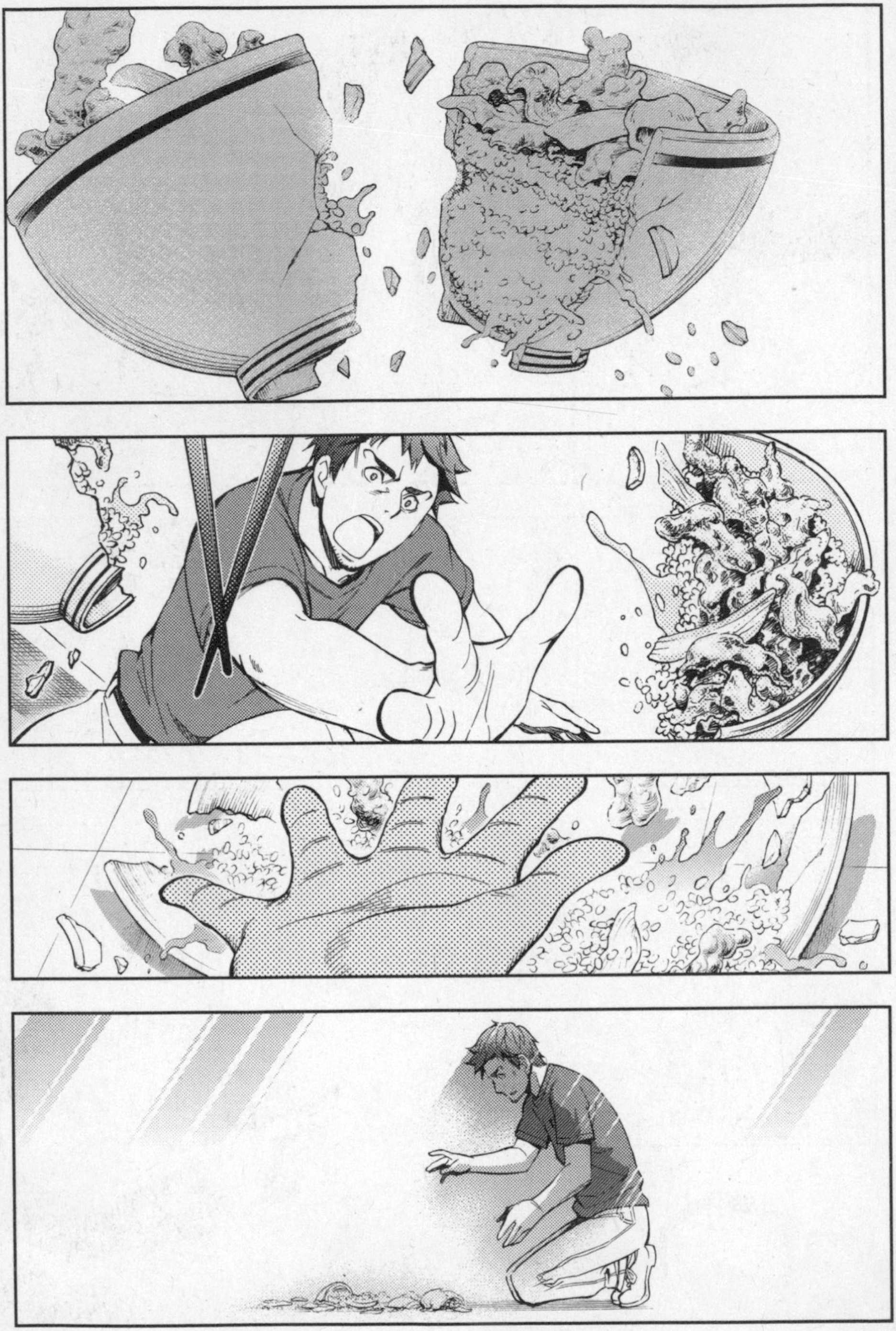

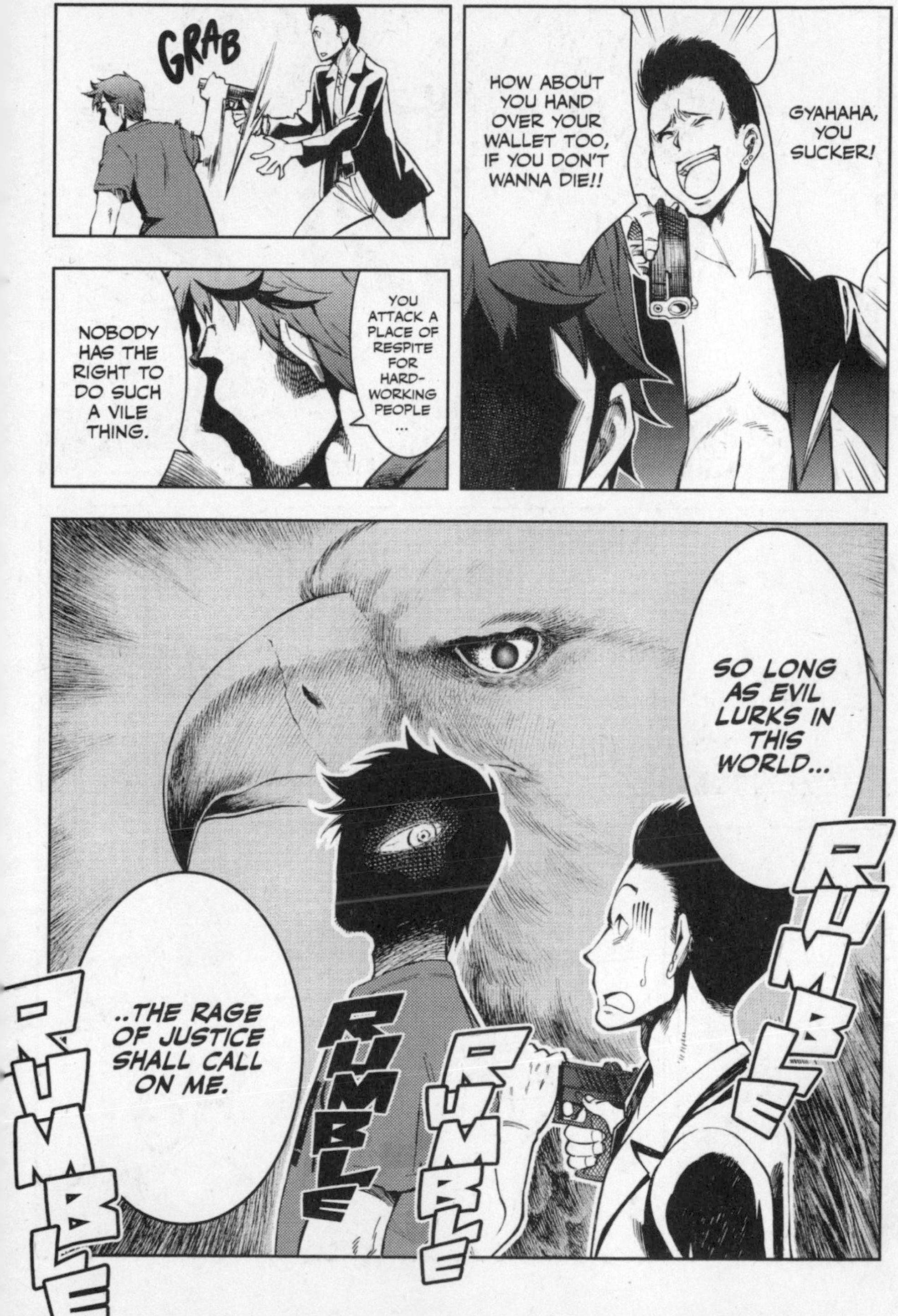
GYAHAHA, YOU SUCKER!
HOW ABOUT YOU HAND OVER YOUR WALLET TOO, IF YOU DON'T WANNA DIE!!
GRAB
YOU ATTACK A PLACE OF RESPITE FOR HARD-WORKING PEOPLE ...
NOBODY HAS THE RIGHT TO DO SUCH A VILE THING.
SO LONG AS EVIL LURKS IN THIS WORLD...
RUMBLE
RUMBLE
RUMBLE
..THE RAGE OF JUSTICE SHALL CALL ON ME.
RUMBLE

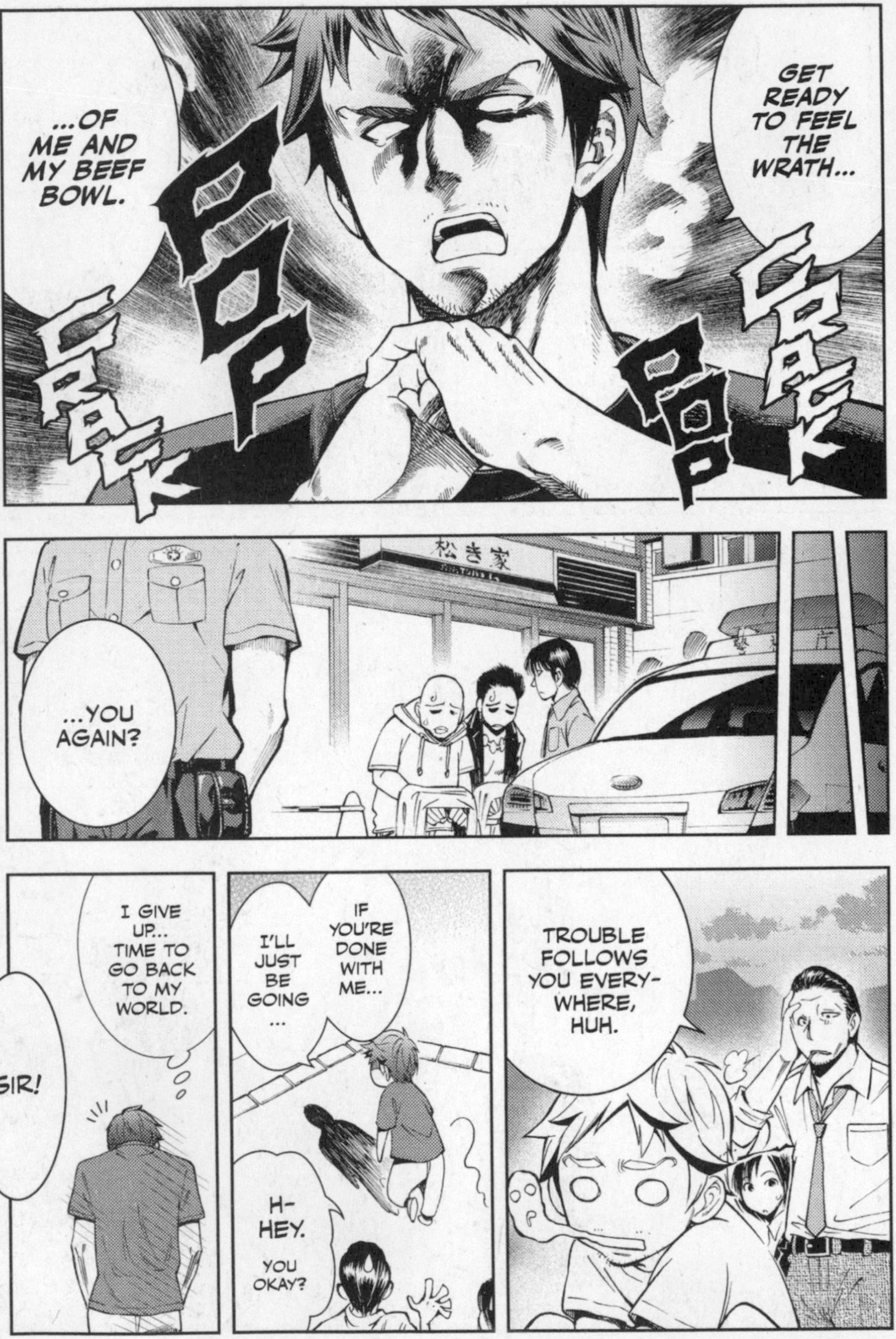
GET READY TO FEEL THE WRATH...
...OF ME AND MY BEEF BOWL.
CRACK
POP
POP
CRACK
松き家
...YOU AGAIN?
TROUBLE FOLLOWS YOU EVERY-WHERE, HUH.
IF YOU'RE DONE WITH ME...
I'LL JUST BE GOING ...
H-HEY.
YOU OKAY?
I GIVE UP... TIME TO GO BACK TO MY WORLD.
SIR!

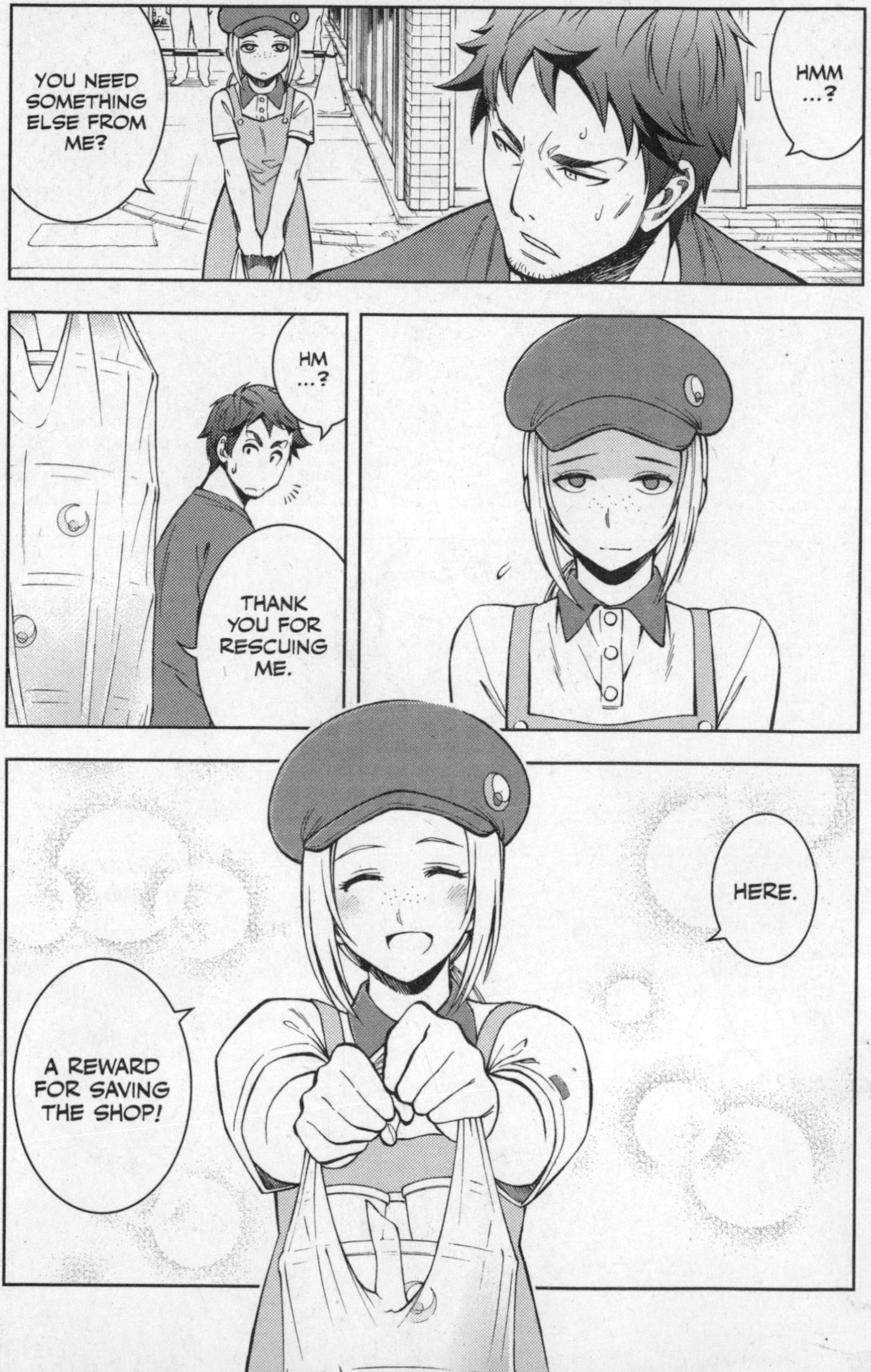
HMM ...?
YOU NEED SOMETHING ELSE FROM ME?
HM ...?
THANK YOU FOR RESCUING ME.
HERE.
A REWARD FOR SAVING THE SHOP!

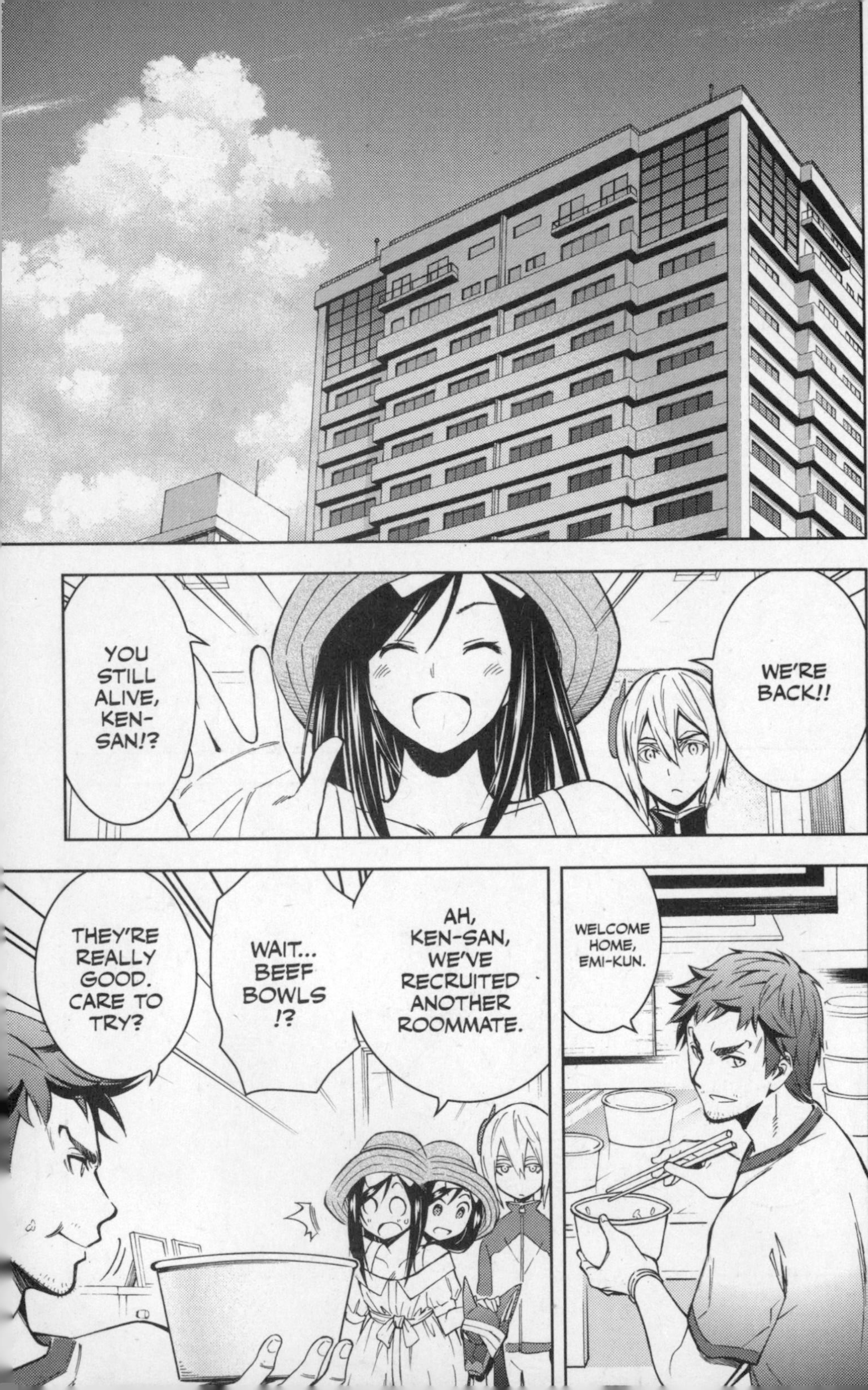
WE'RE BACK!!
YOU STILL ALIVE, KEN-SAN!?
WELCOME HOME, EMI-KUN.
AH, KEN-SAN, WE'VE RECRUITED ANOTHER ROOMMATE.
WAIT... BEEF BOWLS!?
THEY'RE REALLY GOOD. CARE TO TRY?

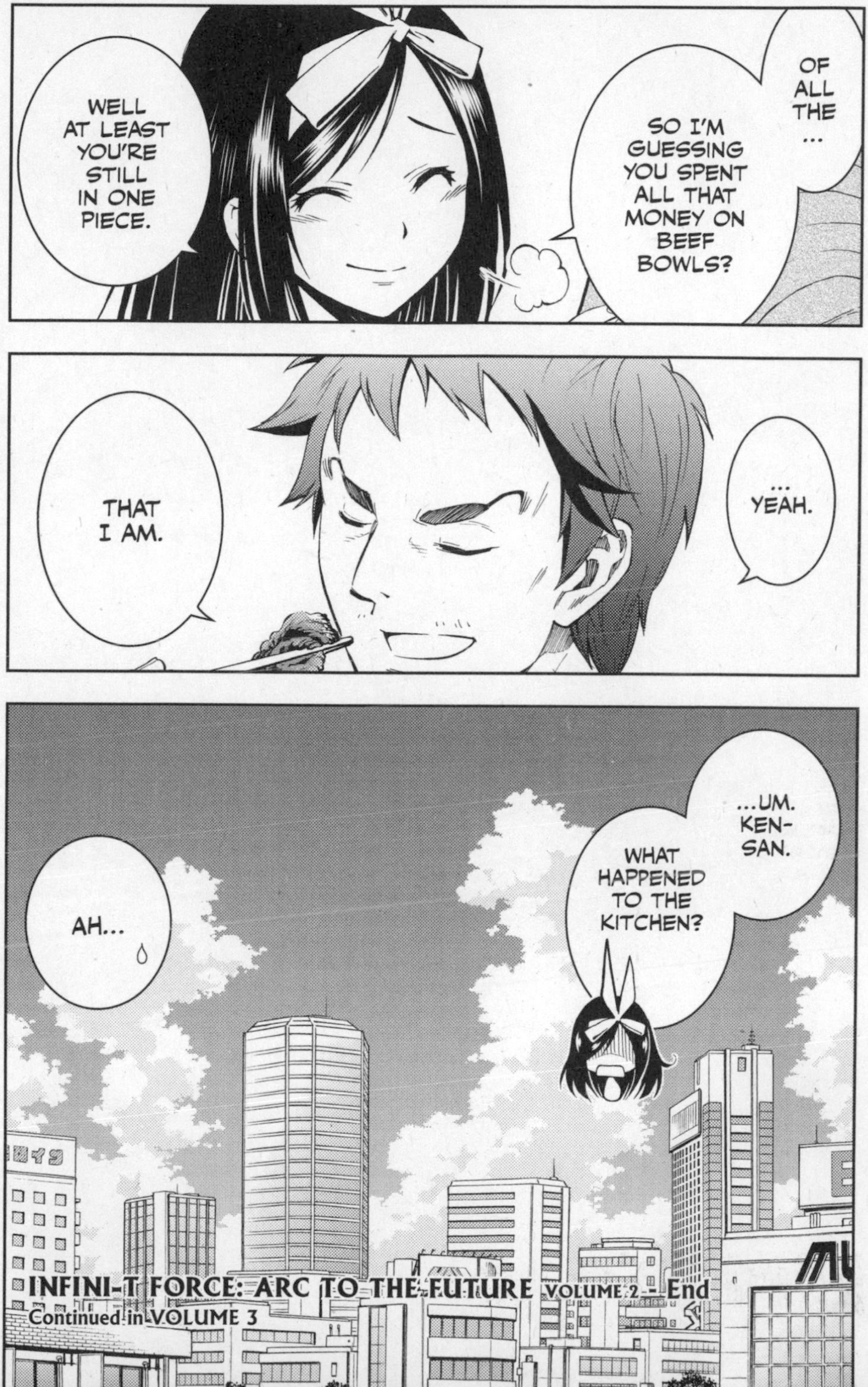
OF ALL THE ...
SO I'M GUESSING YOU SPENT ALL THAT MONEY ON BEEF BOWLS?
WELL AT LEAST YOU'RE STILL IN ONE PIECE.
... YEAH.
THAT I AM.
...UM. KEN-SAN.
WHAT HAPPENED TO THE KITCHEN?
AH...
INFINI-T FORCE: ARC TO THE FUTURE VOLUME 2 - End
Continued in VOLUME 3

...UM. KEN-SAN.
WHAT HAPPENED TO THE KITCHEN?
AH...
完。

Infini-T Force
インフィニティフォース
ARC TO THE FUTURE

**Infini-T Force** インフィニティフォース
▶未来の描線

# Infini-T Force

インフィニティ フォース

▼ ARC TO THE FUTURE

## '02

ORIGINAL
TATSUNOKO PRODUCTION
STORY
UKYOU KODACHI
COMIC
TATSUMA EJIRI

## STAFF

小太刀右京（チーム・バレルロール）

江尻立真

葛葉ヒロユキ
田中晋士

上原暁
古賀周太郎
柴本哲平
水清十郎
帝ェ門
中村祥子
長谷川真也
八田正男
松浦ショウゴ

## COLOR ASSISTANT

黒木崇文

## EDITOR

小林範善
木村大介

## DESIGN

内古閑智之＆CHProduction

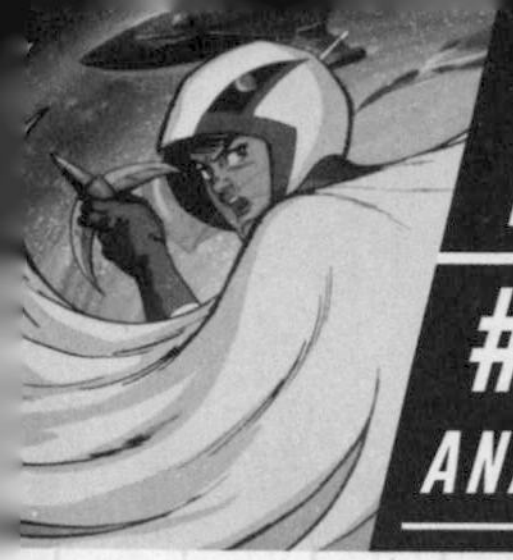

# Infini-T Force PLUS

## #01 SCIENCE NINJA TEAM GATCHAMAN

### ANALYSIS OF TATSUNOKO HEROES!!

## THE TEAM OF JUSTICE THAT OPPOSES GALACTOR - THEY ARE THE "SCIENCE NINJA TEAM"

### GATCHAMAN POINT 01

ANALYSIS OF TATSUNOKO HEROES

### THE RICHLY WRITTEN AND ILLUSTRATED WORLD APPEALED TO COUNTLESS FANS

*Science Ninja Team Gatchaman* began airing in 1972 as one of Tatsunoko Production's flagship sci-fi action series. The straightforward pitting of a team of justice-seeking heroes against a wicked organization plotting global domination looked at first glance to follow the orthodox tropes of good versus evil.

However, some of the core themes brought up in the series included the ramifications of technological developments and the light and dark sides of their use.

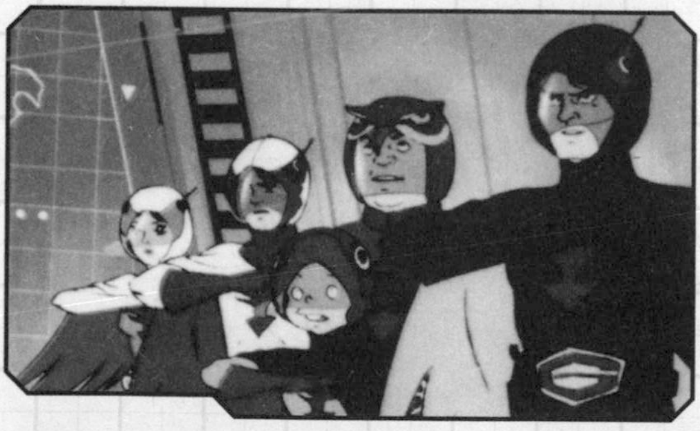

*These five assemble in the name of justice. Gatchaman isn't the team's name; it's just an alias for Ken.*

### GATCHAMAN STORY

ANALYSIS OF TATSUNOKO HEROES

The massive intergalactic crime organization Galactor schemes to rule the Earth, and they begin with an invasion. Dr. Nambu of the International Science Organization detects the coming threat and orders the top secret squadron, the "Science Ninja Team", to move out. Each young member of the team has his or her own bird motif and codename. There's Joe the Condor, June the Swan, Jinpei the Swallow, Ryu the Horned Owl, and their leader, Ken the Eagle, also known as "Gatchaman".

*The "Birdarang" was a weapon of Ken's that appeared as early as episode 1. The iconic weapon appears in this manga series as well, naturally.*

The stories of *Gatchaman* reflected the period of rapid post-war economic growth that Japan was experiencing at the time and incorporated plotlines concerning energy development, urban expansion, pollution, and even war. The ups and downs of society in that era were used as shockingly honest backdrops for this fresh action series.

The show also dug deep with all its characters, exploring their inner conflicts and growth as people. In an age when anime was still largely aimed at children, *Gatchaman* won over older fans with its dramatic plotlines and rich character portrayals. This popularity won the show its renewal, allowing it to run for two years and a total of 105 episodes.

## GATCHAMAN POINT 02

ANALYSIS OF TATSUNOKO HEROES

### OVER 40 YEARS AFTER IT AIRED... THE LEGEND LIVES ON

Fans kept asking for more after the series ended, which led to a theatrical release in 1978, as well as a direct sequel series titled *Science Ninja Team Gatchaman II*. The following year saw the release of *Science Ninja Team Gatchaman F (Fighter)*. In the 40 years since, there have been remakes, parodies, live action films, and entirely new versions of this legendary hero franchise.

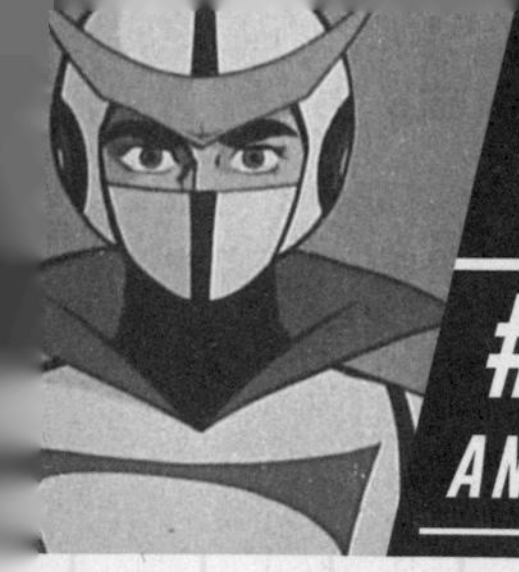

# Infini-T Force PLUS

## #02 NEOROIDER CASSHAN

### ANALYSIS OF TATSUNOKO HEROES!!

## FOR THE SAKE OF HIS FATHER AND ALL OF HUMANITY, SOLITARY HERO "NEOROIDER CASSHAN" WILL GIVE UP EVERYTHING IN ORDER TO FIGHT

### CASSHAN POINT 01

ANALYSIS OF TATSUNOKO HEROES

#### CAN A TRAGEDY BORN OF SCIENTIFIC DEVELOPMENT SERVE AS A WARNING TO MANKIND?

*Neoroider Casshan* began airing in 1973. As *Science Ninja Team Gatchaman* had received an extension the year before, there were two Tatsunoko hero series running simultaneously. *Casshan* was another show that reflected the times, and like *Gatchaman*, it sought to warn audiences of the dangers of taking scientific advancements too far.

The source of all Casshan's troubles, Buraiking Boss, was originally developed to help counteract pollution, creating an ironic plotline where something created to fix humanity's mistakes wound up becoming an even bigger threat.

### CASSHAN STORY

ANALYSIS OF TATSUNOKO HEROES

When master roboticist Dr. Azuma's android creation BK-1 is hit by lightning, it becomes self-aware, donning the name "Buraiking Boss" and leading the Android Army against humanity. Hoping to clear his father's name, Tetsuya Azuma sacrifices his flesh and blood body to become an advanced "neoroider". As Casshan, he fights the Android Army and seeks to make the world peaceful once more.

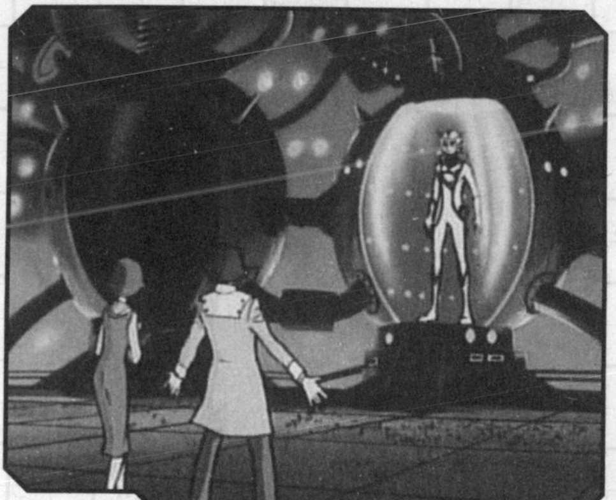

*In order to right his father's wrongs, Tetsuya gives up his human body to become "Neoroider Casshan" and fight the Android Army.*

## CASSHAN POINT 02

ANALYSIS OF TATSUNOKO HEROES

### WHAT MOVES THIS SOLITARY HERO TO ACTION IS BOUNDLESS LOVE

The series takes this concept a step further and shows that the only thing that can stop scientific catastrophes is human love. Though Tetsuya Azuma knows he will never be truly human again, he volunteers to become a neoroider, exhibiting a sort of self-sacrificing spirit not seen in other species. Casshan fights out of a sense of duty to restore peace to the world, but as his father is reviled by society as BK-1's creator, he also fights out of love for family. Humanity comes to see robots as the hated enemy, though, so Casshan must fight while concealing his own identity.

Sometimes, however, conflict does erupt between Casshan and the people he hopes to save, and the series' overall plot rarely lets up with such hard-hitting developments. Casshan struggles but never gives up, always fighting for his family and for the world. In *Casshan*, the very nature of humanity is explored via a hero who's anything but human.

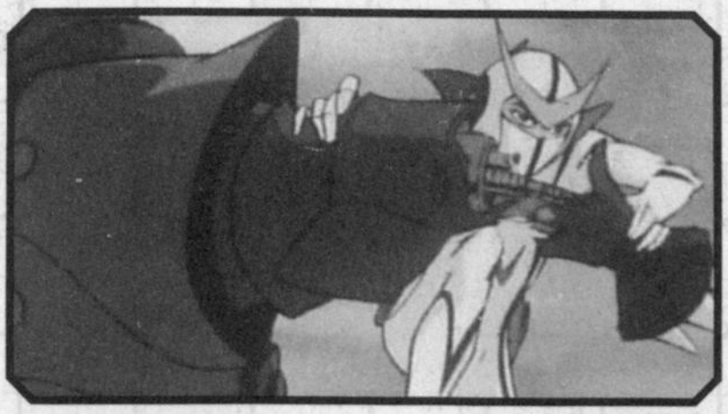

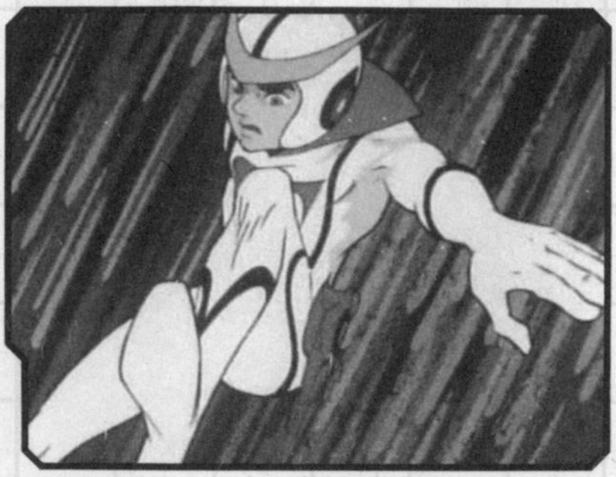

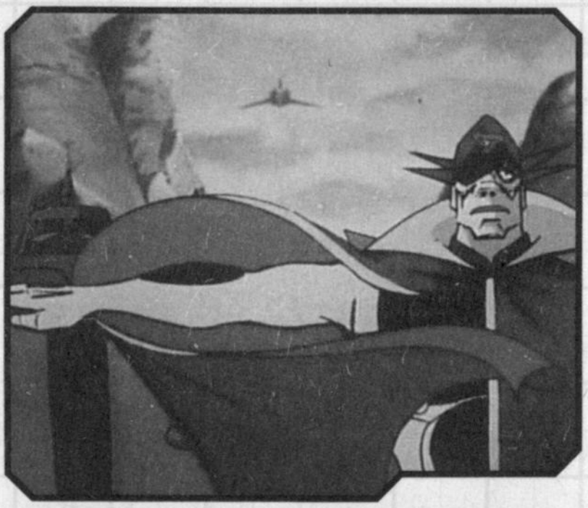

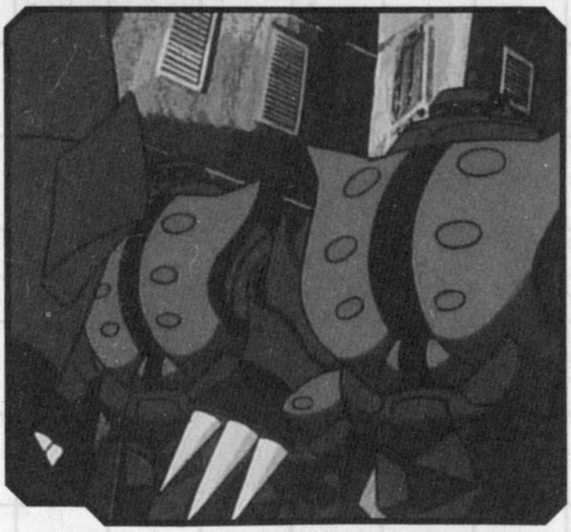

*When robots made to follow humans' orders become self-aware, they turn into a force that threatens all of humanity.*

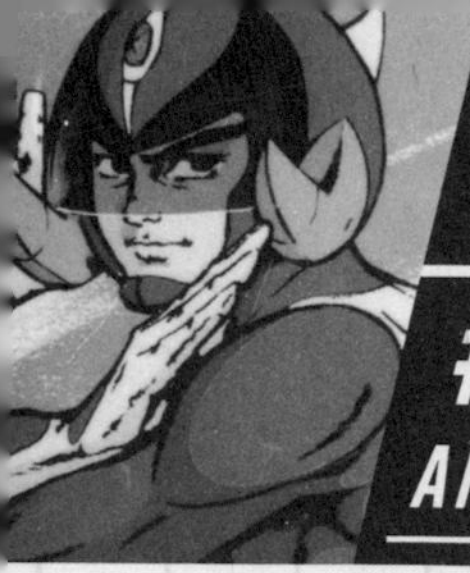

# Infini-T Force PLUS

## #03 HURRICANE POLIMAR

### ANALYSIS OF TATSUNOKO HEROES!!

## WITH HIS CRIMSON COSTUME AND HONED FISTS, "HURRICANE POLIMAR" IS READY TO TAKE DOWN EVIL

### HURRICANE POLIMAR STORY

ANALYSIS OF TATSUNOKO HEROES

Takeshi Yoroi is a third-rate detective recently hired by Joe Kuruma's private eye agency. He looks to be a lazy, shiftless young man, but when he dons a special "polymet" helmet equipped with a transformation device, he turns into the crimson-garbed superhuman, Polimar. While keeping his hero identity secret from Joe Kuruma and friends, he uses his unique "Hurricane Style" moves to lay down the hammer of justice on the villains that run rampant throughout the city.

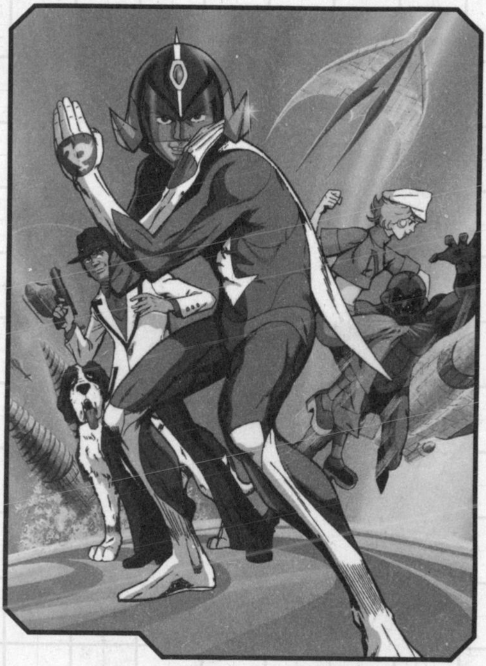

*Takeshi leads a quirky cast; the rich characterization is definitely one of HURRICANE POLIMAR's highlights.*

### POLIMAR POINT 01

ANALYSIS OF TATSUNOKO HEROES

### THE THIRD HERO MAKES A DEPARTURE FROM THE SERIOUS TONE OF THE OTHERS FOR A MORE COMEDIC APPROACH

In 1974, *Hurricane Polimar* followed *Science Ninja Team Gatchaman* and *Neoroider Casshan* to become Tatsunoko's third hero series. Whereas *Casshan* dealt with more serious topics, *Polimar* took the opposite approach by incorporating plenty of lighthearted gags and other comedic elements.

The protagonist, Takeshi, plays the part of a bumbling, unremarkable guy who can't help but get on everyone's nerves.

Other lead characters include Joe Kuruma, who's largely incompetent but thinks of himself as a great chief detective, and Teru Nanba, the strong heroine who serves as the detective agency's secretary and owner. The everyday interactions between the cast of quirky characters and actual detective work constituted the first half of each episode and consistently delivered.

POLIMAR POINT **02** ANALYSIS OF TATSUNOKO HEROES

## SHOCKING BATTLE CRIES BORROWED FROM THE KUNG FU BOOM

*Takeshi makes good use of his unique "Hurricane Style" to beat down the forces of evil. The pulse-pounding action is a must-see!!*

The action scenes are, of course, indispensable when it comes to a hero series. Bruce Lee's *Enter the Dragon* was released the year before *Polimar* started airing, sparking a worldwide kung fu boom. Polimar took that inspiration in the form of his wild battle cries and smooth, flowing fighting moves.

The viewer can feel each visceral hit as Polimar drives his fists into hordes of enemies in fresh action scenes. The strange blending of comedy with action is just another charming aspect of *Hurricane Polimar*.

# Infini-T Force PLUS

## #04 TEKKAMAN: THE SPACE KNIGHT
### ANALYSIS OF TATSUNOKO HEROES!!

## FLYING THROUGH SPACE ON HIS NOBLE MOUNT, IT'S THE BRAVE HERO, "TEKKAMAN"

### TEKKAMAN POINT 01
ANALYSIS OF
TATSUNOKO HEROES

#### EARTH IS ALREADY DOOMED... BUT A THREAT FROM BEYOND THE STARS SPURS A NEW HERO TO ACTION

*Tekkaman: The Space Knight* was Tatsunoko's fourth hero series and began airing in July of 1975, just four months after *Hurricane Polimar* ended. As the title implies, the main theme concerns space. Set on a futuristic Earth, the story concerns humanity's efforts to find worlds beyond our solar system. This premise, along with attacks by hostile aliens and interactions with the more friendly variety, lend the series more of a sci-fi flair than the previous ones.

### TEKKAMAN: THE SPACE KNIGHT STORY
ANALYSIS OF
TATSUNOKO HEROES

The Earth is on the verge of ruin thanks to environmental destruction and dwindling resources. Humanity sends scouting teams into space in search of a new world to call home, but those efforts are thwarted when the vicious Waldarian aliens of Waldaster attack. When his father is killed by Waldaster, the young Joji Minami dons a powerful suit of armor to become the superhero "Tekkaman". As one of the "Space Knights" who oppose Waldaster, Joji charges into battle, staking all of humanity's survival on his victory.

*A fearsome enemy threatens an Earth already on the verge of destruction. Tekkaman is humanity's last hope.*

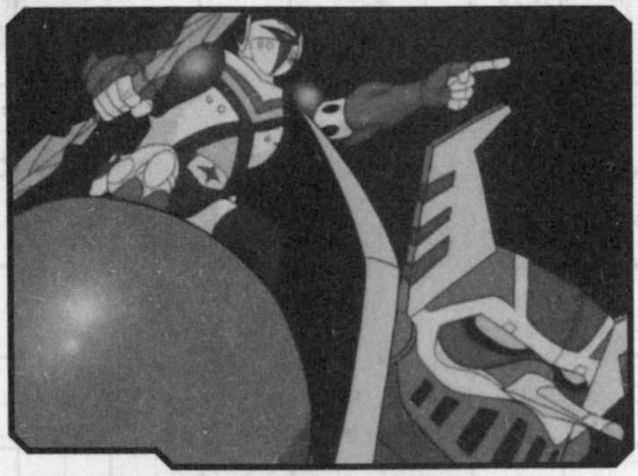

Following in the footsteps of *Gatchaman*, *Tekkaman* takes the concept of scientific advancement gone wrong to the extreme.
The Earth itself is set to become unlivable in just a few years thanks to environmental destruction, and the attacks from Waldaster mean that humanity is fighting for survival on two fronts in what seems like a losing battle.

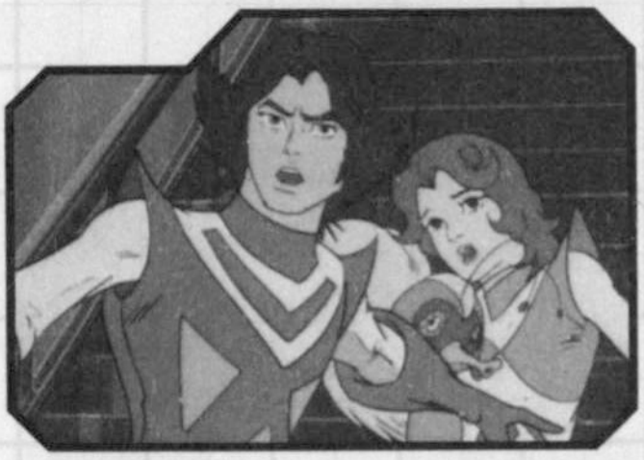

## TEKKAMAN POINT 02

ANALYSIS OF TATSUNOKO HEROES

### ONLY THE SPACE KNIGHTS CAN STAND AGAINST DESTRUCTION AND DESPAIR

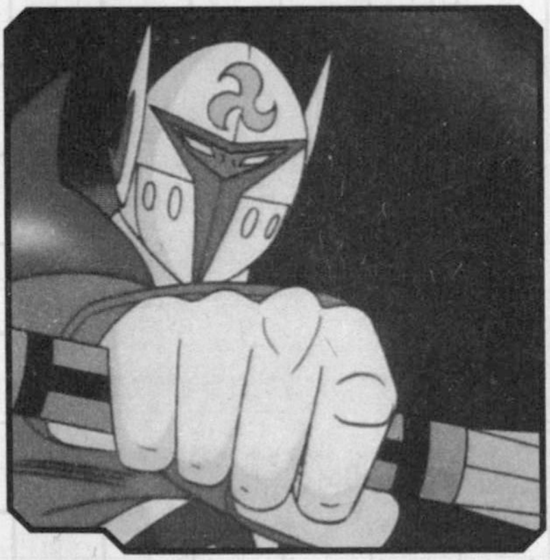

It takes a hero of unprecedented power to combat the greatest imaginable threat. When Joji Minami transforms into Tekkaman, he gains not only a suit of armor but also a superhuman body. The armor and helmet he acquires by strapping into A-Robot Pegas' system looks distinctly Western. Pegas also serves as Joji's faithful steed, allowing him to rocket through space while mowing down one enemy ship after another with his spear and whip. This gallant fighter is worthy of the title "Space Knight" and represented an altogether never-before-seen type of hero.

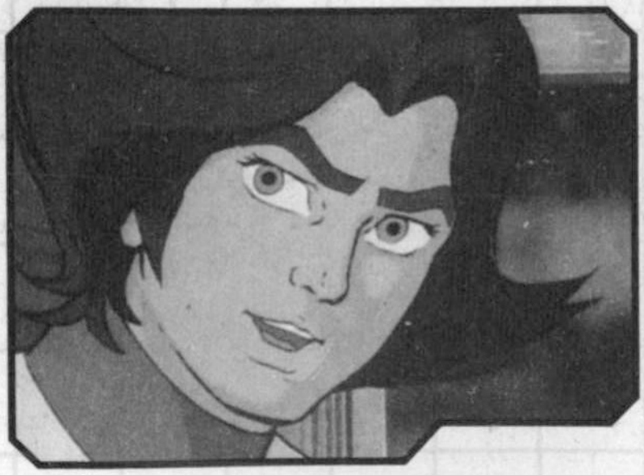

*The "Tekset" system allows Joji to transform into Tekkaman.*

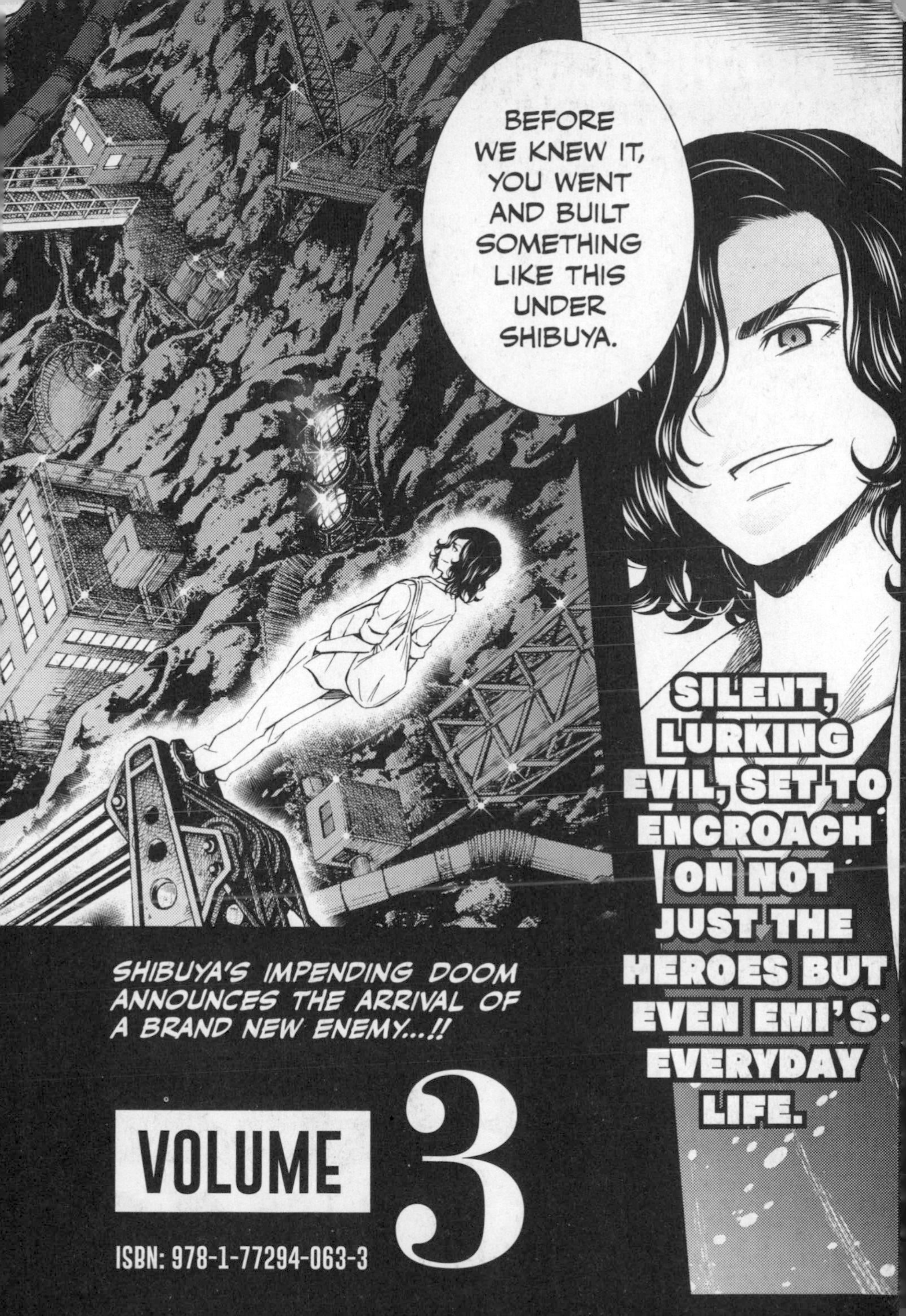
BEFORE WE KNEW IT, YOU WENT AND BUILT SOMETHING LIKE THIS UNDER SHIBUYA.
SILENT, LURKING EVIL, SET TO ENCROACH ON NOT JUST THE HEROES BUT EVEN EMI'S EVERYDAY LIFE.
SHIBUYA'S IMPENDING DOOM ANNOUNCES THE ARRIVAL OF A BRAND NEW ENEMY...!!
VOLUME 3

ISBN: 978-1-77294-063-3

## NEXT VOLUME

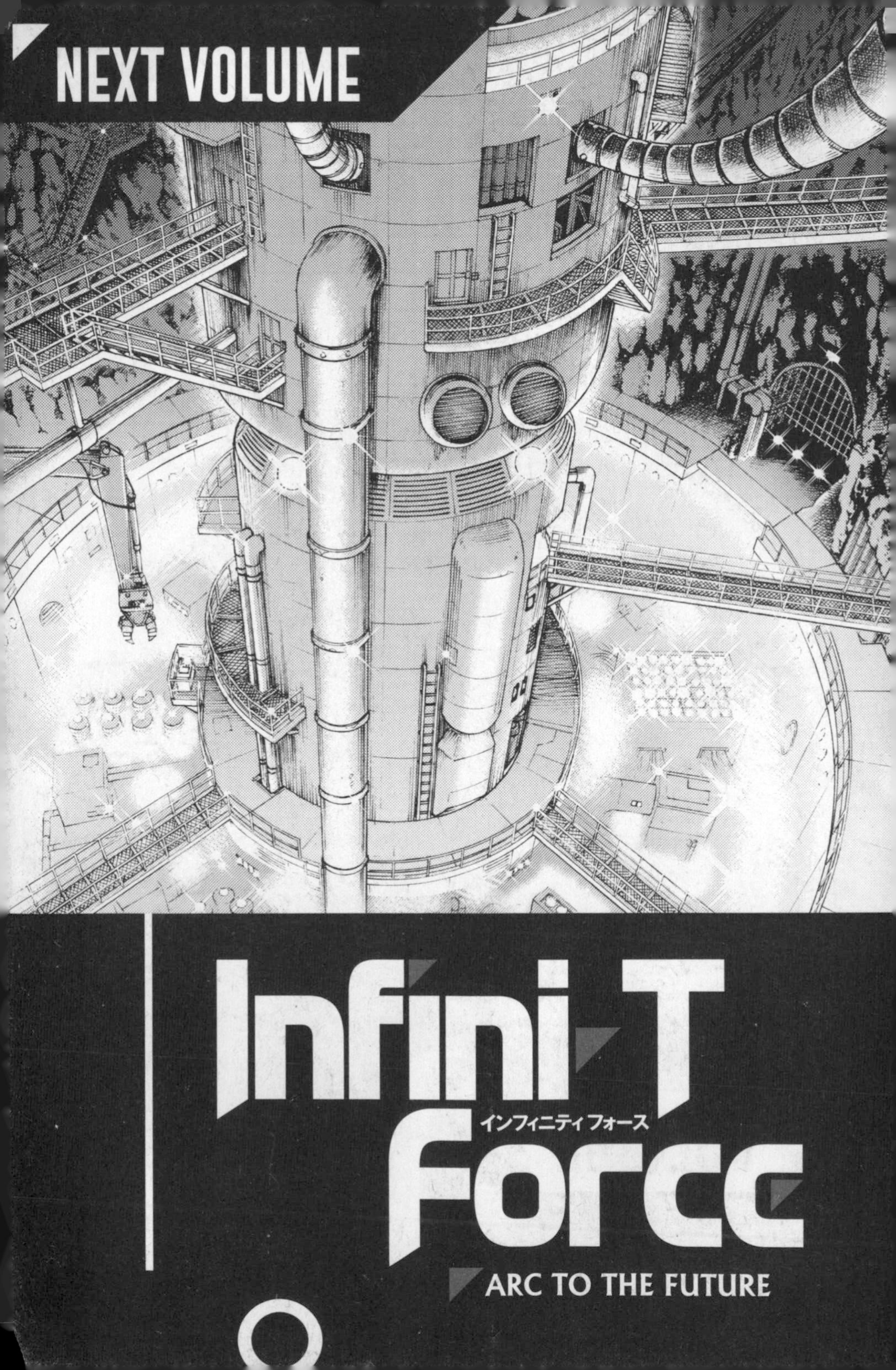

# Infini-T Force

インフィニティフォース

ARC TO THE FUTURE

# Infini-T Force インフィニティフォース 2

## ▼ ARC TO THE FUTURE

EB D. COOK
O HOSOYAMA
EANNIE LEE
Art Touch-ups: MERIKO ROBERT
Associate Editor: M. CHANDLER

**UDON STAFF**
Chief of Operations: ERIK KO
Director of Publishing: MATT MOYLAN
VP of Sales: JOHN SHABLESKI
Senior Producer: LONG VO
Marketing Manager: JENNY MYUNG
Production Manager: JANICE LEUNG
Japanese Liaison: STEVEN CUMMINGS

INFINI-T FORCE Volume 2

© Tatsunoko Production, Ukyou Kodachi, Tatsuma Ejiri 2016
ALL RIGHTS RESERVED.
First published in 2016 by HERO'S, INC., Tokyo, Japan.
English translation rights arranged with HERO'S, Inc.

English language version published by UDON Entertainment Inc.
118 Tower Hill Road, C1, PO Box 20008
Richmond Hill, Ontario, L4K 0K0 CANADA

## www.UDONentertainment.com

First Printing: January 2018
ISBN-13: 978-1-77294-051-0
ISBN-10: 1-77294-051-8

Printed in Canada